Vygotsky and Cognitive Science

Vygotsky and Cognitive Science

Language and the Unification of the Social and Computational Mind

William Frawley

Harvard University Press

Cambridge, Massachusetts, and London, England | 1997

Copyright © 1997 by the President and Fellows of Harvard College
All rights reserved
Printed in the United States of America

Library of Congress Cataloging-in-Publication Data

Frawley, William, 1953–
     Vygotsky and cognitive science : language and the unification of
the social and computational mind / William Frawley.
          p.   cm.
     Includes bibliographical references and index.
     ISBN 0-674-94347-3 (cloth : alk. paper)
     1. Cognition—Philosophy.   2. Cognitive science—Philosophy.
3. Psycholinguistics—Philosophy.   4. Vygotskiĭ, L. S. (Lev
Semenovich), 1896–1934.   I. Title.
BF311.F72   1997
153—dc21   96-30021

For Christopher and Emma

Contents

Acknowledgments

The epigraph is from *Collected Poems* by Wallace Stevens. Copyright ©
1936 by Wallace Stevens and renewed 1964 by Holly Stevens. Reprinted
by permission of Alfred A. Knopf, Inc., and Faber and Faber Ltd. Some
of the arguments in this book, in earlier forms, can be found in the following publications: "The Theoretical Importance of Private Speech,"
Signo y Seña, in press; "Vygotsky and Developmental Computationalism,"
in *Language and Thought in Development: Cross-Linguistic Studies*, P.
Broeder and J. Muure, eds. (Tübingen: Gunter Narr, in press); "Texts,
Disciplines, and Metaconsciousness," *Proceedings of the Poetics and Linguistics Association*, J.-L. Martinez, ed. (Granada: University of Granada
Press, in press).

I want to thank the following people for various kinds of support, suggestions, criticisms, ideas, and suspension of disbelief: James Lantolf, Roberta Golinkoff, Barbara Landau, James Wertsch, Robert Frank, William
Idsardi, Mary Richards, Raoul Smith, Peter Cole, Tony Whitson, William
Stanley, Deborah Hicks, Charles Scott and the staff at the A. I. DuPont
Children's Hospital, and two reviewers for Harvard University Press. An-
gela von der Lippe, Kimberly Nelson, and Kate Brick of the Press have
been of enormous help in getting this book into print. I must also thank
a decade of students for letting me run these ideas by them. My wife,
Maria, deserves much thanks for her love and support and for doing her
part to keep the family stable and organized (and quiet!) during the ordeal
of writing. I am also grateful to Emma and Christopher for their love,
happiness, enthusiasm, and willingness to engage in an occasional informal
experiment.

Finally, I owe an incalculable debt of gratitude to Richard Fischer, M.D.
When I first began to think seriously about writing this book, my son,
Christopher, came down with a neurological disorder that left him with
impossibly slim odds for recovery. In helping to cure my son, Dr. Fischer
put a whole family's shattered life back together. Without his hard work,
I am certain that I would never have been able to write this book.

And what we said of it became

A part of what it is . . . Children,

Still weaving budded aureoles,

Will speak our speech and never know

Wallace Stevens,
"A Postcard from the Volcano"

Introduction

When I was in graduate school two decades ago, I spent several years taking what was then, and probably still is now, a strange concoction of courses. Half of each day I studied formal linguistics, computational models of text understanding, and information-processing theories of language learning and breakdown. I studied the abstract human language machine. The other half of each day I spent learning about Vygotsky, Luria, Leont'ev, and their theories of the sociocultural determinants of speaking persons. I came to understand that the human computational inside had an equally complicated, and no less influential, outside world of speech positions.

These two views of the human—as a device and a person—never seemed at odds to me. Thanks to the integrity of my teachers, they were never put at odds. That was reserved for the partisan and often dangerous world of the profession, where suggestions that the computational and the sociocultural mind not only went together but *belonged together* met with a few worried looks.

I have written this book to tell the story of the reconciliation of the linguistic device and the linguistic person. In my mind there is such a thing as a *Vygotskyan cognitive science,* and it requires an honest assessment of the insights and limits of both traditional computationalism and trendy sociocultural contextualism. The idea can be put simply: social and computational mind come together in the way certain parts of language, perched on the mind-world boundary, are used by computational minds to mediate inside and outside during thinking. That is, some parts of social language are computationally effective. This is what I think of as *sociocomputationalism.*

Why should the social and the computational mind go together? And why should Vygotskyan sociocultural theory and standard computational cognitive science be the suspects? Here are three reasons.

1. They often study the same problems, unaware of each other's findings.

1

Vygotskyan theory and computational psychology have a long-standing interest in the frame problem: the puzzle of how beliefs globally constrain thought, limit it to what is relevant to the mind's interests, and even define *relevant*. Vygotskyans generally have no sense of the ingenious solutions in the computational literature for limiting inference. Nor do computationalists have much sense of the sociocultural units Vygotskyans claim constrain problem solving. Similar missed opportunities can be found in their mutual concern for cognitive control and consciousness.

2. Each way of thinking about mind has something of what the other lacks. If they would only talk to each other in the right way, some real progress might be made.

A number of schools of thought in cognitive science downplay the mind as a manipulator of internal representations: for example, situated action (Suchman 1987), embodied cognition (Varela, Thompson, and Rosch 1991), and existential cognition (McClamrock 1995). Some cite Vygotsky to bolster their view of the importance of externals and the contextual embeddedness of mind. But this gesture to Soviet theory is very misguided. Situated action, for instance, has the mind directly apprehending the external world, and invokes Vygotsky for support, but Vygotskyan theory requires that some of this apprehension be mediated by symbolic, internal, social representations. The lesson here is that accounts of mind in context, which call on Vygotsky for perfunctory support, must have a very rich theory of the inside to use him properly.

But the knife cuts both ways. Vygotskyan theory badly lacks a believable account of implemented units of mind. Vygotskyans often go to great lengths to display scientific rigor in identifying sociocultural units of mind (e.g., Zinchenko 1985), but it is often hard to see the units' exact boundaries. If we say, like good Vygotskyans, that speech has an inhibitory function, then we have to show how this inhibition is implemented. What are the inhibitory units the mind manipulates, and how are they manipulated? Computationalism has had a long, successful obsession with working models, and Vygotskyan sociocultural theory would benefit from the pressures of proposing an *implementable* theory of mind.

3. Each can be read in terms of the other. There is nothing intrinsically noncomputational about sociocultural mind, and there is nothing inherently asocial about machines.

If context has any bearing on mental life, then it must be computed in some fashion. This is the ultimate argument for individualism—the belief that mind can be explained through properties wholly internal to the organism. No matter how external, sociocultural units must be registered in a brain/mind to be effective, and all the evidence seems to be in favor of the brain/mind as a computing device.

Nor is there anything anticomputational in Vygotsky's theory. He proposed a protocybernetic account of mental control processes. Indeed, much of Luria's neuropsychology was devoted to finding the brain bases of Vygotsky's ideas. Vygotsky died long before the first computer was ever built, but that hardly seems reason to think of him as anticomputational.

The six chapters that follow use these motivations to argue the unity of social and computational mind. Several concepts essential to the argument are broad cover terms and must be clarified. The first is *Vygotsky*, which I use to stand for all Soviet and Russian sociocultural theories of thinking and personal identity. Grouped under this rubric are the theories of Vygotsky, Luria, Leont'ev, Gal'perin, Zinchenko, and others. (Bakhtin is not so included because his theories and Vygotsky's are really quite incompatible. Bakhtin is more a postmodernist than Vygotsky, the unrepentant rationalist.) I recognize the dangers of such a wide embrace, and it is not done to downplay disagreements (e.g., Vygotsky versus Leont'ev and the Kharkov school). But there is enough commonality to refer to them all in the same way, and certainly Vygotsky himself was the source of many of the ideas.

Similarly broad is the term *computational*, which covers all views of thinking as the manipulation of data structures. Computationalism is the basis of cognitive science, with its focus on minds as devices in abstract code: "Cognitive scientists view the human mind as a complex system that receives, stores, retrieves, transforms, and transmits information" (Stillings et al. 1987: 1). Jackendoff (1987: xi) echoes the view: "I take very seriously the motivating premise of contemporary cognitive science—that the mind can be thought of as a biological information-processing device."

There are many different competing, and unfriendly, schools of thought that qualify as computational: connectionism, symbol manipulation, hybrid connectionist-symbolic architectures, situated action, and so on. Calling them *computational* does not change their disputes or smooth over their commitments to computational psychology. As a group they are the typical foil to Vygotskyan sociocultural psychology. What could be more different than mind units in neural software and mind units in a community of speaking persons? (They are not so different, I would argue.)

The last two cover terms are *internalism* and *externalism*, which refer to scientific ideologies that place the major burden of explanation on units and processes either inside or outside the head. *Internalism* is not to be equated with nativism, which is only one kind of internalist account. Nor is it the same as computationalism, though such accounts of mind usually stress facts inside the mind-world boundary. *Externalism* privileges the outside over the inside and comes in many forms—empiricism, behaviorism, or some such outward-looking school of thought. But it is possible to be an externalist *and* a computationalist, as any one of the many new theories of embedded mind attests.

The fact of the matter is that there is no such thing as pure internalism or externalism. Innate ideas, those classics of internalism, must be triggered by input; behavior, that classic of externalism, needs a memory, no matter how schematic. There are plenty of schools of thought that fill out the line between, but none, so far as I know, that is neither internalistic nor externalistic. Vygotsky leans to the outside, as does connectionism; Chomskyan genetic determinism leans to the inside. The internalist-externalist split is a just way of organizing the explanatory preferences of competing research programs. The real issue is where and how the ideologies draw the mind-world line.

Part I of this volume explores the bases for unifying Vygotsky and computationalism. In Chapter 1 I sketch out the prevailing ideological disputes in the study of mind, showing that cognitive science is dominated by an internalist approach to explanation that wrongly excludes Vygotsky's brand of externalism. This is not to deny the ideological power—or the truth—of internalism. Surely we are in some sense isolated neurobiological subjectivities. Perhaps the most telling piece of evidence for this is that the neural mechanisms that make consciousness unified and seamless operate even during REM sleep and anesthesia (Flanagan forthcoming), with the remarkable implication that dreaming, the bellwether internal state, is by definition conscious experience. Consciousness can occur without an outside world!

But mental life is full of instances that require externals for adequate explanation. One day when my son was about three, he spontaneously sang a song he had learned at school. I asked him to continue singing, but he said he could not remember the song. I conceded and assumed the incident was finished. But then he said, "*You* sing it!" I did not know the song, and he had never heard me sing it because I did not know it. He insisted, however, that I sing the song. In a world explained by the young child projecting experience totally outward from the private, egocentric self, this behavior does not make much sense. But, as Vygotsky observed, because part of the child's mind is first social and external, not egocentric, my son insisted on my singing the song not because he believed that I was indistinct from him but because he believed that *he was indistinct from me*. It was an issue of perspective. Since his mind was mine, I must know the song too! He had to learn to become an individual, a private person behind the mind-world boundary.

This is the Vygotskyan lesson that could easily be lost in knee-jerk internalism. Once Vygotsky is properly understood as promoting an account of sociocultural metaknowledge, control, and internalization, he meshes nicely with psychologists and computationalists pursuing metaprocesses and the frame problem (Wellman and Hayes) and philosophers struggling with mind-world trade-offs (Dennett and Wittgenstein).

The legitimation of Vygotsky and externalism is the motivation for Chapter 2, which proposes a framework to integrate externalism and internalism. The reigning paradigm in cognitive science, Plato's problem (how we know so much from so little), can be supplanted by Wittgenstein's problem (how we manage both the internal virtual machine and the external real machine).

Current answers to Plato's problem side with radical internalism and construct ever narrower virtual machines: genetically determined, universal grammars of language, space, music, taste, mathematics, and so on. But Wittgenstein's problem, built on an argued continuity between the two Wittgensteins (1, *Tractatus;* 2, *Philosophical Investigations*), links the virtual machine (logic) with the real machine (action) and assigns language the crucial role in mediating reason and value. Wittgenstein, Vygotsky, and cognitive science come together in Vygotsky's concern for higher thought through particular instances of self-speech in on-line frame building.

Chapter 3 then presents the basics of both Vygotsky and cognitive science and some remarkable convergences. For example, the standard computational finding of input-output asymmetry has a correlate in the Vygotskyan idea of production running ahead of development. Similarly, Vygotskyan insistence on the material basis of consciousness has an analogue in neurobiology as the arbiter of proposed mental units in cognitive science.

Computationalism and sociocultural theory both have a vested interest in what might be called *architecture-context trade-offs*. Inner computational code interacts with external cultural context in different, but predictable, ways, depending on whether context subsumes or interacts with architecture. Does sociocultural context, in the form of metaknowledge, intervene in the processing of code and "preselect" results? Or does it just operate very fast after the fact, giving the impression that processing is continuously sensitive to context? Is it Orwellian or Stalinesque, to use Dennett and Kinsbourne's (1992) terminology? The answers to these questions depend, in turn, on how a language and culture make the cut between code and context and differentially manage mental and behavioral control.

With the foundations for a Vygotskyan cognitive science laid out, Part II explicitly integrates Vygotsky and cognitive science, focusing on three issues in which each has traditionally had a long-standing interest: consciousness, on-line thinking, and breakdown. In Chapter 4 I argue for the legitimacy of consciousness as the object of study and propose that subjective experience has three modes: nonconscious processing (automatic, deterministic computing of input), consciousness (awareness of the results of nonconscious processing), and metaconsciousness (deliberate awareness for mental and behavioral control). Vygotsky provides an account of the last, what he called *osoznanie* (something like 'meta-co-knowing').

Vygotskyan metaconsciousness has at least two benefits for cognitive science at large. First, it clarifies the properties and dependencies of the other subjectivities. For example, Crick and Koch (1990) have shown that, neurobiologically, language plays no essential role in conscious awareness. A nonspeaking brain in a vat—or a sufficiently intelligent thermostat—could be conscious. From the standpoint of Vygotskyan cognitive science, this makes perfect sense: language is computationally effective only in metaconsciousness because this kind of subjectivity requires a community of speakers engaged in mutual and self-directed regulation. Perhaps a thermostat could be conscious, but it would not realize it—and could not put its awareness to any use—unless there were a community of thermostats helping it talk itself into the thermostat it always dreamed of being. Seen in this thought-talk light, with a speech community arbitrating truth and action, Vygotsky sounds very much like Donald Davidson, though predating him by half a century.

The second benefit is that metaconsciousness can be used to clarify and reinterpret findings in the cognitive science literature on the social and experimental contexts of domain-specific problem solving and inference. These externals have long been known to have varying "metaeffects," depending on their uptake in on-line thinking and the uses to which they are put by individual problem solvers to regulate their behavior and thinking activity. The units and processes of sociocomputational metamind, as revealed by a Vygotskyan cognitive science, show how certain kinds of contexts can inhibit behavior, focus solutions, unexpectedly interfere with successful problem solving, and mediate the transition from expert to novice (and back again, according to the difficulty of the task).

How does context regulate thinking? The answer lies in the way language mediates metaconsciousness. Chapter 5 gives a computational interpretation of private speech as a symptom of the run time of thinking: the language *for* thought. Metaconsciousness is built on the resources a language has to call attention to its own representational capacities: metarepresentational forms such as focus, discourse markers, evidentials. Private speech—self-directed language for metaconscious control—is organized around these reflexive forms, which vary according to how a language trades off architecture and context in its semantic and pragmatic structure.

Interestingly enough, computing systems have a clear analogue to self-directed regulatory speech: control. Programming languages have a variety of metacomputational devices to monitor data flow, regulate the interactions of subroutines, and manage the system's responses to external influences and interruptions. So Vygotskyan private speech finds a home in computational psychology as the mind's metacomputational regulator.

The *language for thought* is the human analogue of computational control, mediating the progress of mental-computational activity. (This is, of course, what Vygotsky said fifty years ago, but without the vocabulary of the machine paradigm.) Different languages and cultures accord their speakers different means to this activity by the way they cut the architecture-context line for metarepresentation. Under this view, linguistic relativity becomes a hypothesis about the ways different languages mediate architecture-context relationships for mental and behavioral control.

Nothing shows presence better than absence, and nothing more clearly demonstrates the existence of a mental phenomenon than its systematic disruption. If there is metaconsciousness, and if it is driven by a language for thought, are there metaconscious breakdowns, disorders of the language for thought? Chapter 6 describes a number of such congenital control disorders: Williams syndrome, Turner syndrome, spina bifida with hydrocephalus, autism, and several other unnamed syndromes.

A close look at the linguistic behavior associated with these disorders shows that they disrupt linguistic metarepresentation and leave individuals with computationally ineffective speech for thought. For example, Williams children engage in much private speech during problem solving, but none of it is in normal form or has any effect on behavior. Likewise, autism, which has been explained as a deficit in the child's "theory of mind," disrupts the linguistic link between representation and metaconsciousness and affects the vocabulary for private mental states which an intact "theory of mind" requires. One might argue, then, that these disorders affect computational control, which would in turn account for the concomitant deficits in planning and inhibition, both earmarks of metaconsciousness.

It is important for the development of a Vygotskyan cognitive science that these syndromes are all *design disorders*. Insofar as cognitive science is concerned with the intrinsic properties of mental representation systems— what Dennett (1987) calls the *design stance*—these congenital disruptions of language for thought suggest that control is part of the design of higher thought. We could imagine a genetically given schematic computational control mechanism that heavily relies on exposure to social speech in order to be effective. These syndromes appear to affect this very internalization process by dissociating the two essential components of any algorithm: representation and control.

The issue of design leads to a final question: if the social and computational mind—two traditionally antagonistic views—so easily come together, is any study of the mind cognitive science? The Epilogue to this volume answers no. Only work that ultimately describes the mind's design properties, its representational and metarepresentational engineering, is cognitive science. Hence, the link between Vygotsky and cognitive science via sociocomputationalism—a place where external social speech can have an internal computational landing site—is the essential building block of a Vygotskyan cognitive science.

Writing a book has its hopeless side. New and important ideas continue to come out as you desperately try to finish your own writing, and you are ashamed not to include them. You also discover older papers you should have read but missed, and when you read them—assuming you have time—some turn out to be unrelated to the book and others embarrassingly on the mark. This book was completed in January 1996, so the arguments reflect a reading program that essentially stopped in 1995 while, of course, the work on social and computational mind pushed ahead.

There is much in evolutionary psychology, for example, that dovetails with Vygotsky and merits comment. Cosmides and Tooby (1994) argue that humans have evolved a rudimentary social-exchange module as an adaptation to the assessment of the success of small group interaction. This, they claim, is the computational locale of innate social representation (see also Jackendoff 1992), which confers the evolutionary advantage of an internal packet of social reasoning.

Could sociocomputational control be the same sort of adaptation? Since control is not representation per se, and certainly is not built on the representation of exchange, it seems unlikely to be a spin-off of the essentially internalist solution that Cosmides and Tooby propose for social knowledge. Indeed, they give an elegant account of half the sociocultural algorithm: its data structures. What about control? What problem is the language for thought an evolutionary solution to? What advantage could a mind have in regulating its own thinking from the speech of others?

It might be useful to be able to remind yourself of the contents of your own mind and that others are out there to help you just in case the world is too hard cope with by yourself. While social representations may have persisted because they confer the advantage of an idealized cost-benefit assessment of the minimal social community, control confers the advantage of portable order.

There are many other recent ideas that merit further scrutiny: the work of Karmiloff-Smith et al. (1995) on metaprocesses and Williams syndrome, the ever-growing literature on theory of mind (Baron-Cohen 1995), detailed inquiries into domain-specificity (Hirschfeld and Gelman 1994), and important basic work on computationalism (Llinás and Churchland 1996) and the social mind (Searle 1995). These advances all point to the need for at least one more book on how a human is both a person and a machine.

I

Foundations for Unification

Part I establishes the bases for unifying social and computational approaches to mind through language. In Chapter 1 I outline the current metascientific landscape and look at the frame problem, where social and computational approaches to mind have a mutual interest but conflicting accounts. The internalist/externalist dichotomy that presently drives cognitive science falsely pits computationalism against socioculturalism and unnecessarily precludes the cooperation of social and computational views. In Chapter 2 I examine the reigning sloganized paradigm in computational mind science—Plato's problem: internal mind exceeds its external context. An alternative framework is proposed: Wittgenstein's problem, where the virtual machine and the real machine come together. Wittgenstein's problem subsumes Platonic internalism and external social action and so transcends the false dichotomy described in Chapter 1. In Chapter 3 I spell out the basic issues of both cognitive science and Vygotskyan theory and link the two, arguing their unity in terms of context-architecture relationships: the ways that language manages and codes mind-world trade-offs. Context architecture relationships translate Wittgenstein's problem into the empirical arguments of social and computational accounts of mind. The unity of internal and external accounts in Wittgenstein's problem, enacted in architecture-context relationships, sets the stage for a Vygotskyan cognitive science focused on three aspects of mind: subjectivity, real-time operation, and breakdown.

1

Internalism and the Ideology of Cognitive Science

1.1 Luria's Peasant and the Frame Problem

In the early 1930s, the Russian psychologist A. R. Luria traveled to Uzbekistan and Kirghizia to study the psychological effects of the social changes of the Russian Revolution. He asked the local people to engage in a variety of cognitive tasks. Here is one of the typical protocols from a counterfactual problem-solving task performed by a thirty-six-year-old, slightly literate peasant (Luria 1976a: 127):

> Experimenter: It is twenty versts from here to Uch-Kurgan, while Shakhimardan is four times closer. [In actuality, the reverse is true.] How many versts is it to Shakhimardan?
>
> Peasant: What! Shakhimardan four times closer?! But it's farther away.
>
> Experimenter: Yes, we know. But I gave out this problem as an exercise.
>
> Peasant: I've never studied, so I can't solve a problem like that! I don't understand it! Divide by four? No . . . I can't . . .
>
> [Experimenter repeats the problem.]
>
> Peasant: If you divide by four, it'll be . . . five versts . . . if you divide twenty by four, you have five!

How does the peasant solve the problem? How can we explain his behavior, that is, predict it in a simple and clear way that fits with both the empirical evidence and existing theory?

One kind of explanation is an *internalist account,* which casts the so-

13

lution mainly in terms of what goes on inside the peasant's head. This is the sort of explanation that appears in textbooks on problem solving. The subject sets up an abstract problem space; he plans and executes a method within that problem space, much like the operations of an expert system; he outputs a solution (see Holyoak 1990). His performance shows that he can represent abstract mathematical quantities in his head and successfully process these representations—increase, decrease, and transform them—according to the rules and inferences of mathematics. On the internalist account, the peasant gets the right answer because he can do mental arithmetic. His self-report is the most compelling evidence: "If you divide twenty by four, you have five."

If the internalist explanation is on target, it should predict behavior on future tasks. Indeed, when asked to solve the same problem, but with distance converted to time (five versts in an hour), he says, "Twenty versts by four . . . if you put it that way . . . five versts in an hour, so twenty versts would take four hours" (Luria 1976a: 129). Here the peasant looks very much like a production system (Anderson 1983)—a rich internal logic machine constituted by algorithms in "if-then" form—and the internalist account thereby assumes the added force of received cognitive theory.

Here is another account, one that describes the solution principally in terms of what goes on *outside the peasant's head*. The peasant's world does not fit the problem world, which is reason enough for him first to reject the whole scenario: "No . . . I can't." But the recent introduction of schooling into his environment has changed his sociohistorical circumstances, making the possibility of logical problem solving a new cultural fact. His experience has shown him that if he complies and accepts school-like problems, he can do things that otherwise are contrary to his actual world. So he acknowledges the demands of the situation, allows the task to be defined as a school problem, and divides twenty by four to get five. On this *externalist account*, the very execution of the task follows from the peasant's external circumstances, which can themselves be reliably and simply identified. As with the internalist explanation, the peasant's own words are the most compelling evidence: "I've never studied, so I can't solve a problem like that!"

The externalist account also has compelling explanatory value. The struggle between conflicting cultural facts—life with school and without—predicts his future behavior. On the same problem with distance converted to time, which he ultimately solves successfully by simple arithmetic deduction, he first rejects the whole task: "How should I know how long it would take? . . . I can't understand you anymore. This problem calls for someone who has studied in school" (Luria 1976a: 128). Like all trustworthy explanations, these external facts find their place within a more encompassing theory, in this case one of social cognition (Luria 1976a: 1–19).

Certainly both accounts leave much unsaid. For example, each weakly presupposes the other (see the discussion of individualism in section 1.21 for more on this). The internalist account is not purely internalist since, after all, the peasant must have been exposed to mathematical information in order to solve the problem internally. But even given this exposure, most of the weight of the internalist account lies in characterizing what goes on inside the peasant. Conversely, the externalist account is not purely externalist since the cultural circumstances that carry the burden of explanation must be cognized by the peasant. Nonetheless, the crux of this account lies outside the peasant, in what surrounds him, not his mental manipulations.

Since both accounts of the behavior of Luria's peasant are arguably good explanations, they ought to have equal status in the study of mind. But for mainstream cognitive science, internalism is clearly the explanation of choice. For cognitive science, which studies mind as biologically constrained, formal intelligence, the causes of the peasant's problem-solving behavior lie in *what he held in mind and how he computed it*. A mind is what is inside its boundaries. The externalist account—that the peasant's world first makes him see that the problem is not even worth computing and then disposes him to play along, that thinking is determined by and traceable to external facts—seems, if not totally wrong, quaintly behavioristic.[1]

The illegitimacy of an externalist account such as Luria's is at once both understandable and odd. On the one hand, it evokes recidivistic anti-rationalism, the sort of thing thought to have been left behind with the critiques of Skinner (Chomsky 1959) and Ryle (Fodor 1975, Dennett 1987). If the externalist account applies to anything, it does so most readily to nonhumans, which seem to lack consciousness and thus do not have interesting insides to begin with—though Griffin (1981, 1984) raises serious problems for this view (see also Gallistel et al. 1991).

On the other hand, the behavior requiring explanation brings out one of the central issues of cognitive science: the celebrated and intractable *frame problem*—the puzzle of stating clearly and totally the overriding conditions, attitudes, or beliefs that globally constrain the decisions an intelligent system makes. There is little difference between Luria's peasant and the behavior described by McCarthy (1980; see also McCarthy and Hayes 1969), the inventor of the term *frame problem*, in his anecdote of the famous missionaries and cannibals puzzle (quoted in Dennett 1984a: 143):

> Three missionaries and three cannibals come to a river. A rowboat that seats two is available. If the cannibals ever outnumber the missionaries on either bank of the river, the missionaries will be eaten. How shall they cross the river? . . .
>
> Imagine giving someone the problem, and after he puzzles for a while, he suggests going upstream half a mile and crossing on a bridge. "What bridge?" you say. "No bridge is mentioned in the statement of the problem." And this dunce replies, "Well, they don't say there isn't a bridge" . . . So you modify the problem to exclude bridges and pose it again, and the dunce proposes a helicopter, and after you exclude that, he proposes a winged horse or that the others hang onto the outside of the boat while two row . . .
>
> You now see that while a dunce, he is an inventive dunce. Despairing of getting him to accept the problem in the proper puzzler's spirit, you tell him the solution.

Why is McCarthy's version seminal to cognitive science while Luria's is rarely mentioned? An important volume on the frame problem in cognitive science (Pylyshyn 1987) recounts McCarthy's examples and claims in great detail without a single mention of Luria, which is surprising, given that Luria's neuropsychological work makes him very familiar to the cognitive science community. The privileging of McCarthy's version is not traceable to the correctness per se of any of the proposals. After all, no one has solved the frame problem. It is, rather, a function of *the kind of account allowed in the field*. For this reason, Putnam, hardly a peripheral figure in the discipline, is not always taken as a serious voice in internalist, computational-representational views of mind. He has frequently offered equivalent frame-evoking anecdotes (see Putnam 1988: 110–11), but they are rarely cited because of his belief that not all mentalism need be internalism.

There are two standard approaches to the frame problem in cognitive science. One is to eliminate it, as, for example, Fodor (1983) does by relegating global beliefs to the mind's central processing, which he also sees as not amenable to rigorous or scientific study. Ironically, Dreyfus and

Dreyfus (1986, 1987) use the same eliminative strategy, and in this respect make unlikely bedfellows with Fodor, who wants to save computationalism by drawing its boundaries. But the Dreyfuses want to get rid of computationalism altogether, and the frame problem is just another gambit in the project.

The other approach is to propose internalist solutions, such as presolving the frame problem by equipping machines with large-scale knowledge structures that limit decision making by predetermining the available contexts in which an intelligent system finds itself (e.g., Schank and Abelson 1977). Even though these structures have shown limited effectiveness and plausibility—fatally so for critics of computational psychology (e.g., Dreyfus 1972)—they are tenable in cognitive science because they place the causes for frame behavior inside the organism and meet the demands of the world from the inside out.

More recent computational proposals follow the same internalist line and propose clever, high-level, but nonetheless brute force and noninterpretive solutions (e.g., Janlert 1987, Glymour 1987). Haugeland (1987), in a totally internalist view, suspects that the frame problem is a false issue on the grounds that it is a consequence of the interaction of internal subsystems. Even Dennett (1984a), an otherwise ardent supporter of psychology-connected-to-the-world, seems to see frame solutions lying principally within when he casts the problem as nonmonotonic, ceteris paribus reasoning *in people*. And Searle (1992: 175–96), not at all a friend of computational psychology, states the frame problem in characteristically clear fashion as the problem of "the Background" of thought; he looks principally inside the head for a solution.[2]

1.2   The Deprivileging of External Causes

The grip of internalism on behavioral explanations, and hence on cognitive science generally, long precedes the paradigmatic critiques of Skinner and Ryle that have given rise to the popular view of thought as the manipulation of an inner code (Fodor 1975). Flanagan (1991), though he does not use the term *internalism*, traces the idea to Kant's need in principle for transcendental reasoning and a priori knowledge. Accepting the validity of Hume's skeptical observation that only sense data, not notions such as causality or time, are experienced directly, Kant argues that inferences resulting in unobservables, such as causes, require a logic that goes beyond the merely empirical (and is thus transcendental). Cognitive science then appropriates the results of transcendental logic to its canonical "doctrine of unconscious mental representations" (Dennett 1987: 214), where the a priori is a given property of the mind/brain, not a property of some transcendental world waiting to be grasped. As Flanagan (1991: 185) writes, "Kant made the crucial substantive and methodological moves which make cognitive science as we know it today both possible and respectable."

This inward turn, if we follow Flanagan's account, is inherited by cognitive science via the theorizing of Brentano and James, which forms the basis of modern cognitive inquiry. Five properties characterize mental life on the James-Brentano view:

1. *intentionality*: thoughts are beliefs with goals and purposes; they are beliefs *about* things
2. *consciousness*: experience involves an awareness or subjectivity
3. *privacy*: mental states are personal or unique
4. *continuity*: subjectivity flows in a unified self
5. *selectivity*: the mind attends only to certain features of the external world

The truth of these properties is less important than their connection to the internalist idiom. Features 2, 3, and 4 are self-evidently internalist, but so are 1 and 5, which on the surface seem more tied to the external world. Flanagan (1991: 29) notes about intentionality "The fact that we are capable of having beliefs, desires, or opinions about [even] nonexisting things secures the thesis that the contents of mental states are mental representations, not the things themselves." Similarly, even though the mind selectively attends *to the external world,* this filtering is done by the internal mechanisms that experience the world. The world does not filter itself.

The James-Brentano properties of mental life are so essentially tied to internalism that *both* their acceptance and rejection by contemporary cognitive science preserve the internalist stance. Consider intentionality, that humans have beliefs and wants about the world. Stich (1983, 1991) and the Churchlands (Churchland 1985, Churchland 1986) reject the idea because of the connection of beliefs and intentionality to naive folk psychology, which in their view should be drummed out of psychological theorizing. Stich argues that beliefs, content, and folk psychology as a whole disappear when a fully and purely syntactic, formal theory of mind is worked out; the Churchlands eliminate intentionality since it has no neurological counterpart: brains do not allow intentions. (Nor do they allow syntactic minds, either, for that matter. But that is another story.) Neither the formalism of Stich nor the materialism of the Churchlands vitiates internalism. Beliefless mental syntax and intentionless neurological networks still remain *inside the head*.

Even connectionists, who pride themselves on sensitivity to external patterns and the embeddedness of mind in the world, have a very impoverished view of what the external world is; they spend much of their time building and justifying rich, adaptable, intelligent, *decontextualized* internal networks. Van Gelder (1992) argues that connectionism essentially embraces mainstream cognitive science ideology and builds a mind from within; the external world is an idealized, *virtual* context. The connectionist gesture to externalism is thus pretty much a token gesture.

The dominance of internalism also comes through clearly in the work of Dennett (1987), an ardent supporter of intentionality. He characterizes his well-known *intentional stance* as the prediction of behavior by attributing beliefs, desires, and other mental states to a system as a rational agent: a human is intentional *because of* hopes and beliefs about things, but (as Brentano might have said) a table is nonmental because it is not about anything. Even though we must make our intentional attributions about others from outside the minds of these putative rational agents, "we are [still] concerned with determining the *notional world* [my emphasis] of *another*" (Dennett 1987: 153).

The internalist-externalist split is not a replaying of some standard epistemological dichotomy, such as mind/body dualism. Internalism cuts a broad path across cognitive science and is blind to the details of the field's subdoctrines, uniting in stance even those who might otherwise disagree on the methods, facts, and explanations. Internalism is totally compatible with either mentalism or nonmentalism, materialism or idealism, connectionism or representationalism. It is simply the belief that the crucial factors for behavioral explanation lie inside the head, whether that head is a mind or a body, a network or a formula, both or neither (see also Varela, Thompson, and Rosch 1991: chap. 1).

It is, however, very much like the problem of individualism in the philosophy of psychology. For a variety of reasons, I do not want to cast my distinction in these terms. Not only will the terminology become confusing (e.g., Vygotskyan theory makes much use of the term *individual*, but in a sense that is totally unlike the philosophical problem here), but also many of the philosophical points scored in the debate are irrelevant to the issue at hand. Nonetheless, the larger lessons of the individualism debate are instructive and deserve some comment.

1.21 An Aside on Individualism

Individualism is the doctrine that the psychology of an organism can be explained entirely by reference to properties internal to the organism. Theories that do make reference to properties of the environment are said to be *nonindividualistic*. The issue centers on the role of content—reference to the world—in describing mental states. More philosophically technically, do the predicates of mental state descriptions have a semantics?

A purely syntactic, structural theory of mind could in principle be individualistic. This is apparently what Stich (1983) seeks, and it is found in the earlier versions of Fodor's (1975) proposed language of thought. It is a position bolstered by Fodor's (1981) arguments for "methodological solipsism," whereby psychology can be carried out singularly and autonomously, since explanation of mental states by reference to more than one mind is unnecessary if the core of mind is purely internal stuff and genetically the same in all instances of humans: if you've seen one mind, you've seen them all! But it is also clear that a representational theory of mind must in some way be nonindividualistic, since the very idea of representing requires something to be represented and some motion toward the outside world for interpretation. This notion is partially behind Heil's (1981) critique of the formalist tendencies of all symbolic information processing.

Accounts that reject individualism accept the crucial influence of environment on psychological explanation. The classic position derives from Putnam's (1975) Twin Earth problem and variations thereon (see Burge 1979, 1986). If there is another world exactly like ours, where my Twin Earth double is the same as me, molecule for molecule, are my thoughts about my cats, the same as his thoughts about his cats since our internal properties and worlds are exactly the same? No, my thoughts are about *my* cats, his about *his*. My double and I are individualistically—internally— the same, but our thoughts are not, no matter how close and how much about the "same thing," because the context of our thoughts differentiates the content. The external facts bear on the content of mind even when the purely internal properties are held constant. Because of the effect of the whole context on mental states, nonindividualism is said to be *holistic* about the meaning of mental predicates, or to evoke *wide content*.[3]

For three reasons, I do not want to cast the distinction between internalism and externalism as the problem of individualism. First, many of the philosophical arguments, and especially the crucial thought experiments, are not relevant to the empirical issues. Burge (1986: 22) recognizes this when he says that mere invocations of philosophical technicalities and failed demonstrations of their applicability to empirical matters blunt all the effects of philosophical critiques of psychology. Who cares about my Twin Earth double? What about the actual cases of reasoning, such as Luria's peasant (or McCarthy's dunce, if he is real)?

Second, nothing is entirely individualistic or nonindividualistic. Burge (1986: 24) puts the matter another way: "Any attitudes that contain notions for physical objects, events, and properties are non-individualistic," no matter what their formal structure. Still, content, no matter how wide, must be internalized. The facts of psychology demonstrate that even information that is uncontroversially external is transformed and recoded into something with individualistic properties, whether a shared language of thought, a probabilistically weighted network, or neurochemical impulses.

This leads to the third reason. The issue is not really whether psychological explanations can be individualistic, but rather *how and where the world matters* to thinking, that is, when and where nonindividualistic explanations apply as the ultimate cause. As Dennett (1987: 151) writes, "Two people narrowly construed as being in the same state can be reconstrued as being in different states if we redraw the boundaries between the people's states and the surrounding environment." How the world-mind line is drawn—what effect context can have on thinking—is the interesting and empirical question. Burge puts the issue clearly when he says that we must concern ourselves with the precise effect of the environment on mental states (1986: 13): "What supervenes on what has at least as much to do with how the relevant entities are individuated as with what they are made of. If a mental event *m* is individuated partly by reference to normal conditions outside a person's body, then, regardless of whether *m* has material composition, *m* might vary even as the body remains the same."

At this point it becomes clear how a psychology such as Vygotsky's can play a critical role in cognitive science. As I will argue later in this chapter, his work is not an account of the external so much as it is a theory of the *internalizing of the external,* a theory of *internal-external relations.* Toulmin's (1979) critique of purely internalistic views of mind is relevant here. In taking interiority for granted in our acceptance of the inwardness of thought, we fail to see that our inner lives are products. We *develop* inner lives; our internal states are so only insofar as "they have been internalized—only, that is, to the extent that we have had reason to internalize them" (Toulmin 1979: 8). And reasons lie just as much in our external circumstances as in our interior decisions.

In Vygotsky we find a theory of *internalizing*, not pure interiority or the pure outside world either, for that matter. The internal is not necessarily personal, private, or solitary. Consequently, to follow Toulmin's (1979) advice, we must look beyond philosophy and psychology to social history for explanations.

Vygotsky's goal is to explicate the symbolic nature and origins of subjectivity in and from context, and so his work is more properly understood as the study of the role language plays in the boundary conditions of mind and world. In more contemporary phraseology, his theory is about the relationship between contexts and mental architecture as it is played out in actual cases of speaking subjects executing their awareness. Put this way, Vygotsky's work raises basic issues for cognitive science, some that we even know a fair amount about (see, e.g., Chapter 3); it is also something to which Vygotskyan theory can contribute and from which Vygotskyans can learn.

1.22 *The Ideological Status of Internalism*

Dennett (1987: 7) sets out the internalist landscape most clearly when he argues that the majority of human behavior, if understood through recourse to the sciences of the external, is "hopelessly unpredictable from these perspectives." But he is also a wise and candid observer of his field and his own actions therein, and he notes how the epistemology of internalism, what he calls *the intellectual stance*, has come to serve the ends of academic territorialism: "The reigning ideology of cognitive science sets itself so defiantly against Ryle [an antimentalist] that it might be with some justice called the intellectualist stance . . . Cognitive science speaks openly and unabashedly of inner mental representations and of calculations and other operations performed on these inner representations" (214). Fodor, the spokesman for the language of thought, is "a leading ideologue of cognitive science" (Dennett 1987: 214).[4]

Like all human activity, science is first of all a system of rhetoric, power, and regulating activities, *a regime of truth,* to use Foucault's phrase, subject to the overarching constraint of ideological formations and practices. How we know the truth—epistemology—is subordinate to how we count something as a legitimate question or answer and control the production and reproduction of legitimated knowledge through academic programs and institutions, granting agencies, journals, conferences, and so forth. In more fashionable terms, the discourse of science precedes the truth of science.

To say, then, that internalism is the explanation of choice in cognitive science is to say that it is the dominant ideology. This is not to demean internalism; there is nothing wrong with being an ideology, which is, after all, just a cover term for a collection of received views and a truth-making/ truth-regulating apparatus (see Apple 1982). Indeed, some of the received views of internalism are empirically correct: there probably are universal, biologically determined grammars of language, vision, music, and so on (see Jackendoff 1992). But we must see these truths in terms of the ruling apparatus of internalism to understand it fully as an explanatory *movement*. In this way we can recognize the territory that it stakes out (its ontology, its justifications, its academies and forums), its power commitments (who can speak as a leader, where it is legitimate to study, who controls and gets the funds), its legitimate competition (who is allowed to change the field, what is a legitimate critique), and the character of its statements (its claims to truth, its totalizing statements).

The privileging of internalism entails the depriveleging of its competition, which can be seen in the explicit ideological complaints of those partial to the subordinated ideology of externalism. Thus, Putnam (1988: 55–56), long an advocate of looking to the outside, observes: "We have all seen one social or human science after another—psychology, sociology, economics—come under the sway of some fad. In the United States such fads were more often the product of a reductionist idea of what it means to be 'scientific.' The idea that nothing counts as a contribution to 'cognitive science' unless it is presented in terms of 'mental representations' (and these are described 'computationally') is just another case of this unfortunate tendency!" Less caustically, but no less critically, Toulmin (1979: 5) notes: "Once the interiority of all our mental activities is taken for granted, the problem of developing any adequate conception of the external world (question-begging phrase!) is like the problem facing a life-long prisoner in solitary confinement who has no way of finding out what is going on in the world beyond the prison walls . . . As a model for explaining the inwardness of mental life, a computer in the cortex is no improvement on an immaterial mind trapped wherever Descartes or Newton originally located it."

The subordination of externalism has forced it into into its own corner, where it has naturally developed its own truth-making apparatus. Just as no mainstream cognitive scientist—no self-respecting internalist—has looked forward to the latest issue of *Soviet Psychology*, so no Vygotskyan has pored over the latest volume of *Connection Science*. In Flanagan's massive and wonderful survey *The Science of the Mind* (1991), there is not a single reference to Vygotsky; the single citation of Luria is to his popular book *The Man with a Shattered World*, not to his work on the neuropsychology of consciousness and metathought. But the knife cuts both ways. Wertsch's (1985) excellent and influential study of Vygotsky has not a single mention of Fodor. Dennett (1987, 1991), caught in the middle, speaks as if he is quoting Vygotsky and Luria, but cites neither. Externalism is clearly as illegitimate to the "science" of the mind as internalism is to the "science" of society. Neither can contribute to the discourse of the other. But, after all, why should they?

In my view, externalism and internalism are talking about compatible facts and must work with each other for cognitive science to have an accurate picture of human thinking. But the apparatus of each explanatory movement has prevented synthesis for reasons that have little to do with rational discourse. This is not to deny that there may be very good reasons for separating the two opposing schools of thought on certain issues. For example, if each lays claim to *the same territory* and does so in commensurable ways, then such conceptual disagreements necessarily prevent synthesis and are resolved only through empirical or theoretical argument and demonstration of the adequacy of one over the other *on the same facts*. Thus, Ryle and Skinner arguably staked out the same territory as the mentalists, and so deserved some of the drubbing they got.

In the places where Vygotsky does address the same facts as modern internalists—for example, in conceptual structure, the effects of context on thinking, and the relation between biological and social development (see Wertsch 1985: 196–98 for the latter)—his theory needs revision in light of internalist advances. But this is not so for his externalism. Vygotsky inhabits epistemological territory that is very different from Ryle's, Skinner's, or even that of currently respectable externalists, whose citations of Vygotsky often startlingly misfire.

Typical of this problem is the use of Vygotsky in situated action theory, a version of cognitive science and artificial intelligence that views thought as directly tied to the external world and minimizes the role of preexisting symbolic cognitive plans in the generation of behavior. According to situated action, thinking is not, as in purely internalist-representationalist accounts, the deployment of a rich inner code that mediates inner brain/mind and outer social action, but is rather the organism's perpetual reinvention of strategic behavior in a world context, or, as Clancey (1993: 90–93) puts it, "our ability to coordinate our activities without mediating theories."

Vera and Simon's (1993) decisive objections to this movement notwithstanding, situated action appears to be totally insensitive to Vygotsky's brand of externalism. It calls on him to justify its account of the on-line construction of knowledge by an agent situated in the external world: direct and interactive thought as action (Greeno and Moore 1993, Agre 1993). But in fact, Vygotsky looks more like situated action's antagonists than its adherents. His theory is about higher thought—metaconsciousnesss—but situated action does not make the distinction between cognition and metacognition (Brooks 1991: 148). He argues for symbolic, mediating mental plans that precede action, which situated action also denies (Suchman 1987, 1993). What situated action regards as the thinking agent's ongoing action in the external world, Vygotskyan theory sees as symbolic locations in the service of inner control. There is no better illustration of the fundamental divergence of Vygotsky and situated action than on this very point. Clancey (1993: 91) says that one central claim of situated action is: "There is no locus of control in human activity, either neurobiological or social." Nothing could be further from Vygotsky's ideas, which identify both neurobiological and social control sites.

Whatever situated action is, it is not a very rich (or even accurate) theory of the intersection of cultural knowledge with computationalism. Similar points hold for other versions of externalist cognitive science, such as Gibson's (1979) theory of affordances, which involves the direct perception of external objects, but, as Margolis (1987) observes, lacks entirely an outer *social* world. What is needed is to bring computational and cultural psychology together in the sort of internalism that Garnham (1993) and Vera and Simon (1993) outline—*situated symbolic thought,* something that is entirely compatible with mainstream representationalism and that lets some outer social facts bear on internal representations.

In the face of these prevailing winds—the polarization of internalism and externalism, the dominance of the former, and the dubious Vygotskyan sympathies of official versions of the latter—I want to defend and promote the externalist stance, advocate the sort of externalist, social psycholinguistics that Vygotsky proposed, and argue for its incorporation into contemporary cognitive science. This project requires an updated, computationally sensitive reading of Vygotsky, with an acknowledgment of the proper place and limits of social explanations; likewise, it requires an acknowledgment of the narrowness of computational accounts and the recognition that while we might just turn out to be brains in a vat or Turing equivalents, there are people, institutions, and things out there, too, and they influence our thinking in a determinate way.

How can we develop an internalist idiom that allows for an externalist idiom in the proper place and in an equal way? There is a simple lesson in Luria's peasant, whose problem solving illustrates the complementarity of externalism and internalism.

1.3 Luria's Peasant, Again (and Fodor on Vygotsky)

In solving the problem presented to him, Luria's peasant does two things: he *orients to* it, and he *represents* it. In the former activity, he passes judgment on the nature of the situation and the relevance and solvability of the task at hand. What is this task? What are you asking me? Can I do it? What is needed here and why? In orienting, the peasant essentially confronts the frame problem; he *realizes* that the task is a division problem, a judgment that precedes and organizes the subsequent deployment of mental arithmetic and computations (though, crucially, without determining their content, in my view).

Critical to the peasant's orientation is how his circumstances run through his metatalk. He orients by identifying the task and his position in it, and he essentially talks himself into solving the problem: "I've never studied, so I can't solve a problem like that! I don't understand it! Divide by four?" This is very curious speech. For one thing, it is monologue disguised as dialogue. For another, it is blatantly false. He claims not to understand the problem, but he understands it perfectly well, as his articulation of the correct representational procedure ("divide by four") and successful subsequent solution illustrate. He must mean *understand* in its evidential sense of 'realize' or 'come to accept as an allowable, relevant action or fact'. His language is less truth-conditional than symptomatic of perspective and action, of how he is positioning himself. It is precisely the mechanisms of this orientation to the task, the locating of framing determinants in the external world, and the translation and execution of these determinants in self-directed metatalk that Vygotskyan theory is all about. When the peasant is given the same problem converted to time, he concedes to the task and says, "If you put it that way," an explicit acknowledgment of the frame and the external facts.

In the second activity, representation, the peasant carries out the mental abstractions and computations necessary actually to produce a solution. Just as the internalist account sheds little light on the peasant's realization of the task, so the externalist account says nothing of how the peasant actually divides twenty by four to get five. There is nothing external about this procedure, which requires that the peasant be able to distinguish actual numbers from abstract quantities and process these quantities according to the rules of arithmetic (i.e., hold items constant, understand the effects of arithmetic operations on equivalence, etc.). The solution itself depends on memory, abstraction, and processing, not on taking a perspective. To follow Dennett's (1984a) phraseology, the correct division of twenty by four to get five is something that he *knows*, not something that occurs to him; things that people know are unquestionably in the province of traditional cognitive science.

Crucially, neither explanation gets in the other's way. Only an internalist account fits the representational aspect of the problem: it would be very strange indeed to say that the peasant infers five from twenty via the division of four because that is how the world works—though perhaps it does in Katz's (1981) world! It would be just as bizarre to say that the peasant orients to the problem because he can think mathematically. Why does he decide to think mathematically? His world makes that decision for him.

Just as crucially, *both accounts* are needed if we are to understand the peasant's behavior fully. The same holds for an explanation of the hypothetical solver in McCarthy's missionaries and cannibals problem, as well as for the many documented cases of contextual biases of induction (see, e.g., Tversky and Kahneman 1974). Rationality is not solely deductive closure (Dennett 1987); as Leiber (1991: 41) says, thinkers must be logicians *and* good guessers.

In a complete picture of rationality, externalism and internalism will get in each other's way only if allowed, an unfortunate scenario that is played out clearly in Fodor's (1972) reading of Vygotsky, and that typifies the out-of-hand dismissal of cultural psychology by mainstream cognitive science. Now, it is unfair to criticize Fodor twenty years after the fact, especially since his critique centers on the first edition of *Thought and Language*, the seminal but cryptic Vygotskyan text. Nonetheless, an examination of Fodor's critique, now that we are more informed about both Vygotsky and cognitive science, can tell us much about why social and computational psychology have not dovetailed and why they now can and should.

Fodor argues that Vygotsky has a hopeless solution to the acquisition of word meaning because he believes that "word meanings evolve" (1972: 88), which invokes the paradox of emergent complexity: if children's meanings must change in kind, not in degree, to become adults', they must be couched in an inner code that itself evolves; but in order to change, the code must already be powerful enough to represent the change, and so cannot increase in complexity. The problem, however, is not one of complexity but one of meaning itself. As Wertsch (1985: 95–97) points out, incorrect translations of Vygotsky's Russian into technical English blur his distinction of three kinds of meaning: *predmetnaya otnesennost'* ('object relatedness', or something like 'extension'), *znachenie* ('knowledge', or something like 'intension' or 'sense', what translations of Vygotsky's works often call 'meaning'), and *smysl* (something like 'understanding'). Fodor's criticisms apply to the first two, probably correctly. Vygotsky did think that 'intension' (*znachenie*) developed over time and derived from external features of the referent. This failure to attribute intensional development to rich internal principles with full computational power is a shortcoming of Vygotsky's work (see Wertsch 1985: 102).

Of greater importance to Vygotsky's concerns with meaning is *smysl*, overall cultural, psychological, and personal significance (see Leont'ev 1978: 20 n. 3)—"the sum of all the psychological events aroused in a person's consciousness by the word. It is a dynamic, complex, fluid whole" (Kozulin 1986: xxxvii; cf. Vygotsky 1986: 244–45). *Znachenie*, 'meaning', is stable, while *smysl*, 'psycho-cultural significance,' is inherently variable; it is the individualized meaningful perspective that a word carries, how a word contributes to orientation. This kind of meaning always changes. As a cultural derivative that serves individualized consciousness, *smysl* is crucial to development as a whole since it is part and parcel of how external speech becomes internalized to drive cognitive growth. *Smysl* is orientational semantics, the meaning of inner speech.

Here is where Fodor and Vygotsky—read cognitive science and cultural psychology—simply misunderstand each other. When Vygotsky talks about meaning, he is ultimately concerned with, to use more contemporary cognitive science phraseology, external facts in lexical cues to the frame problem. When Luria's peasant says, "I don't understand it," he is to be taken as signaling, 'I don't admit it as legitimate, given my experience with schooling'. This culturally derived, individualized significance keyed by the word *understand* is tied to the concrete situation and serves the peasant's consciousness in the act of problem solving. Orientational meaning can change and grow because a "word acquires its sense [*smysl*] from the context in which it appears; in different contexts, it changes sense [*smysl*]" (Vygotsky 1986: 245).

Two other misunderstandings, likewise traceable in part to translation errors, fall under the larger heading of problems with "higher thought." Fodor criticizes Vygotsky for equating thought with problem solving (1972: 84) and divorcing consciousness from knowledge (1972: 95). Neither of these characterizations is correct. As to the first, Vygotsky draws a distinction between elementary mental functions, which have natural and biological bases, such as perception, and higher mental functions, which are goal-directed activities of the individual, mediated through speaking by the internalized, symbolic, sociocultural tools in the individual's environment (something like what we now understand as *metacognition*). Vygotsky is concerned with the latter (see, e.g., Vygotsky 1978: 52–57 and Wertsch 1985: 24). More properly, then, Vygotsky does not equate thought with problem solving. He ties *higher thinking*—the on-line activity of mind—with problem solving (as is well known, the more accurate title of his classic book is *Thinking and Speech*, which reflects his view of thought as activity; see Wertsch 1985: 234 n. 8; Rieber and Carton 1987: v–vi).

As to the second, Vygotsky does indeed distinguish knowledge from consciousness. As we will see in Chapter 4, he gives a three-part account of subjectivity: *znanie* ('knowing'), the most elemental subjectivity; *soznanie* ('co-knowing'), situated subjectivity that needs others and is often translated misleadingly as *consciousness*; and *osoznanie* ('about co-knowing') or something like *metaconsciousness*, what Vygotsky calls "the consciousness of being conscious" (1962: 91). (Vygotsky gives this definition one line above what Fodor quotes disparagingly; it appears that Fodor has not read Vygotsky closely enough here.) The real focus of Vygotsky's theorizing is *osoznanie*, which is a type of *soznanie* (Wertsch 1985: 188). Vygotsky is thus concerned with the experiencing of co-constructed experience (Lee and Hickmann 1983: 347)—that is, higher thought *(osoznanie)*—which *is* different from both knowledge *(znanie)* and consciousness *(soznanie)*.

When Vygotsky's translators make him say that a word's *sense* is the locus of *consciousness* and totally varies with context, he sounds like a deadly mix of William James, Benjamin Lee Whorf, and Jacques Derrida—three thinkers far removed from Fodor's computationalism. But he is really arguing that the personal and idiosyncratic senses of a word, tied to cultural significance, are the vehicles of voluntary thinking. Seen in this light, he is at the very least saying something arguably worth pursuing, even empirically testable.

A final misunderstanding, which makes sense as such only if we appreciate Vygotsky's concern for higher thought, centers on cognitive similarities between children and adults. Fodor criticizes Vygotsky for drawing a developmental line between children and adults in one case, as in the learning of word meaning, and then making distinctions which suggest that children and adults are exactly alike: "The remarks he makes about the way children operate at 'lower' developmental levels are exactly applicable to normal adult thought. This is, of course, a way of saying that Vygotsky's stages do not correspond to anything *in rerum natura*" (Fodor 1972: 94).

In higher thought *(osoznanie)*, children and adults do perform very similarly. In a difficult problem-solving situation, an adult resorts to (meta)cognitive strategies that are characteristic of children—for example, seeking external memory aids—precisely because *the difficulty of the external circumstances redefines the adult as a novice*. The adult then *reorients* and recovers developmentally earlier, more concrete, successful problem-solving tactics. In a direct test of this reaccessing of earlier strategies, Tul'viste (1982) finds animistic thinking as prevalent among adults as among children and observes that this similarity is a function of the continuity between children and adults in higher thought: "If a child acquires its reasoning from culture, how can that reasoning be qualitatively different from the reasoning of adults?" (4). For Vygotsky, the idea of demarcated stages loses its significance in higher thought, and Fodor's observation becomes curiously accurate: in (meta)consciousness adults do behave like children.

Fodor reads Vygotsky as if he were a computational internalist, competing with the cognitivists and offering commensurable accounts. But Vygotsky is only partly that; he is mostly interested in how speaking itself bears on metathought, a characterization that surely still fails, in any case, to recommend him to Fodor. This is because the sorts of things that Vygotsky is concerned with are those that Fodor (1983) relegates to central processes—integrative global thought tied to the world outside the head. Crucially, Fodor also believes that there can be no rigorous or scientific study of these processes—because they are Quinean, subject to perpetual disagreement about their criteria for identification. Thus, even granting the appropriateness of their misunderstanding, the Vygotskyans could never lie down with the Fodorians. Something has to give when, to modify

Varela, Thompson, and Rosch's (1991: 207) point, "intelligence shifts from being [only] a capacity to solve a problem to [include] the capacity to enter into a shared world of significance."

1.4 Vygotsky and the Frame Problem

The frame problem persists because the internalist ideology of cognitive science limits legitimate inquiry to structural intelligence. We cannot have a complete or even accurate picture of thinking until we spell out the mechanisms that humans use both to represent and to realize the applicability of computational processes in the first place. Fodor (1986) puts the matter by saying that a complete theory of mind must formalize the line between arbitrary and nonarbitrary facts, between mechanisms that arbitrarily and automatically deliver fewer hypotheses than might reasonably be true (such as mathematical inferences) and those that make our beliefs correspond to the world. Vygotskyan psycholinguistics, which studies subjectivity as the unification of intellect and affect, is an account of the latter kind of mechanisms. Seen this way, it strikes a curious chord with recent views of consciousness in mainstream cognitive science, such as Flanagan's (1991, 1992), in which consciousness itself is the linking of emotion and data processing (see Chapter 4 for more discussion).

Dennett (1984a) lists a number of issues that surround the frame problem, or, as he says, how we think before we leap. The frame problem is a question of neither induction nor deduction, not a matter of inferring across representations. It is, rather, a question of how nonmonotonic reasoning—how the addition of information influences the evidentiary status of the conclusions—can inhibit or rule out inferential options. Even the ardent internalists recognize the inhibitory function of the frame (Pylyshyn 1987). Why doesn't the solver of the missionaries and cannibals puzzle just rule out bridges? Why doesn't Luria's peasant inhibit his non-school knowledge? Vygotskyan theory has not only a solution but a method.

Humans talk to themselves—mostly silently but sometimes predictably overtly—during problem solving. This private speech encodes the individual's unique internalization of external social and cultural significance—*smysl*, the meaningful perspectives, the evidence, relevance, and attitudes that frame the individual's decisions. Speaking drives thinking. This *language for thought*, the framing of the inferential language of thought in which the solutions are finally computed, has an inhibitory function, ruling out options and giving a direction to the representational thinking. Thus, when Dennett characterizes humans as inveterate self-controllers (1984b) and self-talkers (1987: 112), in whom "foreknowledge is what permits control" (1984b: 54), it is curious that he does not mention Luria's (1976b, originally 1932) work fifty years earlier on the same problem: "Our [Vygotsky and Luria's] researches convince us that . . . control comes from without" (Luria 1976b: 401), but "the adult cultured human may achieve this by a special apparatus—one of his most important functions—which may be used for auto-stimulation and the organization of behavior. This function is speech" (412).

How do we know about this control function of speech? For Vygotskyans, one of standard the methods of experiment is to interrupt behavior by introducing a difficult task and then observing how the subject regains cognitive control. In this righting of the self, the subject uses private speech as an external symbolic guide, and what surfaces are linguistic cues to the individual's grappling with the cognitive frame. As Dennett (1984a: 133–34) says, the best way to find out how the frame is operating is to rummage "around backstage or in the wings, hoping to disrupt performance in telling ways."

An interesting comparison with the work of B. F. Skinner underscores this view of the frame problem. It is easy to dismiss Vygotsky as a behaviorist, especially with Vygotsky's talk about thinking as speaking to oneself and citations to Watson. But this would be accomplished with a superficial reading of both Watson and Skinner.

One way to think about Vygotsky is as a (mild) behaviorist comfortable with mentalism. As is well known, the successes and failures of behaviorism center on its blind externalism. On the one hand, the radical empiricism of behaviorism puts verifiability and rigor at the forefront of psychological explanations and thus confronts ghosts in the machine. On the other hand, the same empiricism runs like a loose cannon and threatens itself, since behaviorism falters on matters of novelty, purpose, and the undeniable existence of other minds, much less one's own. But in the canonical dismissal of behaviorism, there remains one point where its arguments continue to have bearing on cognitive science.

As Flanagan (1991) observes, Skinner argues that self-knowledge is learned, more particularly that subjective terms have a public origin. Thus, "competence in a language of private events is in some important sense a necessary condition for knowledge of one's own private events" (103). The lesson of this doubting of the Cartesian method—that "self-knowledge is simply not there for the asking" (103)—has been brought entirely into contemporary cognitive science in the developmental "theory of mind" school, but with no mention of its behavioristic predecessors. Perner (1991), Wellman (1990), and a number of others have argued that normal cognitive development involves children acquiring a mental theory about their own and others' internal states; this naive epistemology is tied to the kind of language they have for representing mental states, that is, how they use the words *know, believe, want,* and so on. In fact, disruptions in metacognitive performance appear to be associated with concomitant failure to acquire a rich vocabulary of subjective experience (see Chapter 4).

Although I discuss the theory of mind literature in detail later in the book, I note here that this view of thinking is precisely the goal of Vygotskyan theory. Higher thought, metaconsciousness in Vygotsky's sense, and self-knowledge are tied to cultural externals mediated by that part of language that conveys personal-cultural significance—*smysl.* The sense of private-state words might thus be said to drive private-state knowledge. Vygotsky's work is both a parallel to current work on children's theory of mind and a vindication of Skinner's story about private states, though without being other-mind blind.

In this way Vygotsky strikes a marked contrast with Ryle (1949), another out-of-fashion theorist. Ryle sees mental states as dispositions to external behavior; Vygotsky sees the states of higher thought as derivatives of external behavior. That is, some mental states require world states, those that are associated with evidence, relevance, attitudes, and all the things that current "theory of mind" schools take as crucial to the grounding of the representational mind.

Vygotsky is not a pure externalist and so avoids the pitfalls of radical behaviorism. His is a theory of *internalization,* the connection of the external with the internal. For Vygotskyans, not all causes of behavior are environmental; elementary mental processes are entirely compatible with neurobiological evidence or some interactionist theory such as Piaget's (Wertsch 1985: 44–46). Environmental factors apply fully to only some forms of thinking, the kinds that play directly into those subsumed by Dennett's intentional stance.

Dennett (1987), we should recall, claims that we predict behavior by attributing to a system beliefs that are relevant to the system's interests. This purely internalist account leaves open a prior question, which Dennett (1987: 28–29) appears to recognize. How do we decide what beliefs are *relevant* to the system's interests? Vygotsky's answer fills out the unexamined presumption of the intentional stance: look at the society and culture and see what parts of it are appropriated by the language and used in metatalk to control behavior. That is, look at the parts of language that mediate cultural knowledge and metaconsciousness. Thus, while computers may or may not have beliefs, since the jury is still out on what counts for the attribution of rational behavior to machines, they most certainly *do not have relevant beliefs* since they lack a culture and a self-directed language to internalize that culture's interests.

To understand the compatibility of Vygotskyan theory with cognitive science, we need a framework that gives language a role in both the social and computational mind. This, I believe, can be found in an integrated view of Wittgenstein. But this approach in turn makes sense only with a prior examination of the existing internalist framework which accords language an internal role and takes a decidedly anti-Wittgenstein tack. This brings us to *Plato's problem,* which systematizes, expands, and intellectually situates cognitive science's inward turn.

2

From Plato's Problem
to Wittgenstein's Problem

2.1 Plato's Answer: The Inward Turn

How do we come to have such rich and effective knowledge of the world when the evidence presented to us through our senses is so fragmented, meager, and inconclusive? The data on which we develop our visual knowledge, for example, are variable and indeterminate. We are never apprentices to the total human visual experience, and so we do not learn to see just by seeing all things. This situation is, as Chomsky (1986) calls it, *the poverty of the stimulus*, and it underlies what has become sloganized as *Plato's problem*: how do we know so much from so little? What makes the *insides* of our minds so full and systematic when the *outsides* are so motley?

Plato's problem is certainly the central, if not the only, question about mind (though it would be wrong to see it originating with Plato: Buddha, for one, taught that the fragmentation of the phenomenal world causes error in reasoning and that the trained mind can transcend this fragmentation and grasp the unified whole). More important to cognitive science than Plato's problem is *Plato's answer*: we are equipped with an inner system of universal truths implanted in our reason from exposure to the world of pure, ideal forms. The influence of this internalist answer can be seen not only in the choice of it over competing internalist and externalist responses, but also in the willingness of schools of thought to adjust their claims to retain it.

Solutions to Plato's problem do not necessarily require Plato's answers. One response to the question of how we know so much from so little is to say that we do not know very much. Thus, Gorgias (483 B.C.) doubted the existence of everything and argued that if anything did exist, we would not know it, and even if we did, we would not be able to tell anyone about it. Such relentless skepticism turns into its opposite in the long run. As

Wittgenstein (1969: 18e #115) writes, "If you tried to doubt everything you would not get as far as doubting anything."

Another non-Platonic answer to how we know so much from so little is to deny that it is so little. This is the approach of radical behaviorism and other schools that trace most of our insides to our outsides. There is no need to retell the case against this view; it is enough to note, as Chomsky (1959) does, that much of our behavior is stimulus-free, and so even if the world is not so little, it is not clear that it enters into the composition of our mental states in any significant or determinate way.

In cognitive science the received responses to Plato's problem are also Plato's answers. We know so much from so little because we already know a lot. Different Platonic responses diverge on how much we know and what it looks like. Some hold that we come to the task of learning with minimal prior equipment that is nonetheless powerful and general. This idea is behind associationist schools, including the most fashionable, connectionism. Others hold that we have very powerful and specific prior equipment that operates blindly, as argued by the Chomsky-Fodor school (see Chapter 3 for a review).

Plato's answers to Plato's problem motivate cognitive science because of their connection to internalist discourse. As Leiber (1991: 10) notes, "Plato asked two of the most central questions of cognitive science and gave the beginnings of an answer to both." What do we know and how do we know it? Our minds come to the world equipped with a rich, predetermined system of necessary truths: timeless, idealized, unchanging, absolute, self-evident forms brought to consciousness by introspection, not developed through mimesis or other such copying of the outside world. Thus, we can do geometry because we already know the truths of geometry; more quotidianly, we know what water is because our minds have prior exposure to the world of ideal forms where ideal water was implanted in our reason.

Some of this, of course, is very hard to swallow. Where is this world of ideal forms, anyway? But we can dismiss part of the ontology and retain the gist of Plato's answer. As Leiber (1991: 11) writes: "Many if not all cognitive scientists would strongly endorse Plato's whole line of thought. His questions are the right questions. His answers, as far as they go, are the right answers." They are uncontroversially rendered in the modern internalist idiom, which proscribes explaining our insides as copies, even shallow copies, of our outsides.

The mind is a genetically disposed virtual machine (Pylyshyn 1985: 70) that has presolved much of the task of learning. Every individual inherits the same architecture, with built-in abstractions for which the vicissitudes of the world have little consequence. Thinking is the algorithmic manipulation of formal objects under the dictates of logic (freedom from contradiction, compositionality, truth-functionality, etc.). Cognitive science is thus the study of biological devices, their design, and their decision-making properties (Jackendoff 1987: xi); thoughts are formal results. Admittedly, different schools of thought construe the virtual machine in different ways—some seeking a brain machine over a mind machine, others building more or less in—but all are quite compatible with Plato's answer, conceiving of ourselves as equipped with an inner system of universal truths from the world of forms.[1]

The strongest reason for us to accept Plato's answer to Plato's problem 2,400 years later is that it is correct to a certain extent. Let us examine several cases that adopt Plato's answer to see how it dovetails with internalist discourse and how theories adjust to retain their commitment to internalism.

2.2 Universal Grammars

The search for the genetically transmitted virtual machine has gotten considerable support from advances in work on language, vision, music, action, and other cognitive domains, where researchers have uncovered universal grammars that underlie such capacities. These minimal, essential, and invariant systems of data structures and procedures appear to be available and operative from birth.

The work on language is among the most well known and convincing. While there is no need to review this work in detail, it is instructive to consider the gist and thrust of the findings, especially insofar as they typify and evoke similar architectural, virtual machine problems and accounts elsewhere in the cognitive system.

2.21 Language and Learnability

The goal of formal linguistics is to identify the presumably finite information that all children use to determine, within a very short period of time, the entire structure of the language they hear. In terms of the machine version of Plato's answer, formal linguistics investigates the basis on which language is *completely decidable,* a formal result with no revisions.

More technically, this is known as *learnability* or the *logical problem of language acquisition.*[2]

The theory of learnability specifies the relative contribution to the decidability of language of (1) input, (2) a class of languages to be learned, (3) the internal structure of the learner, and (4) a criterion for success (see Gold 1967, Wexler and Culicover 1981, Wexler 1982, and Baker and McCarthy 1981). The grammar problem is thus solved on the basis of the interaction of data, a target grammar, a procedure for relating the data to the target grammar, and some measure for choosing among equivalent intermediate solutions to the data-grammar problem. (Wexler and Culicover 1981 also add *feasibility*—that the decision could be one actually made in real time by real learners; see also section 2.31.)

Different views of acquisition stress the richness and importance of these four components. For example, information-processing accounts (Ingram 1989, O'Grady 1986) emphasize the innate learning component at the expense of the other factors. Such theories place the burden of attaining adult grammar on the power of general computing principles, such as serial processing, hierarchical chunking, memory limitations, and so on.

Information processing, however, downplays the role of specifically linguistic information, and so is not the received view in formal linguistics. Chomsky (1986) articulates the linguistic view clearly in saying that the learnability question centers on how the child constructs an internal language—I-Language—out of the interaction of innately given universal grammar (the initial linguistic state of the system) and other humanly learnable systems. Noticeably absent in this process is the external language—E-Language, the observable forms in the language as a corpus. Chomsky (1986) excludes the E-Language because it is an artificial, unstable epiphenomenon, derived from the presumptions of those who describe language. More crucially, the E-Language is not even the input into the learner. The child is given finite data, not a corpus, and so the input into the learner is decidedly less determinate than even what an E-Language corpus might be. The E-Language plays no role in language acquisition because it is not even real; only the I-Language is the true language.

With the learnability problem now cast as *an entirely internalist issue,* linguistics signs on to the task and seeks to identify universal grammar, the conditions that define the initial linguistic state of the system and permit the decidability of language. The most influential and successful approach is government binding theory, which tries to make explicit the abstract principles (formal constraints on data structures) and parameters (data structures set like switches in an on/off fashion) that constitute the initial state of the learner.[3]

The remarkable success in this work testifies to the essential correctness of the approach. For example, whatever their language or culture, children universally begin forming their sentences by omitting pronominal subjects—"Ø want milk," "Ø ride car," and so on. The pervasiveness of this phenomenon suggests that they come to the task of learning syntax with the hypothesis that languages do not express pronominal subjects—more technically, that the *null subject* parameter is positively set in the initial linguistic state (see, e.g., Jaeggli and Safir 1989). This behavior does not depend on whether the language to be learned requires subjects to be expressed (as in English and French) or is itself null subject (as in Spanish, Polish, Mandarin, or Italian). Nor is it a function of the requirements of communication, where subjects, which typically encode known information, are deleted because of their deducibility, since children do not universally delete forms that encode given information even though they consistently omit subjects. And certainly the absence of these subjects in children's speech cannot be uniformly traced to externals—the input— because children who hear sentences with these subjects expressed nonetheless delete them in their own speech. The facts suggest that children's initial syntactic decisions are internally constrained to omit subjects. What internal principles explain this condition on the learnability of these initial data structures?

Answers to this question center on the formal constraints that allow null subjects under the assumption that children come equipped with these conditions and a preset parameter which they either verify or modify, given the language to be acquired. Hyams (1992) proposes that the null subject parameter is preset positively and conditioned by two principles, one that determines where null subjects can structurally appear and one that states the means by which the value for the null subject is determined. These conditions correspond to the two basic decisions the child has to make: is there an absent subject in this data structure, and if so, what is it? In Hyams's (1992) account, the answer to the first is keyed by uniform morphology (as in Italian, Spanish, and Mandarin, which have regular verbal agreement and delete the subject); the answer to the second is determined through either the agreement-inflectional system (as in Spanish, where the absent subject can be identified from verb endings) or through linking to another noun, such as the sentence topic (as in Mandarin, which has no verbal morphology and is thus uniform, but also has regular linking of the null grammatical subject to the noun that encodes the discourse topic). On this account, then, children universally omit subjects because they come to the task equipped to do so. Morphological uniformity and identification by nominal topic or agreement decide null subjects for them.

English-speaking children exhibit behavior which suggests that they conform to these preconditions even in the presence of disconfirming evidence—namely, adult English, which requires subjects. They drop inflections across the board and so have uniform morphology, and they link their subjects to topics (see Gruber 1967, Lebeaux 1988); in a very real sense they begin producing E-English on the basis of something like I-Mandarin. But their input, adult English, is morphologically nonuniform, with inflections on some verbs but absent from others. So they eventually get evidence that they have to reset the parameter for English and learn how the language varies from the predictions of the initial state of universal grammar. Remarkably, they solve this problem at a very young age, by three or four, and never revise the decision.

Hyams's explanation is used here as an illustration only and not necessarily an endorsement; indeed, there is much dispute over its details and even its correctness (Weissenborn 1992, Bloom 1990, Gerken 1991, Lillo Martin 1992). Hyams herself has cycled through several explanations of the phenomenon (Hyams and Wexler 1993). As crucial as these disagreements are, they nonetheless concern *the nature of the innate principles* and so do not shift the explanatory commitments away from Platonist discourse. The decidability of language by the virtual machine remains unchanged as an account.

Learnability also holds sway in explanations of other features of syntax, as well as for the rest of the components of language. For instance, very early on, children have knowledge of the principles of binding, which state the structural domains in which the antecedents of pronouns can be found (Lust 1986). They also appear to know quite early the formal properties of bounding, which state the constraints on the movement of elements of a data structure, or, better, how elements of a data structure are interpreted as belonging in positions other than those they occupy. For example, in the sentence *What did you see?* the question word *what* has been moved to the front of the sentence and must be interpreted as belonging to a slot after *see* since it refers to the object: *What$_1$ did you see X$_1$?* Goodluck (1991: 91–92) reports that three-year-olds know there are limits to what can be moved and know how to interpret the displaced elements. The best explanation for these results seems to be that the behavior is constrained by the children's knowledge of the formal conditions on the size and accessibility of the domains that constitute sentential data structures.

While these syntactic claims illustrate the formal nature of universal grammar, they do not speak directly to the putative biological properties of the virtual linguistic machine. Knowledge of binding and bounding by age three is impressive, but it *is* three years after birth and could conceivably have been learned in that time, not preprogrammed. But similar formal results hold for phonology and semantics, which show that very young children have quite specific knowledge about sound and meaning systems. By the age of four months they can distinguish voice onset time, the acoustic cue that universally differentiates voiced and voiceless consonants. By six months they have learned the range of allowable cues for their particular language (Ingram 1989: 88–96). Children thus appear to be biologically disposed to categorical phonetic perception.

Semantic acquisition, too, implicates learnability and formal constraints on what we might call *the denoting machine*. Golinkoff and associates (1992, 1994) describe six principles of lexical acquisition that appear to be operative from the first year on and suggest the formal character of the assignment of content to expressions (though Golinkoff would not endorse this entire interpretation). For instance, very young children know that their words apply to the world, or denote (the *principle of reference*), and that denotations first apply to whole objects and events (extensions) and only later to their parts or properties (the *principle of object scope*).[4]

Children's initial semantic behavior suggests that they come to the task of learning meaning equipped with the two formal properties of denotation and extension. These qualities make their linguistic denotations quite different from their nonlinguistic, gestural referring (Pettito 1992), and so children's initial semantic competence cannot be reduced to pointing or some other nonverbal mechanism for denoting.

The algorithmic and deterministic quality of children's performance in all areas of language—even to the apparently nonformal area of content—is strong evidence that Plato's answer is correct for the structure of language. But though language is important to the human character, it is not the only property, and, furthermore, is not the only one explained as a biologically given, virtual machine.

2.22 Taste

The problems of learnability, and consequent explanation through Platonist, internalist discourse, are found in other cognitive domains that are equally likely to be biologically given and so constituted by deterministic computation. The natural place to look for instances is in the senses. These informational systems at the very boundary between mind and world are indisputably built-in and automatic, blindly delivering canonical output whatever their input.

Visual and spatial knowledge are among the most thoroughly studied subfields of cognitive science, with the results widely known, even paradigmatic to Plato's answer and internalist cognitive science. When is the last time you saw a new *kind* of object—not a new object itself, which happens all the time, but a new type, such as one without edges, one that is neither solid nor nonsolid, or one that has no internal consistency (Marr 1982, Yuille and Ullman 1990, Biederman 1990)? When did you ever see a new kind of motion or some new type of relation between an object and its location (Spelke 1990, Jackendoff 1992)? These universal truths of object form, place, and motion are products of our neurobiological makeup, not open to revision.

Visual and spatial knowledge provides the paradigmatic arguments for Platonism. But similar evidence can be found in work on other senses, research rarely cited in cognitive science. The findings on taste offer independent support for Platonism and internalist explanations. (The entire discussion that follows is based on Scott 1992, a comprehensive survey of taste.)

Taste poses a problem isomorphic to that of visual and linguistic knowledge. How does the organism convert degrees of chemical input into categorical representations of taste? How does it taste so much from so little? This problem can also be posed as one of gustatory learnability. Since the behavioral function of taste is feeding, how does the organism distinguish toxins from nutrients? The answer to both questions is decidedly Platonic: gustatory learnability and taste are presolved. As Scott observes, "The capacity to perform [analysis of quality and intensity of incoming chemicals] is genetically endowed" (275).

The basics of taste read like the basics of vision and language, with taste knowledge invariant, underdetermined, modularized, and obligatorily computed by dedicated neural structures. The four primary tastes—salty, sweet, sour, and bitter—have unrelated but determinate stimulus properties. For example, the lipophilicity (greasiness and fattiness) of a stimulus partly explains its bitterness, but lipophilicity is totally unrelated to the other three basic tastes.

The four primary tastes are keyed to localized receptors, which are disposed to the chemical properties of the input and send information along specific neural channels. The chemical properties of the input trigger changes in cell membrane conductance and depolarize receptor cells; the depolarization spreads up the cells in taste coding pathways—a sweet channel, a sour channel, and so on—in an informational transduction, instantiating by activation the gustatory neural code.

The primary-taste neural channels lead to the hindbrain, an evolutionarily primitive area of the central nervous system, and have neural connections to other lower brain areas, such as the limbic system (unsurprisingly), which is associated with emotion. In primates there are also neural connections to higher cortical areas, such as that for vision and the frontal cortex. This neural distinction appears to underlie behavioral differences between primates and nonprimates with respect to the hedonic value of tastes. In rats, for example, value and taste are closely tied. Their simultaneity—both good *and* nutritious, bad *and* toxic—makes sense in relation to the rat's concomitant inability to regurgitate food (Scott 1992: 231): if it is going to taste good, it had better also be nutritious, since the rat has no way of expelling what has been ingested. In contrast, taste and value are neurally differentiated in primates (e.g., the connection to the visual system offers visual preference), and so motivation and food preference are independent of taste. Likewise, humans and monkeys can regurgitate food that might taste good but actually be toxic.

The linking of value and taste again points up the learnability problem and Plato's answer thereto. Some organisms are predisposed to solving in one fell swoop value-taste decisions for feeding; others are predisposed to compute them separately. But in each there is no question that these things are inherent to the gustatory neural code; they are unrevisable results (Scott 1992: 275).

The four primary tastes are to the gustatory system what objects and motion are to the visual system and what the binding and bounding theory are to the linguistic system: inherent representational constraints. If anything, the gustatory neural code evokes Plato's internalist answer for cognitive science more directly than vision or language. Scott (253, 275–79) points out that while the taste system is poised on the line between world and mind, its essential goal is to assess the consequences of ingestion. The function of taste representation is not to have a record of the environment, as with the visual system, "but to sample the chemical environment discretely" (253) to verify the acceptability of input and "to maximize hedonism" (278). It is thus an essentially internalist representational system in both its construction and its goals.

As Chomsky (1986) might say, taste is I-Taste. The mental representation is the only real and true taste system. Where, after all, are the tastes in the external world? Nothing is a taste unless it is I-Tasted. Just as E-Language and E-Space are ad hoc, so taste stimuli can give only finite, fragmented, and impoverished data to the organism. How do we taste so much from so little? Neurobiology preanswers the question by equipping us with underspecified ideal tastes and dedicated physical mechanisms for computing them.

2.3 Troubles in Paradise

The virtual-machine paradigm has taught us a great deal about the mind as a device. But these gains have not been gotten without cost. The expenses point up the line between Plato's problem and other essential problems about human thinking that have their own answers. The feasibility of Plato's answers and the gradual shifting of the learnability factors in response to the encroachment of the world alter the balance between the virtual machine and the real one. These troubles in Platonic paradise are especially relevant in explanations of language, which is the linchpin of the relation between social and computational mind. Problems with feasibility suggest the need for an inclusive ideology for cognitive science, one that respects the gains of Plato's answer while complementing it with real-time action. Before we examine that paradigm, Wittgenstein's problem, we need to appreciate some of the troubles with language.

2.31 Feasibility

The feasibility of Plato's answers to Plato's problem has come under attack from two camps which are otherwise sympathetic to the general program. (This differentiates them from adversaries outside the internalist camp, many of whom propose counters that simply miss the mark.) On the one hand are those who see the virtual machine as *not Platonic enough*. On the other are those who see the virtual machine as promising but, in its present form, psychobiologically implausible.

2.311 PLATONIC FEASIBILITY
Katz's (1981, 1990) position against Chomskyan universal grammar is the benchmark Platonist objection. He points out that the goal of Platonism and traditional philosophical rationalism is the discovery of necessary truths—constancies beyond the contingent regularities of the material

world. But the currently fashionable stripe of rationalism, conceptualism (which formal linguistics endorses), situates universals in material psychobiological facts and thus preserves contingency in the universals it proposes. Conceptualism can never be more than mere nativism since its necessary truths remain time-bound, that is, in a material mind/brain. This, in turn, allows idiosyncratic aspects of psychology to constrain theorizing. For Platonists and true philosophical rationalists, such an account always falls short of giving an accurate picture of what is essential to language because it fails to treat language as an ideal, abstract object.

Presumably these objections hold for other universals proposed by conceptualist cognitive science. Universal properties of form and motion and the four primary tastes are as bogged down in their real-time clothes as the null subject parameter. All the rest of cognitive science has a Platonism problem, since its constancies are too much situated in the world.[5]

What are we to make of the objection that universal grammar falls short of true Platonism? In one sense, the truth of the objection has very little impact. The conversion of cognitive science to pure ideas entails only the elimination of psychological data. Such results have never played a central role in formal linguistics, for example, where they have been used as justification, not as axioms. In another sense, it underscores the power and dominance of the internalist ideology. Katz's (1981, 1990) objection is that universal grammar—even in its presently rarefied formal state—is still *too contextualized, too attached to the world*. How, then, are we even aware of these Platonic forms? In Katz's view, we grasp them by pure Kantian intuition, an internalist mechanism with no causal history. Or, as Frege argued about our awareness of the truths of logic, our minds "see" them but do not construct them as such (Leiber 1991: 38). There is no way into the world with this "advanced Platonism," as Katz (1981) calls it. The invariants of objects and motion, the binding theory, the null subject parameter, and the four primal tastes are like numbers and the necessary truths of logic. Our minds have them as objects of intuitive apprehension (Katz 1981: 203), but they appear against the backdrop of another reality of ideal forms. Truly rational cognitive science needs the external world even less than we might imagine.

2.312 PSYCHOBIOLOGICAL FEASIBILITY

A different kind of complaint comes from within the psychobiological camp. Lieberman (1991: 130–34) puts the objection by observing that, in the case of universal linguistic grammar, the proposal that all humans are born with the same rich, tightly interconnected set of principles and parameters is genetically implausible. The central role of variation in genetic transmission requires that some of the proposed universal code be absent in some children. Just as there is, for example, color blindness—and taste blindness (Scott 1992)—so must there be syntax blindness.

There are, in fact, cases of the selective genetic preservation of formal grammar (Yamada 1990), as well as claims of its selective loss (Cromer 1981). Pinker and Bloom (1990) cite evidence for more wide-ranging variation in formal capacities (though some of their arguments rely on performance factors only). But even with these disclaimers, the thrust of Lieberman's point remains. Universal grammar builds in a great deal and links it up too tightly to be a plausible psychobiological hypothesis.

Recent modifications in formal grammar are instructive responses to these feasibility troubles because they reveal the tendency of cognitive science, under attack, to draw the mind-world line even more narrowly on the mind side and so accentuate the tension between internalist and externalist explanations.

One misgiving about universal linguistic grammar is that it is too abstract. More than a little suspension of disbelief is necessary to accept that the child comes into the world with, for example, a null subject parameter. Innate grammatical subjects are very different from innate edges or saltiness. We can perform a physical reduction on the latter two and trace them to light and chemical gradations with corresponding physical receptors. But subjects, anaphors, and bounding conditions? What is their neurochemistry?

The response in formal grammar has been toward *more abstraction,* that is, *minimalism* (Chomsky 1992)—the postulation of only what is absolutely essential, and a closer connection between abstract representations and the output expression. In the minimalist program, universal grammar consists of a computational system that projects minimal structural representations up from the idiosyncrasies of learned words (the lexicon); these representations optimally interface with two performance modules: articulation/perception (phonetic form) and conceptualization/intention (logical form). Universal grammar has no constructions, nothing like (genetically implausible) verbs or subjects, but rather invariant principles and conditions with built-in options for variation.

The details of minimalism are less important here than the overall approach. Universal grammar has two abstract properties—economy (representations are simple and minimal) and realization (they come factory installed, in optimal form for execution). Seen this way, universal grammar strangely recovers some plausibility. Kean (1992) argues that to be neurobiologically feasible, formal grammar must be organized not in terms of discrete components with direct neural correlates, but by mediating areas—linguistic and cognitive interfaces. The minimalist format gives a more believable alignment of linguistic and neurobiological structure and better accommodates data from language disorders, which tend to affect a range of linguistic phenomena at once, that is, those joined by an interface.

The theoretical advance of minimalism in formal linguistics, while very likely correct as a modification to the computational account, illustrates an essential point about the virtual machine's response to problems. *It pulls mind back further from the external world* by drawing the mind-world barrier very narrowly and limiting its domain to *core mind*. In so narrowing mind, such proposals shift the balance of the learnability factors because they further restrict the contribution of the inherent properties of internal structure.

2.32 The Encroachment of the World

If universal grammars of language, taste, and vision markedly underdetermine knowledge, then the other learnability factors of input and learning assume greater importance in explaining the acquisition and functioning of these capacities. Researchers in visual and spatial knowledge and taste have appreciated the consequences of this retrenching. Spelke (1990) observes that while knowledge of stereoptic depth depends in some way on maturation and inherent knowledge of kinetic depth, binocular *experience*—input and learning—plays a significant role in the development of depth competence. In work on the gustatory code, Scott (1992: 260) observes: "An animal's experience has a pronounced and lasting influence on its behavioral reaction to taste stimuli," especially in taste aversion, where, for some animals, experience modifies taste neurons (263). For space and taste, externals impinge in a more than trivial way.

Similar findings hold for language, though their effect on overall theorizing has been less influential. Choi and Bowerman (1992) and Bowerman and Choi (1994) have shown that while minimal a priori semantic content universally underdetermines verb denotations, children are sensitive to the language-specific denotations in their input much earlier than previously assumed. Morgan (1986) and others have argued that children's syntactic decisions are influenced and facilitated by (what Morgan calls) *bracketed input*, E-Language with explicit phonetic cues to the abstract constituency of I-Language. If there is such prosodic bootstrapping, then the learnability problem for syntax is radically altered, with input taking on more of the work and reducing the role of innate structural knowledge (though McRoberts 1994 has seriously questioned the reliability of such cues). Hirsh-Pasek et al. (1986) have suggested that children may get some cues to negative evidence in their syntactic input. This is an important result because Plato's answer to the learnability problem emphasizes the decidability of language from positive instances only—no negative feedback. With negative evidence—that is, direct information that hypotheses are wrong—anything can be learned, and so the putative absence of negative evidence in the child's input would underscore the powerful role of preformed knowledge. If children's syntactic errors can be flagged by surface cues such as pauses and reformulations, information external to the learner may be more structured and facilitative than a purely Platonist answer might desire.

These encroachments of the world on Plato's problem deemphasize the innateness component of Plato's answer. Responses to the encroaching world from the internalist camp bring to the surface the tension between internal and external explanations and take us full circle to the problem with which this book began.

There are three ways that Platonism can deal with the encroaching external world. One is to externalize Plato, either by externally situating all knowledge (a return to behaviorism) or by locating knowledge in an objective ideality (as in Katz's Platonism). For reasons already discussed, neither of these is acceptable.

A second solution is to further Platonize the external world. This is done by expanding the domains of universal grammars to include ideal, decontextualized knowledge of a broader range of inputs and so further underdetermine the external world from within. A variety of proposals have this expansionist flavor. One from linguistics is the maturationist hypothesis (see, e.g., Borer and Wexler 1987). In this view, universal grammar grows just like other biologically determined organs. The stages of linguistic development are accountable to the gradual unfolding of internal, idealized knowledge, and so what look like mismatches between input/learning and given structure—which might otherwise support the influence of externals—are really places where internal knowledge is just waiting to catch up.

In large measure, the same internal expansionism, though without innateness, underlies linguistic proposals for communicative competence (ironically, since adherents of communicative competence are often decidedly anti-Chomskyan). Algorithmic rules of conversation (see, e.g., Sacks, Schegloff, and Jefferson 1974) and idealized inferences about intentions (see, e.g., Searle 1969, 1979) are communicative versions of the virtual machine. Just as language learners stop revising their syntactic decisions, so there comes a point when they never experience a new conversational move or communicative intention. As Staten (1984: 131) observes, "Searle's account . . . gravitates toward Chomsky's picture of grammatical competence" because, even though Searle and Chomsky disagree markedly on most else, they share an important epistemological strategy in seeking to identify the *necessary conditions of language* (Searle 1992: 243 acknowledges the convergences). The learnability questions thus apply to communication as well, where they are presolved by theories that equip the speaker with minimal models of all contexts (cf. Cosmides and Tooby 1994).

A third way to deal with the encroachment of the world is to accept it and put experience and the virtual machine in détente. This requires drawing the mind-world line throughout cognitive science in a way that some work on vision and taste has already done: by assuming the truth and importance of *both* the psychobiological code and experience. It also requires an overarching ideology that allows the legitimate cohabitation of both core computational mind and real-time action. For language, this would join grammar as a universal decision problem with speech as the internalizing of the vicissitudes of the social world in individuals. Can we link the internal, virtual machine with the real-time machine and its externalist idiom?

Such an ideology cannot be found in the MIT worldview, which excludes language and social connections from linguistic theorizing. What Chomsky (1986) calls *Orwell's problem*—how we know so little from so much because our political systems restrict access to all the evidence—is socially situated, but it remains an entirely political concern, not a linguistic one. Moreover, Plato's answer does not let language enter into action because universal grammar is not a causal or dispositional theory of behavior. Chomsky (1986: 241) argues that it is not at all clear just how, or whether, computational mind enters into real-time performance. This separation of language from action is bolstered by his claim that language has evolved not as a product of selection but as a side effect of other genetic changes. In such a view, universal grammar is arbitrary and disconnected from the functional purposes of the organism as a whole, the modern genetic version of objective ideality (but see Pinker and Bloom 1990 for counters).

There is a program that embraces *both* language as computed form and language as action. This is what I will call *Wittgenstein's problem*. Contrary to the popular view of Wittgenstein—and his dismissal from linguistics (Chomsky 1986) and computationalism generally (Fodor 1975)—the tension between inner form and overt action belies a unified theory of mind. Just as Plato's problem legitimates the inward turn, so Wittgenstein's problem links core mind and action through language. It is on these grounds that we can build a Vygotskyan cognitive science.

2.4 Wittgenstein's Problem

How do we coordinate the idealized, homogenized experience of the interior, virtual world and the motley, lived experience of contingent, outer circumstance? Goldman (1990) argues that the compatibility of these two "is an important issue *for* cognitive science, because it concerns the ramifications of this discipline's approach to human beings" as both "underlying principles . . . orderly, lawful patterns . . . [and] . . . persons as freely choosing agents" (319, 317).

If this is a problem for cognitive science, it was no less one that dogged Wittgenstein (1968: 227): "Of course, in one sense mathematics is a branch of knowledge—but still it is also an *activity*." His *compatibilism*—to use the modern ethical term for the doctrine that allows both determinism and freedom (ter Hark 1990: 212)—lies in his concern for how language fits in the management of reason and acting.

2.41 How Many Wittgensteins?

Wittgenstein is commonly viewed as a philosopher of two distinct minds. The first, the Wittgenstein of the *Tractatus* (1974a, originally 1921), is a logician, exploring, in a prooflike style, the form and meaning of propositions under the conditions of determinate truth. The second, the Wittgenstein of the *Philosophical Investigations* (1968, originally 1953), is a natural historian, speaking discursively about the uses of statements under indeterminate conditions on truth and meaning. Characterized as such, the two Wittgensteins do seem diametrically opposed, but this bifurcated view fails to appreciate that Wittgenstein always worked at the border between determinacy and indeterminacy. From that single theoretical vantage point he explored each side, focusing early on logic and later on use. For this reason, some have attributed a *dialectical unity* to Wittgenstein, thus defusing the whole issue of a *choice* between continuity or discontinuity (Dixon 1987: 60, Margolis 1987).

The case for Wittgenstein's unified program can be made in a number of ways. Textual work shows that many of the ideas associated with his early writings continue into his later work and, conversely, that ideas usually attributed to his later theorizing are found in his first studies. For example, ter Hark (1990: 1–24) observes, from studying Wittgenstein's manuscripts, that the idea of the language game, so crucial to the later work, appears in the manuscripts of the very early period. Indeed, in *Philosophical Grammar* (1974b, originally 1932–34), written in the transitional period between the *Tractatus* and the *Philosophical Investigations,* he argues for both arbitrary, autonomous formal systems and family resemblances (see also ter Hark 1990: 262–63).

Curiously, the most compelling argument for the unity of the two Wittgensteins—and the one that bears directly on forging a Vygotskyan cognitive science—can be seen in his ethics. According to Janik and Toulmin (1973), Wittgenstein's goal in both the *Tractatus* and the *Philosophical Investigations* is to draw the line between fact and value by first investigating the essence and limits of formally determinate knowledge, and then holding up the purely demonstrable against the results of an inquiry into the essence and limits of real-time speech and action. The continuity in Wittgenstein is his desire to rescue moral behavior by determining the boundaries of reason in coherent and meaningful speech. The difference between the two Wittgensteins is one of focus: in the *Tractatus* he assumes the self-evidence of the language-world connection; in the later work he sees self-evidence as mediated by the social world, with necessity arising out of contingency (see Harré 1987).

The later Wittgenstein most certainly spoke in explicit contrast to his earlier work. In the preface to the *Philosophical Investigations* he writes, "I have been forced to recognize grave mistakes in what I wrote in that first book" (1968: vi). Still, he never rejected his early work, but simply acknowledged its limits and saw his inquiries as a seamless, integrated whole. Five lines prior to his acknowledgment of "grave mistakes" in the *Tractatus,* he writes, "It suddenly seemed to me that I should publish those old thoughts and the new ones together" (vi). The *single Wittgenstein* manifests perpetual tension between representation and acting, between the formally computable and run time in the real world. Wittgenstein's problem concerns the limits and codetermination of each, not the reduction of one to the other. As Wright (1989: 237) observes, Wittgenstein was pulled in *two directions simultaneously*: to nondeliberate experiences (Cartesian internalism) and to dispositions by external causes (Rylean externalism). Hacker (1990), perhaps Wittgenstein's most thorough interpreter, argues that he sought to transcend the dichotomous, inner-outer conception of mind (ter Hark 1990).

While this justification of a single Wittgenstein might sound like a stretched apology for a theorist who simply changed his mind, it is important to remember that Wittgenstein's ethical inquiries occur in the context of a long philosophical tradition of studying the tension between logic and morality. Kant sought the borders of fact and value as two sides of a single coin by examining the limits of reason from within. His linking of reason and value by charting logical limits runs headlong into the views of Schopenhauer and Kierkegaard. For Schopenhauer, fact is split from value, and ethics is based on what is, not on what ought to be; the world of ideas (necessity and logic) differs from the world of will (morality and desire), and morality becomes an empirical pursuit. Kierkegaard takes the fact-value split as a decisive one, relegating reason wholly to fact and linking moral choice to absurd leaps of faith and value decisions in the actual, lived world.

Wittgenstein's philosophy can be thought of as a struggle with Kant's, Schopenhauer's, and Kierkegaard's ethical problems all within a history of (failed) critiques of language. Kant is to the *Tractatus* what Kierkegaard is to the *Philosophical Investigations*; Wittgenstein the truth-table logician is the other half of Wittgenstein the moral individualist (Janik and Toulmin 1973: 22). Wittgenstein's problem is how language fits into the relation between machines (determinate facts in computable form) and persons (value choices under indeterminate rules).

How this tension is played out in Wittgenstein is instructive to our larger goal of replacing Plato's problem with Wittgenstein's. There is no need to review Wittgenstein's entire work, which the burgeoning Wittgenstein industry has already done with ample insight. Instead, I briefly examine the essential ideas of the *Tractatus* and its isomorphism to Plato's answer. I then move on to a similarly brief study of the gist of the *Philosophical Investigations*, as a prelude to the linking of the later Wittgenstein with Vygotsky through deconstructionist philosophy.

2.411 WITTGENSTEIN 1: THE VIRTUAL MACHINE

In a section of the *Philosophical Investigations* (#193–94) where he is concerned with models and causal determination, Wittgenstein notes two ways to view a machine: as an abstract symbolization and as an actual apparatus. The virtual and the real machine differ in that the parts and function of the former are idealized and completely determinate while those of the latter distort under actual operation. The properties of the virtual machine are inherent equipment. They are in it from the start, and so "the movement of the machine-as-symbol is predetermined in a different sense from that in which the movement of any given actual machine is predetermined" (1968: 78 #193).

This is a striking rendering of the tension that underlies Wittgenstein's problem, especially because it directly evokes the machine analogy that motivates cognitive science. The *Tractatus* is a book about the virtual machine and the inherent properties of ideal objects. The partiality of the early Wittgenstein to Plato's problem and Plato's answer can be seen in a much later book, *Remarks on the Foundations of Mathematics* (1956). Wright (1989: 238), noting the remarkable convergence of Chomsky and Wittgenstein on this point, cites the passage (from *Remarks* 4:48): "And here we see the mathematical machine, which, driven by the rules themselves, obeys only mathematical laws and not physical ones . . . But might it not be said that this sentence is grammatical, and has the meaning it does, even if no one ever considers it? For that is what one would like to say—and here we see the language-machine which, driven by the rules of language themselves, obeys only linguistic laws and not physical ones." Wittgenstein the logician was thus concerned with the necessary properties of the language machine, and, moreover, did not abandon this concern when he later focused his attention on the language machine in use (ter Hark 1990).

The goal of Wittgenstein's logical work is the elucidation of the form of thought and displayed truth. He began this pursuit within an intellectual milieu dominated by the conflict between the stability of internalist proposals (e.g., Kant's forms of judgment) and the near-nihilism of observations of the dispersion and vicissitudes of the external world (e.g., Mauthner's proto-deconstructionism). This conflict is a version of Plato's problem: how can the vicissitudes of the external world be so determinately modeled by thought? Wittgenstein 1 believed that the answer lay in *the nature of the models*, the exact approach of modern internalist cognitive science, and so (again as in cognitive science) he took the Kantian approach by studying reason from within.

Crucial to this inquiry is the nature of propositions—expressed thoughts—which is the focus of the *Tractatus*, where he examines the relationship of propositions to one another and to the world. Both tasks are problems of inner form and displayed truth. The relationships of propositions are determined wholly on the basis of the form of the propositions and are shown formulaically (in truth tables). Propositions get truth by retaining the configuration of the world in their form. They exhibit their truth.

But just how do thoughts as propositions show their truth? How do they model the world? As cognitive science might say, given that mind is a modeling device obeying the specifiable laws of form, just what is a mental model? (Johnson-Laird 1983 devotes a whole book to this question.) For this answer, Wittgenstein turned to the then current theories of empirical models because these, like the mechanics he knew so well from his training as an engineer, combined mathematical ideality with links to the world. This mathematics of language was potentially an overarching critique of mind since it would yield all the possibilities of language itself— its models—without the distortions of real-time psychology and history.[6]

Wittgenstein had two accounts of models at his disposal: Mach's, in which models have a physical basis and are distilled sensorial copies, and Hertz's, in which models are logical constants, abstract possibilities from which actual facts derive, not rarefied copies of the world. The difference lies in the world-mind relation: do facts limit the possible models, or do the models limit the possible facts? The latter, clearly Plato's question and answer, is the one Wittgenstein adopted: "[We have] a priori *knowledge* of the possibility of a logical form" (1974a: 67 #6.33), and "For all that happens and is the case is accidental. What makes it non-accidental [logic] cannot lie *within* the world" (1974a: 71 #6.41). "Logic [i.e., the study of models] is transcendental" (1974a: 65 #6.13). Logic makes the world possible by giving it form (Janik and Toulmin 1973: 188).

Thoughts and/or propositions anticipate and construct experience; they do not copy it. Representations preserve the form of the world by already containing the possibilities, much as the actual movements of the real machine inhere in the virtual-machine model. The early Wittgenstein is a possible-worlds theorist for whom propositions occupy a position in logical space, which is presupposed in its totality.[7]

In the end, the *Tractatus* encounters its own limits. Not only do the limits of my language mean the limits of my world (as the sloganized Wittgenstein goes)—that is, the necessary boundaries of my representing point to the necessary boundaries of what I can think—but "a picture cannot . . . depict its pictorial form" (1974a: 9 #2.172). Thought may be a logical picture of the facts, but this picture cannot explain why it is so. Unlike, say, chemistry, which also gives a certain kind of picture of the (chemical) facts but can call on independent demonstrations of its validity (e.g., through mathematics or language), the applicability of logic to language (and then to the world) must be validated in language itself.

Here is where the virtual machine ends and the real machine begins. In the search for value from within, the inherent, determinate, totalized form of thought displays its own boundaries (see Worthington 1988).

2.412 WITTGENSTEIN 2: THE REAL MACHINE

In his logical investigations, Wittgenstein hopes to save ethics from proof by examining the structure and limits of decontextualized, logico-linguistic calculi. In the *Philosophical Investigations,* he articulates "the rule-conforming behavior by which such calculi acquire some external relevance" (Janik and Toulmin 1973: 224). Wittgenstein is still concerned with the link between the formally decidable and the unsayable, but his focus shifts from inner to outer. He now concentrates on the connection of decidable systems to significance, speaking in action, not static demonstrable truth.

One way of understanding this work is as an attack on the reduction of language and thought to essences. In reconsidering his own statements in the *Tractatus* about the essence of propositions, he writes, "One thinks that one is tracing the outline of the thing's nature over and over again, and one is merely tracing round the frame though which we look at it" (1968: 48 #114). His goal in the *Philosophical Investigations* is "an order with a particular end in view; one out of many possible orders; not *the* order" (1968: 51 #132).

This movement away from essences, though still part of his general program of delimiting the boundaries of the sayable, requires him to rethink the verification practices of his logical work. The *Tractatus* relies on ostensive definition and assumes a direct and self-evident world-word relation; the later Wittgenstein argues for *meaning as use,* an axiom that has been popularized to confusion and so requires two clarifications.

First, Wittgenstein's actual statement about meaning as use is: "For a *large* class of cases—though not for all—in which we employ the word 'meaning' it can be defined thus: the meaning of a word is its use in the language" (1968: 20 #43). In line with his attack on essences—and against the frequent current use of Wittgenstein as a totalizing social functionalist—he did not hold that the meaning-as-use axiom applied everywhere to language and was the essence of meaning. Naming, the very relation of the assignment of words to, as he says, their bearers—or reference itself—is another matter. "For naming and description do not stand on the same level: naming is a preparation for a description" (1968: 24 #49). It "gives this object a role . . . ; it is now a *means* of representation" (1968: 25 #50). As in a game, the use of a piece makes sense only in relation to a prepared place in the game for the piece (1968: 15). Wittgenstein thus rejects not ostension and reference but only its self-evidence, and so Wittgenstein-the-functionalist does not merely supplant Wittgenstein-the-logician.

The second clarification is that in talking about meaning as use, he was more precisely talking about the word *meaning* and not the concept 'meaning'. As Staten (1984: 87–89) points out, if Wittgenstein were definitively characterizing 'meaning' itself, this would have been a hypocritical gesture toward the essentialism he was calling into question; rather, he was depriviteging and reflexivizing the word *meaning*, making it just one among other ordinary words and thereby calling attention to its position as a role focuser in all its situations of use. For Wittgenstein, the role of the word *meaning* is to signal that the roles of all other words are on the table and under scrutiny.

These clarifications of meaning-as-use return us to Wittgenstein's larger project. He has not eliminated the centrality of language-world relations; he is still concerned with symbolic representations—models—but has modified their mechanisms for verification. What once were necessary, self-evident formal relations are now the contingent procedures governing actual words in real time. He had earlier "paid too little attention to the steps by which formalized representations are put to use in real-life linguistic behavior . . . So, from now on, Wittgenstein focused his attention instead on language as behavior" (Janik and Toulmin 1973: 222, 223). The truth of virtual machines now lay in their implementations.

Remarkably, this shift from the virtual to the implemented machine is also a strategy basic to the verification procedures of cognitive science. The goal of computational theorizing is to produce explanations in effectively computable form—precise, explicit, and hence computable. As Johnson-Laird (1983: 4) observes, all models should be working models. Anderson (1987) sounds as if he were mimicking Wittgenstein when he says that the value of implementation lies in its consequences for discovering true accounts in cognitive science.

Whereas Wittgenstein's internalism in the *Tractatus* runs him into the necessary metaphysical limits of the sayable, his externalism in the *Philosophical Investigations* runs him into actual bounds. As he writes, "We can draw a boundary—for a special purpose" (1968: 33 #69). The limits of rationality and logic do not depend on anything for their delimiting; they just limit. Universal grammar, the four basic tastes, and the elementary computations of vision do not deliver their respective representations for any reason: they just represent. But real-time boundaries *are drawn for reasons*. How we position ourselves in the act of speaking does depend on why we are speaking at the moment. Luria's peasant, we might recall, acts as he does for a special purpose.

2.42 From Wittgenstein's Problem to Vygotsky's Answer via Derrida

The role of language in the tension between reason and action in Wittgenstein's problem offers a new, broader foundation for cognitive science. Persons and machines are compatible. But Wittgenstein was not a psychologist and so had no research program in which to formulate empirical solutions. Fortunately, Wittgenstein 1's quandaries are strikingly analogous to Plato's problem and answer, and so internalistic computational psychology provides a rich set of theoretical and empirical results for Wittgenstein 1. When we turn to solutions for Wittgenstein 2, we see that we need a social psychology of action. Where do we find that?

Perhaps, like Varela, Thompson, and Rosch (1991: xviii), who call for a cognitive science that links both reductive, internalist mind-science with a "hands-on, pragmatic approach to experience with which to complement science," we could turn to Buddhism for an account of mind embedded in the external material world. Remarkably, this gesture to the East keeps the ideological blindness of the West and passes right over Russia, which, in the Vygotsky-Luria-Leont'ev school, has a long tradition of studying mind embedded in the sociocultural material world; it is a tradition, moreover, with results already articulated with those of Western psychology.

More sensitive to the Vygotskyan tradition, Margolis (1987: 146) points out that Wittgenstein 2 is a natural link between social psychology and developmental structuralism because of the *unifying tension* between the two Wittgensteins. Vygotsky's social psycholinguistics of action is the research program for Wittgenstein 2 and so fills out the prospects of Wittgenstein's problem. But to appreciate this, we need to see Wittgenstein 2 himself as an action theorist, which can be done in reading, as Staten (1984) has done, Wittgenstein 2 through postmodern theory.[8]

2.421 DECONSTRUCTING WITTGENSTEIN 2

The usual interpretation of Wittgenstein 2 is as a social-competence theorist who can be assimilated to discourse and speech act theory (Staten 1984: 156). Instead of buying into Wittgenstein 2 as a proponent of a communication calculus arbitrated by omniscient social truth, we can, like Staten (1984), see him as an early deconstructionist. He is not a social or psychological theorist, or even a philosopher for that matter, but an action theorist, one who subverts the status quo by holding up ontological opposites—for example, the received view and the marginalized, the object and its absence—and examining the play of meaning in the self-reflexive speech of the postmodern moment.

While it may seem extraordinary to call Wittgenstein a proto-deconstructionist, it is worth noting that a number of others have made similar, independent characterizations, though not in such fashionable terms. Ter Hark (1990) remarks that the views of Wittgenstein 2 cannot be readily linked to competence theories of psychology because he does not separate (internal) understanding from (external) action. Searle (1992) uses Wittgenstein as a base from which to argue for a complete revision in psychological theorizing along the lines of mental action, without a split between homogeneous inner rules and variable outer behavior.

Like Derrida, Wittgenstein 2 is concerned with action, and on these grounds he clearly links up with Vygotsky. As Wertsch (1991: 119) points out, Vygotskyan sociocultural theory explains mind as "human action . . . situated in cultural, historical, and institutional settings . . . [T]he key to such explication is the . . . person(s)-acting-with-mediational-means," chiefly the mediation of speech. In seeing the theoretical value of the action of the moment of speaking, Wittgenstein 2 evades Platonism and turns into Vygotsky via Derrida.

2.422 AN I FOR AN i, A TRUTH FOR A truth?

The best way to understand the convergence of Wittgenstein and Vygotsky via Derrida is to look at the origins of Derrida's deconstructionism in Husserl's phenomenology. Two of Husserl's major concerns were the stability of knowledge and the meaning of the objects of experience. How do we ground our experience and speak coherently given that our minds operate in the flux of external particulars? (Recall Plato's answer to this question.) For Husserl, experiential stability lies in the ideality of the perceived object, or the *noema*. In experiencing actual objects, the mind constructs an essence, which gives experience its continuity and repeatability. In more cognitive terms, the vagaries of sensation are idealized by perception. Thought stabilizes, and has priority over, experience per se.[9]

Phenomenology anchors perceived objects by assigning them meaning through reference to actual objects. We ground our knowledge in internal ideality, which makes phenomenology a form of idealism; but ideality has meaning in reaching back out to the world, which gives phenomenology the flavor of naive realism.

To Derrida, Husserl is only partially correct and, in many respects, has the whole story backwards. In classical phenomenology, the stability of knowledge and the possibility of meaning are grounded in being (the presence of an object). Derrida, in contrast, claims that being itself is sensible only in simultaneous contrast to non-being, or absence. So, whereas Husserl grounds knowledge in being, this partial truth actually presupposes grounding in the deconstructive interplay and codetermination of presence and absence. To put this in less ponderous terms, we know an object not because it exists as such, but because its presence to our consciousness simultaneously evokes its absence. We know it because we deconstruct it.

Moreover, if being itself is secondary to simultaneous presence and absence, meaning is then freed from its traditional attachment to objects. To Derrida, Husserl has it backwards: words do not follow being; being follows words. Derrida locates meaning in what he calls the free play of signifiers, the moment of signification and the interplay of actual words. These are the things that embody in a single speaking moment both presence and absence. Again, in less technical talk, meaning is not the recovery of objects from words as signals of things but the tension between what words in themselves both say and do not say at any given moment.

In large measure Derrida's project is a rejection of all the idealism of phenomenology and an affirmation of particulars and externals. Totalizing Truth follows particular truths; the omniscient, interpretive I follows particular interpreting i's. This reinvests mind in real-time operation and action, and this is where Wittgenstein 2 enters the picture. According to Staten (1984), Wittgenstein is a kind of proto-Derrida. There are three points of convergence between the two.

First, both are concerned with "how one situates oneself . . . as [a] linguistic subject" (Staten 1984: xvi), a project traceable to a more fundamental recognition of the role of form in the determination of knowledge. In answering the ontological question of what we can know at all, we clarify what we can speak about coherently. The objects of knowledge are such only insofar as form gives boundaries to their substance and individuates them as objects of knowledge. Both Derrida and Wittgenstein dedicate much effort to an examination of the limits of form by perching on the boundary itself and looking at each side. Wittgenstein wants to save ethics and the unsayable by studying both the ideality of logical form (in the *Tractatus*) and its contingencies (in the *Philosophical Investigations*); Derrida saves being through non-being, and vice versa, by holding up the line dividing presence and absence as the ontological vantage point from which we can speak coherently: privileging a position on one side of form literally misses the mark and leads either to the assertion of mere presence (e.g., Husserl's positive being) or its negation (e.g., nihilism). The ethical continuity of the two Wittgensteins leads directly to Derrida, with Wittgenstein's positioning problem very much Derrida's. In rejecting essences but retaining form, both learn how to act with an awareness of the limits of what can be known and said at all.

A second point of convergence is that both are concerned with *the importance of the particular* in identity and continuity leading to consensus. For Derrida, identity comes from the iteration of particulars that change ever so slightly because of the different moments of their existence, not because of a constant essence. For example, a word has the same meaning in different contexts not because it carries with it some semantic essence, but because it bears similar relations to its contexts at different times.[10]

This potentially radical semantic indeterminacy is constrained, however, by the pressures of past practice. Words, for example, bring with them a history of signification and the authority of past contexts to constrain their changes. Continuity thus comes from the repeatability of instances, not from some prior ideal determination. The place to look for constancy—or the "hardness of the law," as Staten (1984) calls it—is in the particular, material cases themselves.

The connection to Wittgenstein can be found in his view of the nature of rules, perhaps the most thoroughly discussed but least understood of his positions. It is popular to say that for Wittgenstein, meaning is use in a language game, itself constituted by rules and subject to the conditions of "forms of life." Staten (1984) argues, however, that this makes Wittgenstein a kind of social reductionist, proposing hierarchies of rules for language function, with "forms of life" as the ultimate ontological category. In fact, for Wittgenstein, rules are not self-identifying forms or instantiations of socially or conceptually given templates. They are mere instances; rules are *case-by-case rulings,* acts, the operations of real machines, not forms or timeless strictures.[11]

Rules are followed by obedience in particular circumstances, not by a mind interpreting them. This view puts an end to interpretation in action and avoids the infinite regress of interpretive rule-following. If a mind follows a rule by truly interpreting it, what truly interprets the mind that truly interprets the rule, and so on? Only idealism needs an I for every i, and a Truth for every truth.

The upshot of this account is that meaning for Wittgenstein 2, as for Derrida, is the open-ended, momentary activity of application, or, as Staten (1984) observes, the indication of a path to follow, not the preconceived goal (Russell 1987 makes a similar point). This is why the proper understanding of the Wittgenstein slogan "meaning is use" is to be understood as "particular instances of the word *meaning* call for an examination of their use." There is no final system of rules: "We are not equipped with rules for every possible application" (1968: 38 #80). Meaning is not *predeterminate:* "The application of a word is not everywhere bounded by rules" (1968: 39 #84). Regularity lies in the external particulars: "If there has to be anything 'behind the utterance . . .' it is particular circumstances, which justify me in saying I can go on" (1968: 60 #154). Consensus and stability are not a precondition for talk but an emergent property of actual words in actual patterns of sign sequences (see also Searle 1992: chap. 10).

The third convergence between Derrida and Wittgenstein is their belief that minds are not constituted by language, though it would be easy to believe the opposite. Derrida appears to privilege speech over being, and Wittgenstein seems to link the knowable with the sayable. But Staten (1984) convincingly argues that neither sees mind as made up of language; nor is either a linguistic philosopher for that matter.

For both Derrida and Wittgenstein, language is *a symptom of acting, not its constitution.* In deconstruction, material language embodies simultaneous presence and absence, but it is the subversion and self-reflexivity of language itself that leads to the more important ontological and epistemological discoveries. This is typified in Derrida's proposed pseudo-word *différance* as the material indication of the deconstructive attitude. *Différance* is at once both a word and a non-word, and in a single instance evokes 'difference', 'deferral', 'dispersion', and, since it is not a word, 'nothing at all'. *Différance* is neither a word nor a concept but an unfolding mark (Leitch 1983: 39–45).

Similarly, when Wittgenstein uses language as the object of both logical analysis and social action, he is not trying to establish the primacy of language in thought (Staten 1984: 22). On the contrary, he is using language as a symptom of the borders of language and thought and as an instrument in the struggle between saying and doing. The essence of language lies neither in logical form nor in social practice but in the codetermination of its essence by accidence and vice versa.

Derrida and Wittgenstein are linguistic philosophers only in the sense that they use language as a gambit in their epistemological and ontological work. Their focus on language does not thereby mean that they are asserting that we cannot get outside language. For Wittgenstein and Derrida, in fact, we have to get outside language to grasp the roots of their insights.

2.423 VYGOTSKYAN ALLIANCES

Wittgenstein and Derrida gesture toward the actual and the viability of externalism. Their mutual concern for the position of the linguistic subject, the free run of particulars, and the view of language as symptomatic of mind rather than constitutive of it immediately strikes a chord with the Vygotskyan view of higher thought and internalizing. Although I consider Vygotsky's ideas in much more detail in the next chapter, here I can point up the bases for the Wittgenstein-Derrida-Vygotsky alliance.[12]

Let us recall from section 1.4 that Vygotskyan theory looks at how the individual speaking subject constructs and maintains an inner world, what we might now (half a century removed from Vygotsky) call *a self*. (Vygotsky did not speak in such terms, and this way of talking is best understood as a post-Vygotskyan interpretation rather than as elucidating something located in Vygotsky's writings per se. I thank James Wertsch for this observation.) The individual does this by internalizing external particulars and consciously deploying nonconstitutive, private speech in the moment of acting—in a nutshell, *higher thought through on-line frame building*. Crucial to this metaconsciousness *(osoznanie)* are the Vygotskyan versions of the three Wittgenstein-Derrida commonalities.

First, the epistemological resources that languages give their speakers to situate themselves as speaking subjects (evidentials, metadiscourse markers, etc.) linguistically position the self as a viewpoint. Vygotskyan social psycholinguistics studies the individual as a positioned ethical subject. Second, *smysl*, inherently variable and actively constructed psychocultural significance, is the meaning iterated on-line, in particular cases, to construct the individual's position. Third, the language for thought—private, regulatory self-directed monologue—mediates but does not constitute metaconsciousness. Speaking drives thinking; it is not coterminous with mind.

The significance of the particular momentary act of self-speaking in constructing a viewpoint links Vygotsky to Wittgenstein via Derrida. Harré (1987: 227) puts it cogently: Vygotskyan self consciousness is "the ability to play a certain language game, that of self ascription." Perhaps the best illustration of the convergence of the three can be found in Wittgenstein's own writings. In a well-known section of the *Philosophical Investigations* (1968: 59–60 #151), where he considers the meaning of *understand* and *know* in their usual senses, he remarks:

> But there is also this use of the word "to know": we say "Now I know!"—and similarly "Now I can do it!" and "Now I understand!"
>
> Let us imagine the following example: A writes a series of numbers down; B watches him and tries to find a law for the sequence of numbers. If he succeeds he exclaims: "Now I can go on!"—So this capacity, this understanding, is something that makes its appearance here.—A has written down the numbers 1, 5, 11, 19, 29; at this point B says he knows how to go on. What happened here? Various things may have happened; for example, while A was slowly putting one number after another, B was occupied with trying various algebraic formulae on the numbers which had been written down. After A had written the number 19 B tried the formula $a_n = n^2 + n - 1$; and the next number confirmed this hypothesis.
>
> Or again, B does not think of formulae. He watches A writing numbers down with a certain feeling of tension, and all sorts of vague thoughts go through his head. Finally he asks himself: "What is the series of differences?" He finds the series 4, 6, 8, 10 and says: Now I can go on.
>
> Or he watches and says "Yes, I know that series"—and continues it, just as he would have done if A had written down the series 1, 3, 5, 7, 9—Or he says nothing at all and simply continues the series. Perhaps he had what may be called the sensation "that's easy!" (Such a sensation is, for example, that of a light quick intake of breath, as when one is slightly startled.)

What better illustration of the frame problem than this? Wittgenstein's number-series solver has a difficult task, and struggles to "go on." He speaks to himself—"What is the series of differences?"—and the psychocultural significance of his words positions him in the momentary act as a speaking subject. This self-directed question serves the same nonrepresentational purpose as it does for Luria's peasant telling himself that he does not understand his own task. Of course he does not know the series of differences. That *is* the problem! Thus, his speech cannot constitute the thinking, since that would be either trivial or contradictory. *The framing action in speech,* however, lets the number-series solver continue—"Now I can go on." Remarkably, the German original of this passage shows that Wittgenstein was struggling with the psychocultural meanings of evidentials and discourse markers in German private speech. A great deal hangs on the German metapragmatic particles in Wittgenstein's examples: *ja,* 'yes', and *jetzt,* 'now' (see König 1991: 173–85).

Luria's peasant, McCarthy's dunce, and Wittgenstein's number-series solver have the same problem. Indeed, they are in the same quandary as "Putnam's counter," who illustrates what he sees as the foundational battle in cognitive science between objectivism and conceptual relativism—determinate fact and conventionalized value:

> Suppose I take someone into a room with a chair, a table on which there are a lamp and a notebook, and nothing else, and I ask, "How many objects are there in the room?" My companion answers, let us suppose, "Five." "What are they?" I ask. "A chair, a table, a lamp, a notebook, and a ballpoint pen." "How about you and me? Aren't we in the room?" My companion might chuckle. "I didn't think you meant I was to count people as objects. Alright, then, seven." "How about the pages of the notebook?" (Putnam 1988: 110–11)

They all are, as Searle (1992) says about Wittgenstein's project in general, struggling with the background of consciousness.

Putnam's solution, internal realism—that we allow fact and value to coexist—relies on the characterization of "a sufficiently well placed speaker" (1988: 115). Wittgenstein's solution likewise reaches out to the actual world in real time:

> But are the processes which I have described here *understanding?*
> . . . [D]oes it follow . . . that I employ the sentence "Now I understand . . ." or "Now I can go on" as a description of a process occurring behind or side by side with that of saying the formula [for the number series]?
>   If there has to be anything "behind the utterance of the formula" it is *particular circumstances,* which justify me in saying I can go on. (1968: 60, #154)

So how, then, should we think about understanding?

> Try not to think of understanding as a "mental process" at all—For *that* is the expression which confuses you. But ask yourself: in what sort of case, in what kind of circumstance, do we say, "Now I know how to go on." . . . [U]nderstanding is not a mental process. (1968: 61 #154)

Vygotsky would have put it like this: Try to think of metaunderstanding not as an internal mental process but as a way that external social speech has come to be internalized for personal use.

Wittgenstein's problem with Vygotsky's answer can inform cognitive science on how to draw the line between the mind's minimal equipment and its context. Platonic I-Tastes, the null subject parameter, and the binding theory do not drive a self any more than the evidentials and metapragmatic markers that do the work of self-talk deliver an object's surface or delimit the interpretation domains for pronouns. In Wittgenstein's problem, computation and subjectivity can live peaceably and productively.

The virtual machine of internalist, Platonist discourse is compatible with the externalist idiom of the real machine and social mind in action. They come together in a single Wittgenstein. Vygotsky, read through postmodernism, becomes the empirical research program that the unified Wittgenstein lacked.

How, then, can we speak in more empirical terms about the person-machine? How can we get a cognitive science that allows us to talk about units of mind that are neither wholly internal nor external—perched on the mind-world line—yet compatible with the mind as an acontextual device and a contextual agent? The answer can be found in the ways both computational theory and sociocultural theory use certain parts of language to manage the trade-off between internal mental architecture and the external context in which the architecture operates.

Architectures and Contexts: Unifying Computational and Cultural Psycholinguistics

3.1 Incommensurability and Unity

In Chapter 1 we looked at the internal-external clash over the direction of explanation in cognitive science. In Chapter 2 we considered a framework in which the clash disappears and the merger of inner and outer comes to make sense. This framework, Wittgenstein's problem, stakes out the meta-theoretical high ground and forces us into the specifics of the cooperation between computationalism and culture.

This project evokes Bernstein's (1983: 68) work to bridge the false dichotomy between "either permanent standards of rationality (objectivism) *or* arbitrary acceptance of standards or practices over against its rival (relativism)." In choosing one side of this division—for example, by siding with just Plato and Wittgenstein 1 (rock-bottom reason) *or* Wittgenstein 2 (real-time action)—we would remain trapped in what Bernstein calls *the Cartesian anxiety:* perpetually on guard to defend computationalism against culture and vice versa (see also Varela, Thompson, and Rosch 1991). But the dialectic of Wittgenstein's problem points us beyond both ahistorical computational absolutism and free-for-all cultural relativism because we are not collapsing the virtual and the real machine into each other but just asking them to live and work together.

Bernstein justifies his move by distinguishing three barriers to epistemological alignment that are instructive to keep in mind as I outline the fundamentals of cognitive science and Vygotskyan theory and argue their unities. The first is *incomparability.* Two accounts are incomparable if there are no identities across them, whatever the status of a common ground for evaluation. The second barrier is *incompatibility,* which applies to accounts that claim the same ground but with logically exclusive results; incompatibility produces *real conflicts* (Bernstein 1983: 88). Finally, there is *incommensurability,* Kuhn's (1962) voguish and much misunderstood proposal whereby two scientific paradigms diverge because their theories disagree on basic problems and accord their practitioners different conceptual networks and worldviews. To be commensurable, two paradigms require point-by-point theoretical identities and the same basis for measurement. But since no theory is ever complete (Brown 1990: 196), no paradigm is ever fully commensurable with any other (despite ceteris paribus escape clauses or "in principle" caveats; see Bernstein 1983: 66–68), and so most of the burden in practice falls on incommensurability alone.

These three kinds of divergence clarify the linking of computational and cultural psycholinguistics under Wittgenstein's problem and afford us unity despite (or because of?) contrast. Vygotskyan theory and cognitive science are clearly comparable. For example, insofar as deconstruction provides the grounds for comparing Vygotsky and computationalism under Wittgenstein's problem, the two can be held to the same metric. Globus (1990, 1992) notes that the emphases in connectionism on "knowledge how" (versus "knowledge that"), continual real-time updating of knowledge, and close world-mind connections (see section 3.2) are formal analogues of Heidegger's *Dasein:* situated, embodied being. Connectionism's appeal to emergent properties and unit differentiation by opposition strikingly evokes Derrida's notion of *différance,* with its infinite deferral of meaning and codetermination of being and non-being (Globus 1992; see also section 2.422).[1]

As for compatibility, in some places cultural and computational psycholinguistics are incompatible, as in the genuine conflict between Vygotsky's views of concepts and current theories of conceptual structure. But some competing ideas only seem incompatible, and we do not have to choose between them. This is the case for language-and-thought questions and the particular contrast of (Fodor's) hermetically private mentalese and (Vygotsky's) publicly verified inner speech (see Chapter 5). Here we let two sleeping dogs lie.

Finally, although computational and cultural psycholinguistics share controversies, such as the frame problem, they do so from markedly different vantage points (e.g., the directionality of explanation) and so are basically incommensurable. Nothing would necessarily be gained by commensurability anyway, since, as Wittgenstein's problem shows, there is nothing especially troubling about the incommensurability of the virtual and real machines.

Vygotsky died of tuberculosis in 1934 at the age of thirty-eight. If he had lived twice as long, until 1972—not an unreasonable possibility—he would have seen computational psycholinguistics firsthand. He would have been very partial to cognitive science, with its origins in cybernetic control mechanisms and its alliance with materialism. His work would have appealed, on the one hand, to symbolic functionalists because of its concern for representation and, on the other, to subsymbolic connectionists because of its focus on learning in context. He would also have been very much against some aspects of cognitive science, particularly the pure formalism and autonomy of certain versions of computationalism.

A few cognitive scientists have even reached back those many years to Vygotsky. Bechtel and Abrahamsen (1990: 248–49) point out that the focus in connectionism on problem solving and external tools directly evokes Soviet cultural psycholinguistics. The theory of situated action, with some incorrect citations of Vygotsky (see section 1.22), touts the rediscovery of the mind's world as the latest promise for progress in computationalism. Clark's (1993) work has some suggestive correspondences with Vygotsky, especially on matters of what he calls "macrostrategies" and the connection between self-diagnosed errors and externally diagnosed errors (71). But even his work seems to side with internalism in the long run; that is, the units of mind lie essentially in the code.

Still, incommensurability is friendly to compatibility and comparability. Indeed, progress is made by the tension of incommensurable accounts. This is a modern statement of the old Vygotskyan axiom that we do not need identity for unity. Productive cooperation comes when we overlook our sameness and let our differences drive the inquiry.

What are those likenesses and differences? Here I sketch out the basics of computational and cultural theory to show how the two can work together.

3.2 Cognitive Science: A Primer

Cognitive science has many divergent schools of thought, each with its respective apologists. To do full justice to them all means to do them injustice simultaneously. Instead, I survey cognitive science broadly, pointing out the leading ideas of the field. Since language is the ground on which cultural and computational theory come together, the focus is on the place of language in analysis and explanation.

As Dinsmore (1992: 1) observes, cognitive science is driven by a combative relationship between its two main paradigms: *representationalism,* which views mind as a symbol manipulator, and *connectionism,* which sees mind as a pattern associator.[2] For all their unkind words about each other, the two schools are not so divergent as their advocates claim (Dinsmore 1992), and each has quite serious problems in the very features that supposedly recommend it over its rival. For example, mind in the representationalist view consists of language-like rule subsystems. This kind of architecture accounts most perspicuously for actual human behavior, such as generalization and rapid, relatively error-free learning (see, e.g., Pinker and Prince 1988). But it also works best in very sharply circumscribed cognitive domains (Mellor 1989), is brittle and breaks down under the common conditions of noise and anomalous input (Dinsmore 1992: 5), and does not look anything at all like the brain in which it supposedly lies (McClelland, Rumelhart, and Hinton 1986). In contrast, connectionists argue that the mind is a huge, ruleless, pattern-matching, associative network. This model accommodates a broad range of knowledge and evinces properties of actual brains in real-time learning operations (see, e.g., Rumelhart and McClelland 1986, Bechtel and Abrahamsen 1990: 1–20). But connectionist architectures succeed because they learn in very limited, artificial contexts (Dinsmore 1992: 10), have limited generalization capacities (Pinker and Prince 1988, Barnden 1992), and do not look anything at all like actual brains despite pretensions thereto (Aizawa 1992).

In spite of these tensions and mutual shortcomings, the discussion that follows is frequently organized around the representationalist-connectionist dispute because it sets off the basic issues of cognitive science against one another very clearly. No single approach to computationalism is championed here. The purpose, instead, is to show what makes cognitive science cognitive science and how the commonalities in otherwise competing views of language and mind could possibly reach out to cultural psycholinguistics.

These competing schools of thought converge in four areas: the *inner code* (the nature and function of mental representation), *computation* (data structures and processing mechanisms), *architecture* (mind as the format of domains), and *hardware* (the neural substrate, or the *wetware,* to use the fashionable term). Each of these speaks to the core of cognitive science and in so doing lays out straightforwardly the possibilities for comparison and compatibility with Vygotskyan theory.

3.21 Inner Code

For just about all versions of cognitive science, mind is an interior code.[3] Unlike, say, a blender, which does not convert matter into a model in order to chop it, mind reduces and transduces input into the abstractions of inner life. (No doubt this position is traceable to the partial source of the field in cognitive psychology, which is predicated on the view that mind lives by its own terms.) A riskier way of saying this is to claim that all cognitive science is representational, but this would surely elicit howls from some connectionists, who (wrongly, I think, as we shall see) differentiate themselves from their opposition on this very count. I will therefore keep to the (I hope) uncontroversial claim that mind is an inner code.

Representationalism views the inner code as symbolic and language-like, a position most closely and persistently argued by Fodor (1975, 1981, 1983, 1989), who reasons as follows. To learn, the mind must be able to represent its hypotheses to itself in a form that allows them to be verified. The most robust, systematic, and productive—that is, the best and most accurate (for reasons I shall outline)—representational system is language-like, constructed out of symbols organized into formulas under the constraints of rules. The inner code not only is *but has to be* a propositional language of thought.

Connectionism's response is to agree that the inner code must be robust, systematic, and productive, but to disagree that it has to be in language-like symbolism. More fundamentally, connectionism rejects the idea that learning is the testing of mental hypotheses, and without them there is no need for a propositional language of thought to give them form for verification. Instead, the inner code is a huge learning network of nodes and connections, constructed out of simple units with levels of activation, joined to one another by weighted connections that either inhibit or excite other nodes. The entire network is subject to certain general conditions on learning. Input activates input units, which are keyed to properties of the input; these are connected to hidden units, intermediate nodes that recode input information and that in turn are connected to output units, which produce desired behavior. Unlike representationalist minds, where inner codes are symbols, formulas, and rules, connectionist minds are patterns of activation constantly adjusting to new input on the basis of input history and target behavior.

These sketches of representationalism and connectionism are clarified by a linguistic illustration. In English syntax there are forms that are interpreted as belonging to a position in a sentence far removed from where they actually occur. In *What did you say you believed John saw?* the interrogative, *what,* appears at the beginning of the sentence but is understood as belonging at the end, as the object of *saw: You said you believed John saw what?* How do we know this long-distance association? The standard answer in representationalist syntax is to say that we mentally match the sentence to an abstract formula made up of traditional grammatical symbols, such as S, NP, and VP, and not-so-traditional but necessary ones, such as *operator (what)* and *e* (the empty slot left behind by moved elements). In this formula the operator *(what)* has moved from its original position after the last VP *(saw)*, leaving behind the trace *(e)*; it moves by rules that displace it one clause at a time, subject to a more general rule that prohibits movement if certain other symbols are passed in the process (the condition known as *subjacency*). According to this account, we know what the sentence means because the formula in our inner code links the operator with the empty category under the rules and proscriptions of successive displacement.

The inner code in a connectionist account of this same process, however, has no rules or formulas. The system trains intensively on examples of the structure and stores associations among the actual words to which it is exposed. The long-distance dependency between the interrogative and its position of interpretation is a pattern extracted from the data as a stable relationship among actual words in real-time instances. There is no formula made up of abstract grammatical and logical symbols; the link between *what* and its position of interpretation is an inherent property of the network, not movement constrained by rules. It is an activity, not a hypothesis.

Each proposal is supported by significant linguistic and psycholinguistic evidence (for the representationalist view, see Haegeman 1991: 335 and McElree and Bever 1989; for the connectionist account, see Elman 1992 and Pickering and Barry 1991). The code in a representational account is a rule-and-formula list, while in the connectionist view it is a geometry or a state space. Nonetheless, both presuppose some sort of inner code because the code itself has certain intrinsic properties that yield undeniable benefits.

3.211 STRUCTURE FOR REGULARITY AND GENERALIZATION

Why do humans generalize and think systematically? In Fodor and Pylyshyn's (1988) view, the constituents of mind can be regularly manipulated and recombined to yield generalization. Humans do what they do because their *mental code has internal structure.*

Representationalism locates mental constituency in the inherent structure of mentalese as a language. The symbolic units of mental formulas are the basis of regular inference, just as in classical logic. Connectionism is often charged with failure on this count (Fodor and Pylyshyn 1988), but it also clearly has a structured code. Input units, hidden units, and output units are, after all, *units,* and, as Pinker and Prince (1988) and Lachter and Bever (1988) note, they look awfully symbolic no matter how much they are labeled otherwise (e.g., subsymbolic; see Smolensky 1988). Connectionists have come to recognize the representational character of their proposals and acknowledge the role of structure in regularity (see, e.g., van Gelder 1990, Horgan and Tienson 1992). But they do prefer to see it as something other than symbolic, like a tensor product (Horgan and Tienson 1992: 207, citing Smolensky), and they insist that the structure of the inner code is not a syntax in the representationalist sense (van Gelder 1992: 190–93).

Whatever the details of the competing models, the intrinsic structure of the inner code underlies the regularity of human thought. Computational psycholinguistics thus accounts for regularity through representational constituency.

3.212 THE CODE *IS* THE KNOWLEDGE

Not only is the inner code structured, but it is also the locale of the knowledge. Now, this may seem an odd thing to assert, but a little thought shows that it does not have to be true. The inner code could be some sort of conduit or all-purpose processing system through which input merely passes. Why can't the mind be like a blender, with knowledge of chopping intrinsic to its blades? The answer is that the blender has no knowledge to begin with, precisely because it has no inner code. The structure of the code *is the knowledge,* and so by identifying the inner code as such, we also identify mind.

There are three contrasting ways of looking at how knowledge is located in the code: *explicit versus implicit, local versus distributed,* and *hard versus soft.* As we might expect, these options cleave the representationalists from the connectionists. Consider again the regularity that the interrogative in *What did you say you believed John saw?* refers to the inferable object of *saw.* How does this appear in the code? In the representationalist account, the knowledge is explicit, a stated regularity between moved operators and their traces. In this view, mental processing is stable and regular because the code is expressly so. But in a connectionist account, regularities are implicit in and emerge out of the system's activation. They are thus said to be *emergent properties.* The regular interpretation of initial interrogatives is not stated overtly anywhere in the network, but is implied by how the network stores the patterns to which it is exposed. In this way syntactic knowledge is an implicit physical property of the mind.

Closely related to this distinction between explicit and implicit knowledge are the contrasts between local and distributed knowledge and hard and soft code. If knowledge is explicitly stated, it can in turn be *situated exactly,* that is, respectively local and hard. The units, formulas, and rules of a representationalist language of thought are like specific addresses in the inner code. This implies that in cases of damage and breakdown, the inner code should crash decisively for the simple reason that it is easier for a disorder to hit a stationary target—a local and hard one—than a moving one. Indeed, instances of such patterns of breakdown are cited as strong evidence for symbolic mentalese (Fodor 1983).

Connectionists argue precisely the reverse. If knowledge is minimally stated in the units of the network with regularities implicit and emerging out of the operation of the system, then knowledge is really not anywhere in particular. It is *distributed* throughout the network, much as the solidity of an object is not located anywhere in particular in the object. Moreover, the code is not hard and fast but flexible—*soft,* as it is said—because the patterns of activation that constitute the code-as-knowledge are in constant update, depending on input. The stability of knowledge, like the liquidity of an object, is just one of the regular states into which the system settles. Consequently, breakdown should be not a decisive crash but a flexible degradation, since the knowledge itself is not a specific address and so cannot be damaged in one fell swoop. Connectionists cite clinical examples of gradual breakdown in support.

3.213 GROWTH OF THE CODE

All cognitive scientists agree that the code must accommodate learning, but, depending on the commitments of the adherents, different schools view growth differently and attribute to it varying significance. One safe generalization is to say that representationalists minimize learning, while connectionists maximize it.

In symbolic accounts, learning is testing the hypotheses of the language of thought; growth is the development of the propositional structure of the inner code. Fodor (1975, 1981) takes this to the logical, if extreme, conclusion, arguing that the inner code can never increase in power because that would presuppose that the code can already symbolize what it needs to learn in order to grow. In Fodor's scheme, humans come with all the inner code they ever need, and learning has a minimal affect on the language of thought.

This is not by any means the received view. Alternative representationalist accounts hold that the symbolic inner code grows by a kind of mitosis of existing specialized code into other specialized code (see, e.g., Carey 1985, Keil 1992 for a counter, and Clark 1993 for a third version). Another position is that general-purpose code is retooled for specialized processing. This is part of Bever's (1992) argument that specialized linguistic knowledge is an overlay on neuropsychological structures originally dedicated to processing the relationship between discrete units, whatever their type.

There are at least two commonalities across such accounts. One is that growth of the inner code is task-specific. Since mentalese either is already dedicated or comes to be dedicated, mind learns those tasks it is bound to learn. Second, learning may have great impact on the code but *does not have to*. All models are compatible with minimized learning, where the world can impinge by triggering existing code into life, not by changing it in any significant way.

Here the connectionists both diverge and converge. They place great emphasis on learning, since their simulations succeed by exposure to highly structured situations under intense supervised training with significant feedback. The network has the form of a general-purpose learning device and adjusts the code markedly on the basis of the input, registering knowledge as the probabilities of the occurrence and co-occurrence of phenomena. This means that connectionist learning is also task-specific, but for reasons quite different from those in its rival paradigm. Since knowledge is the activation patterns of the network, which in turn are derived from exposure to situation-specific input, the inner code is task-specific because of its learning history, not its essential or a priori dedication. In connectionist models, then, the code significantly grows by constantly updating from input. In a real sense, *knowledge is growth*.

For cognitive science, the inner code is coterminous with mind. In a representationalist account it is explicit, local, hard, and dedicated; in a connectionist account it is emergent, distributed, soft, and adjustable. These properties have interesting consequences for the link with Vygotskyan psycholinguistics. Is metaconsciousness a code in itself or is it bootstrapped up from consciousness, or from explicit parts of the inner code? What parts of the code are situation-specific and culturally determined?

Are regularities and generalization part of the boilerplate of interior code? How does culture affect the computational units of mental structure? How does the code break down? Can metaconsciousness be split from the code by trauma? In short, where and how is the mind-world line drawn, and how is it developed and sustained?

3.22 Computation

Functionalism, the dominant metatheory of cognitive science, holds that the mind is the program run by the brain, and a program consists of code and its running orders.[4] Code and computation are thus intimately connected, or, as Fodor (1981) has axiomatized it: no computation without representation. What mechanisms and instructions are used in the mind to run the inner code?

There is no shortage of answers to what computation is (Johnson-Laird 1988, Pylyshyn 1985). Mellor (1989), in a paper essentially opposing the conquest of mind by computation, puts the matter as follows: computation is the causal manipulation of the intrinsic properties of input tokens of true/false types to produce output tokens that correspond to states of affairs. In other words, computation takes in actual stuff (tokens) that stands for things (true/false types), effectively arranges and rearranges this actual stuff on structural considerations only, and produces actual stuff that also stands for things. This homely rephrasing implies, more technically, that computation is both syntactic (it operates on things by means of its and their structural features) and semantic (it takes in and produces things that have truth).[5] This also implies that computing can be carried out in any form, serial (one causal manipulation after another) or parallel (many causal manipulations at once), by any device (brain or blender), with or without rules and formulas (representational or connectionist), just as long as these criteria hold.

3.221 CODES AND PROCESSES: SOME CHICKENS AND EGGS

What in mind is generally computational, and what is essentially tied to the code? An answer would tell us how much of our mind is content-specific and how much is global in organization. It would also help us decide between theories in which the inner code develops out of general computational procedures and those in which dedicated code emerges on its own. Unfortunately, such answers are immediately complicated by the fact that the best computational processes are those that are code-sensitive, and the best code is that which hooks up directly to its computation. The chicken and egg both come first here!

We can see this by returning to an earlier linguistic example. A representational model of sentence initial interrogatives (as in *What did you say you believed John saw?*) works by successive movement of the operator up through the structure, clause by clause, under specific stated conditions; this is very much in accord with representational processing requirements. As Elman (1992: 173) points out, "It is entirely consistent with a stack machine," a computing device in which information is stored and accessed in "vertical" piles: one domain is stacked on top of another, and access proceeds incrementally and sequentially. The code in the representationalist account is thus a perfect counterpart to the computational processes that have to implement it. Significantly, this is also true of the connectionist account of the same structure. The absence of successive movement in the connectionist code has its counterpart in the absence of informational stacking in the network, where all information is simultaneously accessible (Elman 1992: 172–75).

In the context of discussing processing limitations in cognitive models, van Gelder (1992: 187) remarks on the importance of the closeness of code and process: "One of the pivotal issues in thinking about the plausibility of various kinds of cognitive architectures is whether these kinds of performance limitations should be seen as somehow built into the architecture, or whether such limitations should be seen as resulting from (relatively uninteresting) resource restrictions on the mechanisms which are themselves, in principle, truly productive in nature." That is, are processing limitations traceable to the processes as code, or are they intrinsic to the processes as independent operations? Solutions once again split the representationalists from the connectionists. Maximizing the gap between code and computation is the strategy of representationalism, in which data structures have a life of their own and are implemented by procedures. In this way, experimental results and breakdowns can be attributed to (relatively independent) computational performance that leaves the code unaffected. Minimizing the gap is the connectionist strategy, in which the code is in many ways an outgrowth of the very procedures. Here computational performance matters to the code. Both approaches have their respective support but nonetheless converge in forcing us to see processing and code as codependent. That is, looking at the properties of one opens up the properties of the other.

3.222 THREE PROPERTIES OF PROCESSING SYSTEMS

Computing systems have a number of general features. All are time-sensitive, for example. All change in informational demands as processing unfolds because difficulty decreases as predictability increases. Since predictability is low at the beginning of input and higher at the end, processing systems show clear effects at these points (related to the *primacy and recency effects* in traditional psychological accounts). Three properties in particular help us make the link between computational and cultural psycholinguistics: speed, input-output asymmetry, and strong-weak equivalence.

Computation is capacity-driven. Because the contentless manipulation of units is a physical and real-time process (two decided advantages, according to Sterelny 1989), it is conditioned by resource allocation. Human working memory has quite definite limits (e.g., Miller's famous $7 +/- 2$ units), and computational systems have small active windows because not everything can be held in mind or on-line at any single time.

Capacity limitations on computation give rise to a robust and reliable measurement of processing: *speed*. Easy manipulations of the inner code take up less processing space and so need less time; difficult manipulations need more space and so take longer.[6] Now, there may be many reasons why manipulations are easier/faster or harder/slower. For instance, in a matching task, the input and inner code may be identical, and this will facilitate processing; alternatively, in the same task, with the input and code still matching, the system may be burdened elsewhere, thus causing a reduction in speed for an otherwise easy task because of overall draw on capacity. So, speed is clearly not a singular variable but depends on other things that might also affect the capacity properties of the computation.

The second property is *input-output asymmetry*. In simple terms, reception and production are not two sides of the same coin because output is not produced by reversing the procedures for input. Speech perception, for example, places less demand on working memory than does speech production because in the former, the goal is to empty working memory of actual forms as quickly as possible in order to convert input into the representations of long-term memory. But in production, the actual forms of speech matter crucially and so have to be tracked as the speech is generated (see Romani 1992 for neurological evidence). Input and output mechanisms have very different computational requirements, and so the processing system is not a unified, task-independent device in this respect.

The third feature is *equivalence*. Two computational systems may be equivalent through identical code and computations (and, by implication, identical output) or just through identical output, whatever their respective inner codes and procedures. The former is *strong equivalence,* the latter *weak equivalence.* This distinction is critical in artificial intelligence, where human thinking can be simulated by replicating the actual grammar of thought (strong equivalence) or just by producing output or behavior that is indistinguishable from human output or behavior (weak equivalence or Turing's criterion).

The issue once more splits the representationalists from the connectionists, this time along the lines of universality and variation. For biological reasons, the language of thought is the same in all individuals, and so at the level of formal mind we are all strongly equivalent. In connectionist accounts, however, where the network is tied to its external circumstances and input, and where target output is more important than a universal means to achieve it, weak equivalence holds sway and individual variation in code and computation are accorded higher status.

The connection of these ideas about computation to Vygotsky is quite revealing. Speed is a crucial factor in Vygotskyan theory, where cognitive framing is slow and deliberate. We might in fact get a measure of how discourse and orientation dovetail by looking at the speed of discourse processing. Input-output asymmetry is an axiom in Vygotsky's work, where the individual's performance can exceed competence, and speech production can run ahead of and inform thinking. The tension between the individual and the universal is also a hallmark of Vygotsky's thought but lacks a sophisticated way of drawing the line. Perhaps one way of showing that two individuals are identical in their metaconsciousness is by observing similarities in what they deploy as output in private speech. That is, selves could be weakly equivalent cultural constructs.

3.23 Architecture

The computing of inner code is constrained by the overall layout of the system, that is, what flows into what, and whether and how codes and processes of one type can affect codes and processes of another. This format of mind is the *cognitive architecture* (Anderson 1983, Pylyshyn 1985), or, as it were, the management structure of thought. Is the mind subdivided into areas of processing responsibility? If so, how are the boundaries drawn? Do some domains have to report their output to others, or is mind a sort of libertarian free-for-all?

3.231 MODULARITY

Symbolic language-of-thought accounts are usually *modular*.[7] The format that conditions computation and code is a composite of dedicated processing areas, or modules, each with its own requirements and content and essentially immune to the requirements and content of other dedicated domains. Hence, there are autonomous languages of vision, taste, music, and so on, and each of these may likewise have a modular internal format. Within the language module, for instance, there may be syntactic and phonological (sub)modules, and within those there may also be (sub-sub)modules for various kinds of (sub-sub)domain-specific processing.

The most fully articulated and thoroughly discussed version of modularity is Fodor's (1983). He draws a distinction between peripheral and central processes (roughly the difference between sensation and perception on the one hand and cognition on the other) and argues for the modularity of peripheral *input systems*, which take information from sensation (what he calls *transducers*) and send it up for further processing. Input systems are fast and automatic because they are hardwired (unlearned and built-in); they are unaffected by processing in other domains (*cognitively impenetrable*, to use Pylyshyn's 1985 term); they have characteristic patterns of breakdown because they are automatic, hardwired, and so on. These modular properties contrast with those of central processes, which receive output from input systems and deploy all knowledge, all the output of every domain, to fix belief. Central processes are therefore nonmodular, or *interactive*. They are slow, learned, and cognitively penetrable (isotropic and Quinean, as Fodor 1983 says: i.e., indeterminate).

While almost all these claims have been criticized in (Maratsos 1992 is a good review), the idea of modularity as a format nonetheless persists, no doubt because it is probably true in some form. A substantial portion of the literature on grammatical parsing, for example, supports a modular view of syntactic processing, that is, that grammatical decisions are made rapidly and without information from any other domain, such as semantics (see, e.g., Frazier 1987, Clifton and Ferreira 1987, Weinberg 1987). Analogous support comes from work on lexical processing, where access to the format of meaning in the lexical code appears to be rapid and unaffected by context (see, e.g., Tanenhaus and Lucas 1987, Jones 1989).

Fodor's version of modularity, while certainly influential, is not the only such proposal (see, e.g., Gardner 1983). Alternatives raise the more general issue of what exactly constitutes modularity (see Maratsos 1992). The basic problem is whether contextual information can intrude on processing by feeding back information from a higher domain to a lower one during processing. That is, where is the mind interactive? Here connectionism throws in its bet: everywhere.

3.232 INTERACTIONISM

In a connectionist architecture every piece of information can potentially impinge on every other. Since knowledge is a distributed pattern of activity with any place in the network in principle accessible from any other place, the format itself is inherently interactive. Lexical context can influence phonological processing, syntactic context can influence lexical structure, and so on. Domains of linguistic knowledge are no more autonomous in mental organization than is any other information.

The idea that everything mutually constructs and interdetermines everything is such common sense that it seems self-evidently true. It also plainly has its advantages. If some part of the system should break down, then potential access to that part from all other points should facilitate recovery. In fact, it seems counterintuitive to have dedicated modules with interfaces that make information from one domain computationally visible to another by translating between modular codes. In the connectionist "state representation . . . all of the information . . . is contained in a state vector . . . This state vector is *entirely visible to the processor*. Thus, all the information is available simultaneously" (Elman 1992: 174).

Psycholinguistic work in the connectionist vein provides a striking contrast to the received modular view of both lexical access and grammatical parsing. Glucksberg, Kreuz, and Rho (1986), for example, have argued that context constrains lexical access for ambiguous words, inhibiting the initial overgeneration of lexical code and sorting out meanings by context prior to response. Just and Carpenter (1992) have argued a similar line with respect to grammatical parsing. In their view, modular and interactive effects are the consequence of individual differences in working-memory capacity: the higher the individual's capacity (as measured by independent memory tests), the more likely the appearance of interactive parsing, since such individuals can hold many options on-line, including information from context and domains other than syntax. In this view, parsing is not the result of the inherent structure of mental architecture but an emergent property of real-time computation.

As with all the discussion thus far, the purpose here is not to promote one view over another but to point out how they illustrate cognitive science and computationalism at large. Nowhere is their unity clearer—or more ironic—than in the claims of each for biological and evolutionary plausibility. Modularity is held by its proponents to be evolutionarily superior to interactionism because its divide-and-conquer approach delegates the cognitive work to special-purpose mechanisms that come "knowing" the circumstances in which they apply. General mechanisms, of the sort that connectionists prefer, are at a perpetual disadvantage, always chasing an ever more general solution to ever-changing general circumstances.

Connectionists argue precisely the same point with opposite affinities. Churchland (1986: 388) says: "The enthusiasm for cognition as sentence-crunching [modular, language-of-thought models] seems insensitive to evolutionary considerations. Sentence-crunching is certain to have been a cognitive latecomer in the evolutionary scheme of things . . . [S]entence-crunchers have no cognitive heritage from earlier species, which is also implausible given the evolution of the brain." Interactionism sees evolutionary advantage in flexibility and sensitivity to learning-in-context. Special-purpose processors are not intrinsically beneficial because domain-specificity resides less in the processor itself than in the problems to be solved and the learning environment (see Kirsh 1992: 308.). The biological superiority of interactionism lies in its ability to *adjust to,* not presolve, the environment.

Modularity and interactionism may both be evolutionarily advantageous because it may be that they both occur. Tanenhaus and Lucas (1987), Seidenberg and Tanenhaus (1986), and to some extent Arbib (1989) have argued that modularity and interaction are really *effects* of code, context, and feedback, not prespecified formats or intrinsic properties of the layout of the mind. For instance, those parts of the lexical code that allow feedback from higher context look interactive, as in the effects of word structure on phonological processing. But other parts of the code do not allow such contextual penetration—for example, syntactic context does not facilitate lexical choice—so here modular characteristics emerge (see Tanenhaus and Lucas 1987, with more detail later in this chapter).

The possibility that modularity and interaction are both effects takes us to a Vygotskyan cognitive science. Codes exhibit modular or interactive architectures depending on whether and where they allow the intrusion of context via feedback. In more Vygotskyan terms, how and where can context situate thinking? If computation takes place within the context of culture, how and where does the latter feed back onto the former? Does metaconsciousness, for example, have access to the content of thought as it unfolds, or does it select thought? Is there a culture-mind interface or interaction, or both, depending on the nature of the information?

3.24 Hardware

Just as the structure of a computer program does not have to make explicit reference to the structure of the machine on which it is implemented, so a computational theory of mind is not obliged to exhibit point-by-point identity to the brain. To radical functionalists this gap between software and hardware is significant since it bolsters the autonomy of cognitive and computational psychology (see Pylyshyn 1985). The freedom of the software-hardware gap nonetheless carries the responsibility that programs have *some* connection to their machines. Try to run a PC program on a Mac with no bridge software, and the immediate crash will drive home the point. So, while a theory of mind does not in principle require a theory of brain, it would be a very good idea for computationalism to recognize and identify neural analogues.

This is not a call for reductionism. "Functionalists can be true blue functionalists without naysaying reduction" (Churchland 1986: 358) because the recasting of mind stuff into body stuff does not have to be *mere reductionism*—cognitive states and processes as *merely* brain processes.[8] The functionalist's truth of multiple realizability—that a functional state (such as a mind) can be implemented in many ways—works hand in hand with the neuroscientist's truth that the brain has a functional structure (small pieces of mind stuff do not have very specific neuro-addresses). The leeway in each is subservient to the ideological condition that respectable mind science must embrace materialism.

3.241 NEURAL COMPUTATION

The brain is an information-processing device. While it is obviously not a computer per se—since it fails on size, the nature of information transmission, and architecture (for instance, there is no separate memory)—it nonetheless can be organized into groups of input-output mechanisms with internally regulated operating states (Baron 1987). As Sejnowski

(1986: 372–73) puts it, the fact that the brain computes is less controversial than its *style of computation* because the close association of hardware and software in the brain affects the way computation can be performed.

I have already defined *computation* as 'the causal manipulation of the units of a meaningful inner code on the basis of their intrinsic properties'. Each part of this definition has a neural correlate. The *units* of neural computation appear to be neuron groups (Crick and Asanuma 1986), though computational modeling has implicated the single neuron as the smallest neuro-computational unit (Smolensky 1986: 393), and neuroscience has suggested that subneuronal units may also be involved (Baron 1987). The code itself, neural information, is the spatial, time-varying pattern of the rates of neural firing—"the propagation of a 'spike' or 'action potential' " (Crick and Asanuma 1986: 335)—which is transmitted across neurons by the depolarization of cells and chemical transfer. The meaning of the code—what makes it information as such—lies in the neural pattern itself: "Information has meaning because neural networks are designed to process it in a well-defined way. Static information patterns are spatial arrangements of molecules in neural networks and dynamic information patterns are movements of molecules, hence waves of activity, in neural networks" (Baron 1987: 508).

The *effective manipulation* of neural code can be seen in a number of ways. Some neural pathways merely send information along, without modifying it. Others act as switches to redirect information, and still others (receptor cells) convert nonneural information into neural code. Neurons and neuron groups also manipulate the *intrinsic properties* of the code to vary input-output relations. Some neural processing is passive, with no change between input and output. Some processing is adaptive, with the output changing according to history of inputs; as Smolensky (1986: 385) remarks, the "cortex . . . can be partially reconfigured with experience." Other processing is active, with input subjected to control from elsewhere in the neural network, which changes the output. Neural processing, then, like computation, is the causal manipulation of units of an inner code.

Neural computation not only fits the definition of computation per se but also evinces a number of the characteristics of all computational systems generally. In the brain, the code is the knowledge. Baron (1987: 508) remarks: "It is only because neural networks are designed to process patterns in specific ways that they, the arrangements of molecules or the waves of activity, convey meaning. This structure—the neural networks and their coupling parameters—and function—the way the networks encode, store, and process patterns—cannot be understood independently." Moreover, speed, capacity, and time-sensitivity are essential to understanding the manipulation of neural code (Smolensky 1986: 393 tabulates neural, mathematical, and processing factors). This can be seen in the inherent processing limitations of neurons themselves: "The average discharge rate of neocortical neurons is . . . 50 to 100 spikes per second, though the rate for a brief time can rise as high as several hundred spikes per second" (Crick and Asanuma 1986: 366).

A spectacular example of these hardware capacity limitations can be seen in human iconic memory. Brains apparently make an exact and continuous visual and auditory record of experience; under electrical stimulation of the cortex with local anesthetic, patients recall past experience in vivid, scenario-like form, dictating sequences of events that they are unable to recall explicitly in a nonsurgical state (Penfield and Roberts 1959 is the classic work). This kind of permanent memory trace—like a computer's read-only memory (ROM)—appears to be organized in temporal packets of twenty seconds and moves only forward in time. That is, chunks of memory narratives in these patients persist for up to twenty seconds after the termination of stimulation and never go backwards, but always follow the serial organization of real time. Remarkably, these memory narratives do not contain evidence of metamemory: patients do not recall actually making decisions or plans. This suggests that these experiments tap latent (neuro)consciousness, which is physically separate from (neuro)meta-consciousness.

3.242 NEURAL ARCHITECTURE

What kind of neural computing system is the brain? Is it modular or interactive? What is the neural format? Unfortunately, for those seeking in the brain the ultimate arbitration of representationalism and interactionism, neural computation appears to have both modular and interactive qualities.

The most striking evidence for modularity is the well-known and uncontroversial fact that the brain has dedicated cortical processing areas that receive input via specific channels: a visual cortex, a motor cortex, various speech areas, an area for face recognition, and so on. Hence, there are specialized domains of neural code, a fact that even the most ardent interactionists acknowledge: "Different areas of cerebral cortex are specialized for processing information from different sensory modalities" (Sejnowski 1986: 372).

And yet, these dedicated areas cannot be more specifically localized than in a broad, fish-scale neural topography. For one thing, cortical areas are not uniform in structure (Crick and Asanuma 1986: 353), and for another, the neurons in one domain have multiple connections to neurons and domains elsewhere; moreover, the cortical domains on one side of the brain appear to have correlates on the other side (Luria 1973). Where, then, *is* a domain? All this uncertainty makes it difficult to claim that the architecture of the neural code is straightforwardly modular (Crick and Asanuma 1986: 356).

Nonetheless, there is something like dedicated neural processing, and this corresponds roughly to neural structure for peripheral and sensory input. As Crick and Asanuma (1986: 368) note, sensory processing (like immediate visual perception) is keyed to features of the input, but "as one proceeds further, the mapping of the periphery becomes more diffuse . . . [and] . . . it becomes increasingly difficult to discover exactly what feature a cell likes best." Thus, Sejnowski (1986: 380) sounds like a proponent of deterministic representationalism when he says, " 'Single-shot' algorithms that converge in one pass through a network . . . remain attractive . . . for the early stages of visual processing." But the interactive side persists. Sejnowski (1986: 374) notes that dedicated, local intrinsic processing of visual information is restricted to the classical receptive field; information outside this field (so-called *surround effects*) appears to involve long-range connections and information spread in a typically connectionist manner.

Perhaps the best way to make sense of these conflicting claims for neural format is to return to my earlier discussion of computational format. There I noted that the overall layout of information may be more a property of the codes, contexts, and process themselves than some inherent organization or structural overlay into which knowledge is placed. Using this idea in more specifically neurocomputational terms, we see that the brain does and does not have a classic computational architecture, depending on what it has to do and where and how it has to do it.

For example, there is no separate central processing unit (CPU) in the brain, as there is in a classic computer, but there are local central processing–like areas that handle their own kind of *neural code control*. The frontal lobes are associated with planning, deliberateness, and volition (see section 3.34), but these are codes in themselves and do not overarch the entire neurocognitive computational system; they can, in fact, be dissociated from all else by trauma and so are arguably distinct at some level. Similar control properties can be attributed to the thalamus, a gland located just below the corpus callosum which acts as a kind of cortical gateway by modulating nearly all information that comes to the cortex. The hippocampus, too, has executive properties; it appears to control whether information is stored in long-term memory, probably by assigning storage indexes and addresses to the spatial coordinates of experience for recall (see Baron 1987: 488).

Significantly, none of these controlling functions has a privileged or physically superordinate position. The neural architecture embodies the omniscient CPU in various local cpu's (no I for all those i's). Whereas a classic computational system separates control from content, the brain either does or does not do so, depending on what the content is and what kind of control is needed. But this is so because the overseeing functions of a CPU do not have to be totally localized to have a local effect.

These truths about neural computation and architecture speak to two Vygotskyan concerns: materialism and control. The Marxist backdrop to Vygotsky's thought makes it essential to locate the material base of consciousness and metaconsciousness. For Vygotsky, the sociohistorical conditions of thought are as material as the neural ones because a culture is as objective and tangible as a brain. While Vygotsky principally pursued the cultural-material basis of mind, his colleagues, especially Luria, investigated the neuropsychology of culture, under the assumption that "the functional systems underpinning specifically human forms of behavior involve 'extracortical' components, external supports, including cultural objects in the world (which, for Luria, included human language)" (Cole 1990: 25).

Computational brain and linguistic-cultural mind are natural allies not only in material constitution but also in their control function. Metaconsciousness is in fact defined by its control properties. But since materialism does not require specific locales, distributed executive functions of the sort found in computational neuroscience are entirely compatible with the neural analogues of Vygotsky's work (see section 3.34); indeed, Luria's research on the frontal lobes continues to be essential to Western neuroscience. Perhaps the deconstruction of Wittgenstein 2 and the analogues with Vygotsky illustrate the point best: the lack of a material central overseer does not preclude material central overseeing.

3.3 Vygotskyan Theory: A Primer

Just as there is no shortage of surveys of cognitive science, so the growing Vygotsky industry offers many useful syntheses in addition to the reissues and new translations of the original Russian texts (for the former, see, e.g., Wertsch 1985, Valsiner 1988, van der Veer and Valsiner 1991, and Newman and Holzman 1993; for the latter, see, e.g., Vygotsky 1962, 1986, 1987). We need less to repeat the ideas found elsewhere than to distill them with an eye toward computationalism.

In this section I look across the various (then-)Soviet schools and include in a single picture the ideas of Vygotsky, Luria, Leont'ev, and their colleagues and students.[9] This is not to deny the very serious differences among these thinkers. For example, Vygotsky and Leont'ev had a falling out that led Leont'ev to form the Kharkov school. Nonetheless, they also have a common thread in four overriding ideas: the goal of their work *(development);* the processes by which development is carried out (*control, mediation,* and *internalization*); the context for development *(activity);* and the neurological correlates of development (the *brain bases of higher thought*).

3.31 Development

Vygotsky's work is predicated on *change and growth* (Valsiner 1988: 328), a guiding principle he states outright in *Thought and Language* (1987: 51): "What unifies all these investigations is *the idea of development.*" If change seems an odd rock on which to build a theory, it is nevertheless quite understandable in the context of the Marxist discourse that grounds Vygotsky's work and stresses individual and social progress through labor. A comment from a lecture of Vygotsky's on thinking and development underscores this intertwining of labor and growth: "The child's *work on a word is not finished* [my emphasis] when its meaning is learned" (Vygotsky 1987: 322).

Even though Vygotsky stresses change and development, he never falls into radical relativism or self-defeating nihilism. That is because he accepts both the historical and cultural groundedness of development and the classic Marxist view that development is teleological—progress toward a better, ultimate state. This doubly anchors development to the world.[10]

3.311 HIGHER THOUGHT

If the basis of cultural psycholinguistics is development, then *what is development the development of?* As we saw in Chapter 1, higher thought, or metaconsciousness, develops. Thinking is something to be mastered; rationality lies in the marshaling of personal meaningfulness (what Leont'ev called *lichnostnyi smysl,* 'personality-bound significance'; see Valsiner 1988:

218) in the service of the voluntary control of thinking and behavior. Vygotsky (1987), in a lecture on the development of memory, puts it succinctly: for young children, who are in the early stages of the development of higher thought, *to think is to remember*, as higher thought develops, the child then *remembers to think* (see also Vygotsky 1978: 50).

Metaconsciousness, or what Gal'perin (1979, originally 1941) called *the role of orientation in thought,* has three essential features. First, it is learned, and so it is contingent on both the environment and individual performance. Second, since it is a learned behavior, its content lies in the external sociohistorical and cultural context of the learner. The analysis of metaconsciousness therefore requires the determination of units of sociocultural information *outside the mind*. Third, it is domain-specific. Higher thought is not a general mental process that cuts horizontally across cognition because it is learned and tied to the circumstances of its acquisition and so retains the features of the tasks in which it develops. Luria (1976a: 164) remarks that his studies in Central Asia show that the cognitive frame "depend[s] utterly on the basic forms of social practice," and Vygotsky (1987: 301–10) rejects the then-current associationist views of memory because they are predicated on domain-general laws of recall. Domain-general thinking is less a defining feature of higher thought than *a consequence of it* (Vygotsky 1987: 198), since it develops out of the generalization practices in the external circumstances of the learner.

Higher thought as learned, task-specific, sociocultural content leads to cognitive science in a number of ways. One important link is in the domain-specificity of higher thought (see Hirschfeld and Gelman 1994). The successes of both representational and connectionist models are in large part attributable to the task-specificity of the models and processing. Higher thought merges intellect and affect in tasks and so gives motivating representations (Bozhovich 1979; see also Valsiner 1988: 225). We now need to know more about the nature of external tasks and how this information is internalized and used in motivation.

3.312 THE INDIVIDUAL AND THE GROUP

How does higher thought develop? If higher thought is sociocultural, then common sense should tell us that metaconsciousness emerges as individuals become socialized. Children, whose worlds and thought radiate outward from their ego centers, *assimilate into society* by learning to conform to the conditions of their surrounding cultural milieu. The direction of metacognitive development is thus away from the individual to the practices of the group. What could be more uncontroversial than that?

In Vygotskyan theory, this view is totally backwards. The individual is not swallowed up by a homogenizing society; on the contrary, *society precedes the individual* and provides the conditions that allow individual thinking to emerge. Metaconsciousness is first of all a property of the social group which is then appropriated by the individual, who can in turn relocate metaconsciousness in the group, depending on the task at hand. Higher thought is both double and fluid, flowing from the group to the individual and back again to the group.

Initially, this account is difficult to accept, especially with respect to children, because, as Piaget remarks, there seems to be "no real social life between children of less than 7 or 8 years" (quoted by Newman and Holzman 1993: 116). Vygotsky demolished this solipsistic view of development in many places, most notably in his criticism of Piaget's account of egocentric speech (which I discuss at length in section 3.321). But here I can give a simple observation and demonstration.

The child is born into a prestructured world. Group influence on the child begins long before birth, in both the implicit, historical and sociocultural circumstances that individuals inherit, and the more obvious explicit, physical and social preparations that groups make in anticipation of the individual. All these exert their force even in simple, everyday tasks requiring the management and deployment of individual action.

Like Luria's peasant and McCarthy's dunce, we all lay out the tools we need, we ask for help, and we talk to ourselves. We seek to frame the problem in terms of the larger *prearranged social resources made available to us by our culture*. In a real sense, two minds are better than one, even if this means that both of the minds are our own: a private, internal mind and a public, external one.

Vygotsky (1987: 339–49) puts the whole matter nicely in his observations on the development of children's imagination. Children's solitary thinking is traceable not to "a pure state of consciousness that does not know any reality other than itself" (343), but to a failure to distinguish mental activity originating within from that originating externally. What to Piaget (and common sense) looks like the voraciousness of the *private I* is actually the absence of a self and the dissipation of metaconsciousness into the group. As Bozhovich (1979) says, the child must learn to distinguish his subjectivity from all else and so is the last one to become conscious of his own actions (Valsiner 1988: 143).

The view that the multiplicity and diversity of social context ground the individuation of thinking has a number of consequences. First, it means that the line between adult and child is very porous in matters of higher thought. Once speech overlaps with thought and thinking becomes mediated (see section 3.322), there is nothing *essentially* adultlike or childlike, since everyone has the same problem of managing individuation in relation to the group. The nature of the thinking task may redefine the adult into a child or vice versa. The categories of 'adult' and 'child' are therefore not ready-made for verification in an experiment, but are emergent properties of on-line metaconscious performance.

Second, we must reconsider the nature of the group. It is easy to think of the group as a homogenizing consensus, the place where individual differences are smoothed out in the service of a common goal. Valsiner (1988) outlines the various definitional struggles on this matter within Soviet psychology, and he settles on the view that the group is a system of distributed work wherein the component individuals' interpersonal relations are mediated by a common goal and task. This last characteristic, common goal and task, misses a critical fact and continues to situate both group and individual idealistically. Individuals do not need a shared goal or task in order to belong to a group. What matters for unity, as Putnam (1988) observes, is the willingness of individuals to *discount their differences,* whatever their likenesses. This is why intersubjectivity, joint consciousness in the service of problem solving, requires only on-line joint work retaining the diversity and differences of individuals. Development proceeds by differentiation and contrast, not by reproduction of similarities.

Third, we must strike a balance between dynamic, socioculturally situated higher thought and universals. If both the individual and the group are emergent properties, can there be constancies in the development of higher thought? There are undoubtedly structural constancies across cultures that bear on the construction of higher thought. For example, all cultures provide their members with a ranked hierarchy of legitimate evidence for belief. In some cultures the best evidence is firsthand knowledge; in others it is mythical and transcendent evidence. What is important for our task of linking computation and culture through language is that these kinds of information and their ranking are encoded in the evidential markers of speech, which in turn are crucial to the regulatory processes that constitute higher thought. So the dynamic nature of the individual and group is orthogonal, not contrary, to the existence of sociocultural universals.

3.313 UNEVENNESS

Any developmental theory is bound up with the idea of stages of growth. In the Vygotskyan view, development proceeds unevenly (see van der Veer and Valsiner 1991: 309); metaconscious progress, like social progress, is revolutionary, with massive, instantaneous, qualitative shifts. As Wittgenstein 2's number-series solver remarks when the frame dawns on him, "Now I can do it!" (see section 2.423). In this respect, cultural psycholinguistics is remarkably similar to some versions of computational psycholinguistics, such as Chomskyan Cartesian rationalism, in which humans are markedly differentiated from nonhumans by their linguistic capacities; it also accords with the evolutionary theory of punctuated equilibria, in which change occurs in spurts and bursts, while gradualism and the evenness of development are imposed by the viewer in retrospect (but see Pinker and Bloom 1990: 711–12).

Two features of the unevenness of development are important to the unity and use of Vygotskyan theory: *recovery* and *convergence*. As in Marxist theory, where history remains in contact with the present and so grounds the future, metathought can always reaccess past practice because development unfolds in real time, where the past and future are mutually determinate and infused in any single present moment. Vygotsky's (1978: 65) celebrated statement of this, borrowed from Blonsky, is: "Behavior can be understood only as the history of behavior" (see also Scribner 1985, Valsiner 1988: 124–25). The adult recovers the child; the child approaches the adult. The external social world is internalized in individuated metaconsciousness only to be reaccessed when a subject in difficulty redirects itself to the social group. In Vygotsky's (1986) phrase, the past *goes underground* for reaccess; it does not disappear. So, one part of the development of higher thought is the subject's management of the simultaneously explicit and implicit.

The other part is the convergence of distinct lines of development. Speech and thinking are originally parallel, and at "a certain point, these lines meet, whereupon thought becomes verbal and speech rational" (Vygotsky 1962: 44). Thought and language are initially opposed, not only because they originate in different locales but also because they have different goals. Speech is external and moves in development from the smaller to larger, from the word to the phrase to the sentence; thought is internal and moves from the larger to the smaller, from the synthetic whole to the individuated analyzed concept. When the parallel developments of outer speech and inner thought converge, metaconsciousness and the voluntary control of thought and language result (see Vygotsky 1987: 311–24).

Remarkably, this account is a virtual copy of that proposed by a foundational figure in cognitive science. Donald Davidson, in "Thought and Talk" (1975), argues that speech—by which he means actual words, Saussure's *parole*, not the system of speech, *langue* or competence—gives the best evidence of rationality because, like the attribution of thought to others, it requires interpretation. That is, speech, at least, has an objectively applicable theory of meaning in which to ground interpretation. (This is a sort of speech-based version of Dennett's 1987 intentional stance, with rationality lying in words instead of attributed intentions.) Crucially this account relies on seeing speech and thought as equally primary and parallel. Davidson (1975: 10) writes: "If thoughts are primary, a language seems to serve no purpose but to express or convey thoughts; while if we take speech as primary, it is tempting to analyze thoughts as speech dispositions . . . But clearly the parallel between the structure of thoughts and the structure of sentences provides no argument for the primacy of either, and only a presumption in favor of their interdependence." When Davidson considers the prospect of a subject's having metaknowledge—as he says, *knowledge of belief*—he sounds remarkably Vygotskyan: "A creature must be a member of a speech community if it is to have the concept of belief" (1975: 22).

3.314 METHOD

Vygotsky was generally occupied—indeed, motivated in his very career as a psychologist—by problems of method. He thought that psychology as a whole was misdirected because the field had unnaturally split causal-scientific accounts from descriptive-intentional ones. In privileging the former, it had also split experiment from development (see van der Veer and Valsiner 1991: 141).[11] Vygotsky believed that all psychology was necessarily developmental and that this metascientific fact should permeate the very practices of observation, experiment, and analysis.

Observation and experiment must enact a developmental microcosm. Analysis must be of the on-site emergence of higher thought through individual-group relations; the goal of experimentation itself is to precipitate development—not simply record it—by bringing higher thought into existence for controlled examination. The method of experiment is *microgenesis*, that is, short-term, on-line growth and change (Wertsch 1985: 54–57).

Complementary factors—breakdown and help—guide microgenetic experimentation. Since higher thought emerges in situations where, because of difficulty, the subject must frame the task, the search for control can be induced in a variety of ways. But all experimentation must preserve functional breakdown and consequent orientational behavior, whether by giving subjects a problem that is difficult from the start, by giving them simple problems and disturbing performance, or by observing natural cases of psychological and neurological dysfunction.

The other side of breakdown is help. When in our everyday lives we undergo ordinary breakdown, we redirect our actions to the group and external social circumstance for assistance. So, in the experimental situation proper, the experimenter must provide help in order to fill out the natural social structure to which the struggling individual can turn for metaconscious aid. In this way experimenter, subject, and experimental situation form a unified working social group. Vygotsky criticizes experimentation that is preceded by practice sessions since this is neither socially significant nor natural as a course of development (who has practice for life?): "In our experiments, the problem is put to the subject from the start and remains the same throughout," and so the "problem solving . . . follows the same path as it takes in real life" (Vygotsky 1987: 104, 105). The experimenter then gradually introduces assistance (e.g., verbal directions or external tools such as memory aids) to help the subject do the task correctly. This allows the experimenter to "study not only the final effect of the operation, but its specific psychological structure . . . the means and methods the subjects use to organize their own behavior" (Vygotsky 1978: 74).

In constructing a situation in which all subjects succeed in developing new means to an experimentally given end, Vygotskyan experiments seem very fashionable and, at the same time, antithetical to current methods. As to the former, the mutual involvement of the experimenter and subject in the co-construction of an act evokes modern ethnographic work that uses the case study in hermeneutic, interpretive experiments. As to the latter, help in the service of total success sounds like old-fashioned cheating. We tend to think that subjects ought to sink or swim; in fact, the better they swim without help, the more promising they are deemed to be. Vygotsky's views of the nature of help are discussed in more detail in section 3.32. I note here that Vygotsky thought that sink-or-swim studies start well past the point where the experiment actually begins—at the subject's *choice of tactic and orientation*—and they often discard the most interesting and crucial data—that is, *where the subject seeks and uses help*—because of inordinate fears of conflation and bias.

When Dennett (1984a) remarks that the best way for cognitive science to study consciousness is to rummage around in the wings and backstage of life, trying to interrupt performance in revealing ways, he is more accurate and historically significant than he might imagine. But the flip side of the freedom to interrupt is the responsibility to help recovery, and Vygotskyan theory argues for both in any experiment or observation.

3.32 Developmental Processes

Having looked at development itself, I now want to specify the means by which it is carried out. Here I examine three features of the way an individual constructs and maintains metaconsciousness: internalization of external social relations and meaning, principally through speech; mediation of thinking and action; and control of thinking and action.

3.321 INTERNALIZATION

The study of internal-external relations in mental activity has a long history; arguably, it is the only thing ever studied! The Vygotskyan view of the matter can be understood only by drawing significantly on the work done after him, since his explanations of internalization were very sketchy.

Higher thought originates in the internalization of external social relationships and meanings (Valsiner 1988: 140, quoting Vygotsky). This process is not the mere copying of the external into the internal, as if sociocultural metamind were a disguised iconic theory of thinking (Wertsch and Stone 1985, Zinchenko 1985, and Gal'perin 1969 argue this point in detail). It is, rather, the recoding—what Vygotsky called *the transposing*—of the essential meaning structures of social activity into a distilled, syncretic form via semiotic activity, speech in particular. In the more popularized version, interpsychological activity becomes intrapsychological activity.

A look at the actual Russian terms clarifies this point considerably. One technical term for 'internalization' is *vrashchivanie,* which means literally 'ingrowing'. The dynamic and developmental character of the notion is lost by the English nominal translation. *Vrashchivanie* implies that higher thought emerges out of the active, nurturing transformation of externals into personally meaningful experience. Two other Russian terms support this interpretation. The term for 'meaning', as we know from Chapter 1, is *smysl,* but more specifically *osmyslivanie,* 'significancing'; experience is *perezhivanie,* literally 'living through', but probably best rendered as 'lived experience' (see van der Veer and Valsiner 1991: 316). Thus, when we speak of internalization in Vygotskyan theory, we are more accurately describing the ingrowing of lived experience into personal meaning.

Internalization is carried out by the abbreviation of interactive social speech into audible speech to oneself, or *private speech*, and ultimately silent speech for oneself, or *inner speech*. Social dialogue condenses into a private dialogue for thinking.[12] Vygotsky incorrectly believed that only verbal language worked this way. We now know that higher thought can be accomplished by the internalization of any *symbolic system;* for example, deaf signers sign to themselves, and other cultures privilege nonverbal but still culturally derived symbolic means to solve problems (for the latter, see Wertsch 1991: 31). Nonetheless, because my goal in this book is to examine the role of language in linking computational and social mind, I focus on the major insights gained by looking at speech.

Vygotsky (1987) argued that self-directed speech preserves the psychological predicate (what the speech is asserting) while deleting the psychological subject (what is known), and so the course of abbreviation in internalization follows the informational structure of speech. Wertsch (1985) recasts this argument in the more modern terms of the given-new organization of social discourse and holds that private speech abbreviates the given at the expense of the new. We shall look in more detail at the structure of private speech in Chapter 5 and see that it is driven by a variety of pragmatic and discourse phenomena. But these details are less important at this point than the more general observation that speech for one's own metathought originates in, and preserves features of, dialogic speech for others. The claim that social dialogue abbreviates to private dialogue goes hand in hand with earlier observations about the emergence of the individual from the group. Vygotsky's well-known demonstration of this point is worth recounting here.

Piaget argued that children's private speech—what he called *egocentric speech*—derives from their own cognitive autonomy and disappears when they become socialized. Vygotsky countered that since children are initially social and have to learn to be individuals, their private speech is not egocentric but essentially social. He then observed that young children use private speech in the presence of other young children, but not alone, and so their private dialogues preserve the social conditions of dialogue. The reverse is true for adults, who use private speech alone because they, unlike young children, have already internalized the dialogue and so have no need for recourse to the social group. Moreover, private speech does not disappear but goes underground in development, resurfacing in both child and adult, depending on the task at hand.

The initial location of private speech for thinking in the social context, then abbreviated as it is internalized for autonomous functioning, returns us to the foundational issue of internal-external relations. Davydov and Radzhikovskii (1985: 56) remark that Vygotsky saw "a resemblance between the structure of [external] labor activity and the structure of [internal] mental processes." This characterization curiously evokes the appropriateness of Wittgenstein as a guide to a unified cognitive science. Wittgenstein 1 is concerned with how the semantic structure of the external world is preserved in the structure of the propositions that constitute our mental life. The picture theory of meaning in the *Tractatus* reads like a logical account of the organization of internalization. From the preservation of structural relationships in the mental code, Wittgenstein 2 goes on to fill out the structure in the personal, lived experience of the subject. Vygotskyan internalization, the ingrowing of the personal semantic structure of lived experience, has a clear correlate in the unity of logic and action found in Wittgenstein.

3.322 MEDIATION

Higher thought is instrumental and involves the deferral and recasting of the external world, never its direct apprehension in its own terms. Gal'perin (1979: 97) puts this point by saying that an "object is present not to consciousness, but to the personality," and so distinguishes the neutral things of our awareness from their transformation into positioned objects by the self. Speech *mediates* this semiotic construction of metaconsciousness (see Davydov and Radzhikovskii 1985, Lee 1985, Wertsch 1991).

The instrumentalization of higher thought by signs, specifically verbal ones, clarifies the relation between language and thought. A quick reading of Vygotsky leaves the impression that he is a radical linguistic relativist, but he says outright that language and (higher) thought are not coextensive—"Thought and word are not cut from the same pattern. In a sense, there are more differences than likenesses between them" (Vygotsky 1962: 126)—and he explicitly criticizes Watson's equating of thought with inner speech (Vygotsky 1986: 84; see also Lee 1985: 78–79). Language equals thought no more than a vehicle equals transportation. Linguistic mediation of higher thought makes speech a go-between, not a reductive substitute. Vygotsky frequently observes that words do not equal concepts but instead steer toward them (van der Veer and Valsiner 1991: 265); words mediate and complete thinking but do not express it (van der Veer and Valsiner 1991: 370). Speech is a language *for* thought, not a language *of* thought.

Once we see speech as a tool *for higher thought,* we can focus on the tools at a speaker's disposal, that is, the features of culture appropriated by language for use by speakers to individuate themselves in metaconsciousness. Culture and individual meaning link up in evidential systems, focus structures, markers of discourse position, and so on, and languages vary markedly in how they systematize these things. This means that speakers of different languages have divergent—perhaps incomparable—learning tasks in constructing metaconsciousness through alternative resources for regulating the self. In this way we get a new view of linguistic relativity, one where "Vygotsky has something to offer Whorf" (Wertsch 1991: 45).

The mediating—that is, nonreductive and nonconstitutive—character of speech strikes a chord with my earlier comparison of Vygotsky and Wittgenstein through Derrida. In deconstruction, the material sign, actual speech, is a symptom of action and runs ahead of meaning because it is not tied to any particular signification. In observing that children's use of the material word precedes their understanding (and so their performance exceeds their competence), Vygotsky (1962: 47) notes that "the child learns relatively late the mental operations corresponding to the verbal forms he has been using for a long time." Moreover, for Derrida the material word is a metaphysical microcosm because it embodies both being and nonbeing simultaneously. Vygotsky would have concurred: "Thought is not expressed in the word, but is completed by the word. One might therefore speak of the becoming (the unity of being and nonbeing) of the thought in the word" (quoted by van der Veer and Valsiner 1991: 370).

3.323 CONTROL

The purpose of higher thought is the control of thinking and action, and internalization and mediation are means to achieve this goal. Three features of control are relevant to the unification of computational and cultural psycholinguistics.[13]

The first is *planning.* In development, the language for thought initially co-occurs with action and thinking, but as it takes on metafunctions, it anticipates and so regulates action and thinking. Vygotsky (1978: 27–28) observes:

> The greatest change in children's capacity to use language as a problem-solving tool takes place . . . when socialized speech (which has previously been used to address an adult) *is turned inward* . . . The crucial change occurs as follows: At an early stage speech accompanies the child's actions and reflects the vicissitudes of problem solving in

a disrupted and chaotic form. At a later stage speech moves more and more toward the starting point of the process, and so comes to precede action.

Evidence for the planning function of metathought, mediated by speech, is wide-ranging, from observations of children naming their pictures after drawing and then reversing the process (Vygotsky 1978: 28–30) to the use of self-directed speech as a clinical technique in remediating dysfunctions of behavioral control (Luria 1976b).

The second feature is *inhibition*. Higher thought works as a kind of cognitive filter to limit options and thereby let the individual proceed. Vygotsky (1978: 28) writes, "The specifically human capacity for language enables children to . . . overcome impulsive action . . . and to master their own behavior." The inhibitory function of metathought plays a central role throughout Luria's work: in the analysis of the culturally derived language for thought that gradually develops an inhibitory function in children (1982), in its surfacing in normal adults in difficult situations (1976a), and in clinical applications for the remediation of hyperactivity (1976b).

The third feature is the *locus of control*. Where does the individual get the information used to regulate thinking? It is important to phrase this question in a spatial way because Vygotsky, in his cultural-historical emphasis, equated causes with the *sources of behavior* (Vygotsky 1978: 62). Metaconsciousness can have three locales: in objects, in others, and in the self. Vygotsky (1978) observes: "Children confronted with a problem that is slightly too complicated for them exhibit a variety of responses including . . . direct verbal appeals to the object" (30), "appeals to the experimenter for help" (29) in which the "path from object to child and from child to object passes through another person" (30), and finally "appeal[s] to themselves" (27). Thus, higher thought, which seeks control through mediation and internalization, can be object-regulated, other-regulated, or self-regulated.

These three sources that individuals use in "applying a social attitude to themselves" (Vygotsky 1978: 27) bring out two important points. First, they have a developmental order, from object to other to self as the highest form of control. But since all developmental stages are symmetric and recoverable, an individual can traverse this sequence at will (literally), given the demands of a task. An adult's metaconsciousness may thus be object-regulated in one circumstance and self-regulated in another.

Second, it recalls my previous discussion of linguistic and cultural relativity. *Object, other,* and *self* are not neutral terms but semiotic phenomena subject to cultural construal. What counts for a self or legitimate object in one sociocultural circumstance does not count likewise in another. Moreover, different languages will track object, other, and self in different ways, for example, by privileging object-evidence over self-evidence and encoding this distinction in pragmatic markers for self-directed speech.

The connection of control to computationalism is straightforward. The frame problem is built on the possibility and nature of cognitive inhibition and control. If McCarthy's dunce had only had metaconscious planning, the options he proposed to the cannibals and missionaries problem would have been limited from the start. He would thereby have been rational! Vygotsky himself posed the frame problem in the very context of control, when he read Spinoza's account of Buridan's ass (see van der Veer and Valsiner 1991: 239). Although the story may be apocryphal and is traceable, if at all, to Aristotle more than Spinoza, Vygotsky found it in the work of his favorite philosopher and thought it typified his whole concern for psychological study: an ass caught between two equal bales of hay starved to death because it could not decide which one to eat! If the animal had only had a culture, an awareness of other animals and things, and a language that appropriated some meaningful pieces of its environment for use in self-talk, it could have ruled out one bale and eaten the other.

3.33 Context

Development and its component processes construct the subjectivity of an individual, but this is appreciable only against the subjectivity of the group *in context*. We therefore need an account of the conditions under which, to use Wertsch's (1985: 158–83) phraseology, individuals achieve intersubjectivity by establishing a common definition of situation. Leont'ev's *activity theory* provides such an account by spelling out the practical relations of the individual with the environment and group and their impact on the emergence and control of higher thought.

Before beginning, I should clarify two points. First, the theory of activity comes out of the Kharkov school (Leont'ev, Luria, Zaporozhets, Gal'perin, among others), which diverged from Vygotsky on a number of issues (see, e.g., van der Veer and Valsiner 1991: 289–92). But in spite of these serious disagreements, Vygotsky and the Kharkovians concur on the fundamentals, and so activity theory here can be viewed as broadly Vygotskyan (see Valsiner 1988: 208–19).

Second, the discussion that follows associates activity theory and the zone of proximal development. This is more a marriage of expository convenience than a theoretical claim, since both are concerned with the conditions under which the individual develops. But it should be noted that the zone of proximal development is not typically thought of as a correlate of activity theory.

3.331 THE THEORY OF ACTIVITY

The theory of activity is concerned with the way the individual engages the environment and the conditions under which an individual's thinking changes. Since I have already examined *thinking* as *higher thinking* and *change* as *development,* I now need to clarify what is meant by *conditions* and the more complicated phrase *under which.* The former leads to units of analysis and the latter to causal explanation.

Activity theory has a direct analogue with Vygotskyan work on the locus of control by identifying three kinds of conditions under which individuals engage their circumstances: interaction with objects, with others, and with the self (Valsiner 1988: 209). These conditions form the backdrop of practical activity, not the direct reducible causes, because individuals may persist in holding views despite conditions that steer them to the contrary.[14] For example, an individual may be caught between the authority of others and the authority of objective evidence without choosing between the two in a strictly causal way (see Valsiner 1988: 210). Object, other, and self frame and motivate the orienting activity—as suggested by the Russian term *obuslovlivaetsia,* 'caused by setting up conditions'—and are therefore not different forms of thought per se.

More specifically causal factors are found in the theory's three levels of analysis (see, e.g., A. N. Leont'ev 1978, 1981). Individual behavior may be characterized by its conditions of execution, its goals, or its motives, respectively, as an *operation,* an *action,* or an *activity.* Consider, for instance, problem solving as an operation, and so analyzed in terms of the concrete actions carried out by the problem solver, for example, writing out the problem. As an action, problem solving is described by its conscious purposes, say, for performance on a test; as an activity, problem solving is analyzed in terms of the reasons and personal meanings of the solver, say, for personal gain.

There is some dispute over just what the units are and what role circumstances and individual belief play in defining these levels (see, e.g., Wertsch 1981). Indeed, it is not clear whether activity theory concerns objective or methodological units; for instance, are operations real or imposed on reality by the analysis? In spite of these problems, the value of activity theory is that it admits purposes and reasons into mental life and, coupled with the vocabulary of object, other, and self, provides more precision in analyzing the context for intersubjectivity.

Consider, for example, two individuals solving a school problem who situate their metaconsciousness in another—say, the teacher—by asking directly for help. Despite these commonalities, they may diverge on motive: one may genuinely seek help by asking a more knowledgeable other, while the other one may ask for help just to demonstrate publicly compliance with and knowledge of the rules of school. If they have different motives and goals, they are engaged in quite different tasks, even though the locus of control and regulation is the same for both. Thus, the frame problem is different for each because "a person's orienting activity in any new situation involves the formation of a 'psychological model' of the situation (and the tasks to be performed in it), which further directs the subject's actions in that situation" (Valsiner 1988: 211). Goals, purposes, and conditions work hand in hand with the locus of control to determine different orienting activities. We will see how languages encode and privilege certain of these at the expense of others to provide individuals with the resources to construct subjectivity in context.

3.332 ZONE OF PROXIMAL DEVELOPMENT

Vygotskyan theory is very specific about how to look at the prospects for individual growth in any one instance of intersubjective activity. This is to be done through examining the zone of proximal development (hereafter ZPD), which is "the distance between the actual developmental level as determined by independent problem solving and the level of potential development as determined through problem solving under adult guidance or in collaboration with more capable peers" (Vygotsky 1978: 86). While this definition admittedly leaves much unsaid—What is actual growth? How does one measure help?—subsequent studies have operationalized these terms (see, e.g., Rogoff and Wertsch 1984), and the ZPD emerges, more generally, as the intersubjective context for growth via help.

Two features of the ZPD speak directly to our overall concern with unifying the cultural and computational mind via language. The first is that the ZPD can be either natural or deliberately constructed, just as long as it reflects a difference between actual and potential growth. Obviously school-based tasks have this difference, but so may any ordinary, practical framing activity, as well as play. Vygotsky (1978), in fact, devotes particular emphasis to the latter because play allows the child to engage in activity that is "well above his head" but with no direct social consequence for failure. The study of mental life thus need not be restricted to experimentally contrived situations, since any situation built on the difference between actual and potential development is a microcosm of growth.

The second feature is the finer structure of the ZPD, which must be intersubjective but asymmetric. As to the former, an individual must engage in joint attention with at least one other; by discounting their differences and thereby functionally deriving a shared definition of situation, they have intersubjectivity and prospects for on-line growth. As to the latter, one person must be more capable in the task and so lead the other beyond the actual level of growth. What is important is that both intersubjectivity and asymmetry can be constructed and maintained by language. Different cultures accord their speakers alternate ways of signaling common ground (e.g., through presupposition, deixis, and switch reference) and asymmetry of power (e.g., through pronouns and honorifics).

The theory of activity and the ZPD give us a way of analyzing the individual's relations with the world. We can identify the cultural context of mental life more precisely than just by saying that minds are contextually situated. Some parts of language track the goals and motives of individuals; indeed, they give individuals ways of objectifying, and thereby realizing, their goals and motives. A context is less a determinant of thinking than a locale where individuals speak to manage the gap between their own abilities and those of more capable—and helpful—peers.

3.34 Brain Bases of Higher Thought

We have thus far considered the purely psychological aspects of Vygotskyan cultural psycholinguistics. Just as computationalism seeks neural hardware correlates to bolster its claims about the programs of mental life, so Vygotskyan cultural psycholinguistics has a material side in Luria's theories on the neurological substrate of higher thought. In many ways Luria's work attempts to substantiate directly Vygotsky's and Leont'ev's psychological claims through an account of the brain as a functional system (see, e.g., Luria 1980: 28–36). In Luria's view, the brain is organized into three functional levels: *tone*, which is dedicated to attention and wakefulness and is associated with lower-level neural structures such as the reticular formation; *information processing,* which is dedicated to cognitive and representational mechanisms and is associated with cortical structures such as Broca's area; and *regulation,* which is dedicated to controlling and selecting information and is associated with the frontal lobes (Luria 1973).

The frontal area has all the earmarks of the brain basis of the self (Brown 1991). Here we find the neurological mechanisms for cognitive control, guidance, inhibition, integration, planning, monitoring, selection, sequencing, goal-directedness, persistence, and self-awareness (see, e.g., Luria 1980, Stuss and Benson 1987, 1990). We know these facts from the unfortunate occurrence of disorders and lesions in the frontal areas. Luria's (1976b, 1980) celebrated examples of diffuse narrative protocols by individuals with frontal lobe disturbances underscore these control properties. PET scans show that routinized behavior fails to engage the frontal lobes and remains subcortical, suggesting that the frontal areas are associated with voluntary activity; disturbances there, *control aphasias,* are neither purely linguistic nor cognitive, but seem to involve speech-thought interrelations and executive control over the uptake of external symbolic information (Stuss and Benson 1990).

As Cole (1990: 18) points out, the central Vygotskyan ideas of inhibition and externalism come together in Luria's argument that the frontal lobes are connected to culturally learned, symbolic systems that act as functional barriers to action. Since the orientational system differs both functionally and neurologically from the representational system, Luria can be taken as arguing that *the language for thought is dissociable from the language of thought* (see Chapter 6). We can see this in four fairly predictable consequences of frontal lobe lesions.

3.341 REPRESENTATION AND ORIENTATION

Frontal lobe disorders appear to split representation from orientation. Stuss and Benson (1987) and Goldberg and Bilder (1987) observe that frontal lobe patients can identify, learn, and recall information, but cannot deliberately do so. They have normal IQ's and can process abstractions, such as metaphor, and so are normal in formal-computational intelligence. But they cannot translate this knowledge into action or use it as an external monitor to guide the self. For example, one patient shown a picture of the Vatican could say that Roman Catholics use it, but when asked to define the Vatican directly was utterly at a loss. One way to interpret this failure is to say that the frontal lobe patient can perform well on representational tasks but not on *metarepresentational* (orientational) ones.

Goldberg (1987) tries to cast these facts into a larger account of the functional suborganization of the frontal lobes. The lateral portion is said to regulate the flow of information from the outside to the inside; the medial regulates the opposite flow, from the inside to the outside. Significantly, alien hand syndrome, a disorder in which an individual's limbs act without voluntary control (much like Dr. Strangelove's self-strangulating hand), occurs when the medial area is affected, where motoric representations are initiated into action. In other words, the motor representations themselves are preserved but disconnected from their selection. Hence, intentionality can be decoupled neurologically from the program to be executed; or, better, the language *of* motoric thought and action is dissociable from the language *for* such thought and action.

3.342 DOMAIN SPECIFICITY

Pribram (1990) remarks that frontal lobe disturbances affect processing across domains of knowledge. Significantly, they do not merely disrupt the general computational operations of the mind/brain, such as serial processing, which can be disturbed by a lesion anywhere. Rather, they disturb horizontal control across knowledge domains and vertical control of levels within such domains (Goldberg and Bilder 1987, inadvertently echoing Fodor 1983). This means that the behavioral consequences of frontal lobe disorders can help us draw the boundaries between representational domains because we can observe how their effects on control processes allow information from one level or domain to intrude on another.

Clear examples of what I will call *representational leakages* are given by Goldberg and Bilder (1987). They observe that some frontal lobe patients asked to draw the sequence of a cross, a circle, and another cross draw the first cross and circle successfully. But when they draw the second cross, it appears in block form, suggesting that the patients fail to inhibit the circle's property of geometric openness from intruding on the subsequent simple line drawing of the cross. A similar failure to inhibit component properties within a domain on a serial task can be seen in cases in which subjects are given an equal sign and asked to draw a dot, but produce a colon because they fail to inhibit the property of duality in the equal sign from intruding on the singular dot. Also observed are cross-domain problems, as when subjects draw a geometric figure and include the first letter of the word for the object—for example, a circle with the letter *c*—which shows an inability to separate linguistic and visual information.

This behavior suggests that the frontal areas are the brain/mind's border patrol, policing the interfaces of domains of knowledge and overseeing the boundaries of tasks. Significantly, this apparent modularity can be an emergent property of the brain/mind, a consequence of the nature of the domain and representations to be manipulated, not necessarily something built in. As Brown (1990) observes, the structure of the brain/mind is a consequence of the relationship between components more than an inherent arrangement (cf. Tanenhaus and Lucas 1987 and further discussion in section 3.4). So both modular and nonmodular properties may emerge as an effect of component relationships monitored by the frontal areas.

3.343 CENTRAL PROCESSING

Brown (1987, 1990) essentially argues that frontal lobe disorders show that the mind has *central processing without a central processor.* Frontal lobe disruptions give patients an altered feeling of agency, but not because the self is somehow affected as the instigator of action. Quite the contrary: these disorders illustrate that there can be disruption of volition without disruption of initiation, as in the case of alien hand syndrome, and so central-processing disorders do not implicate the *I for an i,* or the originary cognitive mover.

In Brown's (1987) view, volition inheres in action. Neurologically, the initiation of an act occurs well before any activation of the motor cortex: awareness of the action and feelings of agency *follow* the act. The function of the neurological self thus appears to be to inform the organism of things already initiated, and so is very much like Dennett's (1991) constantly updating narrative voice. The self does not propel action and thought so much as it keeps us posted on how action and thought transpire. (This, in fact, is how I view the relationship of private and inner speech to thought: not as causing thought but as informing or *mediating* it.) The neurolog ically correlated self and central processor are not central in the sense that they receive all information or oversee mental life as an omniscient executive, but that does not mean that they are any less regulatory.

3.344 CONSCIOUSNESS AND SELF-CONSCIOUSNESS

Frontal lobe disturbances substantiate Vygotsky's psychological distinction between consciousness (*soznanie*) and symbolically driven metaconsciousness (*osoznanie*). Brown (1977: 151) draws the distinction as follows: "The separation of the world [from self] leads only to consciousness of the world and of the self qua object in that world. Self-awareness requires a further distinction within the self. Language fulfills this need." In his view, the neurological evidence indicates that "when one is conscious of being conscious, the object of consciousness is not the self but an idea or description of the self in a state of consciousness" (Brown 1991: 62). "Language enhances this trend and helps to build up and protect the self concept" (74).

Stuss and Benson (1987, 1990) document the split between consciousness and self-consciousness. They note that frontal lobe patients have awareness and self-knowledge—they know that and who they are—but not self-consciousness; they cannot integrate and monitor their knowledge. The same split characterizes Capgras syndrome, whereby the patient believes that the individuals around him or her are duplicates of the original. Stuss and Benson (1987: 147, 1990: 34) describe such a case, caused by frontal lobe damage, and note that the patient is conscious of the impossibility of having duplicate families and accepts this impossibility as theoretical knowledge, but refuses to apply it to his own case. He also verbally expresses a desire to return to work but never makes the slightest move to do so.

In short, frontal lobe damage may result in the decoupling of consciousness from self-consciousness. The patient can be aware of the world and his own position in it; indeed, even "total aphasics still appear to be *conscious* [my emphasis] in a human way" (Brown 1991: 63). But the frontal lobe patient cannot use any of this information in a self-directed way to change or monitor his own beliefs. These kinds of pathologies of the self, as Brown calls them, are possible because symbolic "commentary on events is not an essential feature of consciousness" (1991: 63) but of meta-consciousness.

The brain bases of higher thought in the frontal lobes are perhaps the most obvious connections that cultural psycholinguistics has to computationalism. Here we find the same theoretical vocabulary (e.g., *inhibition* and *control*), the same evidence (neural areas and pathways), and the same purposes for explanation (a functional account of brain/mind). Perhaps this lesson can be turned back on the culture-computation link through materialism. Culture is no less objective and causal than computation so long as each is understood in its proper bearing on mind.

3.4 Architectures and Contexts: Three Prospects for Unity

The synopses of cognitive science and Vygotsky thus far provided could be the basis for a quick marriage of computation and culture if cognitive science were left to the mind's formal structure alone and Vygotskyan theory to its noncomputational complement. But this would be an arrangement headed directly for the rocks. While cognitive science buys heavily into computationalism, there is nothing inherently noncomputational about Vygotsky's humanistic view of language, culture, and the self. Metaconsciousness surely has its computational and coding limitations. Frame decisions and mental orientation might, in fact, be profitably studied as the computing of representations at the language-culture interface. (Part II is devoted to the details of this idea.)

The old saw that mind occurs *in* culture may help us make better sense of the two. More specifically, *architecture* (the codes and processes that constitute the form of inner mental life) is *situated*. Vygotsky and cognitive science might productively come together under a theory of the (linguistic) relationship between architectures and contexts. Fortunately, such an account can be found in proposals in cognitive science and cultural psychology regarding the ways in which contextual information can bear on code.

Essential to this work is the view that architecture is not "built into the language processing system as a design characteristic, but rather . . . may result from the relationship among representations" (Tanenhaus and Lucas 1987: 231; see also Tanenhaus, Dell, and Carlson 1987: 106). The crucial factor is how some representations situate and provide feedback for (i.e., *contextualize*) the processing of others: "Different feedback patterns will be associated with different types of contextual information" (Tanenhaus, Dell, and Carlson 1987: 105). Where representational context predetermines the processing of another representation, connectionist properties surface; where context does not so predetermine, behavior looks modular. An architecture is *the effect of informational relations and congruity of code and context*. Consequently, the same code can exhibit different architectural characteristics depending on how it adjusts to or accepts feedback from the information that forms its context.

These architecture-context relationships speak directly to the connection between Vygotsky and cognitive science because, to repeat and modify the old saw, inner mind occurs in the context of outer culture. But how so? Is inner mind *in* culture the way sounds, for example, are *in* words or words are *in* syntax?

3.41 Mind-Context Relations

To answer these questions, we need to make some headway into the complicated issues of the nature of cultural context and its effects on mental code. Furthermore, to make this information the basis for a believable link between computation and culture via Vygotskyan theory, one must show how some parts of language mediate the mind-context relationship by selecting aspects of context to bridge culture and code.

3.411 WHAT IS A CONTEXT?

Answers to this question have filled entire books, so we might confidently cast our defining nets narrowly, expecting to bring up a nice catch with little effort. My experience, however, is that work on the nature of context is frequently overtechnicalized and packed with putative, detailed units that, if appreciable at all, are usable only by their inventors. Curiously, despite the intense work on the subject, an explicit definition of *context* very often goes unstated (as Butterworth 1993: 6 notes). I think that it is possible and necessary to talk about (cultural-linguistic) context without overstating the facts and without resorting to mindless technicalities.

Following work by Butterworth (1993, in turn leading back to Cole's) and Mercer (1993), a simple definition of *context* is 'the setting for thought'. Context is not just the spatiotemporal locale of mind but its whole informational surround: the configuration of who, what, where, when, why, and how. This definition moves us away from seeing context as a body of *shared* ideas (as Mercer 1993 nicely counters) and more as a common opportunity for individuals to discount their differences in order to operate *as if* there were shared knowledge. In this way, context is neither a singular notion—thought is not in *a* context but in many (Goodnow and Warton 1993)—nor a simple determinant of thought: thought may change context (Mercer 1993). Context heads off and arbitrates the puzzlement of individuals in their ordinary encounters with one another by spelling out the normal state of affairs. This default information setting is neither simply real (i.e., it is not just past contexts) nor hypothetical (i.e., it is not all possible ones) but *authentic*: it has its effects by being believably *real*, that is, imagined but instantiatable (Butterworth 1993).

How, then, does culture speak through the authentic, normal-state, nonmonolithic settings for thought? Culture scripts contexts by arranging their occurrence; associating different contexts with one another; and assigning different responsibilities to contextual components of who, what, where, and so on (Butterworth 1993).

Consider what happens in school, the setting of formal, instructed thought, which Western culture scripts as the context of universal knowledge. School accords more frequency to some settings than others, directly links some situations at the expense of others, and arranges people, events, things, and outcomes in a pecking order. A clear example is the way American culture scripts mathematics learning in the primary grades: it privileges individual problem solving and contrasts that with group busywork; it removes mathematics from everyday contexts and relegates it to scientific settings; it invests the asymmetric teacher-student relationship with authority, assigning ultimate power to the instructor.[15]

The empirical evidence appears to indicate that context—scripted for frequency, co-occurrence, and internal configuration—bears on thinking by *focusing the attention* of the participants. It is well known that adult logical reasoning is affected by the language of the problem to be solved and the familiarity and concreteness of the objects reasoned about. In formal logic, for instance, an implication (if *p* then *q*) can be efficiently verified by affirming the antecedent (*p*, therefore *q*: modus ponens) or by denying the consequent (~*q*, therefore ~*p*: modus tollens). But when adults are given the implication *if you clean up the room* (p), *then you can go outside* (q), and asked to take the perspective of either a parent or a child, those in the former setting look for antecedent violations while those in the latter look for consequent violations. This is because, as Girotto and Light (1993) argue, the parent context focuses on room cleaning, which obligates the result, while the child context focuses on going outside, which is obligated by the antecedent. The different personal stances induced by the description of the settings change the motives and goals of the reasoners and so draw attention to some parts of the events at the expense of others.

What is crucial here is not the familiarity or concreteness of the problem but the different viewpoints impinging on the task as an activity, to use Leont'ev's term. The reasons and personal meanings of the individuals play a critical role in the task as the context differentially organizes the events (Roazzi and Bryant 1993). Here the effects of language come to the fore in explicitly tracking aspects of the informational surround.

3.412 HOW DOES LANGUAGE HIGHLIGHT PARTS OF CONTEXT?
Language focuses attention and codes perspective through devices that function expressly to bridge the context-code gap. Experimental work shows that *explicitness of context* has the greatest bearing on thought (Roazzi and Bryant 1993), and so those parts of language that make contextual factors overt by giving them form, and thereby marking focus, can be a guide to how a speaker navigates the line between inner mind and outer world.

We will look at many examples of the linguistic structures that carry out this attentional work in more detail in Chapter 5. But here we can consider a simple illustration. In Spanish, parts of objects that are inalienable (generally thought of an nonremovable) are signaled as belonging to their possessors by the definite or indefinite article *(the/a)*, not, as in English, by the possessive adjective *(my)*. So *la mano*, literally 'the hand', means 'my/your/his/her/its/our/their hand'; *mi mano*, literally 'my hand', is rather odd-sounding. This does not mean that speakers can never use possessive adjectives with the body parts, but doing so signals that the expression is the focus of attention and is asserted in explicit contrast with the contextual givens and the normal state of affairs.

With this in mind, let us consider this discourse, which illustrates two four-year-old children (M and C) drawing pictures of their families and simultaneously talking to themselves during the task (after Ramirez 1992: 210–11):

M: Y sus manos. ('and her hands': possessive adjective)

C: Mi mama en la foto. ('my mother in the picture')

M: Y le hago un corazón. ('and I make her heart': article)

C: Un corazón. ('her heart': article)

M: No. ('no')

C: Las orejitas. ('her little ears': article)

What is interesting here is M's initial coding of the possessor–body part relation by the possessive adjective *sus*. She uses the focus marker at the point where she has to begin the task and hence contrast her speech and action with the speech and action of C and the rest of the ongoing state of affairs. The possessive adjective is a symptom of how her perspective on the present situation holds against the background of the drawing task. Her drawing emerges against all others, and thus her first utterance is more accurately 'and HER hands, in contrast to all those others that are or could be drawn and talked about here'. This focusing device frames the task at hand and signals her motive and goal to differentiate her work from all others. When M no longer needs to make the contextual frame and the focus of attention explicit—when she has no need to invoke the context because she is no longer positioned, so to speak, at the culture-code boundary—she, like C, uses the non–focus marking via the article.

Spanish allows its speakers this means of explicitly coding the focus of attention for use in the deliberate exercise of metaconscious control. M deploys this resource to mediate her thinking activity and give her voice a position (Wertsch 1991). Different languages will code more and less— and in different ways—about context-mind relations and so position their speakers differently. Some languages commit their speakers to specifics about the configuration of context and its connection to on-line thought and action, for example, by marking and denoting the culturally determined significance of why, when, and how the setting focuses attention. Other languages are less explicit, signaling only that a speaker is focusing attention.

These variations show that speakers of these languages take a perspective and make parts of context explicit in quite different ways. Since these languages cannot mediate metaconsciousness comparably, they arguably accord their speakers different means to metathought. In all cases, however, the languages themselves provide their speakers ways of bridging context and architecture through certain linguistic forms.

3.413 HOW DOES CONTEXT IMPINGE ON MIND?

As Butterworth (1993: 12) observes, it is not enough to say simply that context surrounds thought. Code-context relations of *feedback, storage,* and *retention of source* help us examine the congruity of culture and mind through language.

Tanenhaus and Lucas (1987) and Tanenhaus, Dell, and Carlson (1987) claim that the influence of context (what they call *higher-level information*) on contextualized information (what they call *lower-level information*) depends on how the latter is embedded in the former. If context has a *part-whole* relationship to contextualized information, then the influence is by *feedback,* activating contextualized information *during processing* and modifying it in terms of speed and content. In this way the processing itself evinces properties of an interactionist architecture, where surrounding information intrudes to *predetermine* the most contextually appropriate result. But where there is a *set-membership* relation between context and contextualized information, context influences processing *only after* the contextualized information has been processed. This *postprocessing selection* of information for contextual appropriateness does not affect speed and content and evinces properties of modular architecture, where one piece of information has access to another only at input or output, not via feedback.[16]

Does culture feed back onto computational mind, or does it select the contextually appropriate behavior? In more specifically Vygotskyan terms, does orientation determine the content of representations or simply frame them? Does the frame border or outline the task, or does it change the content and processing of the task itself? The answers—to which the next three chapters are devoted—lie in how and where some parts of language mediate culture and thought, and this turns on whether cultural orientation has a part-whole or set-membership relationship to computational representation.

Proceeding in this way requires concessions on the part of both Vygotskyans and cognitive scientists in their typical mode of inquiry. The former must acknowledge that some aspects of cultural context do not entirely determine the content of thought. Culture acts on minds by *either* selecting or predetermining. The latter must accord the individual a legitimate place in the investigation and admit a vocabulary of subjective states—such as motive—into the analysis.

These different feedback properties are related to the more general organization of data structures (Tanenhaus and Lucas 1987). Part-whole feedback relationships are *stored;* that is, context and contextualized information occur together in explicit subsumption because the cost-benefit ratio of feedback is best when there is a small set of contextually appropriate choices for the feedback to activate. To put it another way, feedback is contextual prediction, and this process is most effective when the items to be predicted are relatively few. (Unlimited prediction is not prediction at all but omniscience.)

Set-membership contextual relations are not stored but computed: context and contextualized information are separate and have rules for interfacing or construal. Contexts that cannot absolutely predict information have a high cost-benefit ratio since they must select from a large number of potentially appropriate choices. So the system compensates by according context and contextualized information separate status, making set-membership contextual influence orthogonal to contextualized information and requiring rules for negotiation between the two.[17]

Is the culture-mind congruence one of storage or computing? The answer depends on how and where culture influences mind. In cases where cultural context predetermines the content of mind, the options for influence should be relatively few. In contrast, where cultural context selects mind, the number of options for influence should be relatively large. Thus, the storage-computing distinction might yield further insight into two kinds of metaknowledge by suggesting the range of options available to each.

Once again, these formal results from computationalism have a Vygotskyan interpretation. The individual is faced with the problem of acting in context—or, more specifically, constructing intersubjectivity with another individual in a zone of proximal development under cultural conditions that legitimize the problem, the activity, and the search for help. How does this transpire? What do individuals negotiate with one another under rules of contextual construal? What do they deploy automatically as given, stored, presolved cultural gambits?

A final characteristic of different architecture-context relations concerns the preservation of features of the source of input. Computed, nonfeedback, set-membership relationships preserve the source of input and its accompanying contextual noise. They do so because information organized into domains linked by interfaces is relatively immune to contextual factors and so does not need to presort input. The world can enter mind as it is, *unfiltered*. By contrast, stored, part-whole relationships filter the source of input and eliminate accompanying contextual noise because the purpose of feedback is to adjust data *before and as* it is processed. In this case the world is continually updated in mind.

The consequences of these distinctions for the culture-mind congruence again come clear. Computed relationships between cultural context and inner mind should preserve features of the context; stored relationships ought to be more anonymous in this respect, with inner code lacking features of its external source. Hence, regulative, inhibitory metaknowledge should retain its connections to the external world, and this connection should be signaled by explicit contextual markers such as deixis and other non–truth-conditional forms. Where cultural knowledge intrudes on mental content, however, the connection to the context ought to be more opaque.

Luria's peasant, once again, illustrates the structural properties of code and context in action. When he rejects the logical task out of hand, his orientation *frames the syllogism from the outside*. He does not make inferences in such a way as to suggest that culture has intruded on the content of the representations. Cultural knowledge appears to select the logic—interface with it—not feed back onto it.

Yet, there are cases in which culture intrudes on the content itself. When Luria (1976a) gives his subjects a categorization task and asks them to sort spoons, saucepans, eyeglasses, and fire into groups of items that are household objects and groups that are not, one peasant puts them all together because, he reasons, you need all of them to cook and eat, and so they are all household goods (Luria 1976a: 96). Here, culture arguably intrudes on inner mind, with the content and relations of conceptual categories activated by higher-level cultural knowledge. In this case culture and context appear to be stored together.

Culture may provide the context for the implementation of logic, but this differs from the way culture provides the context for categorization. To put it another way, part-whole contexts (such as the latter) affect the *truth of the representation,* while set-membership ones (such as the former) affect *non–truth-conditional execution.* This contrast correlates with the fact that set-membership relations are typically inhibitory and aligned with output editing for appropriateness. Part-whole relationships are facilitative and increase the likelihood of a response because they intrude in the processing itself.

Applied again to Luria's peasants, these distinctions might suggest two kinds of metaknowledge, depending on how outer culture provides the context for inner mind. In one sense, culture inhibits and regulates the information embedded in it; in another, it facilitates and invests it with content. What parts of the language for thought serve these inhibitory or facilitative functions? I try to make sense of this difference in subsequent chapters, as we look at the relationship between contexts and mental architecture played out in actual cases by speaking subjects.

3.42   *Three Unities*

This discussion of architecture-context relations leads to three areas where cognitive science and Vygotskyan theory have a vested interest and where language plays a basic position in the equation. These are *subjectivity, implementation,* and *breakdown.* Here I sketch how computation and culture merge on these counts; the next three chapters, respectively, pick up each of these unities.

3.421   SUBJECTIVITY
Both cognitive science and Vygotskyan theory take the nature of personal experience as central to their work. Subjectivity and consciousness have always been a mainstay of cultural psycholinguistics (Vygotsky 1986: 1), and although they have a checkered history in cognitive science, recent

work has accorded them legitimacy for both proponents (Jackendoff 1987, Flanagan 1992) and opponents (Searle 1992) of computationalism.

An instructive lesson for the unity of Vygotsky and cognitive science is found in the way consciousness has reemerged in computationalism. Jackendoff, a modular representationalist, argues that consciousness is a property of the operation of computational input modules themselves. As he says, they *support* subjective awareness by projecting consciousness up, as it were, during the course of modular processing, each module with its own awareness (Jackendoff 1987: 15–27). The idea that consciousness is an emergent property of the operation of the inner code and falls out from mind's action per se is an increasingly popular one and is held alike by advocates of modularity (Cam 1989) and connectionism (Brown 1991), by those caught in the middle (Dennett 1991), and even those who object to it all (Searle 1992).

Consciousness has fared well in recent cognitive science because it can be given a direct computational interpretation, which in turn makes it a genuine object of scientific (i.e., causal) inquiry. Jackendoff argues the computational hard line by saying that only physical and computational procedures are amenable to causal explanations, and so subjectivity that can be bootstrapped up from lower, formal mind—what Jackendoff calls *the mind-mind problem*—is a valid concern for mind science. Phenomenological mind—all other accounts of personal experience in noninformational terms—is a slippery ghost with a long history of ties to externalism and impossible, dead-end accounts of phenomenal causation (Jackendoff 1987: 26).

There are two mistakes here, both recognizable and correctable from bringing Vygotsky into cognitive science. The first is to equate subjectivity with consciousness alone. Subjectivity is *dual*, constituted by both consciousness *(soznanie)* and metaconsciousness *(osoznanie)*. (Jackendoff 1987: 18 recognizes this, and excludes the latter.) The second is to dispose of external causal explanations on ideological grounds and deny them precision. Jackendoff (1987: 320–27) himself argues that language may serve consciousness by stabilizing and differentiating concepts—an old Vygotskyan point, in fact: words steer toward concepts (see section 3.322). But he locates the causal factors internally, in the computational input systems that manipulate the formal structure of language. Vygotskyan work shows, however, that particular units of speech *at the culture-mind interface* drive (and explain) metathought.[18] Cultural psycholinguistics is no less a causal-materialist theory of subjectivity than is computationalism in this respect.

If we open up subjectivity on two counts—its constitution and its explanation—and cast it more broadly in terms of the position of language in architecture-context relations, we might find that the mind-mind problem is complemented by the *mind-mind/mind-world* problem. This returns us to Wittgenstein's composite subject, perched on the boundary between the wholly interior prospects of universal knowledge in logical form (mind-mind consciousness) and the case-by-case rulings of the individual looking outside for help (mind-world consciousness). If Platonic cognitive science makes subjectivity into mental run time, then Wittgensteinian cognitive science adds *deliberateness* to the picture.

3.422 IMPLEMENTATION

Working mind is important to both cognitive science and Vygotskyan theory. For the former, implementation provides the ultimate theoretical test because it is "scientifically more rigorous . . . [and] closer to something relatively 'real'—the actual machine and its properties" (Anderson 1987: 468). For Vygotsky, on-line thinking is equally crucial because meta-thought is identifiable only as it is played out in the speech performance of subjects in real time. In connecting the virtual machine to the real one, Vygotsky could be taken for Pylyshyn (1985: 75), who says that a theory of mind must not only capture generalizations but also "explain how actual instances of behavior are generated."

Real-time processing leads to two syntheses of computationalism and culture. First, in examining the real-time speech performance of individuals, we must also observe progress and growth in the task. The mere deployment of thinking is no more intrinsically useful than is the mere running of a machine. *What is the implementation for? What does it achieve?* Experimental and naturalistic observations of working mind should describe the concomitant changes in subjectivity—uneven spurts of development, metacognitive backtracking, self-direction and psychological distancing in externals. In this way we can link on-line performance with microgenesis.

Second, we concentrate on language at the culture-mind border. Just as machines throw up system commentary as they process, so thinking subjects speak *to, from,* and *of* the cultural contexts in which their activities are embedded. This mediating language for thought is a symptom of (meta)mind in cultural context. Which aspects of this context are marshaled on-line and which are not?

Two features of code-context relations may help here: the preservation of the source and inhibition. Culture can be located in the trappings of public speech in private inhibitory use. For both cognitive science and Vygotskyan theory, *subjectivity is activity*. In a strictly computational view, consciousness is the information processing itself. In metaconsciousness, culture can be tracked in how it affords its speakers psychological distance through pragmatic and metapragmatic coding.

3.423 BREAKDOWN

Cognitive science and Vygotskyan theory have an essential link in a mutual concern for patterns of breakdown. Typically in computationalism, data on how the (mental) system crashes is used to arbitrate claims about architecture. Representationalism, for example, predicts decisive and specific breakdown since the language of thought is explicit and demarcated—an easy target to hit. Interactionism expects the opposite because a self-compensating network of implicit knowledge should gracefully degrade under disruption. In Vygotskyan theory, patterns of breakdown say less about architecture than they do about control processes. The disruption of metaconsciousness results in characteristic loss of cognitive regulation and inhibition through speech.

We can use the joint focus on breakdown in computational and cultural psycholinguistics to see how disruption splits the cultural from the computational. Taking a methodological lesson from Vygotsky, we can first of all see that the breakdown need not be physical in order to count as such. Functional disruption, artificially induced by difficulty, works as well as neurological trauma to trigger the sorts of representational leakages we saw in section 3.342.

Nonetheless, there are a variety of disorders that appear to affect the language of thought while leaving the language for thought untouched, and vice versa. To put it another way, when an architecture in context breaks down, representation and cognitive framing (metarepresentation) can be dissociated by a disruption in their integrating link in (certain aspects of) language. This remarkable result testifies to the ultimate unity of cultural and computational psycholinguistics: only information that is so closely tied could be so specifically and clearly disconnected.

Cognitive science gives an account of architectures, Vygotsky an account of contexts. Vygotskyan cognitive science spells out the details of this relationship. We now turn to the specifics of the three areas where Vygotsky and cognitive science dovetail into a productive *sociocomputationalism*: subjectivity (consciousness and metaconsciousness), implementation (run time, private speech, and computational control), and breakdown (control disorders and dissociations of representation from speech for thought).

II

Three Unities

In Part II I examine subjectivity, control, and breakdown—three areas where social and computational approaches to mind have traditionally had much to say, though not very much to each other. The findings of each are integrated under the framework for unification described in Part I. In Chapter 4 I argue that subjectivity has three modes: nonconscious processing, consciousness, and metaconsciousness. Vygotskyan cognitive science gives the defining features of the third (e.g., inhibition, slow processing), which in turn legitimize and clarify the first two (e.g., qualia, experiential binding). The properties of metaconsciousness are useful in reinterpreting recent experiments in the cognitive science literature on problem solving, metaknowledge, and distributed representation. Chapter 5 gives a computational interpretation of the standard Vygotskyan notion of private speech. Just as computing systems have a metavocabulary for computational control, so are the metarepresentational resources of particular languages used by individuals to regulate their thinking activity. In addition to a language *of* thought, humans have a language *for* thought— a cognitive and behavioral control language. In Chapter 6 I look at how certain congenital disorders (e.g., Williams syndrome, Turner syndrome) disrupt speech for mental and behavioral regulation by delinking the language of thought from the language for thought. The effects of control disorders surface where social language becomes cognitively strategic. These syndromes provide the crucial negative evidence required for all putative mental phenomena by showing that only what really is in mind can be the target of breakdown.

4

Subjectivity: Consciousness and Metaconsciousness

4.1 Consciousness Regained

Consciousness is the Ross Perot of mind science. Is he in or is he out? When he is in, he occupies everyone's attention, turning even axioms into controversies and suggesting that we may just have to do *everything* differently in order to get back to business as usual. When he is out, our feelings run from perplexity to relief. To our astonishment, sometimes he simply vanishes from contention. At other times he takes punishing questions right on the chin, and we are glad to see him go. But then suddenly he is back in again, claiming to be misunderstood and saying damaging things about his inquisitors.

Consciousness is back. A sure sign that it has come back with a vengeance is that it has returned with an unlikely band of supporters. Plain-language philosophers of mind with heavy computational leanings, such as Dennett (1991) and Flanagan (1992), have embraced the idea in restated form, but so have plain-language philosophers of mind who sometimes flash an anticomputational streak, such as Searle (1992). Cognitivists with clinical and social sides, including Neisser (1992) and Baars (1988), have unsurprisingly argued for consciousness as an essential idea. But so have those with no obvious clinical or social axe to grind, such as Jackendoff (1987) and Johnson-Laird (1988), for whom pure computationalism and subjective awareness are entirely compatible. Even the neuropsychologists (Shallice 1988a and b, Gazzaniga 1988, Kinsbourne 1988) and neurobiologists (Crick and Koch 1990) have signed on; these are the heavy artillery, since they accept consciousness for materialist reasons.

This is not to say that there are no more punishing questioners (see Allport 1988, Churchland 1988, Nagel 1986, McGinn 1991, Harnad 1982, Bisiach 1988a). The point is, rather, that it is now possible to accept both consciousness and neurobiological-computational cognitivism and not be drummed straight out of the profession.

Coincidentally, Vygotsky found himself in the same kind of intellectual environment some seventy years ago. In the 1920's, with logical positivism and behaviorism making very hard times for awareness and subjectivity, Vygotsky (1979, originally 1925: 5) spoke out for consciousness: "The psychological characteristics of consciousness have been persistently and studiously avoided in our scientific literature. Attempts are made to avoid even mentioning consciousness, as if it did not exist for the new psychology." He reached back to William James and over the self-righteous scientism of his contemporaries: "Once consciousness has been banished from psychology, we are trapped in our biological absurdity [his term for *eliminative materialism*] forevermore" (9). For Vygotsky, consciousness binds behavior and so is the key to psychological structure (9). Indeed, the problem of consciousness surrounds his major work, *Thought and Language*, as the center of the book's first sentence—"The first issue that must be faced in the analysis of thinking and speech concerns the relationship among the various mental functions, the relationship among the various forms of the activity of consciousness"—and its last:"The meaningful word is a microcosm of human consciousness" (1987: 43, 285).

In coming out for consciousness, Vygotsky, like contemporary thinkers, defended it in terms of the reigning ideas of the day. Then-current theory was reflexology, or the study of behavior as generalized bodily response. Thinking was a reflex with inhibited motoric response, that is, a reaction with no corresponding overt action (1979: 2). The body could serve as a stimulus for itself, and consciousness was a mechanism to translate the reflexes of one bodily domain into another. Consciousness was thus a reflex of reflexes (1979: 19, 32).

The parallels between Vygotsky and modern theorists are striking. For one thing, his account sounds remarkably like current proposals in which consciousness is a cross-modal interface or a central computational workspace (Shallice 1988b, Baars 1988). And just as modern theories bootstrap consciousness up from lower, automatic mind via the inheritance of computational properties (what Jackendoff 1987 calls the *mind-mind problem*), so Vygotsky's account is *indigenous,* with consciousness built out of its own resources—for him, the inherited properties of unconscious reflexes. Vygotsky and the computationalists both see that there must be continuity of structure between lower mind and consciousness—that is, the form of unconscious mind must be passed into consciousness—if we are to avoid dualism (see, e.g., Dennett and Kinsbourne 1992; compare Vygotsky's comments 1979: 8–9).

Even with these parallels, Vygotsky's view of consciousness must be understood on its own terms. As we know from Chapters 1 and 3, *consciousness* is a cover term for several ideas about subjectivity: *znanie, soznanie,* and *osoznanie.* Moreover, Vygotsky drew on a number of traditions outside of psychology for these ideas, and all were conditioned by his acceptance of Marxism. The view of consciousness that is special to Vygotsky, and motivates much of the present discussion, is *osoznanie*—the experience of experience, or metaconsciousness. This is still compatible with his view of the reflexive structure of awareness, but the content of metaconsciousness is tied to the outside world. So while it is structurally indigenous, it is not endogenous. Self-awareness and knowledge of others both rely on the social contract (1979: 29). His work can thus be seen as an attempt to elucidate the social content of self-reflexivity.

These correspondences between Vygotsky and the computationalists are remarkable in and of themselves, but we might wonder if we have not missed a more essential point. Why should we admit a notion such as consciousness at all? And what about Vygotskyan metaconsciousness? What is *that*? The tradition of including consciousness in mind science is counterbalanced by an equally long and respected practice of excluding it as vague and unempirical. Hair color, for example, can be reliably identified and has a material base, but it has no obvious causal role in behavior or evolution. Is consciousness the hair color of the brain?

Consider the phenomenological intuition that our visual consciousness places an object in the foreground against a receding, slightly blurred background. This phenomenological fact is the figure/ground dichotomy of Gestalt psychology, and it feeds explanations in other cognitive domains, such as the conceptualizations behind spatial language (Frawley 1992b: 162–64). Iwasaki (1993) even shows that, neurologically, foreground and background take different routes along the visual cortex. So slippery intuitions about visual consciousness do seem to have hard material support (see Flanagan 1992: 1–85, for what he calls the *natural method*).

But is the background-foreground distinction an epiphenomenon? What possible causal role could it have? Iwasaki (1993) points out that the neural base of the figure is sensitive to high spatial frequencies and low temporal frequencies, while that of the ground is sensitive to the exact complement. This perfect trade-off means that the foreground-back-ground distinction constructs a unified and stable visual field, by anyone's measure a significant factor in visual behavior.

While these findings suggest the essential correctness of the time-hon-ored proposal that consciousness has a fringe and focus, at least in vision, other respected properties of consciousness simply wash out under scru-tiny. We all have the intuition of omniscience: we stand above and monitor all our experience. Unfortunately, there is little cognitive—and no neu-rological—evidence for a unified, central overseer. If there is anything like omniscience, it is *an effect* of subprograms operating in parallel, not a cause, and so not unified and central (cf. Dennett 1991 and the control aphasias described in Chapter 3).

The lesson here is the same that binds the theist: claims of consciousness regained lay the burden of positive evidence on the proponent. The doubter has a much easier time of it and can derail consciousness by show-ing the failure of any or all of the hard support for the idea. According to Flanagan (1992: chap. 1), there are four received classes of doubters:

1. The *new mysterians* (McGinn 1991), who argue that there is no intel-ligible correlation between brain and mind, and so we simply cannot know any of these things about consciousness.
2. The *agnosticists* (Nagel 1986), who concede that we might be able to know what the features of consciousness are, but we do not know them yet, and the prospects look awfully grim for ever knowing them.
3. The *inessentialists* (e.g., Harnad 1982, Bisiach 1988a), who argue that we do not need to know what the features of consciousness are because they are epiphenomenal.
4. The *eliminativists* (e.g., Churchland 1988), who claim that all fea-tures of consciousness are best understood in other "truer" terms, such as neurobiology, whereby consciousness melts into its material base.

There are, of course, standard responses to such doubts. So what if eliminativism demands a material base? How does that eliminate con-sciousness? Suppose that our sense of visual experience as unified and seam-less is entirely derived from the temporal range of normal cortical rhythm at 0.15 seconds (Varela, Thompson, and Rosch 1991: 73). Should we no longer talk about simultaneity in visual consciousness? Should we really be saying things like, "Wow! Those two spots fell in the same cortical inter-val!" In such talk the eliminativists eliminate themselves as their own brains melt into bundles of neurons. Or are they more truly bundles of atomic particles? Or maybe collections of quarks, strangeness, and charm? Or maybe . . . (see also Flanagan 1992, Shallice 1988b).

Even in the face of these classes of objections and counters, three kinds of subjectivity take up the burden of full positive evidence. Furthermore, Vygotskyan theory provides an almost complete account of one kind. If consciousness is back in fashion in cognitive science, so must be Vygotsky.

4.2   From Information Processing to Self-Consciousness

The available evidence supports the existence of three kinds of subjectivity: *nonconscious processing,*[1] *consciousness,* and *metaconsciousness.* Among the believers in consciousness per se, the first two are essentially uncontroversial; the third is less so, and is often overlooked or conflated with consciousness itself. But it is in the third that Vygotsky gets his playing time, so I devote significant effort to this kind of subjectivity.

Nonconscious processing, or what Flanagan (1992) calls *informational sensitivity,* is the automatic coding of input without subjective experience or awareness of the processing mechanisms. Nonconscious processing has had a long and respectable life among psychologists, philosophers, and neuropsychologists as a discrete, identifiable, and viable type of subjectivity. In Johnson-Laird's (1983, 1988) terms, it is the mental life of the *Cartesian machine,* or the shallow—but nonetheless necessary—mediation of input and output. It corresponds for the most part to the operations of Fodor's (1983) proposed input modules or peripheral systems. Work on the neuropsychology of consciousness relies on the existence of nonconscious informational subjectivity as a basic mode of neuropsychological operation (Rugg 1992: 263–66).

Nonconscious processing works like a reflex. Its mechanisms and content are generally immune to inspection. As Rugg (1992: 264) writes, "In saying that a face has been recognized explicitly [i.e., is conscious], no implication is usually intended that the perceptual/cognitive processes that underlie face recognition form part of the phenomenal experience of that face." The operations of face recognition, not the output of the face-recognition module, are thus "below consciousness." For this reason, the results of nonconscious processing are often considered a form of subjectivity "lower" than consciousness and metaconsciousness. But this way of talking about nonconscious processing can be misleading since it suggests that it is subsumed by consciousness, which, as we shall see, is not the case.

The obligatory and generally noninspectable mechanisms of nonconscious processing—such as the determination of edges by zero-crossings in the neurons of the visual system (see Chapter 2)—support, but neither fully determine nor are fully determined by, conscious subjectivity.

Consciousness, in contrast, is *experience with awareness*. Without any need to review the long (and occasionally tedious) history of the concept, especially since I outline some of its criterial features later on, one can say that whereas nonconscious processing is close to raw experience, consciousness is *interpreted experience* (Gazzaniga 1988). In Flanagan's (1992) terms, it is *experiential sensitivity*, and it corresponds roughly to the operation of what Johnson-Laird (1983, 1988) calls a *Craikian machine:* processing that uses symbolic models with minimal awareness of such.[2] In the neuropsychological literature, experience with awareness is characterized by some sort of explicit knowing (Kinsbourne 1988, Rugg 1992). Or, as Shallice (1988a) says, defending consciousness as a viable neuropsychological construct, it is the state that the experimental subject believes he is in and that the experimenters themselves believe registers their experimental instructions. Awareness is the sort of thing that can be reported on and tapped by others' reports.

One way to understand awareness or interpreted experience is though the controversial philosophical notion of *qualia*. Some argue that instances of conscious experience have a "feel" or quality to them (Flanagan 1992 articulately defends qualia; Dennett 1988 rejects the idea). That is, unlike the blind, zombie-like processing of raw data by input modules, at the conscious level there is *something that it is like* to have experiences: they have qualities (technically *quale*, instances of *qualia*).

Consider again the sense that our visual experience is seamless. If this intuition has its material base in the normal temporal interval of cortical rhythm, at that level there is nothing that it is like to experience the input. "Experiential feel" occurs when there seems to be a subject interpreting and reporting on the experience. For this reason consciousness is said to have qualia. But there is nothing that it is like to be a zombie, or an input module for that matter![3]

The third kind of subjectivity is metaconsciousness: the deliberate awareness and marshaling of experience, or, more simply, self-consciousness. Metaconsciousness is the explicit calling to mind or bracketing of otherwise conscious experience. Self-consciousness has had something of a checkered history, not in the least because it is often conflated with simple consciousness. Baars (1988: 349) attributes not only the usual features of awareness to consciousness but also explicit self-representation and self-monitoring. Johnson-Laird's (1983, 1988) computational account of consciousness as a self-modeling operating system is, in reality, an account of *meta*consciousness: it requires the distinction between consciousness and metaconsciousness because it is a *self-modeling* (i.e., meta-) *Craikian* (i.e., conscious) *machine*. Dennett (1991), too, mixes consciousness and metaconsciousness in his *multiple drafts theory*, whereby consciousness is a perpetually updating, internal narrative. These internal narratives not only do the work of experiential binding, but also are deliberately evoked for the *metafunctions* of monitoring and controlling behavior (see Dennett 1991: 277).

The distinction between consciousness and metaconsciousness must, in fact, be sharply made. Self-consciousness has quite specific properties: consciousness is necessarily self-conscious only in the weak sense that both are bounded by the same brain/mind (Flanagan 1992). There is a clear distinction between endogenous monitoring of experience (consciousness) and explicit self-modeling via external speech (Oatley 1988). Neisser (1992), in fact, distinguishes the ecological self (consciousness), which owes little to language, from the evaluated self, which is the imagined, linguistically labeled self as a moral force: the experience that the subject knows he embodies and performs. Ulmità (1988) differentiates consciousness from metaconsciousness on the basis of control: metaconsciousness is not a special form of consciousness but a separate subjectivity. Shallice (1988a, 1988b) argues that the neuropsychological evidence from both intact and disordered brains supports a distinction between ordinary attentional awareness and reflexive consciousness (1988a: 312). Metaconsciousness is here to stay.

4.3 The Organization of Subjectivity

Having identified the three types of subjectivity, I now turn to their relationship via their criterial attributes. My ultimate goal is to integrate the findings of Vygotskyan psycholinguistics with the (now) computationally respectable concept of metaconsciousness. So, at the very least, we need some grounds on which to make the comparison.[4]

Moreover, the rejection of dualism that characterizes all received accounts of conscious experience (Vygotskyan theory included; see Vygotsky 1979: 9) requires that we view the three kinds of subjectivity connected on a continuum of support (see, e.g., Dennett and Kinsbourne 1992: 183–

86). Consciousness emerges out of the purely computational manipulations of nonconscious processes. Likewise, metaconsciousness must be bootstrapped up from and by consciousness.[5] Vygotsky, in fact, argues this line not only by his attempt to ground consciousness with (then-current) reflexology, but also by his contention that mental life has an overall hierarchical organization, with modes of experience feeding into one another and understandable only in terms of how the subcomponents aggregate under a higher-order concept (Wertsch 1985: 189).

An enumeration of the properties of subjectivity illuminates the structure and direction of this indigenous support system: what is shared and what is unique to each kind of experience and how they support each other. For example, there are good cognitive (Neisser 1992) and neurobiological (Crick and Koch 1990) arguments that language is not necessary for consciousness but may be necessary for self-consciousness. Hence, the Vygotskyan claim that a symbolic mediation mechanism (of which language is the usual and most representative form) indexes metaconsciousness forces us to restrict the inquiry to interactions of language with the properties of self-consciousness. For instance, the metaconscious property of deliberateness may be associated with the presence of language. But since both consciousness and metaconsciousness have unity, language probably does not support the binding of experience.

The identification of shared and unique properties also helps us adjudicate proposals that put the three kinds of subjectivity on a single footing. For example, it might be argued that the three are more accurately understood as points on a gradient of attention, with nonconscious processing requiring the least allocation of attention and self-consciousness requiring the most (see, e.g., Velmans 1991). If this is correct, then a reduction or increase of attention should convert one kind of subjectivity into another. But this does not happen. Iwasaki (1993) points out, for instance, that visual inattention does not result in nonconscious visual processing. Ulmità (1988: 343) argues that while attention might be a privileged route for consciousness, it can be controlled and is thus subject to, not constitutive of, metaconsciousness.

The best way to think about nonconscious processing, consciousness, and metaconsciousness, then, is as modes of experience characterized by an assembly of overlapping properties, not as pinpointed, bounded machine states. In the sections that follow I describe the defining features of each mode, grouping the properties into five categories: structure, function, context, universality, and speed. This division streamlines the existing taxonomies of features, shows where the three modes overlap and diverge, and provides a way to link these properties to the claims for computational and cultural psycholinguistics.

4.31 Structure

My examination of the essentially uncontroversial elements of computational mind in Chapter 3 showed that nonconscious processing is structured around relatively fixed representations with local effects and distributed implementation. Their modular or interactive properties depend on the nature and contextual relationship of the representations. Although theories disagree about the complexity of the representations, the degree of fixedness, and the location of the distributedness of the implementation, they all agree that the structure of nonconscious processing is largely syntactic. Still, the representation *is a representation of something*—it is code—and so has content, or, more philosophically, is intentional.

Consciousness is reported to share many of these features. Johnson-Laird (1983, 1988), Jackendoff (1987), and Flanagan (1992: 184) build consciousness on the representational properties of elementary computations. Searle (1992) lists the intentionality of consciousness among its essential properties, and Ulmità (1988: 336) concurs: "Consciousness is a phenomenal experience that refers to the state of an object (i.e., an internal representation)." Dennett's multiple drafts model of consciousness is an account of the aggregate representational effects of otherwise local representations, what he calls "content-discriminations" (Dennett 1991: 113).[6]

Like blind computation, consciousness has local effects and distributed implementation. Each modality has its attendant awareness (Jackendoff 1987) and is part of a distributed collection of local integrators with no necessarily central awareness synthesizer (Dennett 1991, Dennett and Kinsbourne 1992). Although some argue that fragmenting consciousness this way does nothing to explain it (Lloyd 1992), the idea of local and distributed awareness—or consciousness*es*—accords well with the neurological evidence.

Well-known disorders of consciousness split it vertically—delinking it from the subjectivities it feeds and is fed by—and horizontally, disconnecting the awareness of one modality from that of another. Blindsight is the much-discussed illustration of the former, which disrupt the representational continuity of conscious and nonconscious processes, and thus cut

loose the various local and distributed consciousnesses from their indigenous computational bases. Some individuals with cortical blindness report
no awareness of visual input and deny seeing stimuli presented to them,
but they nonetheless behave on subsequent testing as if their nonconscious
visual processors had in fact registered and represented the visual stimuli
(Weiskrantz 1986). Similar effects occur in forms of prosopagnosia, or lack
of face recognition (Shallice 1988b: chap. 16; de Haan, Young, and Newcombe 1987) and a variety of other disorders and traumas, including ep-
ilepsy and achromatopia (lack of color awareness).

These disorders also show horizontal effects: even when such vertical
delinking occurs, the awarenesses characteristic of other modalities are not
affected. Prosopagnosia and achromatopia are very specific disorders and
damage only the representational output mechanisms of those modalities
(Bruyer 1991, Young and de Haan 1990). The amodality or neutrality of
consciousness thus seems to be an epiphenomenon. Even Gazzaniga's
(1988: 233–34) proposal that the left hemisphere contains a kind of neural
assessor that incorporates input into a "unifying input theory" construes
this left-brain interpreter as a roughly circumscribed but structurally distributed cortical area that does not in any way receive and coordinate input
from every other area in the brain (see also Shallice 1988b).

The local and distributed structure of representational consciousnesses
supports both modular and interactive effects. Just as the perceptual modalities are, like the various consciousnesses projected up therefrom, autonomous to the degree their constituent representations allow, so the
various consciousnesses projected up from the perceptual modalities can
be more or less encapsulated, depending on the content of awareness. This
is especially clear in a context-architecture interpretation of Dennett's multiple drafts theory of consciousness.

Dennett and Kinsbourne (1992; see also Dennett 1991: 115) argue that
consciousness is a kind of army of tireless redactors, perpetually revising
and editing input in accordance with some sort of cognitive MLA style
guide: be cogent, simple, and so on. Consider the famous color phi-
phenomenon experiments, in which subjects are presented two light spots
in rapid succession, the first red and the second green. Subjects report the
experience of apparent motion of a single spot that changes color from
red to green. What explains this response?

Dennett and Kinsbourne (1992) outline, and discard, two received neuropsychological accounts. In what they call *the Orwellian view*, the subject
perceives both spots, but the second, green one obliterates the first before

it has the chance to come to consciousness. In this account, the consciousness redactors revise very rapidly after the fact and so produce the idea of a single green spot. An alternative account, what they call *the Stalinesque view*, holds that the green spot feeds back onto the red spot before it is sent up for further processing, thus changing the red spot into a green one fundamentally; here the consciousness redactors interfere with and remake history to give the illusion of continuity.

These alternatives depend, as Dennett and Kinsbourne (1992: 193) note, on the location of the revision: is it post-experiential (Orwellian) or pre-experiential (Stalinesque)? They reject both accounts in favor of the multiple drafts model, which essentially says that all these apparent timing effects are the results the nature of the representations processed. Instead of a radical revisionist "before" (Stalinesque), or very rapid "after" (Orwellian), intrusion of the green spot on the red one, they suggest a constant "while": "The temporal sequence in consciousness is . . . purely a matter of the content represented" (1992: 200). Before- and after-effects turn out to be just that: *effects*. The real explanation lies in the representational processes of consciousness itself.

This is the exact argument made in Chapter 3 regarding modularity and interactionism as effects of the relation between representations and contexts as nonconscious computing unfolds. The color phi-phenomenon has a code-context interpretation in that the green spot provides the context for the interpretation of the red spot. The Orwellian model is modular and selectional: an autonomous and fully perceived red spot interfaces with the context of the green spot, which in turn selects the outcome. The red spot thus *takes on* the context of green. Just as the theory of architecture-context relations predicts that in such circumstances all effects of change should be after-effects (see Chapter 3), so the Orwellian account is post-experiential.

In the Stalinesque model, however, the context of the green spot interacts with and intrudes on the red spot. In feeding the green context back onto the red spot before the latter can actually be brought to consciousness, the Stalinesque model works like a system in which a representation is stored with its context and so is amenable to direct influence by its surround. Indeed, as the architecture-context theory predicts, this relationship should give rise to Stalinesque before-effects.

Now, even more remarkably, Dennett and Kinsbourne's alternative to the received neuropsychological accounts is virtually word for word the theory of architecture-context relationships. In both, before- and after-effects of context lie in the nature of the representations processed. So, the issue for consciousness is really not whether the Orwellian or Stalinesque model is correct, just as it is not an issue in psycholinguistics whether a modular or interactive account of lexical access is better. Both are correct. Indeed, Roskies and Wood (1992) offer an example to show that the Stalinesque, interactionist account withstands all counters, whereas Block (1992) cites work by Potter that supports the Orwellian model outright. Block's (1992) view of the whole matter is exactly that of Tanenhaus and his collaborators in the original proposal of the theory of architecture-context relationships: we can distinguish interactive before-effects from modular after-effects in any representational domain depending on how and where we probe. This is because they fall out from the nature of the representations themselves in their contexts.

So the ultimate point here is that because nonconscious and conscious processing are both fundamentally representational, they are subject to the same overall constraints. Significantly, these constraints—the larger argument from architecture-context relations—are the framework that accommodates both mainstream computationalism and Vygotskyan views of mind-culture embeddedness.

But there is perhaps a simpler lesson here. Locality and distributedness in fact complement each other: a local phenomenon is circumscribed, but its distributed implementation gives it nonlocal effect. So to characterize something as both local and distributed is to say that its structure accommodates modularity and interaction as consequences of organization, not as inherent properties. This same fact transfers to metaconsciousness, as we will see, providing structural continuity. No doubt this agreement occurs because all subjectivity must be implemented in a local and distributed brain. Some continuities simply come with the territory.

I have enumerated a number of structural continuities across conscious and nonconscious subjectivity, but there are divergences as well. These discontinuities give consciousness and nonconscious processing their structural individuality. Perhaps the clearest divergence is that consciousness is often characterized as having a background and foreground, while no such dual structure is ever attributed to nonconscious processes.

The idea of the structural duality of consciousness goes back at least as far as William James, who argued for a psychic overtone or fringe to consciousness, but the same proposal can be found in the work of many current theorists. Flanagan (1992: 163–66) talks about the focus of attention in consciousness against a "halo of relations" (1992: 164). Searle (1992:

chap. 6) notes at least three properties of consciousness that rely on fore-ground/background: its figure-ground organization, its center and periphery, and its overflow (going beyond itself). Kinsbourne (1988) makes a similar claim in arguing that the field of consciousness is integrated by the coordination of breadth and depth—expanse and focus. Iwasaki (1993) has shown that visual consciousness has both figure and ground, with respective neuropsychological substrates.

The foreground-background structure of consciousness can be appreciated very simply. When you sit by a window and listen to the noises outside, at least one of them is salient, while the rest, even though they retain their status as sounds, recede into a kind of noisy blurred hum. You can switch attention and move the previous blur into focus and demote the previous focus to background blur, but even this maneuver preserves the dual structure of focus and fringe. Similar informal experiments bear out this phenomenology in other modalities. Kinsbourne (1988: 243) puts the whole matter succinctly in arguing that while consciousness is organized around focus and fringe, the boundaries of consciousness are not focal. Consciousness is not relentlessly focused attention, but focus against a backdrop of nonfocus. Hence, the limits of consciousness emerge out of the integration of its dual structure. The importance of this point will surface again in the discussion of the unity and persistence of consciousness and the disappearance of metaconsciousness.

When we look at the structure of metaconsciousness, we see a picture similar to the dovetailing and divergence of consciousness and nonconscious processing. Like the two kinds of subjectivity that feed it, metaconsciousness has a local and distributed structure. This may be difficult to accept at first because self-consciousness intuitively feels the opposite: a global but pinpointed executive. Nonetheless, decades of work on metaconscious functioning and associated neurological localization reveal many neurocognitive locales that subserve metaconsciousness, though they principally occur in the frontal areas, and trauma to these areas results in quite specific impairment and behavioral effects despite their distributed implementation.

Shallice (1988b: chap. 14), explicitly acknowledging the heritage of Luria and his relevance to contemporary cognitive science (330), shows that disorders of central supervisory brain systems result in a variety of quite deterministic effects, including failure to use speech to serve intentions, inability to use speech to describe and accomplish tasks, difficulty with novelty, and problems in managing scheduling demands on processing.

Trauma to these supervisory systems often results in perseveration in the systems that feed them. Hence, modular consciousnesses can be delinked from metaconsciousness but preserved; the effects appear as disorders of control over otherwise conscious and nonconscious processing (see Shallice 1988a: 324, Ulmità 1988: 336). These findings, in Shallice's view, are clear counters to Fodor's (1983) argument that nonperipheral systems are isotropic, that is, nonautonomous and unbounded. Quite the contrary: these systems have startlingly specific organization and disruption while they are nonetheless neurally distributed in implementation.[7]

Also like consciousness, metaconsciousness has a foreground-background organization. In the deliberate bracketing of experience, at least one phenomenon emerges as salient and the focus of attention against the backdrop of all else. Vygotsky (1986: 170–71) puts it this way: "The activity of consciousness [i.e., *osoznanie*, 'metaconsciousness'] . . . may illuminate only a few aspects of a thought or act . . . In perceiving some of our acts in a generalizing fashion, we isolate them from our total mental activity and are thus enabled to focus on this process as such and to enter into a new relation to it."

But here the structural parallels with consciousness stop. In self-consciousness, as Ulmità (1988) says, the object of focus can be the agent himself or herself. Although consciousness is not relentlessly focal (Kinsbourne 1988), metaconsciousness is, at least within the capacity limits of foregrounding itself (Shallice 1988a). Moreover, the relationship between the foreground and the background in metaconsciousness is quite different from that in consciousness. In the latter, the focus and fringe are balanced for integrative effect (Kinsbourne 1988); in the former, the focus emerges out of, overrides, and ultimately absorbs the fringe. Again, Vygotsky (1986: 170) puts it aptly: "I have just tied a knot—I have done so consciously, yet I cannot explain how I did it, because my awareness was centered on the knot rather than on my own motions, the *how* of my action. When the latter becomes the object of my awareness, I shall become fully conscious. We use *consciousness* [*osoznanie*] to denote awareness of the activity of the mind—the consciousness of being conscious." Here the knot is initially the focus against the backdrop of the "how of my action." Metaconsciousness expands the focus to include the backdrop ("becomes fully conscious").

An even more striking structural divergence between consciousness and metaconsciousness is that metaconsciousness, unlike consciousness, is not wholly representational. It is not entirely code, not just a second-order representation of the contents of consciousness. While metaconsciousness is grounded in the representational content of consciousness, it is not exhausted by representations. Metaconsciousness is also action and instrument.[8]

Some of Heil's (1992) arguments shed light on this point about action and representation. Heil notes that second-order representation—the representation of representation—does not automatically lead to self-consciousness. For that to happen, the second-order representation must, as he says, register the state of the first *as a representation*. It must *use the first-order representation to some end* and *index the representational aspect of that representation in the act*. Without an awareness of *the manner of representation,* any mechanism of increasingly streamlined representations—for example, an intelligent microwave oven—would qualify as self-conscious.

Metaconsciousness is not just metarepresentation per se, but an appreciation of the *content-as-content* of the various consciousnesses that support it. Kinsbourne (1988: 242) is therefore most certainly wrong when he says that we do not experience how we represent. Perhaps we do not do so at the level of consciousness, where the representational means is not relevant, but we must do so at metaconsciousness (a level which, in any case, Kinsbourne appears to deny).

Under these arguments an account such as Dennett's multiple drafts model seems inapplicable to metaconsciousness. Perpetual revision of representations cannot in itself induce an appreciation of representationality, which requires awareness of the instrumentality of content. In Heil's (1992) view, the appreciation of representationality comes out of the intersubjectivity of the speech community. When we see and learn how others represent experience, and when we communicate our appraisals of such represented experience, we gain a sense of the accuracy and, for that matter, the very applicability of representations themselves. Our intersubjective experience gives us the necessary contrast set to grasp the representational system *as a system* and thereby understand the instrumental side of content.[9]

Flanagan (1992: chap. 10) argues a similar point: one of the purposes of self-representation is understanding through public dissemination. And in Neisser's (1992: 12) view, the structure of the *evaluated self* (his term for metaconsciousness) is tied to public display: we know what our feelings are by labeling them and observing them in others. Oatley (1988) puts it perhaps most succinctly in saying that you can get a model of yourself only from the outside (see also White 1991: chaps. 5–6). All this is remarkably reminiscent of Vygotsky, who, in his classic paper on consciousness (1979: 27), said that you cannot think your own thoughts, and so self-knowledge must look to intersubjectivity for structure: self-awareness and knowledge of others have the same organization in the social contract held together by speech. You cannot be your our own contrast case: "Language is a practical consciousness-for-others and, consequently, consciousness-for-myself" (Vygotsky 1986: 256).

The intersubjective side of metaconsciousness and its association with the instrumentality of representations lead to a third divergence between consciousness and metaconsciousness. Insofar as nonconscious processing and consciousness rely on code, they are indirect and, hence, a kind of mediated experience. But this symbolic mediation is entirely endogenous. Consciousness needs only *intra*subjective mentalese, not public speech.

But metaconsciousness must be explicitly mediated by symbols originally external to mind. Speech is the principal mediational means, since it carries the sociocultural distinctions that underlie self-reflexivity, though any other rich symbolic system, such as sign language or nonverbal cultural symbolism, would do as well. Deficits in metaconsciousness are typically disorders of this external symbolic mediation. Oatley (1988: 384), citing work by Marcel, notes the existence of "people with neurological damage being able to perform actions for which they can supply a personal intention, though they cannot perform the same action if the goal is supplied from the outside." Here, the *intra*subjectivity of intentional consciousness is preserved, but the management of this representation in relation to external factors—its *inter*subjectivity—is disrupted. Shallice (1988b) and Luria (1980) include long catalogues of other such disorders of external-internal symbolic management.

A stark irony of this account of the role of external mediation in self-knowledge is that it can be found in the writings of neurobiological materialists otherwise very much at odds with notions such as the self. Churchland (1985: 73–81) points out that self-knowledge is tied to an ability to spin coherent theories about oneself and others "based on the same external evidence available to the public at large" (79). This is because what brains/minds "know first and best is not themselves [contra a Cartesian account of introspection], but the environment in which they have to survive" (76); they "must set about to learn the structure and activities of [their] inner states no less than [they] must set about to learn the structure and activities of the external world" (80).

Still, in this scenario mind becomes self-intelligible from the inside out. Luria (1976: 144–45) thought this the right result from the wrong strategy:

> Rationalists and phenomenologists share one basic assumption, namely that the subjective world is primary while the reflection of the external world is derivative and secondary. This conviction impels adherents of this view to seek the sources of consciousness and self-awareness in the depth of the human spirit or in the elements of brain structures, while completely disregarding the environment which the human brain reflects.
>
> There is every reason to think that self-awareness is a product of sociohistorical development and that reflection of external natural and social reality arises first; only later, through its mediating influence, do we find self-awareness in its most complex forms.

Metaconsciousness is not wholly the upward projection of inner computational code, but also the correlation of this mind-mind relation with mind-*world* connections.

4.32 Function

The functions of nonconscious processing are fairly uncontroversial. Input systems parse the world to model it. The compelling reason for such a parsing-modeling function is efficient survival. If the world impinges on our minds like a blooming, buzzing confusion, to paraphrase William James, then it is simply too informative in its raw state. The automatic reduction of relevant phenomena via the blind computation of intrinsic code generates manageable information at the point of mind-world contact.

Adherents of competing theories on the organization of nonconscious processing disagree on the details of this modeling function. Representationalists eliminate the immediate and contingent properties of input, while connectionists insist on incorporating such features into the modeling itself; a subgroup of the former, the modularists, believe that the model making is done with no reference to any other information in the mental system, arguing that this autonomy enhances information delivery. Despite these differences, all schools see the function of nonconscious modeling as *persistence:* that is, the most elementary subjectivity works to keep mind relatively upright and constant, like a kind of informational keel.

The functions of consciousness are so numerous that it is surprising that some argue that it has no function (e.g., Allport 1988 and Bisiach 1988a, in part). Like nonconscious processing, consciousness is persistent, at the very least because it is representational and inherits the relatively constant models that input systems deliver. But consciousness has a special kind of persistence, technically known as *binding*. A hundred years ago William James famously noted that consciousness comes to us as an ungapped stream. The seamlessness of conscious experience is a hallmark of all current partisan accounts (e.g., Flanagan 1992, Searle 1992, Kinsbourne 1988, and Dennett 1991). There is a straightforward phenomenological demonstration: when you look out the window, you do not see a tree, then a house, and then a squirrel, and so on. Experience comes to you as an immediately cohesive, regularized scene.

Perhaps the surest argument for experiential binding is that it must be explained even by those who might want to eliminate consciousness altogether (see Allport 1988 and Churchland 1988). Even under the most relentless neurobiological reductionism, the binding of experience in consciousness persists. Crick and Koch (1990) claim that it has a neurological correlate in the 40–70 Hz oscillations of neuronal groups that coordinate input to be sent up for further processing. Neurons firing in synchrony produce reverberating circuits that could be the neural basis of conscious unity. This is an especially important neuro*psychological* finding because the reverberation cycle seems to accompany and gate the delivery of information to short-term memory, the cognitive mechanism that, even to the most ardent eliminativist, is central to the intuition of experiential cohesion (see Churchland 1988: 282).

A particularly clear demonstration of the binding function of consciousness is found in the work of Teghtsoonian (1992), who argues that experience across domains of perceptual knowledge has subjective equality. Individuals experience relative loudness in the same way they experience relative brightness, heaviness, or input from any other perceptual continuum: "It is as if intensity information from all inputs is routed to a single monitor whose output defines the experience of subjective magnitude . . . and it is the maximum range of outputs of this device that makes the brightest light subjectively equivalent to the loudest sound" (224). Consciousness functions as a kind of cross-domain regularizer, calibrating information from different, nonconscious processing domains against a single norm (though without a central calibrator). In this way, input from separate and essentially autonomous modules emerges as an ungapped subjective stream.

Experiential binding is certainly a salient function of consciousness, but it has a frequently noted complement in change. The observations of William James are again relevant: "No state once gone can recur and be identical with what was before" (quoted by Flanagan 1992: 159). Flanagan endorses the observation: "Consciousness seems constantly in flux" (1992: 159). Shallice (1988a: 311) lists change as the very first criterial attribute of consciousness—" 'Consciousness' is always changing"—and Oatley (1988) argues that modification and adjustment are essential purposes of consciousness.

The complementary status of binding and change can be seen in a more general phrasing of the function of consciousness in, as Dennett (1991) argues, the perpetual *updating* of information. If consciousness is in some ways a reviser, then it must balance both flux and consistency. Shallice (1988a: 311) puts this by saying that while change is the hallmark of consciousness, "from waking to sleeping [it] is sensibly continuous" (see also Oatley 1988: 383 and Baars 1988: 349).

More generally, we might say that the function of consciousness is to be inclusive, to render experience from the all-embracing inside. Whereas nonconscious processing delivers models for the purpose of sheer persistence, consciousness binds for the purpose of change. Consequently, the monitoring and control functions of consciousness are often noted (e.g., Ulmità 1988) since balancing cohesion and change requires oversight to ensure the correctly selected response. Even Bisiach (1988a), who otherwise has serious doubts about consciousness per se, sees updating and control as the only possible functional attributes of consciousness with a genuine and measurable causal role in behavior.

When we look to the functional attributes of metaconsciousness, we see a number of convergences with consciousness. The control functions of metaconsciousness can be traced to the monitoring, regulatory, and planning effects of self-conscious awareness. Baars (1988: 349), for instance, lists auto-programming, self-monitoring, and self-maintenance as essential functional attributes (see also Shallice 1988a and b and Ulmità 1988).

But the control functions of metaconsciousness have to be seen in a special light. In Shallice's (1988b) account, the supervisory purpose of metaconsciousness is to *inhibit* the interaction of domains of knowledge and to *gate* information flow across channels of access. Ulmità (1988) notes that the purpose of metaconscious control is to *halt* cognition, not promote it. Oatley (1988), anticipating a point discussed in more detail in the next chapter, associates metaconscious monitoring with breakdown and the computational system of interrupt handling. Thus, while control in consciousness works in the service of experiential binding to inspect the ultimate unity of updated thought, metaconscious control stops, differentiates, and redirects thought; it inhibits rather than promotes.

The control properties of metaconsciousness are, then, only nominally similar to those of consciousness. Vygotsky, in fact, tied metaconscious control not to the simple inspection of smooth mental operation but to direct monitoring, differentiation, and voluntary supervision. This can be seen in his initial writings, as Minnick's translation of the original Russian reveals (Vygotsky 1987: 187, 191):

> The higher mental functions . . . are distinguished precisely by intellectualization and mastery, by conscious awareness [*osoznanie,* 'metaconsciousness'] and volition . . . We master a given function to the degree to which it is intellectualized. The voluntary nature of the activity of a function is the reverse side of its conscious awareness . . .
>
> The foundation of conscious awareness is the generalization or abstraction of the mental processes, which leads to their mastery.

Regulative, metaconscious control is bound up with speech: "To become consciously aware of an operation, it must be transferred from the plane of action to the plane of language" (Vygotsky 1987: 183). Therein lie the special control and monitoring effects of verbal thinking that motivate much of the work of Luria (1982: 87): "What kind of regulative role does [speech] have in organizing volitional acts?"

The regulative characteristic of metaconscious control also sheds light on the way metaconsciousness uses change. Although self-conscious control serves the righting of thought under breakdown (Oatley 1988), the ultimate goal of change in metaconsciousness is not persistence but *dis*appearance. Consciousness may not be relentlessly focal, as Kinsbourne (1988) observes, but metaconsciousness is—and only insofar as it can exhaust itself in the success of its own control function.

Neisser (1992) makes this point in a different way by noting that as an individual's skill in a task increases, the manifestations of the evaluated self decrease. As usual, Vygotsky himself is best read in this respect: "[Private speech, one manifestation of the evaluated self] facilitates intellectual orientation, conscious awareness, the overcoming of difficulties and impediments" (1987: 259), but is destined to disappear: "It is fated to develop into inner speech" (1987: 260).

Just as I was able to phrase more generally the function of consciousness as inclusion, so these observations about the ultimate divergence of metaconsciousness from consciousness show that *metaconsciousness excludes.*

Self-conscious control is, in a very real sense, ad hoc. Although it is grounded in the representational constancies of the other kinds of subjectivity—as Vygotsky (1987: 189) says, "To become consciously aware of something and master it you must first have it at your disposal"—and in the sociocultural regularities infused in speech, it is marshaled for the task and the moment so as to inhibit choices and thereby reestablish the ground for smooth mental operation and behavior.

Nonconscious processing models; consciousness manages foreground and background to bind experience in persistent revision. Metaconsciousness collapses the background into the foreground to drive out alternatives and promote individuated action.

4.33   Context

Nonconscious processing is, for the most part, immune to context—unattuned to all but a very few features of the external world. This is not to say that the rest of the context is not somehow recorded. Indeed, connectionist models emphasize the computational mind's sensitivity to the overall probabilistic structure of the external world. It means, rather, that the features of context that play a causal role in the most elementary forms of mental life are decidedly limited and, for the most part, predetermined. Nonconscious processing does best only what it already knows.

The value of acontextualism has been outlined in Chapter 3. Here I want to stress that contextual blindness gives nonconscious subjectivity a kind of self, an inner life par excellence. As Flanagan (1992: 49) observes, a self emerges when an organism must distinguish inner (me) from outer (not me). But nonconscious self lacks anything like a meaningful point of view, since that would imply a selection of stance at the expense of other available stances. The most rapid elementary computations have only one set of choices, and even the most partisan connectionists acknowledge the determinism of this lowest level of processing. Seeing nonconscious processing as inner experience without a sense of itself *as inner and personal* is another way of saying that it is a self without qualia.

Consciousness, like the subjectivity that supports it, is essentially private. James argued the personalness of consciousness, and Flanagan (1992: 50) dresses the claim in modern phrasing:

Consciousness emerged as a solution to the problem of segregating inner and outer perception. Consciousness emerged with the development of segregated neural equipment [i.e., nonconscious processing] subserving, on the one hand, internal hedonic regulation and, on the other hand, information processing about the state of the external world. Enhancement occurred with the evolution of a memory system capable of retaining hypotheses about what things have or lack hedonic value and projecting them onto novel (possibly even future) states of affairs.

Consciousness thus regulates the balance between inner and outer, though heavily tilted toward the inner. Its internalism renders both input and public criteria unnecessary to its characterization.

The centrality of internalism underlies the frequent equation of consciousness and the self, though, to be more accurate, the self of consciousness is much more contextualized than the self of the nonconscious mechanisms that subserve it. Lutz (1992) nicely demonstrates this point by noting that some aspects of the experiential binding of spatiotemporal consciousness can be contextually determined. She recounts the story of an Ifaluk (Micronesia) traveling in Hawaii and experiencing extreme spatial discontinuity in the taxi ride from the airport. Ifaluk culture and language—that is, the context of Ifaluk consciousness—highly differentiate spatiotemporal organization, and so support the Ifaluk sense of the inherent cohesiveness of the external spatiotemporal world. But the twisting and turning taxi ride obscured the external guides to the cohesion of the spatiotemporal scene and forced the Ifaluk into a frantic and futile attempt to track every directional change of the taxi. As Lutz observes: "To be an adult in an environment such as Ifaluk . . . is to be conscious of space in a different way from, say, an adult in mainland America" (69).

Lutz's illustration of the culture-dependence of some parts of consciousness can be understood through Dennett's multiple drafts model. The Ifaluk is trapped in competing revisions. His default updater looks to the context for support to make the spatiotemporal narrative cohere, but the current context lacks all such support, leaving him on his own to make his latest mental draft. He is caught between a narrative that legitimizes group, external consciousness and one that makes consciousness an individual, internal effort.

This minimal tie to context and the opening up of the purely private self to the outer world give consciousness the rudiments of a point of view, or something like what Searle (1992: 131) calls the *aspectual shape* of intentionality. Input modules do not have a perspective because nothing is relative in automatic computations. But the minimal contextualization of consciousness provides alternatives, as in the example of the Ifaluk.

If there are qualia—*feels* of thoughts—this must be where they lie, at least in part. Indeed, Searle (1992: 131–32) links the aspectual shape of intentionality to subjective feel. It would seem that the combination of experiential binding, which gives conscious states unity, and point of view, which gives individuality, could underlie the experience of peculiar, discrete subjective states.

Metaconsciousness shares surprisingly few contextual properties with consciousness. It involves the same management of inner and outer as does consciousness; it is, after all, a mental state with control functions, and it requires a stance or point of view. But in most cases metaconsciousness magnifies and even refocuses the contextual properties.

Let us begin with the relative contextuality. While nonconscious processing is wholly private, and consciousness mostly private but gesturing to context, metaconsciousness is essentially public. Unlike its supporting subjectivities that reach from inner to outer, metaconsciousness goes *from context to mind*. As Vygotsky (1987: 120) writes, "The development of the child's thinking depends on his mastery of the social means of thinking, that is, on his mastery of speech." This is because speech can mediate direct external-internal contact, and in doing so "it transfers the psychological operation to higher and qualitatively new forms and permits humans, by the aid of external stimuli, to control their behavior from the outside. The use of signs leads humans to a specific structure of behavior that breaks away from biological development and creates new forms of a culturally-based psychological process" (Vygotsky 1978: 40).

It might then be argued—somewhat surprisingly, perhaps—that metaconsciousness is not really about the self at all, but about *persons*. Some of Harré's (1987) positions motivate this argument. He distinguishes the person—"the publicly recognized human individual who is the focus of the overt practices of social life" (110)—from the self, "the still centre of experience, that to which conscious states of all kinds are ascribed . . . the unified subjective organizations of memory, perception, agency, and so on" (99). The two notions must be kept distinct not in the least because different cultures and languages cut the line between private self and public person quite differently. What metaconsciousness concerns, and most surely what Vygotsky appears to be talking about, is how the inner state of self-consciousness emerges out of persons as contextual constructs. Indeed, Harré puts the matter in decidedly Vygotskyan terms: "Most important for selfhood are ways of talking about persons. By imitating the way people talk about us, as public persons, we acquire a knack of talking about ourselves. In picking this up, we are enabled to comment on our own speech acts and other public doings, and particularly on expressions of feeling and other avowals." (110). Reflexive thought, self-consciousness, is not the upward projection of yet another inner order, not a computational model of all our models: "A more economical theory would ascribe the source of that order not to the noumenal realm but to the people-makers of the culture, the parents in whose ocean of talk we all begin our public lives" (110).[10]

The contextuality of metaconsciousness is further supported by its association with a stance or point of view, what Smith (1986) calls the *modality of consciousness*. In Searle's (1992) account, stance is tied to *the background*, the nonrepresentational backdrop of mind. He likens the background to the later Wittgenstein's idea that truth makes sense in terms of an entire system of judgments and beliefs, or Bourdieu's notion of the *habitus*, a presupposed system of regular social and cultural dispositions. Significantly, these are the same analogies that ground the very applicability of Vygotsky to cognitive science to begin with (see Chapter 2).

The public side of metaconsciousness is the external actional and semiotic context in which representational subjectivity is embedded.[11] When Searle (1992: 248) complains "that we need to rediscover the social character of the mind" and urges that we devote research efforts to uncover how "the category of 'other people' plays a special role in the *structure* of consciousness" (127) and to analyze "the structure of the social element in individual consciousness" (128), we might take him at his Vygotskyan word. We need to trace how the publicly determined stances of persons are translated into certain kinds of speech and then used in the service of self-conscious subjectivity (or what Bakhtin called a *voice*). All of the next chapter, in fact, is devoted to this very project: to how reflexive language at the culture-mind border in self-directed speech constructs individual thinking. Here it is enough to note that Vygotskyan theory provides the methods for doing the very thing that Searle and others call for. But, of course, you have to let Vygotsky into cognitive science first.

A final characteristic of metaconsciousness is illuminated by its contextual ties. While conscious states arguably have a feel, metaconscious ones do not seem to. What, after all, is the "in flagrante delicto feel" of recovery from breakdown or the momentary bracketing experience? There may be something that it is like to experience redness, but what is it like to change your mind (Oatley 1988)? The essential *dis*appearance of metaconsciousness suggests that metamental states have nothing like the feel that states of awareness do. This may be because qualia are connected to the binding of experience and a conscious state as a unified mental scene. Qualia seem to appear in the persistence of the objects of our phenomenal awareness. But if metaconsciousness is public, marshaled, and inherently fleeting, it seems unlikely that it should have any durable private character.

4.34 Universality

Sensitivity to context goes hand in hand with universality. Virtually by definition, contexts vary, so the extent to which a form of subjectivity is tied to context should be a measure of its universality. Nonconscious processing is typically seen as acontextual, hence universal. Nonconscious processors may be dedicated to particular input tasks, but this is a trivial tie to context. Their task-sensitivity is nominal since they respond universally to a presolved task.

Issues of universality and fixedness are less clear at the level of conscious processing. In some ways consciousness is less universal—more local—because of its functions of change and updating. As an adjustment mechanism, consciousness would appear to be intrinsically mutable. But the literature on consciousness suggests that it is just as fixed and universal as nonconscious processing.

Flanagan (1992: 194) argues that the mere having of a subjective experience, what he calls *weak self-consciousness* is an inborn property not subject to development. Shallice (1988b: 219) remarks on the startling *lack* of individual variation on this phenomenon, and Neisser (1992: 14) observes that the ecological self (consciousness) has clear limits on variation and change. Thus, even though consciousness is personal in the Jamesian sense, it is *universally personal*. It is shared in the same way by all selves. No doubt this commonality is related to its computational support and derivation from neurobiological hardware.

In contrast, universality is minimized in metaconsciousness, where the local and individual are privileged. What Flanagan (1992: 195) calls *strong self-consciousness* "is not something that we are born with. Maturation, living in the world, being socialized in a life form, and acquiring certain ways of thinking are required." Neisser (1992) observes that all therapeutic interventions to change subjectivity affect just the evaluated self. So the only kind of subjectivity that can be truly adjusted to individual needs is self-consciousness (acknowledging, of course, some cultural impositions on consciousness, as per the Ifaluk example in the preceding section).

Vygotsky (1987: 259) puts the whole matter best: "The central tendency of the child's development is not a gradual socialization introduced from the outside, but a gradual individualization that emerges on the foundation of the child's internal socialization." Variable semiotic context makes variable semiotic persons, and these are the bases of individual, semiotic metaconsciousness. This is not to say that there cannot be a universal structure to higher thought, no more than it is to say that nonconscious processing is entirely devoid of individual variation (consider, e.g., color blindness). We could not study metaconscious processes if there were not regularities. Vygotsky (1987: 43–51, 1978: 58–73) spends much time describing the neutral methods and recurrent units of analysis in the investigation of higher-thought processes.[12]

The real technical worry here is meaning holism, the doctrine that a term is inextricably tied to an *idiosyncratic* network of other terms. Is *metaconsciousness* to be understood holistically? If so, as Stalnaker (1993: 232) puts it, "there is no principled way of distinguishing . . . [its] epistemic liaisons" Thus, related terms such as *person* or *individual* are so contextual, local, and ad hoc that they are useless. The response is that arguments about persons and culture-specificity do not imply idiosyncrasy and do not preclude rigor. Higher thought may originate as an external solution to a particular task, but the legitimacy of task and solution are heavily constrained and circumscribed by the society and culture. This is why Vygotsky thought that a psychology of metaconsciousness was still materialist at the core. Indeed, Shallice's (1988b) work shows, as did Luria's before him, that metaconsciousness is very likely subserved by a (good old-fashioned scientifically analyzable) modular processor, one dedicated to individuation, externalism, and task-specific planning.

4.35 Speed

Speed is among the most robust and respected measures of mind. In a computing device, speed is symptomatic of the quality of the operation. When we look at speed and subjectivity, it turns out that just as universality grades into individuality from nonconscious to metaconscious processing, so the pace of processing slows in the same direction.

One of the trademarks of nonconscious processing is rapid automatic output. Fodor (1983) lists speed among the essential attributes of input modules, making much of the evolutionary benefits of peripheral processors as the mind's rapid deployment force. Dennett (1987: 326) endorses the view: "Speed . . . is of the essence of intelligence. If you can't figure out the relevant portions of the changing environment fast enough to fend for yourself, you are not *practically* intelligent, however complex you are." While it seems a bit overstated to call this speed *practical intelligence*— how practical is it to have the initial point of contact between you and the world mediated by obtuse and dumb computations often tricked by their own speed?—the implication is clear enough: prepackaging, speed, and automaticity all go together.

Estimates of the speed requirements of nonconscious computation have been variously attempted (see, e.g., Sejnowski, quoted in Dennett 1987: 328, Baars 1988: 75, Churchland 1986) and show that the time course of the most elementary subjectivity is very rapid indeed. Most guesses use the speed of neural firing as the baseline—sometimes calculated at up to 1,000 times per second.

In contrast, the pace of consciousness is considerably slower. Flanagan (1992: 83) remarks that it takes from 50 to 250 milliseconds for an object to come to consciousness. Baars (1988) places the minimal conscious interval at around 100 milliseconds. While one-tenth of a second is certainly very fast in absolute terms, relative to the rate of neural firing it is slow indeed. It thus appears that even though consciousness is relatively fixed and universal, it takes time, no doubt because the binding of experience itself takes time.

I am unaware of any studies on the exact time course of metaconsciousness, but all observers seem to agree that self-conscious processes are the slowest. Not only do they need considerably more time to emerge across the span of development (see Chapter 3), but they also slow down the pace of thought in any instance of their deployment. Fodor (1983) presents logical arguments for the slowness of central processes in opposition to the speed of input modules. Jackendoff (1987: 262–72) endorses the fast/slow dichotomy, though not as coterminous with the peripheral/central split. Vygotsky (1978: 72) makes the following observation on the rate of higher thought: "These changes [in the internalization of control] are manifested in the course of the choice reaction experiment. After considerable practice in the choice experiment, the reaction time begins to grow shorter and shorter. If the reaction time of a particular stimulus had been 500 milliseconds or more, it reduces to a mere 200 milliseconds. The longer reaction time reflected the fact that the child was using external means to carry out the operations." The initial slowness is the result of the deliberateness of metaconscious processing, which "imposes a high cognitive burden" (Gombert 1992: 191).

There is an obvious logic to the association of metaconsciousness and slow processing. Deliberate bracketing happens when things are difficult, and hard things make the mind go slower. Rapid deliberateness seems a contradiction in terms. Nonconscious processing, with much of its work prepackaged, has a much easier time of it and so is rapidly executed. Between these two extremes lies consciousness, which is just downright medium, whatever that is.

The actual numbers on speed, of course, do not matter at all. What does matter is speed relative to the overall configuration of the machine/organism and the efficacy with which it deals with the tasks in which it finds itself. Dennett (1987: 326) writes, "In a universe in which the environment events that matter unfolded a hundred times slower, an intelligence could slow down by the same factor without any loss." Jacoby and Kelley (1992) make a similar point in arguing that the automaticity of unconscious response is differentiated from the deliberateness of conscious response as a function of task and test.

Marslen-Wilson and Tyler (1987) give a nice linguistic demonstration of the relativity of speed, which also speaks to claims about architecture. They show that pragmatic and discourse information, usually thought of as slow, central, and isotropic, has the same time course of deployment in sentence processing as does syntactic information, the darling of rapid nonconscious knowledge. In their view, the simple alignment of sections of putative functional architecture (e.g., central/peripheral, e.g.) with certain kinds of knowledge (isotropic world knowledge/reflexive syntax) on the basis of speed (slow/fast) and automaticity (voluntary/mandatory) can be very misleading and, in fact, disappear under exacting empirical measurement. Fast processes are surely mandatory, but not vice versa. Speed, automaticity, and centrality depend on the kind of knowledge deployed, the task at hand, and the overall configuration of the organism in relation to the external task.

These clarifications of the role of speed in turn make contact with Jackendoff's (1987: 265) arguments about the computational substrate of consciousness. In his view, speed is a function not of modularity but of the nature of the representations processed. He notes that there can be both fast and slow modules, but "these processes can be properly differentiated only by paying attention to the representations on which they operate"

(1988: 267). Some learned processes may be very fast (mental multiplication), and some innate ones may be very slow (aging and hunger; see Marslen-Wilson and Tyler 1987: 6 n. 4). But these attributions of speed depend, as I have claimed at several other points in this book for several other phenomena, on the *nature of the information processed* and the relation between the inner state and the context of the organism.

When we associate speed with different kinds of subjectivity or different levels of conscious processing, we should think in a more holistic way. What metaconsciousness slows down nonconscious processing speeds up. But this in turn depends on what each kind of subjectivity is, does, and has access to. All these features are summarized in the table on p. 150.

4.4   Vygotskyan Demonstrations of Metaconsciousness

Here we turn to three demonstrations of the properties of metaconsciousness. These illustrations come from the mainstream cognitive science literature and, while suggestive of compatibility with Vygotskyan theory, remain computational. The findings, however, can be reinterpreted through and adjusted by the arguments just given for metaconsciousness. This lets us embrace Wittgenstein's problem: a human is both a neurobiological device and a person in context.

4.41   External Representations and Distributed Cognition

In a number of papers and books, Donald Norman and his co-workers have been developing an account of thinking in which mental processing is distributed across both internal mind and external context and is supported by explicit representations in the environment (see, e.g., Norman 1988, 1993). In a more recent paper, Zhang and Norman (1994) argue that experimental and theoretical work on problem solving in current cognitive science fails to appreciate a number of important facts: (1) thinking involves the coordination and deployment of both internal and external phenomena and thus is distributed; (2) the external environment contains not just aids to thinking but, like inner mind, representations; (3) experimentation must distinguish internal and external representations, analyze the latter fully, and be aware of the differential effects of each kind of representation on the outcome of the task.

They illustrate their points with various experiments on the well-known

Summary of the properties of nonconscious processing, consciousness, and metaconsciousness

Type of feature	Nonconscious processing	Consciousness	Metaconsciousness
Structure	Local and distributed	Local and distributed	Local and distributed
	Representations as knowledge	Representations as knowledge	Representations as representations
	Modular and interactive effects	Modular and interactive effects	
		Focus and fringe	Focus and fringe
			Mediation
Function	Fix		
	Model		
	Persist	Persist	Disappear
		Bind and change (Update)	Change
		Unify	Inhibit Individuate
		Include	Exclude
		Control as monitor	Control as recovery
			Plan
Context	Acontextual	$+/-$ Context	Contextual
	Self is purely inner	Self is mostly inner	Person is public
	No qualia	Qualia	No qualia
	No stance/ point of view	$+/-$ Stance/ point of view	Stance/point of view
Universality	Fixed	Fixed	Variable
Speed	Fast	"Medium"	Slow
	Automatic		Deliberate

Tower of Hanoi problem (see figure). In this task, the subject must move the three disks from the initial state to the final state under the condition that only one disk can be moved at a time and only smaller disks can be placed on larger ones.[13] This problem has been the subject of intensive research in cognitive science because the moves in its solution can be represented in a decision tree, and the solver's behavior can be explained through the formal decisions that the problem space allows.

Zhang and Norman (1994) point out, however, that this formal representation of the task misses the fact that the problem can be recast in a number of representational schemes, and some of these representations can be more or less external. For instance, the ordinal dimension of the size of the three disks could be coded either by size itself or by color (e.g., red = largest, green = intermediate, etc.). Moreover, size is an external representation since the ordinality of size is physically observable. But since the ordinality of color is not observable and must be stipulated, the representation of relative disk size by color is internal. Similar differences between internal and external representation hold for the other parameters of the problem, such as the location of the disks and the rules for moving them. The Tower of Hanoi problem is therefore not restricted to its physical instantiation but could have a variety of construals, some more or less external, depending on how the parameters of the problem are represented.

Citing much previous work indicating that the nature of a problem's representation affects the speed and accuracy of its solution, Zhang and Norman (1994) manipulate the possibilities of internal and external representations to see the effects of these alternate construals. They find a kind of trade-off between internal and external representation: internally represented problems place more demand on working memory and less on planning; externally represented ones place more demand on planning

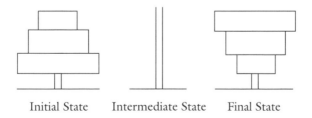

Initial State   Intermediate State   Final State

Tower of Hanoi Problem

and less on working memory. Overall, however, *difficulty decreases with the increase of external representations* because external representation is more explicit, more stable, and more easily checked; externally represented problems display their solutions more readily to the solver.

At the end of their paper, Zhang and Norman (1994: 119) cite Vygotskyan theory as promising related work but do not follow up on its application to their findings. If we do use Vygotskyan theory, we will see convergences between some of their processing claims and the properties of metaconsciousness. But we will also get a different interpretation of certain results and specific predictions about future work.

Even to use Vygotsky meaningfully, we must first appreciate that the Tower of Hanoi problem, like all problems, is *both a task and a metatask*. As a task, the problem states of the puzzle—the configuration of the disks at any one time—remain essentially constant (Zhang and Norman 1994: 94); after all, there are only so many things that any solver can do. But as a metatask, the *sequencing* of problem states is affected by the manner and choice of representation. Some configurations are more likely to be arrived at or skipped, depending on how the problem is couched. The representation of the problem thus calls attention to the task *as a task;* this reflexivity affects task performance in much the same way that computational control structures affect the flow of computation generally (see Chapter 5.6). Vygotskyan claims about metaconsciousness must be understood to apply at the metalevel.

We can see this right from the beginning of the argument, where Zhang and Norman (1994) make much of the fact that external representations are not mere aids to thought but actual representations, and that solvers do not access these representations as such but see right through them to complete the task: "To a task performer, a representation does not represent anything: it is simply the medium" (90). This is another way of saying that external representations *mediate* thinking *without being second-order representations of anything* and *disappear* in this mediation. These are otherwise three essential properties of metaconsciousness informed by Vygotskyan theory.

Note that the mediation does not have to be in language but can be brought about by any kind of symbolization: colors can stand for position. Moreover, what makes external representations external is that *they signal representationality itself* and do not simply refer. Size is an external representation, whereas color is not, because size displays its inherent gradient while any such gradient for color must be stipulated. In other words, size in and of itself signals not only size *but also the fact that an ordinal scale is in effect:* a large object is large only insofar as something smaller is presupposed. Color has no such double life, at least with respect to a gradience: a yellow object does not presuppose a less yellow one, or a green one.

External representations facilitate performance because they simultaneously display their information and their system of information (their representationality). In contrast, internal representations must stipulate their representationality. So to claim that something is an external representation is to claim that it is reflexive, is metarepresentational, and calls attention to itself *as a representation*. It is a tool for metaconsciousness, part of the language for thought.

Consequently, when task performers see right through their external representations, they are engaging the full instrumentality of external metarepresentations. Just as a carpenter sees right through the hammer while nailing, and just as a problem solver thinks right through private speech, so the external representations in Zhang and Norman's study work like Gibsonian affordances, as direct and transparent external means to thought.

Zhang and Norman might thus be said to have outlined the essential features of cognitive orientation. The grounds on which they argue for the role of external representation in distributed cognition are the very grounds on which Vygotskyan metaconsciousness is perched. Now let us turn to the results themselves. How do the external representations function in the task? Why do they make problem solving easier?

The response to the first question involves the contextual and metarepresentational properties of metaconsciousness. In principle, the structure and rules of any problem can be recast into different representational schemes, but in practice these recodings are heavily constrained by the cultural context in which they occur. Zhang and Norman (1994: 105–6) acknowledge this for one of their versions of the Tower of Hanoi, where the objects are recoded as coffee cups, and the cultural prohibition against spilling coffee supports the problem's prohibition of misalignment of coffee cups by size. But the culture-specificity of these external representations cuts deeper.

Suppose that this problem were posed in a culture where an animacy hierarchy structures the potency relations among entities (see Chapter 5.54). In this case, recoded objects would not only represent parameters of the problem, but would also implicate an inherent gradient of effectiveness or independent action. Arguably in these cultures recoded objects would simultaneously convey metarepresentational information. Moreover, if the task were to be carried out verbally, recoding the parameters as color would require a color system with enough terms to accommodate the number of dimensions to be recoded. This would have been very difficult to do in Dani (New Guinea), where only two colors are available. In a culture or language in which color may signal metarepresentational properties, color might be a potential external representational system.

Consider, in this regard, Wassmann and Dasen's (1994) results on counting and problem solving by the Yupno (New Guinea), whose number system goes only up to 33 and the numerals of which correspond to kin and body parts (e.g., 15 is 'stepfather', or 'two hands and one foot', that is, 10 fingers + 5 toes). When asked to count beyond 33 or solve difficult mathematical problems, the Yupno turn to the external representational affordances of their counting system. For example, one informant asked to count 44 sticks remarks that it is one man (33 body parts) and another from the family of the bride, but of these (potentially 33) body parts, the only relevant ones are his first hand (5), his second hand (5), and one toe (1): thus, $33 + 5 + 5 + 1 = 44$ (Wassmann and Dasen 1994: 88). The Yupno number system implicates external, metarepresentational distinctions, such as ready-made groupings, and so facilitates the solution. Hence, the number system in Yupno is a potential source of external representations for distributed cognition *because it is also metarepresentational.* If Zhang and Norman are correct, then, as Vygotsky pointed out, the recoding of problems and the metarepresentational keying of external representations ought to be a function of the culture and language in which the experiment occurs. More simply, metaconsciousness is heavily contextual.

Why do external representations make the problem easier? It cannot be simply that external representations shift the processing burden away from working memory to planning. Not only would we expect this anyway, since, in a Vygotskyan theory of metaconsciousness, externalism and planning are associated.[14] But there is also no reason to believe that planning should be easier than any other cognitive activity. What external representations do is reorganize the *activity* of the task.

As we should remember from Chapter 3, Leont'ev argued that behavior can be analyzed on three levels, as an operation (where its external conditions are relevant), as an action (where its goals are relevant), and as an activity (where its personal motivations are relevant). Operations are the means and components of actions, which, in turn, are the means and components of activities. All the benefits of external representations that Zhang and Norman list (1994: 118–19) lie at the operational level and reflect a modification of the task's conditions: physical memory aids, direct and explicit information, anchoring the structure of the task, and so on. The actions in the task are unaffected: the goal of solving the problem remains the same. Whether the activity of the problem, the personal motivation of the solver, is affected is unclear, but probably not. Thus, all these alterations are confined to the lowest level of the actional structure of meta-consciousness. They are artifactual and material, and they have artifactual and material consequences.

The external representations, however, could modify the goal of the task and so have an effect on the task as an action. For instance, the external recodings of the problem parameters could make the solution of the Tower of Hanoi puzzle a means to another end. In Zhang and Norman's task, the Tower of Hanoi problem is an end in itself: the experiment stops when the solution is reached. Moreover, the personal motivation for solving the task could be changed by modifying the role of the external representations in the activity. If, for example, the subjects had to solve the problem as part of their ordinary lifework, then the conditions of metaconsciousness would be changed in a more complicated way. As Zinchenko (1990: 31) notes in a paper on the relation between activity theory and consciousness, "To give meaning to sense [i.e., to move from an action to an activity] is to delay the realization of a program of action, to play it out in one's mind, to think it through." In a different form of activity, these external representations might have a more serious inhibitory and planning effect, and so might look more or less facilitative.

These ideas about Vygotskyan metaconsciousness give alternative interpretations to two more specific results. First, Zhang and Norman predict (1994: 111) that recoding by size ought to be more facilitative than recoding by color because size is external while color is not. But their results in fact show that recoding by color is not significantly harder than recoding by size. Zhang and Norman explain this by saying that recoding by color is a trivial task, and so its inherent ease fails to differentiate it from the otherwise easy recoding by size.

But there are other explanations that take more precise account of the metarepresentational possibilities of these properties. A division of representations into internal and external may not be so simple as it appears. Certainly what seems to the English speaker to be an arbitrarily referential—hence internal—counting system is to the Yupno a system charged with concrete, determinate external meaning. Color may have external metaproperties that Zhang and Norman do not know about. For the Ngamambo (Australia) fire has no inherent color, and so saying something like *the orange fire* is totally anomalous (Frawley 1992b: 452). But fire does have inherent color for English speakers and so can have external, physically observable associations. Conversely, size may have any number of external metaproperties. Work by D. A. Leont'ev (1990) has shown that the conditions (operations) and goals (actions) under which size is evoked affect the external metarepresentational supports that size provides for problem solving and thinking. For instance, children given tokens that can be used to get candy from a vending machine exaggerate the size of those tokens because the goal (getting candy) affects the construal of the token. Thus, the nature of the circumstances in which the external representation is embedded affects the value of what to Zhang and Norman is a straightforwardly external dimension.

Similar remarks about the false simplicity of external representations apply to the second result. Zhang and Norman (1994: 111) find that recoding parameters of the Tower of Hanoi problem into spatial or visual representations does not have equal effect: spatial locations (e.g., position indicating size) are much more facilitative than nonlocational visual properties. They give a purely internalist solution in terms of differences in brain locale for position and other visual properties (respectively, *where* an object is versus *what* an object is), with data suggesting that locations are more neuropsychologically basic—and so easier.

But this account seems at odds with the otherwise external flavor of their proposals and, in any case, overlooks many external representational factors. For one thing, while there is undoubtedly a neuropsychological differentiation between *what* and *where,* languages and cultures manage a semiotic trade-off between the two with differentiation in the *where* compensated for by simplicity in the *what,* and vice versa (see, e.g., Jackendoff 1992: 122–24). Moreover, different cultures often differentiate spatial and visual categories to a very fine grain, and these distinctions are frequently bound up with other physically observable facts about the culture and appear to affect individual problem solving. Denny (1988: 217) reports on a number of cross-cultural studies in which the highly differentiated locational system of a language and the association of these distinctions with physically-observable, significant aspects of the culture affect the reasoning of subjects in problem-solving tasks. D. A. Leont'ev (1990: 8–10), too, points out that the individual meanings of locations affect the extent to which they function successfully in behavioral tasks.

The point is that the very externality and internality of size, color, and location are not self-evident. Used as representational supports in thinking, these may evoke all sorts of important culture- and individual-specific metarepresentational distinctions and thus afford the task solver many types of external semiotic mediation, the kind of thing that Vygotskyan metaconsciousness puts at a premium.

In point of fact, Zhang and Norman's task and method are virtual copies of Vygotsky's forbidden colors task (Vygotsky 1978: 40). In that task, subjects play a question and answer game under various conditions that prohibit the use of color terms in responses to questions (these are the "forbidden colors"). Subjects are also allowed, to varying degrees, to use colored cards as external aids to their performance. For example, they might spread out all the cards with the forbidden colors as cues to correct answers. What Vygotsky found was essentially what Zhang and Norman find: external aids improved performance as the subjects used the cards as mediating devices. That is, when subjects "saw right through" the objectified colors, the external aids became instruments of thought. So we might say that the Tower of Hanoi problem, as Zhang and Norman have recast it, is really a version of the standard Vygotskyan forbidden colors task to elicit metaconscious performance.

A strong argument can be made that Norman's work on external representations and distributed cognition can be enhanced with an appreciation of the features of metaconsciousness informed by Vygotskyan theory: mediation, representations *as* representations, context, planning, and disappearance. Norman's work does not, however, evoke such canonical Vygotskyan ideas as the individual, the group, and the function of persons in thinking. There is no sense of *human help* in this task, and so it is difficult to judge the use of a Vygotskyan notion such as the zone of proximal development. For the applicability of these ideas to cognitive science, we must look elsewhere.

4.42 *Nonlogical Effects in Inferencing*

Since the 1970s, work on reasoning and inference has revealed a variety of nonlogical influences on an individual's otherwise logical judgments. There is, of course, the well-known work by Kahneman and Tversky (e.g., 1973) on biases in judgment and reasoning, but much additional research has fleshed out these ideas in detail and produced some rather startling findings.

Shafir (1994), for instance, has shown that, contrary to what logic demands, individuals will often suspend inferences even though they are required by the logical form of the problem. Consider the following scenario (after Shafir 1994: 408–10): You have just taken a difficult examination whose grade is important to your future education and career. You also have the opportunity to buy, at a special and very low price, a wonderful vacation package. However, the special price expires tomorrow and the grade will not be available until the day after tomorrow. Do you buy the vacation? In principle, uncertainty about the grade should have no effect on the decision, but in practice, the majority of individuals tested on this problem are willing to incur gratuitous cost just to postpone paying for the vacation until after the exam grade is known. Here uncertainty causes the reasoners to seek out "noninstrumental information" (Shafir 1994: 410) so that the decision can be made in an overall context of maximum certainty. This opting for consistency in conceptual bookkeeping at the expense of logic is at odds with any classical theory of reasoning but is nonetheless robust in everyday thinking.

The irony of this work is that it continues to be done with no awareness of the decades of virtually duplicate research in the Vygotskyan tradition. There is no mention of Luria, for instance, even though over fifty years ago he described and experimented with the same problems. And certainly no self-respecting cognitive scientist makes reference to current Russian work, where the identical issues of nonlogical influence are central to research on reasoning (see the survey in D. A. Leont'ev 1990: 17–18). But if we look in detail at one set of experiments in the non-Vygotskyan vein, we will see not only that the results have a straightforward Vygotskyan interpretation, but also that unexplained phenomena can now be explained and that certain new predictions for the otherwise computational work follow.

Legrenzi, Girotto, and Johnson-Laird (1993) argue that current theories of decision making are either incomplete or inaccurate. Many fail to appreciate the significance of "when one should decide to make a decision, or how one should determine the range of options, or how one should assess the utilities of various outcomes" (37). Others, they say, are insensitive to "how people reach decisions in daily life" (38). In short, the work as a whole overlooks the embeddedness of the machinery of inference in actual situations: Wittgenstein's problem in a nutshell.

In Legrenzi, Girotto, and Johnson-Laird's (1993) view, *model theory* augmented by *focus* addresses these shortcomings. Briefly, model theory holds that human reasoning proceeds not by classical, formal means but by the construction of a mental model of the state of affairs to be reasoned about; the structure of the model corresponds to the situation, not to some abstract formal system. Focus makes entities within each mental model explicit. These factors in combination accord with a number of well-known findings: humans are better at reasoning about problems that match some description of how their actual world works; explicitness of information in the problem facilitates reasoning.

Consider the well-known difficulties with modus tollens reasoning, or denial of the consequent. In a conditional (if p then q), denial of the consequent (not q) obliges denial of the antecedent (not p); so modus tollens is a strict and reliable means of reasoning about a conditional state of affairs. But in practice, humans are very poor at using this strategy. For instance, if told "If there is a tiger, then there is an elephant" (if p then q), subsequently told "There is no elephant" (not q), and then asked to reason further, many subjects say that *nothing seems to follow.* But as Legrenzi and associates (1993) note, if subjects are first told "There is no elephant" (not q) and then presented the conditional, they do perfectly well and reason that the antecedent does not hold: "There is no tiger" (not p).

Why does this informational inversion change the performance? The state of affairs "If there is a tiger, then there is an elephant" is compatible with three models: both tigers and elephants (p, q), no tigers but still elephants (not p, q), and neither tigers nor elephants (not p, not q). (A fourth state of affairs, tigers but no elephants—p, not q—contradicts the problem itself.) Apparently, the initial presentation of the denied consequent, no elephants, focuses it in the mental model and causes all models with elephants to be eliminated. This leaves only "no tigers and no elephants," and so the subject responds with "no tigers" (not p), the correct result by modus tollens, although it is achieved less by logic than by focus in a mental model.

Legrenzi and associates (1993: 51) give a variety of additional—sometimes astonishing—results supporting this line of argument. For example, focusing the conditional with "only if"—"There is an elephant only if there is a tiger"—has a beneficial effect because it brackets the entities in the model. Alternatively, a context that *defocuses* entities can facilitate reasoning by leading subjects away from attractive, but wrong, inferences.

The authors explain their findings simply: "[focusing] can lead to models that differ in what they make explicit about the situation, and this difference in turn can affect the conclusions the reasoners draw" (63).

All of these things make eminent sense under a Vygotskyan theory of metaconsciousness. First of all, as with the Tower of Hanoi illustration in the previous section, we have to appreciate the difference between tasks and metatasks. Focus affects not the representations per se in the mental model but their *manner of representation*. Focus does not construct a second-order representation of the problem—some further coding of an already coded state of affairs. Rather, it brackets and frames the first-order mental model and so works as a commentary on the first-order representationality. It is the *metarepresentational properties of metaconsciousness* that are at issue here.

Given that these results are best understood with respect to metatasks, we can now interpret them in terms of metaconsciousness informed by Vygotskyan theory. Focus signals the difference between foreground and background and accords *perspective* or *stance* to the mental model by singling out entities in the representational structure. Moreover, focus has its effects by making parts of the model explicit and overt: it accords stance by *objectification*.

These are the very mechanisms and effects of *the language for thought*—the private mental control language built on the public semiotic resources of the culture and language. Indeed, as we shall see in Chapter 5, *grammatical focus* is one of the principal linguistic devices that individuals use to structure and drive their metaconscious activity and regulate their own thinking. Thus, it comes as absolutely no surprise that focusing mechanisms, such as inverting the order of presentation of information and enhancing logical problems with "only if," should facilitate inference. Informational inversion and particles such as *only* are standard *linguistic devices* for focus and are structures that English and Italian share (the latter the language of Legrenzi, Girotto, and Johnson-Laird's experiments). We might further wonder if languages with different focusing devices would produce different results.

In any case, the selection of outcomes based on the bracketing of the structure of a mental model of a state of affairs is a standard result in Russian psychology, though couched in different terms. D. A. Leont'ev (1990: 14) reports, for example, that in experiments in which subjects are asked to reason about the causes and effects of their own and others' actions, the judgments match objective probability and neutral cause-and-effect relations when they are about *other people*. When the judgments apply to the subjects themselves, the cause-and-effect relations are distorted as a function of significant personal interests: in this case, subjects "explain success in terms of personal factors and failures in terms of situational factors" (14). To use Dennett's terms, heterophenomenology explains others but applies only to our own losses; for gains, autophenomenology is the best account of the causes and effects. One way to understand this is to say that the structure of the subjects' mental model of the state of affairs is parsed on the basis of the perceived personal significance—*smysl*—of the entities therein: "The personal meaning of objects and phenomena of reality is a component of the images and perception of these objects and phenomena" (21).

Focus has its effects because metaconsciousness is *local, task-specific*, and *contextualized*. As D'Andrade (1981: 188) observes about the relation between cultural and cognitive computation, "human problem solving procedures . . . [are] highly local and content specific, rather than global and formal." To be more precise, it is not the procedures as such but the bracketing and manner of representations on which procedures operate. Indeed, the structure of the mental models underlying reasoning is probably universal. But their deployment *as representations* is task-specific, local, and learned.[15]

When we turn to the effects of defocusing, we find similar convergences of interpretation between Vygotskyan theory and cognitive computationalism. We also encounter phenomena that the latter paradigm is at a loss to explain, but for which metaconsciousness has a ready account. Legrenzi and associates (1993: 52–56) note that context can defocus parts of a mental model as much as put them in focus. To study the effects of defocusing, they test two groups of subjects on decisions during a hypothetical visit to a large city (e.g., "Should I go to the movies, or not?"). Interestingly enough, they allow the subjects to ask the experimenter about the situations presented to get more information on which to make their decisions. The answers given are a crucial part of the experiment: some are presented with no background information, under the assumption that this would retain the initial focus of the problem (control group); some are presented with a context of alternatives, under the assumption that more information about alternatives will defocus any single alternative and hence neutralize the initial bracketing (context group).

As might be expected, the questioning has significant effects on focusing. Moreover, the kind of information provided by the experimenter changes the nature of the decisions made. Answers *without the background context* support decisions on the basis of a decontextualized, idealized instance. Hence, they promote a single focus. But answers *with background information* force the decisions into a comparison with other activities and other alternatives available for the model. This kind of information has a defocusing effect.

This is all well and good and might be understood as supporting the contextual sensitivity of the metatask. Unsurprisingly, context constrains metaconsciousness. But Legrenzi, Girotto, and Johnson-Laird (1993: 56) express their surprise at another result: "One unexpected finding was the close association between asking about alternatives to the focussing action and reaching a negative decision." More simply: "Asking about alternatives was correlated with deciding *not to take the relevant action* [my emphasis]" (55). The context group asked the contextually sensitive questions but then used this information to refrain from response. Why?

The authors give a number of possible explanations: information about alternatives leads to a negative decision (this begs the question); individuals who are about to reject alternatives ask about alternatives (the inverse of the previous); or "some other underlying factors" (56). But a Vygotskyan cognitive science can help to sketch out a coherent account.

First of all, we should remark on the task itself as a social context. Unlike traditional cognitive experiments, this one allows the subjects to ask for help, and uses the experimenter as a participant. Doing so unquestionably changes the conditions of the experiment by making the task a *dialogue* and an *intersubjective* experience. From a Vygotskyan standpoint, the use of help and dialogue is the preferred experimental method, but this in turn requires that the results and explanations thereof be sensitive to these different conditions of elicitation.

In dialogue, the subjects and the experimenter have different material conditions: the mere fact of the availability of another affects the entire definition of situation (Wertsch 1985). The subjects' goals and motivations are also affected by the dialogical structure: subjects can seek explicit information for personal reasons or to reach subgoals that might otherwise be disallowed by a standard sink-or-swim methodology. Consequently, the control subjects, who receive simple information in response to their questions, respond much the same as in a decontextualized state of a typical non-help task. The activity of the task minimizes the significance of the experimenter. But the context subjects have a very different definition of situation because the social context of their tasks is colored by personally meaningful information: indeed, the answers provided to this group were deliberately constructed to tap the individual's perspective and imagination (Legrenzi, Girotto, and Johnson-Laird 1993: 53–54). In short, the conditions, goals, and motivations that frame the metaconsciousness for these two groups differ, and so their task behavior ought to differ.

This is not to say that Legrenzi and associates (1993) do not recognize the effects of dialogue. Quite the contrary: they seek to determine the effects of context on reasoning. But what they do not seem to realize is how these effects are part and parcel of another, more detailed theory with specific predictions and standard explanations. They have created a *zone of proximal development* for their subjects by providing differential help from a more competent participant. Indeed, they note that the experimenter is described to the subjects as "an expert on the city's tourist attractions" (53). They have all the makings of the essence of Vygotskyan higher thought, or microgenesis: dialogue with asymmetric participants; a split between what the subjects bring to the task and what they must get out of the task; differential help during problem solving; modification of the conditions, goals, and motivation of the task. This is the chemistry of development.

The metaconscious effects of thinking in a zone of proximal development are well studied. Help applies differently and has different uptakes and effects depending on things such as the subgoals of the task that the help brackets and the relative intersubjectivity of the experience (Campione et al. 1984; Saxe, Gearhart, and Guberman 1984: 26). What we need to see in the Legrenzi, Girotto, and Johnson-Laird study is precisely what computationalism avoids: qualitative data. What exactly are the questions asked by the subjects? What do they focus on in their requests for help, and what specifically do they say and do in response to the different kinds of help offered? With this information we could give some added explanatory support to what is to a Vygotskyan an *unsurprising* result. The context group decides against relevant action because the help provided has personal significance and so is connected to their individuation *from the group*. Their dialogic experience appears to promote planning and inhibition. But the control subjects are, in effect, undifferentiated from an external group, since the information presented to them as help is impersonal and unelaborated. They might as well have received intelligent, computer-assisted tutoring.

In other words, in a rich semiotic environment, where help is provided from a more competent other (i.e., a person), and in which the information is personally meaningful and significant to the asker, the individual inhibits and refrains from action in an attempt to individuate from the group and context. What the results of the study show is that *metaconsciousness is doing its job and getting in the way of action.*

One cannot help but think that under different conditions—in a context where focus can be achieved in different ways and where the semiotic supports that affect the manner of representation in a mental model are quite different—these results would also be different. In a language such as Sissala (Burkino Fasa; see Blass 1990), which has a number of somewhat free-floating focus particles, or even German, which has a variety of focus markers (König 1991), the resources for bracketing and making explicit elements in a mental model are quite different. Surely in these languages the experiment would take a different shape, as would the results, because these languages offer differential access to the structure of the mental model.

A good illustration of the motivation for this prediction is in Legrenzi, Girotto, and Johnson-Laird's (1993) findings on narrative bias in counterfactual decision making. One of their tasks involves the presentation of a narrative with the actions structured around the protagonist. When subjects are subsequently asked to envisage alternatives to the course of events in the narrative, they "base their models on the protagonist's actions" (57). The authors argue that the narrative focuses the model on *protagonist control* and brackets the decisions in this direction.

But there are plenty of languages and cultures—that is, semiotic environments—in which protagonist control is not the central structural variable. In Russian, as Wierzbicka (1992: 395–441) claims, cognitive style is ordered around *lack of control* and *affectedness by powers outside the individual.* There is also plenty of cross-cultural work showing the interaction between formal, information-processing accounts of problem solving and local preferences for evidence from forces outside the individual's control (Verster 1988). Even closer to home, work on subculture and discourse style shows that the narrative preferences of ethnic groups affect problem-solving performance (Hemphill 1989, Gee 1989).

While none of this would surprise Legrenzi et al. and associates, who would surely acknowledge the relevance of this work, the ease with which such examples can be multiplied suggests that it needs much more than acknowledgment. It is in fact an *architecture-context problem.* Differential and group-specific narrative focusing of elements in a mental model reveals that the line between context (narrative) and architecture (mental model) is cut differently for different semiotic groups. Arguably, protagonist control is simply the default bracketing in the way Western narrative supports the construction of mental models for reasoning, and, it might be argued, this metarepresentational fact is part of the code, built into the mental model. Other semiotic groups might cut the line between coded representations and contextualized representationality quite differently, with clear effects. To put it another way, one benefit of the mental models approach to reasoning is that, unlike formal decision theory, it hooks reasoning up to the actual states of affairs of the reasoner. But we also know that there are no neutral states of affairs. Different cultures semiotically privilege certain entities and structure their states of affairs differently, and so the values for the otherwise fixed variables in the mental models ought to differ likewise.

I have spent some time showing how the results in reasoning experiments can be cast in a different light using Vygotskyan metaconsciousness. But one might, in the end, wonder if the discussion is a only Vygotskyan reclothing of existing sociofunctional approaches to problem solving. After all, there is a growing tradition of studying indigenous (i.e., non-European) and everyday problem solving on its own terms, and explaining the results with a self-conscious sensitivity to the varying sociocultural conditions of the solvers. This variability has been raised to theory by Lave (1991), who argues that cognitive patterns can be traced to *situated patterns of social practice*.

On my reading, at least, Vygotskyan theory *requires the fixed inner mind* and does not dissipate higher thought into community performance. Situating Legrenzi, Girotto, and Johnson-Laird's results entirely in communities of social practice would miss the fact that mental models are part of the fixed computational neurobiological substrate and, in my view, would thereby fail to be true to Vygotsky himself. Radzikhovskii's (1991) rearticulation of Vygotsky's ideas in fact points up the compatibility of the social and computational in Vygotsky's work.

> The more precisely we use a logical language, the more impoverished the psychological content of the corresponding description will be . . . [A] logical language coincides, at least in part, with the immanent language of human consciousness . . . [But] consciousness can be described only using two "complementary" languages . . . [W]e know

only one of these languages: a discrete logical language. The second language can at present be described only from its opposite. (Radzik-hovskii 1991: 18–19)

This is an acknowledgment that Vygotskyan theory requires *two* mental languages: a language *of* thought, immanent logical language of human consciousness—and a language *for* thought—its complement. We must have both for a proper account of mind, as Wittgenstein's problem illustrates. Totally situating the neurocomputational language of thought in social practice for thought may be a fashionable way to proceed, but it simply fails to be true to Vygotskyan principles.

A Vygotskyan interpretation of the nonlogical influences in reasoning supports the existence of a number of properties of metaconsciousness: focus/fringe structure, representationality, inhibition, planning, exclusion, individuation, and stance. These properties also mesh with standard modes of analysis in Vygotskyan theory, such as the zone of proximal development. A final group of experiments in the Western cognitive science vein elicits other features of metaconsciousness and gets a broader interpretation with the units of Vygotskyan analysis.

4.43 Domain-Specific Thinking, Learning, and Teaching

Since the early 1980s Alan Schoenfeld has been studying the behavior of individuals learning mathematics. He has argued that explanations of much of student performance require information "beyond the purely cognitive" (Schoenfeld 1983), beyond internal manipulations of mind code. Beliefs, intuitions, self-awareness, classroom context, self-perception, and self-control all bear on mathematics learning and teaching—and domain-specific thinking and instruction generally—as much as do basic memory and problem-solving processes and technical knowledge of the discipline (Schoenfeld et al. 1992: 294).

Schoenfeld's work is a natural candidate for articulation with Vygotskyan metaconsciousness, most notably because he is one of the few cognitive scientists who explicitly and correctly use Vygotsky. His own work is often perched on the edge of Wittgenstein's problem, balancing mechanistic, information-based accounts of domain-specific knowledge processes (Schoenfeld 1987a) with Vygotskyan work on the social and group origins of higher thinking and action (Schoenfeld 1987b). He admirably uses some of the exact tools of Vygotskyan analysis—such as the zone of proximal development—and he does not just invoke Vygotsky as a social-mind theorist, the usual cognitive science gesture.

The purpose of looking at his (already Vygotskyan) work here is to illustrate how his approach can be enhanced with a fuller use of Vygotskyan ideas. Moreover, it shows how a rich working coalition of Vygotsky and cognitive science can provide an important lesson in reverse for Vygotskyans.

A number of features of Schoenfeld's overall research tack dovetail immediately with the larger arguments of this chapter. Verbalizations during domain-specific problem solving are both data and content: the discourse of protocols reflects and constructs what he calls the *sense making* (something like *smysl;* see Arcavi and Schoenfeld 1992) of the situation and technical domain. His studies show that cognitive science can be built on detailed individual studies that recognize the situatedness of performance without invoking social reductionism. Perhaps most important, his work acknowledges that domain-specific thinking has a significant metacomponent: tasks are simultaneously metatasks, and thinking is enmeshed in metathinking (see, e.g., Schoenfeld 1987b). At least three themes in his work speak directly to the nature of subjectivity and could be given added detail and predictability if the machinery of Vygotskyan metaconsciousness were applied directly.

The first theme is that the advance from novice to expert problem solving in mathematics is associated with a shift in the locus and means of planning. Novice problem solvers are essentially empiricists, governed by the concrete facts of the problem. They see mathematical planning techniques, such as proof, not as a means to a solution but as a way of checking *after the fact* whether the solution is correct. In contrast, expert problem solvers see mathematical techniques such as proof as a "means of discovery" (Schoenfeld 1983: 345); their mathematical plans precede and frame their behavior.

This planning shift has obvious correlates (not noted by Schoenfeld) in Vygotskyan theory. Effective plans precede and inhibit behavior; novice (i.e., childlike) metaconsciousness is object-regulated and must ultimately lose its association with concrete externals in order to facilitate behavior. For the expert, proof makes subgoals explicit, but for the novice, proof is part of the external facts and is applied wholesale and post hoc. Thus, experts and novices arguably have quite *different frames* because of the role of proof. In a very real sense, experts and novices define the situations incommensurably.

How do novice "postplans" shift to expert "preplans"? Here, Vygot-skyan theory can give detail and direction to the analysis. The shift from external to internal relies on semiotic mediation and the language for thought. Since mathematics is a semiotic domain—significantly con-structed out of language (Frawley 1992a)—we should look at the nature and function of technical mathematical discourse (i.e., the mediational means in this domain) in the protocols of the solvers.

Schoenfeld (1983) asks two college freshmen and a mathematician to use only a compass and a straightedge to construct a circle that is tangent to two intersecting lines. After twenty minutes of joint work with nearly a hundred conversational exchanges, the freshmen fail to make the construc-tion. From a Vygotskyan standpoint, their performance is remarkable less for its failure than for the way their discourse functions to support their failure. The students essentially draw diagrams and then use somewhat technical speech *to label the diagrams after the fact of the drawing.*

Early on, they sketch out an informal picture of what they believe to be the result and comment as follows (Schoenfeld 1983: 353):

L: Now, OK, we have to find the center.

T: Of what?

L: Of the circle . . .

T: All right, well we know the point of tangency on this line is go-ing to be right here (points to P) . . .

L: . . . Is it true that if you have a circle like that (see right), and then that (points with finger) would be the diameter . . .

T: The circle has like—no, you don't have a diameter running up through there . . .

L: No, wait: the point of tangency, the point of tangency here . . .

They behave just like the children Vygotsky (1978: 28) observed using language to label, not organize, their pictures. The language for thought accompanies or tags along with behavior; it does not frame it. Interestingly enough, the novices recognize the insufficiency of their technical talk— "That's all being unmathematical, completely disorganized" (Schoenfeld 1983: 355)—and the fact that their unmediated drawings iterate to failure: "I don't know how to do that, without doing it until it comes out right"

(356). This recognition has its upside: it is reflexive and so a sign of prog-ress and promise (see Schoenfeld 1987b).

In contrast, the mathematician has a mediating mathematical language for thought that he deploys prior to behavior. Even though he has not done geometry for ten years, he begins the task of inscribing a circle in a triangle as follows: "Now, what do I know about the center? We need some lines here. Well, the radii are perpendicular at the points of tangency, so the picture's like this" (Schoenfeld 1983: 361). His talk not only is self-directed and technical but also precedes the drawing. This individual is using the semiotic resources of the domain reflexively to model the out-come. Indeed, the expert never actually draws the required figure in the short, eight-unit self-exchange. He simply comes to the point where he could draw it: "I've solved it. Do you want me to do the construction?" (Schoenfeld 1983: 361).

The expert's self-talk is not only effective but also *fluently technical*. He says, at the end, "So the center is on the angle bisectors" (Schoenfeld 1983: 361). This use of *on* reveals the expert's adoption of the epistemic perspective of geometry: the point that is the center of the circle is a de-rivative of another geometrical construct; it falls out of the intersection of the lines. The expert's perspective thus goes *from the lines to the point*. This is in marked contrast to the novices, for whom the center of the circle is a preestablished location, a fixed position: "OK, we need a center and a radius. So how do we locate the center? . . . If you have a center way out there . . . the center has got to be up and over, like here" (Schoenfeld 1983: 354–56). For the novices, perspective moves from the point to the lines, and so they arguably *do not have the proper mathematical stance,* even though they have all the right words and concepts.

These observations about the role of technical discourse in problem solving should not be taken as a recommendation that instruction focus on specialized discourse. The issue is not the vocabulary per se but *how* the technical discourse *as a discourse* is used as a semiotic instrument. Quantitatively, the novices have as much vocabulary as the expert, so they are comparable on matters of strict mathematical content. Mathematical truth is not a factor here. But they diverge on *metacontent via discourse;* that is, they differ in how they construct a mathematical stance and how they mediate their problem-solving action.

Nowhere are these points clearer than in the behavior of intermediate-level problem solvers. After some weeks of instruction, the two novices have gained some fluency in geometry and are asked to construct two circles with the same radius and a common tangent, given the centers of the circles. A look at their protocol shows that they are right in the middle of development—somewhere between post hoc labeling and verbal modeling prior to construction: "What we want basically is this, circles and a line something like this that is going to pass through here (makes sketch)" (Schoenfeld 1983: 357). They produce explicitly self-directed speech for planning and inhibition: "But, OK. Wait, I've got to think for a second" (357). "No. Wait, what am I looking for now?" (358). They engage in reflexive talk about the mathematical discourse: "Yeah, divide it in half . . . Yeah, bisect" (359).

This last point is especially crucial. They spend much time in their protocol sorting out the technical sense of *same,* which turns out to be critical to solving the problem. If two circles have the same radius, does this mean that they have the identical radius (a trivial solution, since they would be identical circles), share a single line but take their radii from different parts of the line, or fall on different lines with the same measurement? Note the following exchange (358):

T: These two radii are the same, right?

L: Except it doesn't look the same, does it?

Their sketches (358–59) show that they are struggling with whether the radius has to be a single line ('same line') or equally measured but different lines ('same line'). This leads to much confusion about the points that are centers and how the circles have to be drawn. Finally, on recovery, one student says: "OK. Since they have to be of equal radius . . ." (358). Here the relevant sense of *same* is articulated, and the solution proceeds. The overall lesson is, however, that *same* has to be appreciated not in its ordinary ontology, 'identical objects', but in its mathematical *epistemology,* 'having identical measurement'. That is, *same* has to be made sense of in the culture of mathematics; the students must grasp the significance *(smysl)* of *same,* not its meaning.

While Schoenfeld admirably uncovers and describes the difficulties and successes on this point, he does so in quite other terms. What Vygotskyan theory affords the analysis is a focus on semiotic mediation and how variable control over this domain-specific resource is linked to variable planning and execution. Vygotskyan theory shows how these individuals construct their metaconsciousness on-line through domain-specific language for thought. Novices and experts thus fall along a continuum of planning and control.

A second theme in Schoenfeld's work is the analysis of self-control. As he points out in many places (1983, 1987b, 1988), an expert is a good self-monitor; she knows what a wild goose chase is and when to stop herself from going on one. Schoenfeld (1983: 345) notes that while novices and experts both evidence monitoring behavior, only the experts use it as a positive force. Consequently, a novice's protocol has a staccato contour—problem solving punctuated by monitoring—while an expert's is seamless and smooth despite/because of the monitoring.

This is another idea that has an obvious correlate in Vygotskyan theory—self-regulation via productive inhibition. But it can be further developed and enhanced by using the theory's predictions about the way self-regulation determines the individuation of a subject from a group. Schoenfeld does not describe in detail the function of the differential monitoring he observes. Here the specifics of Vygotskyan theory offer some analytical help.

In Vygotskyan metaconsciousness, the semiotic (usually linguistic) mediation of interaction and self-direction is a key to individuation and control. While it is true enough that the novices are empiricists and thus at the mercy of the data, their protocols indicate that they are also *at the mercy of each other.* They constantly tell each other what to do, note what each has done wrong, and bemoan the usually dismal consequences of their acts:

> T: Remember on the first problem sheet we had to inscribe a circle on a triangle? Could you do that? I couldn't.

> L: I couldn't either.

> T: We're in pretty sad shape. But just say we draw a triangle even though we don't know how to do it. We will draw a triangle anyway.

> L: So how's that going to help? (Schoenfeld 1983: 354)

This is a true dialogue and genuine exchange. In this problem-solving protocol the two make a coherent *group*.

Such collectivism and exchange are not characteristic of their later protocols, after they have learned more geometry and gotten accustomed to the tasks. In these cases they demonstrate mutual self-control:

> T: OK? These two have to be the same length.

> L: Right.

T: And the thing that is going to determine how long they are is the angle on this line. What I mean like if they are exactly—half way in between the two centers then the line is vertical.

L: Right. (359)

Clearly these individuals have emerged from their previous dialogues as discrete persons. Their mathematical problem solving is less a dialogue than emergent parallel monologues. Interestingly, this protocol has as many conversational exchanges (about one hundred) as the novice protocol, so the quantity of talk cannot be the appropriate measure of performance. Rather, it is the function of the mediating speech in the exchange and the individuation of the subjects from the group.

Schoenfeld (1987b: 210) notes, "A good problem solver argues intelligently with himself." This can happen only if there is an *intelligent group*, "a microcosm of mathematical culture" (1987b: 213), that provides the resources for intelligent self-inquisition. The tension between the group and the individual underlies self-control.

The third and final theme is time. In a number of places, Schoenfeld remarks on the paradoxes of time that characterize the teaching and learning of mathematics. Classroom performance and standardized testing are both oriented to the rapid solution of problems, which in turn suggests that mathematical thinking is more the deployment of quick and effective techniques rather than a slow exploration with lots of wrong turns. It also suggests that problems that cannot be done in a short amount of time are either insoluble or, worse, not worth the effort. As he says (1988: 160), "Students must learn basic facts and procedures, of course, but it is also essential for them to engage in real mathematical thinking—in trying to make progress on difficult problems . . . in learning that some problems take time, hard work, and a bit of luck to solve."

Speed is the opposite of metaconsciousness, which, as we know, must be slow, deliberate, and nonautomatic. The prohibitions against reflection encourage a sink-or-swim version of domain-specific knowledge and locate students in medias res when they might otherwise not even know what the task is. One of Schoenfeld's teaching techniques to combat this attitude evokes an important Vygotskyan principle. He notes (1987b: 200–205) that he asks his students if they all understand the problem before they begin any solution. Many do not but would still have been willing to go along with the classroom practice. The task has to make sense before any technique is deployed or any mathematical principle is invoked, and this cannot be brought about by some pedagogical rapid-deployment force. While this point seems simple enough, it is often overlooked in classroom practice, where we all want to bring the encounter to a coherent outcome.

The Vygotskyan claim that grounds this argument is the insistence that the best data in an experiment often occur before the experiment even begins. This is information that is frequently discarded by experimenters. But it is this initial contact between the task and the individual where the sense battle is waged and where individuals decide how and whether they should commit to the task at all. Unless time is spent on the frame, the frame problem *will* surface. The deliberateness of metaconsciousness is the only effective weapon against the frame problem.

The larger lesson of Vygotskyan cognitive science, then, is not that speed is bad, but that plodding has its virtues. One standard and effective way to slow down behavior is intervention. Much would have been accomplished, for instance, in the intermediate-level protocol (Schoenfeld 1983) if someone had simply told the solvers what *same* meant in that case. This is not an indictment of the experiment, which, for other reasons, required lack of intervention. The point is, rather, that deliberateness can be induced in a variety of ways so long as some barrier to action is introduced. In this way, the study of the computational mind might benefit from its clinical treatment, with effective intervention strategies the order of the day. We should, of course, recall that Vygotsky saw as beneficial the mutual give and take between the study of breakdown/remediation (what he called *defectology*) and abstract theorizing.

Schoenfeld's work interpreted more fully by Vygotskyan theory supports the metaconscious properties of planning, inhibition, mediation, control, individuation, deliberateness, and stance. But there is a reverse lesson for Vygotskyan theory from all this. Schoenfeld (1983: 350) points out that metaprocesses are typically thought of as conscious, that is, the subject is aware of them. But "a person's unconscious beliefs can shape . . . behavior. Moreover, the fact that the individual is unaware of having those beliefs makes them all the more intractable: he or she does not see the difficulties that they cause" (see also Schoenfeld 1987b). In Vygotskyan theory, higher thought appears to be always under voluntary control, but if Schoenfeld is right, then it seems that sometimes metaconsciousness is, somewhat paradoxically, unconscious.

This point might be made in a different way under the guise of introspection (I am indebted to a short conversation with Owen Flanagan for these ideas). It seems uncontroversial to say that conscious and unconscious processes are not all, or always, introspectable. So why should metaconsciousness be any different? Indeed, if subjectivity has three modes, then there is no reason to assume that the "highest form" of thinking is the least intuitive or the most bracketable.

If Vygotsky is correct in originating metaconsciousness in cultural knowledge, and if Schoenfeld is correct in arguing that metaprocesses can be automatic and thus "beneath" inspection, these two points would come together under a standard claim of cognitive anthropology. Despite much overt teaching of the programs of culture, situated knowledge has its greatest effects in its unconscious wielding (see D'Andrade 1981). This in turn would mean that deliberateness, reflexivity, control, externalism, inhibition, mediation, and planning are not necessarily under voluntary control. Metaconsciousness may thus have no essential connection to will, contrary to what received Vygotskyan theory might hold.

In this chapter I have tried to illustrate the integration of computational and social views of mind on an ancient issue—consciousness—long a fashionable concern of sociocultural theorists but increasingly fashionable among computationalists. A tripartite view of subjectivity—nonconscious processing, consciousness, metaconsciousness—whereby the attributes and dependencies of each are made precise yields a productive Vygotskyan cognitive science of metaconsciousness. The tools of metaconscious analysis allow a reinterpretation and clarification of important computational work on external representation, inference, and problem solving.

But these results still leave two questions open: Where, in an otherwise computational mind, is this sort of sociocultural subjectivity? And how is metaconsciousness implemented? In Chapter 5 I try to answer both these questions.

5

Control and the Language for Thought

5.1 The Importance of Reflexivity

In Chapter 4 we saw that subjectivity can have three modes: nonconscious information processing, conscious awareness, and deliberate metathinking. Some of the received accounts of subjectivity exclude language as a necessary feature, while others rest crucially on claims about what language does to construct and maintain certain kinds of subjective experience. The troubling fact about the latter sort of account is that the scanty examples of speech actually doing this work make appeals to language awfully suspicious. When Dennett says that consciousness consists of "narratives . . . under continual revision . . . [with] no single narrative that counts as the canonical version" (1991: 138)—that "Our tales are spun, but for the most part we don't spin them; they spin us" (418)—even the initiated might ask, What on earth does that mean? When Jackendoff (1987: 324) observes that "language might make it easier to think the thoughts one would have anyway" because it confers on the thinker "metaconceptual advantages" (326), the circumspect reader might wonder just how this happens, and, along the way, how this kind of awareness hooks up with good old-fashioned consciousness, which remains "not . . . an especially high-level process" (325).

Here I try to make good on all these promissory notes and spell out the details of linguistic self-management. If, as Vygotsky argued, a self is never purely executed, but needs semiotic instruments to achieve its characteristic distance and control, then how do you know a narrative center of gravity when you trip over one? How *does* language make it easier to think thoughts if, indeed, you were going to have them anyway?

The answers rest in a modern linguistic reading of G. H. Mead's (1934) social theory, where speech converts the subjective *I of consciousness* into the objective *me of self-consciousness*. In plain terms, speech tells you who you are. Still, *how* does language do this? Mead, like most everyone else, has little to say on this important point. But Caton (1993) argues that self-consciousness is triggered by reflexive aspects of linguistic code. Language intervenes in subjectivity because it comes ready for the task. Therein lie the essentials of speech for self-conscious thinking, or the *language for thought*.

Consider the double life of the basic linguistic act of referring. Naming not only invokes semantic information, the truth of the name, but also cues the *manner of truth*—metasemantics. The act of naming signals both the object itself and the fact that the object is nameable. Naming instructs the hearer to pay attention to the semantic system itself and so is inherently reflexive (Lucy 1993; Silverstein 1985, 1993).

Reflexivity bears on our larger concern for the linguistic structure of subjectivity because metainformation cues the limits of characterizability. So if, as Mead says, consciousness names and objectifies itself—if it signals its own status and thereby states its own limits—it has the resources to do so in the speech of the conscious namer. Language turns out to be a kind of toolbox that includes tools to fix tools (see Wertsch 1991 for this analogy).

If this view is correct, then the burden of evidence for the linguistic structuring of metaconsciousness shifts onto just those aspects of language that allow self-referentiality. This in turn adds substance to the sketchy philosophical claim that language has a role in the way thinking generates its own run-time commentary. One way of understanding Dennett's claim that the self is a narrative center of gravity is to say that the language of a speaking subject contains metanarrative forms that signal the existence and limits of narrative itself (e.g., markers of evidence and the shift of speaking subject). Since speakers inherit these forms of conscious mediation from their languages, Dennett's apothegm that our narratives spin us rings truer than he might imagine (see also Wertsch and Bivens 1993: 214–15). Likewise, Jackendoff's point that language makes it easier for us to think the thoughts we would have anyway is made sensible by the fact that the very act of representation bounds the referent and sets off its limits (Cocking and Renninger 1993 and Greenfield 1993 call this the *distancing* function of denoting; see also Jackendoff 1987: 324 and Vygotsky 1986: 256, 170–71).

Similarly, when Mead holds that "the word 'flame' is still not meaningful to the child until it can *say* what a flame is when asked by someone like its mother to 'define' it" (Caton 1993: 326), he sounds like both Wittgenstein, whose recognition of the limits of self-referentiality in logic forced him into viewing language as social action, and Vygotsky (1986: 170): "A preschool child who, in response to the question, 'Do you know your name?' tells his name, lacks this reflective self-awareness: He knows his name but is not conscious of knowing it."

In the discussion that follows, we look in detail at how metaconsciousness is structured around linguistic reflexivity. I begin by defining speech for self-consciousness and clarifying the kinds of forms that count as elements of the language for thought. Much of the existing work on speech for the self has looked in the wrong place in language and often only at English. All metaforms are reflexive and thus have the potential to structure metaconsciousness. This definition and clarification of the elements of the language for thought confer three advantages on our larger project of a Vygotskyan cognitive science.

First, it is easier to trace the ways that social speech gives rise to speech for self-control. As Furrow (1992: 155) points out, not all social functions have to be transferred from communicative speech to inner speech; indeed, the crucial forms are those structural devices that bridge the gap between public and private dialogue, those that can be *both public and private at once*.

Second, the language for thought appears in a more complicated developmental light, its emergence pushed back closer to where a mind and culture first meet. Because the language for thought is inseparable from language for others, children appear to have access to it, and control of it, much earlier in development than is normally assumed (Smolucha 1992).

Third, the social mind can be tied to architecture-context relations and specific computational mechanisms. Different languages carve and code the public-private line differently, some fixing in code for rapid processing what others leave to slow contextual inference. Do some languages code reflexivity directly while others leave it to context? Can these differences be observed in speech for self-consciousness? The organization and function of computational control—that is, the management of data flow, communication across domains of knowledge, error detection, recovery, and notification—have striking analogues in the human language for thought. The similarities between computational control and speech for self-consciousness suggest that it is possible to give an entirely informational account of self-speech, thus according the external language for thought a formal purpose in an otherwise purely internal formal mind.

5.2 Defining the Language for Thought

The language for thought is *falsely dialogic signing for position that mediates thinking*. We need to explore each of the concepts in this definition to appreciate what the language for thought is and does. As we do, we will see that most of the properties of metaconsciousness discussed in the previous chapter have analogues in the functions of the language for thought.

5.21 False Dialogue

The language for thought gives the appearance of communication, but in fact is more like pure broadcasting than the conveyance of information. Consider Wittgenstein's hypothetical number-series solver (hereafter NSS; see Chapter 2.423), whose subjectivity breaks down under the difficulty of completing the series 1, 5, 11, 19, 29. NSS engages in two kinds of actions to reestablish unified subjectivity: self-speech ("Now I know," "Now I can do it," "Now I understand," "What is the series of differences?") and written external aids (representations of the problem, alternative number series, and sketches of formulas). The self-speech has all the trappings of an interlocutor ("What is the series of differences?") but only the NSS as recipient, and so is false dialogue. It merges speaker and hearer in a single instant and uses deictics, *that* and *now*, to code properties of the context and thereby signal the metapragmatic fact that the speech event can be coded. The self-referentiality of language thus does the work for Wittgenstein's NSS in the predicament of objectifying consciousness; this is NSS's language for thinking (see also Goffman 1981: 87–122).

The falsity of false dialogue is traceable to the way the language for thought is *both public and private at once—simultaneously objective and subjective.* Consider the ambiguity of NSS's words *understand* and *know* ("Now I understand," "Yes, I know that series"), which reflect not only the content of a private mental state ('comprehend') but also the external frame in which these private states are situated ('recognize'). The tension between public compliance ('I recognize what I have to do') and private comprehension ('I comprehend it') is, of course, Wittgenstein's problem in a nutshell, and so it is not surprising that the language for thought rests on forms that bridge this public-private gap (see Schiffrin 1987: 228–44).

The language for thought is simultaneously public and private speech. It is subjective and objective at once, speech that calls attention to the coincidence of subjective and objective. The best illustration is free indirect style.

All languages give speakers explicitly reflexive means to report the exact speech of others—direct discourse: *Bob said: "Wow! Tom is crazy!"* Direct discourse is objectified speech and therefore quintessentially public. Languages also give speakers forms to report just the content of another's speech, without overt reference to the speech itself—indirect discourse: *Bob said that Tom was crazy.* Indirect discourse shifts perspective wholly within the mind of the reporter, with objective events reinterpreted from the reporter's position. There is also a third form, free indirect style (or represented speech and thought), typically found in stream-of-consciousness literary narratives, and which, in form and function, lies somewhere between direct and indirect discourse: *Wow, was Tom ever crazy, Bob thought to himself.* Free indirect style retains all the markers of objective, public, contextualized speech that indirect discourse disallows, but also preserves the subjectified, internal viewpoint of indirect discourse. It is thus both subjective and objective at once, simultaneously public and private speech, and so typifies the language for thought. Banfield (1982, 1993), in fact, calls it narrative *speech for consciousness* (the idea is frequently traced to Vološinov 1986, originally 1929; Vološinov = Bakhtin).

A number of structural and functional similarities between free indirect style and the language for thought indicate that the former can tell us much about the latter. Free indirect style is expression without communication (Banfield 1982), narration for narration's sake, not the conveyance of information. In Goffman's (1981: 136–37) terms, it is speech in search not of hearers but of *over*hearers. Free indirect discourse is, moreover, speech with a *viewpoint* but no speaker—or, as Banfield describes it, a self but no subject. A free indirect form (e.g., *Would he be there? she wondered*) has a third-person, objective viewpoint, but the act cannot be attributed to a first-person speaker (note the strangeness of *I said would he be there? she wondered*). Hence, the subject *(I)* is not the same thing as a self (the objective viewpoint of the free indirect speech). In normal speech the two converge (the viewpoint and speaker are the same), but language has the potential to split one from the other. Likewise, the language for thought is built on the possibility of splitting the speaking subject, consciousness, from the objectifiable self in metaconsciousness.

While all these analogies are clear, it is not the case that the language for thought *is* all and only free indirect discourse.[1] The point, rather, is that the simultaneous signaling of public and private is a productive and commonplace fact about language. Consequently, one of the essential characteristics of the language for thought—false dialogue, public speech for private means—penetrates everyday social exchange. This is how the intramental lies in the intermental.

5.22 Signing

If the language for thought is built on forms that code public and private simultaneously and hence give the illusion of purely public discourse, then it can be brought about by *any symbolic means,* not just speech. What is crucial is only that there be ways for the user to gain position via reflexive code.

The emphasis on *speech* for thought is a consequence of a bias to see language as the ideal thinking code and to take its pervasiveness as a mark of privilege. But other sign systems have been observed to play the same code-for-thought role as speech. Wertsch (1991: 31), for instance, cites the work of Rogoff and Kearins on non-Western children's use of non-verbal symbolic mediation in problem solving. Grumet (1985: 186) reports the frequent informal observation that deaf people sign to themselves and so have private signing. Indeed, Wittgenstein's NSS behaves similarly. The recovery of unified subjectivity is brought about not only by speaking but also by objectifying the problem in written code—alternative series of numbers and formulas. Here, nonverbal signing leads to the solution because it, too, can be reflexive: in writing down the formulas, NSS signals that the code of mathematics can itself be invoked and coded.

This focus on signs in general, rather than speech, underlies Vygotskyan work on the development and use of symbolic, external memory aids in problem solving (Vygotsky 1978: 51). But what is remarkable is that the same point, in virtually the same phrasing, has been made by Pylyshyn (1985: 81) in an entirely different context for an ostensibly different purpose, the organization of computational control—how data flow proceeds while a system monitors itself internally and externally (see section 5.61 for details). In computational terms, such external signs can be *interrupts,* signals for a change in processing, "because the initiative for capturing control [may originate] outside the process currently active—in fact, outside the organism" (Pylyshyn 1985: 81). In Vygotskyan terms, objective signs reorient consciousness by directing control outward; the fusion of public and private in the reflexive language for thought allows this possibility. Vygotskyan cognitive science might put the whole matter another way: signing in the language for thought is a kind of content-oriented access key, limiting the beliefs and inferences available at any one time (Pylyshyn 1985: 136).

5.23 Position

The language for thought affords the subject a perspective via the meta-functions of signs. This association of the self with a *linguistic viewpoint* is characteristic of what Goffman (1981) calls *footing:* a stance or projected self (128) cued by linguistic structures with metafunctions (150–51), though Goffman does not use this "meta" terminology. The principal cognitive benefit of position is displacement, decentering, or psychological distance (Siegel 1993). The autonomy and effective operation of a mind emerge as a function of the "space" between the mind and the objects of its attention. The less tied to the objects of its focus—that is, the more bracketed it is, to evoke phenomenology—the smoother its execution. It is important for our argument that one way to view psychological distance is as the discrepancy between two mental stances (Cocking and Renninger 1993, Siegel 1993).

The functions of perspectival discrepancy read like a manual of Vygotskyan cognitive science: it differentiates the self from others, it induces metaknowledge through abstraction, it serves behavioral control, and it establishes beliefs, interests, and values (Cocking and Renninger 1993). Psychological distance is for all intents and purposes a modern analogue of the zone of proximal development. As the optimal mismatch of the known and unknown (Cocking and Renninger 1993), it embodies the very conditions Vygotskyans hold for progress in individual mental functioning (van der Veer and Valsiner 1991; see also Chapter 3.332).

Position, distance, and control are all cut from the same cloth. Metasigns code position; in signaling the code itself, they make the code into an object for the consciousness of the speaker. This in turn induces distance, causing control. Here Wittgenstein's NSS resurfaces. In saying, for example, "Yes, I know that series," NSS indicates much more about NSS than the number series. The expression objectifies the number series and gives NSS a stance by separating NSS's mind from the problem to be solved. In speaking, NSS stakes out the ground, articulates a theory of the situation, and thereby controls both the problem and the problem-solving self. What is important is that the work of this stance making is carried out by forms such as *Yes, I know* and *that*, which focus attention on the context of the speech event itself. They are what Goffman (1981: 153) calls "the structural basis of footing."

5.24 *Mediation*

The language for thought is a *vehicle for thinking,* not a higher-order language *of* thought. It would be easy to think of the language for thought in completely representational terms, as a kind of model of all models. Not only does this evoke infinite regress to the last model, but it is also untrue to the Vygotskyan cause, where the mingling of thinking and speaking in higher thought is best understood instrumentally, not as the ultimate representational content (see Sokolov 1972, Wertsch 1991). Wertsch and Bivens (1993) put it succinctly: mediation involves thinking triggers and the generation of meaning, not just another system of content "one step up in mind" (wherever that step might be!).

If the language for thought were some kind of higher-level representational system, it would be hard to explain why it surfaces when it serves no representational end. Self-speech in schizophrenia, for example, can be explained in completely formal-informational terms as an attempt to reduce the signal-to-noise ratio, not as a failure of higher representational content; similar arguments hold for private speech by "normals" under noisy and stressful situations (Grumet 1985). In other words, the language for thought surfaces as a way of *managing the informational demands of existing representations.*

Nor is the language for thought some kind of think-aloud protocol and certainly should not be studied in such terms. Asking speakers to tell you what is going on in their heads may be a valuable task in some contexts, but this method buys again into a representational construal. Subjects are no more reliable in their reports on metaconsciousness than they are in reporting the content of their phonological representations. For one thing, the language for thought is not a preformed symbolic plan put into words, waiting to be extracted from a speech protocol (cf. Zivin 1979: 35). Moreover, just as some of the contents of consciousness are not amenable to introspection, so some of the contents of metaconsciousness are immune to self-report: deliberateness and volition do not entail access to introspection. Mediation is on-line instrumentation. It is the *style of control* rather than the representation of it.

These points can again be seen in the by now familiar behavior of NSS, who never metarepresents the problem as such, never says anything like "This is a partial differential equation." Instead, all of NSS's effort is devoted to the activity of *formulating* this kind of representation, to everything prior to this sort of coding. NSS says things like "Wait, let's see, now I know, Oh!" NSS's speech for thinking precedes the representational solution and in this way mediates mental life.

5.3   The Limits of Private Speech Research

The definition of the language for thought thus far given leads to some important clarifications in the study of the relationship between speech and self-management. Much work has been done on the nature, function, and development of *private speech*—egocentric, self-directed, acommunicative, regulatory speech during problem solving (see, e.g., the papers in Zivin 1979 and Diaz and Berk 1992). The narrowness of this work has sometimes produced misleading results or focused analysis away from what, in a broader construal, might be more (if not the most) interesting phenomena. As falsely dialogic signing for position that mediates thinking, the language for thought naturally subsumes inner speech and private speech, but also includes *other overt speech dedicated to self-management*.

Private speech is classically defined as abbreviated, overtly self-directed, task-relevant, and preactional. Berk's (1992) excellent review of the literature shows, however, that none of these has to hold for private speech to accomplish its regulatory purposes. Similar discrepancies between definitional criteria and regulatory function are noted by Furrow (1992), Feigenbaum (1992), Frauenglass and Diaz (1985), Azmitia (1992), Frawley and Lantolf (1985), and Rubin (1979: 287). Certainly a child saying to herself, prior to behavior, "Now, go get the puzzle piece," is a very clean manifestation of the language for thought, but other-directed, off-task, concurrent speech has no less a regulatory metaconscious function. Direct questions to interlocutors are regulatory, and putatively off-task comments such as expletives and affective expressions (quite common even among young problem solvers) assist cognitive control by, at the very least, releasing tension (Rubin 1979, Berk 1992). Fuson (1979: 153) puts the issue very well by saying that the nature of the utterance reveals its connection to plans and action, not its fit to a prefabricated category (see also Diaz's 1992 methodological cautions based on the multifunctionality of private speech).

Not only is the nature of private speech clarified by analysis of the language for thought, but so is the frequent appeal to private speech levels to adjudicate disputes about experimental results. The early and influential work by Kohlberg, Yaeger, and Hjertholm (1968) ranked private speech from the "lowest" level of presocial self-stimulating language to the "highest" level of silent or inner speech, with developmental trends linked to these levels. But level of performance is not purely, or even significantly, an age-determined factor (see Frawley and Lantolf 1985), and much of the level-typing of private speech overlooks the regulatory nature of the utterances so classified. In Kohlberg, Yaeger, and Hjerthalm's (1968: 707) work, for instance, wordplay and repetition are not considered regulatory, but this judgment is clearly incorrect since there is no more self-referential speech than wordplay, which is predicated on the acknowledgment of the limits of the linguistic code itself.

Levels of private speech are not a solution because it is not clear what the levels mean. They do not correlate with success, age, or even regulatory function. A more potentially fruitful tack would be to view all reflexive language-for-thought forms equally in their regulatory potential and focus on how they generate a speaker's position in a task because of their meta-functions. Rather than seeing the language for thought as essentially different because of its circumscribed, private, and abbreviated forms, we should look at what it appropriates—or *fails to delete*—from social discourse in order to execute its task of self-construction and management.

This broadening of what counts for language for thought points up a final clarification in work on private speech. When does the language for thought come into existence? The ages proposed vary widely. Vygotsky claimed that inner speech blossoms in the preschool and elementary school years (ages five to seven). Luria suggested that it occurs earlier, from three and a half to five years (Bronckart and Ventouras-Spycher 1979). But Fuson (1979: 149, 161) finds self-guiding comments at ages two and two and a half, as do Furrow (1984) and Smolucha (1992). My own son used regulatory, whispered self-speech at one and a half, telling himself during puzzle-solving things like "OK, there, just one." If we have to wait three years to develop metaconsciousness and control, we might wonder where our subjectivities are prior to that, and how we even start. But if the language for thought is built on all metaforms, and if these occur quite early, then, to return to the computer analogy, our content-oriented access keys emerge with all other speech: back at a point where representational architecture and code make initial contact with metarepresentational culture.

Much private speech research, despite claims to the contrary, appears to adopt implicitly the view that self-speech *represents* higher thinking and so metathought is read off the content of that speech. This view most certainly lies behind the generally unsuccessful attempts to correlate amount of private speech with performance. Private speech does not represent thought but is a *symptom* of it, and so, with respect to performance, reflects both failure and success (see Berk 1986). If anything is to be read off self-speech, it is the style of control, the run time of the operating system.

5.4 A Context-Architecture View of the Language for Thought

This reconstituted view of the language for thought in terms of reflexivity and reinterpreted private-speech research can be cast in the framework of architecture-context relations outlined in Chapter 3. Vygotsky provides an account of the (linguistic) background of thought; cognitive science gives a theory of internal representations. Architecture-context relations specify two ways in which the background can impinge on representations: predetermination by feedback, because the context is part of the architecture; and selection after the fact, because the context interfaces with the architecture. If reflexive language mediates context and code, then an architecture-context view turns on the relative contextualization of self-referentiality. How much of self-referentiality is coded directly and how much is left to inference? That is, how much of the language for thought is architecture and how much is context?

As we know, when a representation and its context are stored together as part of a whole, the context can feed back onto the representation and predetermine output; in this case, peculiarities of context are lost and processing is fast. In short, when context is the code, the architecture is essentially decontextualized. But when a representation and its context are stored separately, they have a computed relationship; here, context is selected after the fact, processing is slow, and peculiar features of the context are preserved. In this case, the representation is relatively contextualized. The difference between the two comes down to the processing work needed to compute independent factors: when a context and representation are coded together, their processing is relatively automatic, but when the two are coded separately, they must be computed separately, as must their interaction.

Reflexivity can be understood in the same terms. It may be coded directly into the semantic structure of a language, or it can be a contextual inference triggered by otherwise representational information. One lan-

guage may code metasemantic and metapragmatic implications into semantic representation, while another may assign them to context and leave
their determination to inference. The activity of metaconsciousness is thus
distributed differently in these languages because the mediational mechanisms require different inferential work for their speakers. For some languages, then, the sociolinguistic background of thought, embodied in self-
referentiality, impinges directly on architecture, making contextual control
rapid and predeterminate; in others, the background bears on thought in
a slow and selective way, as the information that mediates self-maintenance
is left to contextual implication.[2] The language for thought would then
have the attendant architecture-context effects.

Let us consider one clear example of how these differences might be
played out and what their effects might be on the construction of the
language for thought. Some languages have elaborate and productive systems of noun classifiers—forms that code the referential category to which
an entity belongs (Frawley 1992b has a full survey of such forms). In
Yucatec Mayan, for example, the expression *un-ciit chamal,* 'a cigarette',
is literally 'a one-dimensional thing: cigarette' (Lucy 1992a: 75). This
markedly contrasts with the coding in English, where the dimensionality
of the referent is not only unstated but never stated.

Important metafunctional differences hang on this coding contrast.
Yucatec Mayan allows its speakers to signal not only the truth of an expression (e.g., 'cigarette') but also the manner of truth, or how to locate
the truth of the expression. The classifier is a *metasemantic instruction* to
the hearer to access and search a particular referential category: 'find one-
dimensional things and then locate a cigarette'. Further evidence for the
classifier as a self-referential instruction can be seen in its discourse role.
When the referent of a nominally classified entity is known to the interlocutors and is, to use Chafe's (1974) terminology, part of their mutual
consciousness, the noun can be deleted and the reference tracked by the
classifier alone. Thus, Lucy (1992a: 75) points out that in a situation where
the Mayan interlocutors are speaking of cigarettes, it is perfectly appropriate to say *taas ten un-ciit,* 'bring me a one-dimensional'. Use of the
classifier to signal *the means to truth*—categoriality—is a sufficient instruction to the hearer here to recover the truth itself—the category member—
because both are coded.

Such metasemantic signaling and categorial access are entirely implicit
in English. Whereas Mayan metasemantic information about categoriality is part of the semantic representation—that is, the manner of truth

is coded with the truth—in English the same metasemantic instructions are relegated to inference. In fact, metasemantic categoriality in English looks very much like a conventional implicature of the nominal form. The inference that the referent of the word *dog*, for example, belongs to a certain kind of category seems to be given as a matter of the conventionality of naming itself (see Golinkoff et al. 1992). The two languages, therefore, differ in how they cut and code reflexivity, the fundamental element of the language for thought.

This contrast of Mayan and English suggests that it might be beneficial to focus the analysis of language-for-thought forms on the idea of conventional implicature since it stands on the line between code and context. As Levinson (1983: 130) points out, the double personality of conventional implicatures—as fixed meanings of lexical forms, but sensitive to variable discourse context—raises issues about their status as code. Are they in the architecture or in the context? Some theories accord them a kind of selected status and have context filter them out; these accounts work well for languages such as English, in which the forms have a clear contextual distribution. But in other languages, such as Japanese, in which the forms that trigger the implicatures are part of the regular and productive morphosyntax, an argument can be made for their incorporation into the representational architecture. Perhaps the answer is that they can be both, and the language itself determines how they fare in the general architecture-context relationships.

5.5   The Linguistic Structure of the Language for Thought

In this section we turn our attention to specifics of the linguistic organization of metaconsciousness. We look at the meaning, form, and function of six linguistic phenomena and consider their cross-language differences, their early use by children, and their role in the best empirical manifestation we have of the language for thought, private speech.

The last two points converge nicely in work on children's pre-sleep monologues, and offer some important lessons for analyses of speech and thought generally (Nelson 1989b). In self-talk, two-year-olds demonstrate productive control over a wide range of linguistic forms that, according to received accounts, are not supposed to be in their repertoire at this time, such as evidentials (Feldman 1989), tense variation (Gerhardt 1989), and endophoric reference (Bruner and Lucariello 1989, Levy 1989); more formal analysis of the monologues reveals early control over many grammatical operators. Thus, the analysis that follows illustrates not only how metaforms construct subjectivity, and, since one language's code is another's context, how this process varies by language, but also that this happens at a very early age with evidence readily available if we just look in the right places.

The early productive capacities evident in these monologues are very striking. Work in acquisition might significantly benefit from using naturally occurring private dialogue, rather than public dialogue, as a data base. The structure of interaction, in fact, suppresses many forms that young children have clearly mastered. When left alone, children fill in such forms and show remarkable competence: indeed, the mean length of utterance of Emily, the subject in Nelson's (1989b) book, is an incredible 5.4! This puts her at the end of grammatical development by traditional (dialogic) measures when she is in fact just two years old!

5.51 Predication

The structure of language in general provides universal constraints on the organization of self-speech. This circumscription of resources is especially clear in the way linguistic predication grounds and limits private speech.

Vygotsky argued that the essential structural characteristic of private speech is *psychological predication*. Drawing on the analogy of grammatical subject and predicate—traditionally associated with presumed and asserted information—he viewed overt self-regulatory speech as a kind of mental assertion about what is otherwise taken to be in consciousness and thus unsaid, that is, the psychological subject. (Wertsch 1985 interprets this distinction via the given/new organization of discourse; see section 5.52 for an alternate account in terms of discourse focus). He further argued that while grammatical predication is a useful analogy, linguistic and psychological predicates do not necessarily overlap, and so the structure of private speech cannot be read straightforwardly off linguistic form.

The nature of predication and the referential quality of private speech suggest, however, that Vygotsky's view is only partly correct. All psychological predicates are linguistic predicates, but not vice versa, and this convergence is traceable to the universal semantic and structural properties of predicates themselves. In this way, the language for thought turns out to be a kind of natural language since its properties are those of language generally. But thought and speech are not identical and come together just where mental content comes into focus for metaconscious use.

Universally, a predicate is a logical type that denotes a set of properties

(Chierchia 1985, Bach 1989). Under this definition, the words *chair, run,* and *blue* are predicates because they denote the properties of the world that count as 'chair things', 'running things', and 'blue things'—whatever those properties might be, given both the structure of the world and the culture in which the denoting takes place.[3] Logically, then, a predicate is a form that is referential; it collects properties of the world under a single term.

Predicates contrast with other logical types, such as functors, which do not denote sets of properties and so are not referential at all. Instead, functors map property sets onto other property sets (Barwise and Cooper 1981, Chierchia 1985). Consider the word *a,* which does not refer—that is, there are no 'a properties' in the world indexed by the word—but signals the union of all sets of world properties that could be collected under a single name. That is, when we ask what *a chair* might truly refer to, we see that it could be 'the set of all chair properties', since any chair, whatever its peculiar characteristics, will do. Formally, *a* is a function that converts a set of properties into the (union) set of a set of properties.

These logical observations have important ramifications for the structure and analysis of the language for thought. Wertsch (1985) has argued that referentiality itself motivates private speech, no doubt because the crux of self-speech is predication (= reference). Private speech *has to be referential* because it also *has to be predicative.* The inverse observation also holds. Because private speech is referential, there should be no self-talk composed entirely of nonreferential, nonpredicative forms. That is, the language for thought is constrained by a kind of "no functors allowed" rule.

Consider the well-known results from Wertsch's puzzle experiments, in which children putting together a puzzle of a car using a completed model as a guide utter the colors of the pieces needed at particular points in solving the puzzle: "Now purple. Purple . . . White. It's white" (Wertsch and Hickmann 1987: 263). These psychological predicates are also logico-linguistic predicates in that they denote sets of color properties. Similarly, in the private speech of a Spanish child drawing a picture, "la silla . . . la sill—— . . ." (Ramirez 1992: 206), the psychological predicate is again a logico-linguistic one.

What we do not find in private speech are only functors: no subject using English private speech says "the, the, the" or "is, is, is." No Spanish private speech contains just articles, "la, la, la." The language for thought thus appears to have structural limits: psychological predicates must be predicates in the logico-linguistic sense.

Three interesting ideas follow from these observations. First, since the distinction between predicate and functor is not the same as that between open- and closed-form classes, the language for thought cannot be assumed to delete closed classes and retain open ones. In fact, most adverbs (an open class) are functors, not predicates (see Chierchia 1985). Remarkably, private speech appears not to contain adverbs as its psychological predicates. Although I have no systematic data on this, my intuition is that private speech of the form "happily . . . happily" is ungrammatical, while "happy . . . happy," the adjectival (hence predicate) base of the adverb, would be acceptable.

Second, languages instantiate universal predication in different ways (Napoli 1989), thus affording their speakers different routes to psychological predication. Because private speech research has concentrated heavily on Indo-European languages, which are very much alike in their logico-linguistic predicates, all private speech looks pretty much alike. But non-Indo-European languages construe predication in unique ways. In Mandarin, for example, adjectives and prepositions behave more like linguistic predicates than they do in English, and this affects the way private speech is structured. The bilingual Mandarin-English children in Saville-Troike's (1988: 582) study, for instance, say things to themselves like *zhe da* (lit., 'this big'). This expression lacks the copula *shi* that appears in otherwise social discourse (*Exit shi chukou*, 'Exit is chukou', 1988: 581), since there the adjective *da* is sufficiently predicative to preclude *shi*. Indeed, when one child *has to assert* the predicative relationship between two nouns in his private speech, he uses *shi: zhong jian shi no parking de difang o,* 'the middle part *is* the no parking zone' (1988: 582).

Third, functors pattern differently from predicates by having no shortened proforms. There are pronouns *(it)*, pro-verbs *(did)*, and even pro-adjectives *(so)*, but there are no pro-articles or pro-quantifiers. Only forms that are referential to begin with support this kind of reduction in form. This limitation is important to the study of the language for thought because its manifestation in private speech is believed to be controlled by the abbreviation of form, with pronominals an uncontroversial cue to what is in and out of consciousness (Wertsch 1985). If pronouns are symptomatic of universal predication, the abbreviated form of private speech may be a result of its essential predicative structure, a logical matter, not a socio-cultural one.

Does this link between psychological and universal, logico-linguistic predication preclude a Vygotskyan analysis, otherwise allied with cultural relativism? On the contrary, the connection of the language for thought to universal predication anchors subjectivity in reference and thereby evokes an essential principle of Vygotskyan psycholinguistics. Speech for consciousness originates in the external world. It is no surprise that when such speech is reduced to its structural essence, as it were, the elemental connection of speech to the world—*referentiality*—is preserved.

5.52   Focus

For Vygotsky, private speech retains the psychological predicate at the expense of the psychological subject. Wertsch (1979, 1985) interprets this distinction via the information structure of discourse and shows that private speech retains new information and deletes the given. But he acknowledges certain problems in casting private speech entirely in transactional terms because, contrary to expectations, some given information is not deleted in private speech: "All of these utterances [pronominalized or partially deleted forms], then, present a seeming contradiction—they are used to mention new information, but their form meets criteria for given information or the psychological subject" (Wertsch 1985: 144). Wertsch's solution is to argue that the psychological subject—hence, information deleted in private speech—is what is semantically or pragmatically presupposed, and so structural abbreviation in private speech is a function of the contextual recoverability of reference. The implication is that what is retained is what is asserted, and so the presupposition/assertion distinction underlies private speech and hence the language for thought generally.

On closer analysis, however, it appears that the crucial discourse notion for private speech is not given/new but *focus*. The use of focus allows us to subsume Wertsch's arguments about presupposition without putting the issue as the presupposition/assertion split; it also accounts for the apparent retention of new information in private speech since focus and new information typically overlap.

Consider the following example of the emergence of private speech in a Spanish child completing one drawing task and moving on to another (after Ramirez 1992: 206; C = child, E = experimenter):

C: Voy a hacer los libros y la caja y la silla. (continua dirigiéndose al E)

E: Muy bien.

C: Voy a hacer . . . (continua dirigiéndose al E)
(E se aleja lentamente sin contestar, entonces C continua
hablando mientras comienza a dibujar y mira exclusivamente al
papel. Su voz va perdiendo intensidad hasta terminar en un
murmullo.)

C: . . . la silla . . . la sill—— . . .

C: I'm going to do the books and the box and the chair. (continues
directing himself to E)

E: Good.

C: I'm going to do . . . (continues directing himself to E)
(E goes off without answering, and C continues speaking while
he begins to draw and looks exclusively at the paper. His voice
loses intensity and ends in a whisper.)

C: The chair . . . the chai—— . . .

The difficulty of moving from one task to another here classically elicits
self-regulatory discourse from the child, who murmurs *la silla . . . la silla*
as he begins to execute the task. Note, however, that *la silla* encodes given
information, since it has already been uttered and is presupposed. Why
does it surface in private speech if it is both given and presupposed? The
answer is that it is in focus.

By logical definition, a focused item is presupposed as a variable and
asserted as the only item that satisfies that variable (Aissen 1992: 50).
Informationally, the focus bridges both given and new. It is simultaneously
an abstract placeholder signaling the existence of an item in prior discourse
(presupposed as a variable) and new information asserted to give content
to that placeholder in current discourse (satisfy the variable).

Consider again the Spanish example. The referent for *la silla* is presupposed (*voy a hacer algo*, 'I'm going to do *something*'). Indeed, Ramirez
(1992: 207) remarks that it has already been stated in the discourse. But
it is then asserted as the unique value for the presupposed variable (*algo
= la silla*). Here *la silla* is both given and new because it is both presupposed and asserted—it is in focus.

Why should focus be so crucial to the language for thought? For one
thing, the purpose of the language for thought is to provide the speaker

with the means to control subjectivity in the execution of a task, and private speech is the externalized symbolic expression of that means. The language for thought and private speech are the site of the convergence of speech and action, the very embodiment of Wittgenstein's problem. They concentrate the speaker's attention by positioning the subject in relation to the task. Focus is the linguistic correlate of these possibilities since it is the only form that can be externalized (asserted) to satisfy internalized (presupposed) prior social speech. Just like free indirect style, focus lies on the border between full public discourse and abbreviated private discourse because it signals the very information that links the unsaid with the said.

Another reason why focus is central to the language for thought is that it is classically reflexive. Focus can be understood as a kind of metapragmatic instruction to the hearer to recover a referent in prior discourse and then attend to upcoming discourse to fill out the details of that recovered referent (König 1991: 57). It is a way to code both prior and future speech at once.

As we might expect, different languages have quite different means for expressing reflexivity through focus. König (1991: 13) observes that the formal manifestations of focus include particles, prosodic salience, morphology, word order, and specific syntactic constructions. Some languages put the code to work; others leave it to contextual inference. These differences key alternate means to self-construction and self-maintenance.[4]

This is especially clear in languages in which focus controls certain grammatical facts and in those that explicitly signal focus through particles. We turn again to Spanish. The examples that follow are the simultaneous private speech of two children engaged in drawing pictures of their family members (after Ramirez 1992: 210–11):

M: Y sus manos. (habla mientras dibuja)

C: Mi mamá en la foto . . . (susurra mientras dibuja)

M: Y le hago un corazón. (continua dibujando sin mirar a C)
(Mientras dice *corazón* el movimiento de la mano acompaña al trazo con el lápiz.) . . . un corazón (añade al terminar la figura)

C: Su oreja. (dice mientras dibuja)

M: No. (contesta mirando a C)

C: Las orejitas. (continua dibujando sin mirar a M)

M: And her hands. (speaks while drawing)

C: My mother in the picture . . . (whispers while drawing)

M: And I make him a heart. (continues drawing without looking at C)
(While he says *heart*, the movement of his hand accompanies the tracing with the pencil.) . . . a heart (adds to the end of the figure)

C: His ear. (says while drawing)

M: No. (answers looking at C)

C: The ears. (continues drawing without looking at M)

The alternation of the article *(un/las)* and the possessive adjective *(su/sus)* in coding body parts reveals the construction of subjectivity. In Spanish, the unmarked means of expressing inalienable possession is the article, but both M and C use possessive adjectives, *sus manos* and *su oreja,* to signal possession in their initial speech about body parts. These expressions imply something like 'his and no other's'. This implication, moreover, is a conventional implicature of the possessive form. There is no truth-value difference between the article and the possessive. The latter form itself triggers the inference, making the significance of the *un/su* alternation for body parts very much like the status implication of the Spanish *tu/usted* and French *tu/vous* alternations (see Levinson 1983: 129–30).

The possessive forms in Spanish conventionally implicate *exclusive focus,* more particularly *exclusion of the complement* (see König 1991: 98). Thus, M's and C's private speech is better glossed here as 'his and only his hands/ ear and none of the rest of the set of hands/ears spoken about in the past and available to consciousness'. The Spanish possessive works very much like a discourse version of *only,* eliminating from consideration, by implicature, all but what is expressly stated. M's and C's assertions can therefore be seen as uniquely satisfying the presupposed variable of body parts by excluding all other alternatives.

What is important is that this use of focus affects the maintenance of self by the speakers in the task. Once M and C establish the singularity of the object of their drawing through focus, they both return to the unmarked forms in their private speech, *un corazón* and *las orejitas.* Their private speech for thought leads them to action by externalizing the unique verbal solution to the drawing task. The focus forms are symptoms of their position and self-consciousness in the task; focus tells these children that their current speech is a link between what has been said and done and what will be said and done, and so their future action lies in the reflexivity of their self-speech.

This way of focusing, and hence of allowing the speakers to position themselves through their speech in relation to their tasks, is a characteristic of Spanish and languages that allow focus through such formal contrasts. An English-speaking child, however, could simply not carry out his or her speech for thought in the same task in this way. Such contrasts emerge clearly in a comparison of focal pronouns in private speech.

Consider these data from Spanish (the same drawing task, Ramirez 1992: 207) and Mandarin (Saville-Troike 1988: 580, 582):

> M: Yo voy a dibujar a mi hermanito (mira a MF mientras habla) . . .
> pequeñito . . . a mi mama . . . a mis tíos (luego mira el papel y
> dibuja: la última parte, a mis tíos, se profiere en un tono de voz
> muy cercano al susurro). Yo tengo otro hermanito. (añade
> mientras dibuja)

> M: I'm going to draw my little brother (looks while speaking) . . .
> my mother . . . my aunt and uncle (then looks at paper and
> draws: the last part, "my aunts and uncles," is offered in a tone
> of voice very close to a whisper). I have another little brother.
> (adds while drawing)

> S2: (driving around on tricycle) Wo yao dao Chicago le ('I want to
> go to Chicago, and this is currently relevant').

> (playing in a private narrative) Ta jiu xie B, L, M, O, P, O ('He
> then wrote B, L, M, O, P, O').

Spanish and Mandarin are pro-drop languages: they allow deletion of pronominal subjects in their syntax but retain these pronouns under focus in discourse (see, e.g., Li and Thompson 1989: 657–75). Significantly, M's Spanish retains the first-person subject pronoun—*yo voy, yo tengo,* '*I'm* going', '*I* have'—and is therefore best glossed as a signal of M positioning himself as the unique actor in the task. Unmarked social speech otherwise requires the deletion of the pronouns. Analogously, S2 positions himself uniquely in the task by using the first-person pronoun *wo,* 'I'. His subsequent play narrative also focuses the subject *ta*, 'he', at the exclusion of other third-person actors. S2's private Mandarin is therefore better glossed as something like '*I* want to go. . . *He* then wrote . . .'

The point here is not that private speech in pro-drop languages is non–pro-drop since the speech in these language also deletes pronouns when focus is not called for. Rather, it is to emphasize that this option for positioning the pronominal subject explicitly and uniquely through focal contrast is not available to speakers of non–pro-drop languages. Speakers of English, German, Dutch, and French must therefore have other means for constructing subjectivity through focus.

A further cross-language contrast in these options can be seen in the availability and use of *particles*. German has a rich set of such forms (König 1991), and, interestingly enough, they have a central role in German private speech. Consider the data that follow, private speech uttered by a native-speaking German doing a translation task and searching for English lexical equivalents of German expressions (Zimmermann and Schneider 1987: 122):

> Zugaufenthalt . . . hm . . . ahm mit di ri . . . ah . . . ri na . . . wie heisst's hm denn noch ma . . . hm . . . ri . . . relay nee . . . layover layover oder . . . layover . . . quatsch . . . layover. . . doch beim Flug-zeug heisst das so . . . hm . . . na nehm ich das ma eben.

> Layover . . . hmm . . . uh with di ri . . . uh . . . ri . . . no . . . what does it mean . . . hmm . . . ri . . . relay no . . . layover layover or . . . layover . . . shoot layover . . . with an airplane it does mean that . . . hmm well that'll do for now.

In mentally searching for the English equivalent of *Zugaufenthalt*, 'layover', the speaker engages in self-regulatory discourse as he explores what he thinks he knows. He asks himself, *Wie heisst's denn noch ma* ('What does it mean?'), with two focus particles that signal the speaker's perspective and individuation in the task. *Denn*, as König (1991: 185) says, is a metapragmatic instruction to the hearer (the self, in private speech) to indicate that the question is relevant in the current context or that the question continues the perspective of the prior discourse. *Noch* focuses on expectation from prior assumed knowledge and signals that the information in focus is known. These two focus particles convey the speaker's sense of continuity from prior knowledge and discourse to the present discourse. Hence, a more accurate rendering of this segment of private speech is something like 'Given that I think I knew this word once, what does it possibly mean now in this current task?'[5]

The role of focus particles in positioning the speaker can be further seen in *doch beim Flugzeug heisst das so*. Here the speaker is trying to balance the association of *Zugaufenthalt* with train travel and his belief that the potential English equivalent, *layover*, is typically associated with air travel. German allows its speakers to code directly this conflict of perspective through *doch*, which conventionally implicates inconsistency between prior discourse and present assertions—more particularly, inconsistency between "earlier knowledge and the inability to remember" (König 1991: 182). Indeed, König (182) remarks that *doch* is found often "in self-addressed utterances like . . . *Wie heiss er doch gleich wieder* 'What was his name again?' "—that is, speech for thought. All these observations indicate that in this case, the language for thought is more appropriately glossed 'in contrast to what I have said thus far, I believe, on the basis of memory though I'm not sure and cannot exactly recall, that *layover*'s meaning relates to air travel, not train travel'.

There is analogous use of related focus particles in Dutch private speech to signal individuation, perspective, and the management of prior and future discourse. Goudena's (1987: 191) work on Dutch shows a subject saying to himself, *Oh ja, die wordt toch makkelijk* ('Oh, yeah, that one will be easy'): *toch* is the Dutch equivalent of German *doch* (König 1991: 173). The implicature of *toch* seems to point "forwards rather than backwards and the overall effect may be described in terms of creating agreement" (König 1991: 183). So the Dutch expression is best glossed as something like 'Oh, yeah, that one will turn out to be easy after all'.

German and Dutch give their speakers these particular means to externalize perspective and thereby come to terms with the task at hand. My intuition is that equivalent private speech in English would be quite different, carried out by stress, questions, or some combination of both. The closest rendering I can think of for the Dutch example would be something like *Oh, yeah,* THAT'll be EASY, with the implicatures keyed off the stress pattern, not lexically coded, and thus forcing the hearers into different inferential work. Likewise, in the Romance languages, which lack an equivalent class of focus particles (König 1991: 173, 201), these kinds of metapragmatic instructions for inference must be executed in a different way. These languages afford their speakers different regulatory means and hence different self-management possibilities.

If it is clear that focus plays a major role in speech for thought, we might wonder how, where, and when children first come to master these forms. While the implicatures associated with focus seem quite complex on the surface, they appear to pose no particular problem for very young children. Feldman (1989: 103) notes that the twenty-one-month-old in her study has a variety of attention-focusing devices which appear only in mono-logue. My own son had productive control of some focus markers by about eighteen months. He often sat by himself and put together puzzles and block towers, frequently saying to himself in whispered tones, "Just that! Only that." These English focus particles surfaced at points where he had to make crucial choices about the object in the task, and the speech at the very least accompanied, if not guided, his actions.

By age two my son had indisputably mastered one implicature of the exclusive focus particle *just*. To restrict his cookie intake, I often told him that he could have "just one." As I was giving him a cookie one day he said to me, "Just three," and held up three fingers. Now, as König (1991: 101–24) points out, when *just* is used in this way, with a scaled phenom-enon such as a numeral series in its scope, it has two conventional impli-catures. It can denote the exact value and at the same time implicate the exclusion of all values on the scale higher than the one asserted ('no more than'). Or it can denote the exact value but implicate the exclusion of all values lower than the asserted one and thus function as a kind of maxi-mizer, permitting values higher than the one denoted ('nothing less than'). So, when my son asked for "just three," what did he conventionally im-plicate?

He was using the focus particle in the latter sense. When he asked for "just three," I gave him one and then two. Each time, he was very upset and refused to take the cookies, saying with great emphasis, "just THREEEE." Then I gave him four, and he was perfectly happy. I asked him to count out how many he had, and he said, "One, two, three, four." So, four cookies met the truth of his request by being three, and they satisfied the maximizing implicature since more than three were permitted to count for three.

While these observations are admittedly quite informal, they nonetheless suggest a more important point. Children master the metapragmatic in-structions of focus quite early. The rudiments of the language for thought apparently coincide with the acquisition of language generally.

5.53 Evidentiality

Languages give their speakers a variety of ways to signal their epistemo-logical stances, attitudes toward information, and, in general, their viewpoints of, and in, the situation of speech (see Chafe and Nichols 1986, Frawley 1992b: 412–18). As the linguistic signal of a speaker's position and the relative subjectivity or objectivity of the information asserted, evidentiality is a natural correlate of speech for metaconsciousness.

Evidentials depend on self-referentiality and metafunction. Consider the following examples from Makah (a Wakashan language; Jacobsen 1986: 10): *wikicaxa-w,* 'It's a storm', and *wikicaxa-kwad,* 'I'm told it's a storm'. In each expression the root, *wikicaxa,* means something like 'bad weather', but Makah has a variety of suffixes that allow the speaker to code the source of the data and hence the potential credibility of the claim. The suffix *w* signals 'direct evidence', and so the first expression is more accurately glossed as something like 'It's a storm and I know it for sure because I have firsthand evidence'. In contrast, the suffix *kwad* signals 'knowledge from report', making a more accurate gloss of the second expression 'Others have told me that it is a storm'.

One way to think about these differences is in terms of trade-offs between ontology and epistemology, respectively, between what there is in the world (semantics) and how you know what there is in the world (metasemantics). The expressions have identical ontologies—both denote the same event—but they differ, as Silverstein (1985) might say, in the manner of truth. The suffixes are metasemantic instructions to the hearer to search referential space in a particular way to recover the denotation. The marker of direct evidence, *w,* assigns truth to the speaker and so also implies responsibility for the assertion; *kwad* assigns truth to others and so gives the speaker a kind of epistemological escape clause. The evidentials thus tell the hearer how to frame the meaning and interpret the denotation; in doing so, they refer to the system of referring itself.

These facts are observable in the evidentials in speech for consciousness from a wide range of languages. Consider these private utterances from Mandarin-speaking children aged three and four (after Saville-Troike 1988: 580–82):

a. Wo yao dao Chicago le
   I want to Chicago PRT
   I want to go to Chicago
   (more accurately: 'I will be in Chicago')

b. Ta de yinwen wo dou tai nan le
   he poss English I still too hard PRT
   His English is too difficult for me
   (more accurately: 'His English is simply too hard for me')

c. Ting a
   Stop PRT
   Stop!

d. Zhong jian shi no parking de difang o
   middle is no parking poss place PRT
   The middle part is the no parking zone

These utterances crucially rely on sentence-final evidential particles for their force and significance. The first two end with *le,* which signals that the state of affairs expressed has one of five types of current relevance (Li and Thompson 1989: 240–44): a change of knowledge, correction of a wrong assumption, report on progress, determination of subsequent action, or close of the speaker's total contribution to the discourse. Expression (a) carries much more specific information about how private speech constructs the child's stance than what the simple gloss suggests; it implicates any one of the following:

(i) I want to go to/will be in Chicago and I didn't want to/wasn't there before (change)

(ii) What do you mean? I want to go to/will be in Chicago (correction)

(iii) I have been wanting to go to/will have been in Chicago for some time now (progress)

(iv) I want to go to/will be in Chicago, so now I . . . (determination)

(v) So as I've said, I want to go to/will be in Chicago, and that's that (closing)

Speakers have five different positions for action through speech. Alternatively put, evidential *le* conveys five different metapragmatic instructions to the Mandarin self-listener to construct a stance.

The particle *a* has a similar analysis. The third private speech utterance, (c), has reduced forcefulness because of the final evidential (Li and Thompson 1989: 313). This form conventionally implicates friendly self-urging, and so (c) is best glossed not as a peremptory order, but as something like 'Hey, come on, stop, OK?'

The particle *o* in (d) conveys a friendly warning and concern on the part of the speaker. Hence (d) is a caring reminder and is probably best glossed as 'Let me tell you, the middle part is the no parking zone, OK?' The marker itself conventionally implicates that the private speech is used as friendly coercion.

Needless to say, this kind of speech for self is completely unavailable in this form to a speaker of English. Whereas speakers of Mandarin have at their immediate disposal a repertoire of code to construct and regulate the self in a task, speakers of English, because of how the language treats evidentiality, must use tenses, modals, and other devices to signal these kinds of positions and to indicate to the hearer to search context for the correct means to truth.

Most remarkably, children seem to master these evidential signals quite early. Turkish has two evidential suffixes for verbs in the past tense, *DI* and *mIş*, traditionally analyzed as coding, respectively, direct and indirect experience, but implicating associations about the speaker's conscious or unconscious knowledge (Aksu-Koç and Slobin 1986). For example, the suffix *mIş* signals the hearer to search the context for how and where the indirect experience lies on the speaker's fringe of consciousness (Aksu-Koç and Slobin 1986: 163). According to Aksu-Koç and Slobin (1986: 165–67), Turkish children younger than age two understand the complicated meanings and implicatures of these evidentials.

The same results emerge from an examination of the private speech of the two-year-old in the Nelson (1989b) study. Bruner and Lucariello (1989: 88–89) note that at twenty-two months, one-third of Emily's monologues have overt lexical markers of perspective and position, including affectives, epistemic signals, and metacommentary; five months later, two-thirds of the monologues have such forms. In a self-narrative to construct a coherent explanation of observed phenomena (in this case, a broken bed), twenty-four-month-old Emily says, "Actually the bed broken . . ." (Feldman 1989: 109). The positional signal *actually* here is quite remarkable and would never have surfaced in social dialogue, where the situation itself reduces the need for such overt marking of stance. When Emily says *actually,* she is indicating not only a change of state in the bed, but also her recognition of this change against the background of the beliefs she has heretofore fixed.

Not all of Emily's evidential marking, however, is keyed by the lexicon. At twenty-two months she also understands and uses the metafunctions of English tense and aspect. Gerhardt (1989: 186) observes that the simple present and the present progressive are distributed differently in Emily's narratives, with the former essentially confined to monologue and the latter to dialogue. The bare present in self-monologue is an indication of Emily's awareness of monologue as objectifying speech, or speech that adheres to some kind of norm; the progressive, in contrast, indicates that the speech and the events expressed therein are attributed, acted, and carried out. In short, the contrast between simple present and present progressive is connected to speaker stance: the former implies that the information is fixed and decontextualized; the latter indicates that the information is mutable and contextualized.

Interestingly enough, as Gerhardt (1989: 109) points out, it is not the fact of monologue or dialogue per se that conditions this difference, but the nature of the expressed knowledge and the narrator's judgment of the quality of the information represented. When the simple present appears in Emily's dialogue and the progressive in her monologue, they do so as a function of the relative objectification of the narrated information. This suggests two further points about the language for thought. First, self-report is not confined to monologue; it can be either monologic or dialogic, depending on its subjectivity or objectivity. This is an independent characterization of the otherwise Vygotskyan principle that inner monologue originates in dialogue. Second, even a twenty-two-month-old is consistent in the judgment of this distinction and can deploy the grammatical means her language affords her for implicating this judgment. The language for thought therefore begins in the early correlation of architecture and context.

5.54 *Person*

Markers of person—specifically, personal pronouns—are perhaps the most obvious building blocks of the language for thought. They not only code the holders of viewpoints and subjectivity itself, but are also an essential part of other phenomena that constitute speech for metaconsciousness, such as referentiality, information flow, and focus. It is these latter properties of pronominals, in fact, that motivate Wertsch (1985) to recast the traditional Vygotskyan account of private speech into the terms of modern discourse analysis. Less self-evident than their mere place in the language for thought, however, is the way personal pronouns might carry out the functions of speech for metaconsciousness. What they manifestly do not do is provide a way of simply reading subjectivity off language—as if, for example, gender and animacy in speech meant gender and animacy in consciousness. From such an idea it would be little more than a mincing step into the dead end of radical Whorfianism.

Harré and Mühlhäusler (1990: 11–20) put the matter of pronouns and subjectivity differently and more appositely to the language for thought. In their view, the grammaticalization of persons via pronouns mediates the influence of social relations on mental organization, or, as they more technically say, pronouns *index* persons—*not selves,* which are internal. Persons are external individuals, and so pronouns work the ground between public and private mind. Pronouns express, maintain, regulate, and create social relations; they intervene between society and mental structure on the issue of reference to discourse participants and so, like all else in the language for thought, are perched on the border of context and architecture.

The indexicality of reference to persons is reflexive because the content of the reference changes as the system of talk changes. Consider the pronoun *I*, which, in a piece of fiction, might refer to the author, the narrator, a character, a character reported by another character, a character's inner monologue versus public monologue, and so on (see Urban 1989 for discussion of subtle variations). Harré and Mühlhäusler (1990) put it succinctly by saying that personal pronouns are referentially empty and merely evoke concrete instances of persons; for them, a person is a double-sided construct, a spatiotemporal being with a point of view (something like 'the real person in physical space and time') and a placeholder in the network of rights and responsibilities that society builds around physical beings (something like 'the person as moral being').

When we say, then, that pronouns index persons, we mean that the grammar of a language has ways of instructing speakers and hearers to attend to a situational participant as both an empirical entity and an object of social forces and effects. This kind of description admittedly risks charges of hairsplitting and overtechnicalization, but it is in fact essential to the analysis of speech for metaconsciousness. For one thing, languages code and index differently the doubleness of persons. For another, individuals have to master the management of this split in order to regulate their own subjectivity.

Many languages have elaborate systems of kinship and honorifics to code directly the social status and position of discourse participants (e.g., Japanese, Korean, and Nepali; see Frawley 1992b: 105–21). Other languages have little or no coding in this regard and leave the determination of status and position entirely to contextual inference (e.g., English). In the middle are languages that code a few social facts, such as gender and position (e.g., German, Spanish). Harré and Mühlhäusler (1990: 273) note the consequences of this coding scale for the maintenance of subjectivity. Personal pronoun systems with significant coding tend to fix social roles more and provide their speakers with assembled packages of the person-as-social-construct. Indeed, these meanings appear to be conventional implicatures of the forms that code them and so are automatic, relatively decontextualized judgments (Levinson 1983). Languages lacking such code seem to accord greater flexibility in the determination of status, forcing speakers and hearers to compute the social facts, or, as Grice would say, calculate them, and so do more work to avoid ambiguity in the determination of social personhood. Hunt and Banaji (1988: 75) put the difference in more psychological terms: "Languages differ in *the amount of support* [my emphasis] provided for anaphoric reference," which in turn suggests differential working memory loads and differential influence on the mechanics, though not necessarily the contents, of thought (Hunt and Banaji 1988: 74).

These code-context trade-offs for person are complemented by alternate construals of the indexing itself and, consequently, different provisions for mediating mind and social relations via grammar. Many languages organize portions of their morphosyntax according to a hierarchy of the relative agency of the referents of the nouns and pronouns in the language (a so-called *animacy hierarchy;* see Frawley 1992b: 89–98). For example, some languages prohibit passivization if the resultant subject denotes an entity higher in intrinsic agency than the resultant object. But what counts for animacy and potency, and how does this differ by language? While cultures vary markedly on the intrinsic agency of nonpersons, almost all accord highest potency to the self, and the next highest to the other, and so rank the forms for 'I' and 'you' first and second on the hierarchy. But a small number of languages reverse this ordering and have the other, 'you', as the most intrinsically potent; hence they are *other-centered* or *tuistic*.[6]

Such other-centrism appears to affect the double-sidedness of the notion of person in these languages and cultures. Anthropologists have long noted the inclusiveness of the cultures that speak the tuistic Algonkian languages. Straus (1989: 67), for instance, remarks that in Northern Cheyenne, "the self is conceptualized as embedded in a web of relations with other persons": the 'you' determines the 'I'. Murdoch (1988) notes the explicit appeals to the group and the other in the organization of Cree culture, particularly in child rearing, the enforcement of social norms, and cognitive style.

These examples of other-centrism highlight the mediating role of grammar in personhood and return us to the basic conceptual split between 'person as entity' and 'person as social construct'. This split and its coding are recruited by children at a very early age in the development of the language for thought.

In her private monologues at twenty-one months, Emily exploits the indexical character of pronominal reference to make her self-speech internally coherent (Levy 1989). She uses pronouns to refer not only to entities and events constructed entirely in discourse, but also to phenomena that have no interpretable physical referent at all. The referential emptiness of pronouns appears to be no problem for very young children in their own early speech for self-control.

Similar remarks hold for the split between social and physical personhood. Gerhardt (1989) observes that Emily refers to herself in two different ways. In her explicit, monologic speech for self-consciousness, she calls herself *Emmy* and *my*; in her dialogues with others, however, she refers to herself as *I*. In Gerhardt's view, this difference signals two construals of the self. In dialogic public speech, Emily represents herself as a causal agent, an individual bringing about actions. Her simultaneous use of the progressive aspect in dialogue, as noted in section 5.53, further correlates with Emily's sense of herself in public speech as an active, changing, effective entity. In the monologues, however, she sees herself as an experiencer or a recipient of actions. Her use of the simple present in this private speech, again as noted in section 5.53, matches her sense of monologic self as an objective, norm-referenced, static entity.

All of this can be understood in terms of the larger picture of the doubleness of persons, which Emily appears to appreciate quite well. Dialogical Emily sees herself as a physical being in space-time and signals this in forms that code the active, effective self. But monological Emily portrays herself as the brunt of forces and effects, as a social construct. She is also learning the grammar of persons at this time and so takes the straightforward coding solution to these differences. She uses *I* to index the effective agent, the person as being, and her own name and *my* to index the person as constructed form. She must ultimately learn, of course, that English fuses both these indexes into the single form *I* and requires the speaker and hearer to calculate the particulars. Emily does learn this by thirty-two months, but at twenty-one months she codes the indexes separately, and, remarkably, uses the objectifying forms in the service of the speech she uses to drive her solutions to problems, to generate meanings and explanations, and to maintain self-control.

5.55 Discourse Markers

Languages have a variety of ways to bracket the speech event itself and signal the boundaries of units of exchange internal to that speech event.

These framing devices (Tannen 1993), or *discourse markers* (the term I adopt here; see Schiffrin 1987), are forms such as *oh, well, now, anyhow,* and *at any rate*. What makes them a natural class is that their domain of applicability is not the truth of speech so much as the way it is organized and attributed—its representationality (see Blakemore 1987).

Consider the expression *Oh, I thought you were staying at home*. The marker *Oh* appears to signal that the speaker recognizes some counter to expectation, and so the utterance means something like 'I am hereby signaling to you that my belief that you were staying at home has been controverted'. This effect comes about because the discourse marker is associated principally with the speaker and refers to prior discourse or knowledge. But it also reflexively signals the speaker proper since it is intended as a display, and to be taken as a recognition, of reversal of expectation. Other discourse markers can be given similar explanations: they signal the formal structure of discourse by calling attention to the speech itself, the persons to whom this speech is attributed or directed, and the level of exchange at which the speech applies (see also Goffman 1981 on *response cries,* quasi-word interjections such as *Oops!*).

Consider this private speech of an eight-year old putting together pieces of a railroad track (Feigenbaum 1992: 192): "Now . . . Let's see . . . a different road . . . yeah . . . This stays here. Okay! This one . . . No. This one sticks. Where are the straight ones? Oh, yeah. There it is. Okay. Wait! Can't go this way. There. There it goes . . . Hey wait! What did I do wrong? . . . a few more curves . . . should get this one . . . Now this goes around . . . There!" This monologue is characterized by the interplay of referential expressions, such as *this one sticks,* and discourse markers signaling the very execution of speech and action, such as *now, okay, let's see,* and *there*. These latter expressions do not pick out individuals or events in the world but apply to the *discourse as discourse*.

Now signals upcoming discourse focused on the speaker with the current moment of speech as an *initiation point;* for this reason it suggests a break in the flow of information (Schiffrin 1987: 228–46). *Let's see* signals the start of speech and action. *Okay* marks positive uptake or confirmation of a speech act. *There* signals completed speech or action and marks the speaker's removal from the speech event or action unit. Seen in these terms, the discourse markers punctuate the private speech by tying it to its context.

The indexical and reflexive properties of these forms emerge especially clearly if we try to interpret them in entirely truth-conditional terms. The discourse marker *Okay,* for example, has a truth-conditional counterpart, *yes*, which affirms the *content of prior speech*, not the communicative action or the speech event itself. We can see the difference in response to a proposition (content) that may also be an indirect speech act (action/event). If I say *It's cold in here*, and you respond with *yes*, you mean that you are affirming the truth of the proposition. If I intend the same utterance as a directive to get you to close the window, and *you agree to the action*, you are very unlikely to say *yes*; *OK*, the discourse marker, signals not only uptake but also that you recognize that the utterance is intended as an indirect speech act. Thus, if we substitute truth-conditional (non-actional) *yes* for *OK* in the private speech quoted earlier, the monologue sounds very odd: "This stays here. Yes . . . This one . . . No. This sticks . . . There it is. Yes." With *yes* the private speech is content-related and excludes the action necessary to self-management. With *yes*, the speech limits the speaker to a perspective within the events and takes on the air of a report or description. But with *OK*, the speech once again perches on the boundary between truth and action: it reaches out to context while simultaneously keying content.

This difference between *OK* and *yes* speaks to a more general point about the language for thought. The alternation of acceptable and unacceptable forms when the linguistic context is held constant means that there must be something like a system underlying the alternation, a *grammar of private speech*. Thus, private speech gives all evidence of being a surface manifestation of an otherwise abstract underlying system, the system of the language for thought.

This idea of a grammar of private speech supports Schiffrin's (1987: 327–29) observation that discourse markers can take a variety of overt forms, depending on the universals and particulars of the system of discourse marking. For example, Sissala codes the boundaries and salience of discourse units through freestanding particles (Blass 1990: 80–82) and signals echoic interpretive use, a clearly metapragmatic notion, through a discourse marker with a fixed position and a range of prosodic contours (Blass 1990: 97). Toba (South American Indian) signals the completion of discourse episodes by a variety of metapragmatic particles that also correlate with actional pauses (Klein 1986: 216). Unfortunately, there are no data on the private speech in these languages, but their social discourse structure suggests that they are the kinds of languages in which we could test hypotheses about the form of private speech varying with the resources made available to speakers by the language itself.

The best examples of discourse markers in private speech come from languages very much like English. Zimmermann and Schneider (1987: 123–24) note, for example, that the private speech of their German subjects is full of short forms restricted to initial and final position in utterances that signal speaker initiation or completion: *och, tja, also, so, ja, gut, okay, na gut,* and so on. In the middle of a lexical search, one of their subjects says, *Tja, was heisst no ma,* 'Well, what does that mean' (124). Like the English *well,* German *tja* focuses on the juncture between prior and upcoming speech, and signals that the speaker is also defining himself or herself as a listener (see Schiffrin 1987: 323). Thus, the German example is better glossed as something like 'So now that I've said this and will say that, let me tell myself so'. It is not surprising, then, that the subject uses this private speech at a point where he explicitly addresses himself as the recipient of an order: *warte ma,* 'wait a minute' (Zimmermann and Schneider 1987: 124).

Goudena's (1992: 220) studies of Dutch private speech also show the central place of discourse markers. Children in his puzzle-solving task frequently use the form *klaar* (finished) at the point of completion of the task. He analyzes this as abbreviated social speech, but it is clearly a metapragmatic device that signals both the end of speech and the end of action, much like the English *there.* Goudena's subjects are four to six years old, but at the age of eighteen months my own son had productive control over the English equivalent of the Dutch *klaar.* He often sat by himself solving jigsaw puzzles, and when he completed inserting pieces into their proper positions, he would say, in a muffled voice, *there,* or *there we go.* Unquestionably, he had mastered this discourse marker prior to age two and was able to use it to comment on, and guide, his own behavior.

Such bracketers are typical in speech for metaconsciousness and often occur at critical points in the speech-action overlap, places where new speech for action is needed or successful or unsuccessful speech for action has ended. These are points of difficulty and, in the classical Vygotskyan account, require overt mediation. It is thus no surprise that they surface at beginnings, ends, and transitions, places where executive control is necessitated (see Frawley and Lantolf 1985).

5.56 *Metalinguistic Markers*

The last structural feature of the language for thought that we will consider is metalinguistic marking, which allows the speaker to comment explicitly (and, to some extent, consciously) on speech or the speech system. While the structures and forms I have thus far described have a metalinguistic function, those we now consider *overtly display* the objectification necessary for speaker stance and control. These forms are direct signals of representationality.

Before we look at how metalinguistic forms work, we would do well to keep in mind two clarifications proposed by Gombert (1992). The first concerns the alignment of reflexivity, metalinguistic activity, and metacognition. The mere use of self-referential speech does not imply that such speech is put to the service of semiotic metacommentary and self-control. Metalinguistic activity is not coextensive with metacognitive activity.

The second clarification has to do with what counts for legitimate metalinguistic behavior. Gombert (1992) distinguishes *epilinguistic activity* from *metalinguistic activity*. Both involve cognition about language, and both are grounded in the system's own possibilities for self-reference, but only the latter requires conscious control. The distinction ultimately lies in the duality of the notion of 'meta' itself. On the one hand, the objectification, decentering, and distancing that accompany the mere use of a sign are "meta-activities" because they functionally differentiate referents and categories from the individuals that instantiate them. This kind of unconscious meta-activity is *epilinguistic*. On the other hand, there is deliberate, calculated cognition about language that requires reflection. Gombert reserves the term *metalinguistic* for this activity; it presupposes a capacity for self-monitoring and voluntary behavior.

In Gombert's (1992) view, the epilinguistic logically and empirically precedes the metalinguistic. The former is intrinsic to the system and built on the self referentiality of the code; it emerges with the first uses of language and has been documented down to the age of eighteen to twenty-four months. The latter emerges as a function of social and cultural facts; it typically appears in productive form at about six or seven years.

These clarifications return us to our project on three counts. First, we are interested in the properties of the mind's *control language:* whether these properties are epilinguistic or metalinguistic is less important than the linking of metaconsciousness to metasemiotic forms, a connection preserved—indeed, underscored—by the continuity Gombert proposes across unconscious and conscious control. Second, the developmental nature of the control language is crucial. If deliberate language for thought can be traced to the intrinsic, nondeliberate meta-activity of the system, so much the better. The control language has to begin somewhere: people are not immediately self-conscious, as Vygotsky always pointed out. Thus, while most of the children exemplified in this chapter use reflexive forms in private monologue to epilinguistic ends, they are no less "meta" because of it. Third, Vygotsky never linked the control language to strict chronology, and, as Gombert argues, epilinguistic and metalinguistic activity are in *décalage:* that is, given the right circumstances and need, epilinguistic activity may overtake an otherwise fully metalinguistic adult.

A look at the literature on private speech shows many instances of metalinguistic use that typify all these characteristics. Gombert (1992: 21–22) cites studies documenting metaphonological awareness at eighteen and twenty-four months. Indeed, at two years old, my own son made up new lyrics to songs he knew, modifying the syllable structure of the new words to fit the old melody. At the same age, my daughter transposed initial sounds of words in deliberate spoonerisms. Emily, too, also at twenty-four months, engages in metaphonological manipulation: "Raccoon . . . coon. Not rick. Rick, rac-, rac-, raccoon. Not rick. That raccoon. Not like rick" (Feldman 1989: 110). The bilingual Mandarin-English children in Saville-Troike's (1988) study organize their private metaphonological speech by language. Metaphonological manipulation even appears in psychotic adult monologues, long known for their self-directedness and control properties. Ribiero (1993: 98) describes a Portuguese-speaking subject who assumes the persona of a child and modifies the phonetic structure of her speech to reflect her new self. The alveolar flaps and trills characteristic of adult Portuguese become laterals, *senhora* → *senhola,* in the subject's monologues, an alternation typical of Portuguese child speech.

Private speech also capitalizes on explicit metasemantic marking. Gombert (1992) argues that episemantic behavior emerges at about age two—although there is evidence for epilexical behavior at twenty-one months (78)—with metasemantic activity following much later, at about age six or seven. Emily's private speech fits these parameters, though she seems to be closer to conscious control earlier than Gombert has argued she should be. In one monologue where she anticipates the visit of a friend, Carl, she states the converse relationship of the verbs *bring for* and *get (from):* "What if (for) Carl bring Dr. Seuss book for my. Maybe my get Dr. Seuss book from Carl" (Feldman 1989: 109). While it is not clear that this is a deliberate manipulation of the semantic system, it is nonetheless an explicit reference to the logical relationship between these two predicates. This interpretation is further supported by the metasemantic awareness Emily evinces in two monologues on identity. In one she sees her father as an instance of a type, differentiated from other instances of that type: "This is the kind of daddy . . . and this is the kind of daddy . . . but this is not my daddy cause it's funny Mommy gave that Daddy" (Feldman 1989: 110). In another she distinguishes her identity from identities she assumes in a game with her mother (in which she is covered by a blanket and thereby becomes "a mole"): "I don't like the mole . . . But mostly my like the mole, but not really like the mole . . . the baby don't know how, make a mole. But the baby mostly makes mole, but not really was a mole" (Feldman 1989: 111). Remarkably, in both cases Emily is twenty-four months old.

At the border between explicit metasemantic and metapragmatic marking are instances of metalinguistic negation. At age two my son reserved the first slot in his utterances for fixed expressions of metalinguistic rejection and modification. In both social and private speech he would say, "I don't want for some dinner" or "I don't want sing 'dee dee,' " the latter showing that the negative has scope not over the content of the expression but over the form. Drozd (1994) argues that this use of initial position for metalinguistic negation is widespread in social speech at the same age, and younger in many cases. His work also suggests that such metalinguistic negation is not a derivative of internal predicate negation, but one manifestation of the use of the sentence-initial slot for a range of metalinguistic modifications. Indeed, my son's social speech at twenty-eight months supports this view. He used the form *how about* as a fixed pre-sentential indicator of a change in information flow in discourse: "How about Mommy go?" In this behavior he was very much like Emily at the same age: "How about Lance bring book" (Feldman 1989: 109). It thus appears that these explicit metafunctions originate in social discourse, and so the objectification necessary for the language for thought can be traced, as Vygotsky argued, to social speech.

There is extensive evidence for overt metapragmatic marking at a similarly early age. Gombert (1992) locates the epipragmatic at the first sign of speech, twelve months or so, because even then children adjust their productions to truth and context. Conscious pragmatic activities, according to Gombert, surface like all others around the magical Piagetian age of six or seven. But a look at children's private speech shows access to conscious pragmatic manipulation much earlier than this.

My son reported actual speech to himself at about thirty months. He often played alone, engaged in long narratives in which he would state and modify the speech of imaginary others: "And then I said, 'Noooo.' " Identical behavior is found throughout Emily's monologues. At twenty-three months she says, "And Mommy came and Mommy said 'Get up/time go home' [alters her voice as if to mimic another's]" (Gerhardt 1989: 225). Nine months later she continues her use of reported speech forms, appropriating the actual voice of others: "My mom and dad says 'you can run in the footrace,' and I said 'that's nice of you. I want to' " (Feldman 1989: 112) and "But my mommy and daddy . . . thought about it and said 'I don't think it's okay cause your Mormor says it's not okay' " (Feldman 1989: 115).

These examples are remarkable for both their explicit metapragmatic marking (through framing devices such as verbs of report and prosodic modification) and their early appearance. In Hickmann's (1993) study, such metapragmatic behavior does not productively manifest itself until around age seven and certainly not before age four. Perhaps the contingencies of monologue are at work here, since Hickmann's data were gathered in a dialogic format. But monologic speech for metaconsciousness suggests that much more may be going on in a child's private mind than we are likely to allow unless we let the children (literally) speak for themselves.

Finally, overt metanarrative markers also appear to structure private speech. At thirty-three months Emily engages in a *monologue about how to make monologues,* and in it articulates "the instructions for how to construct monologues for fantasy play: 'So they can be . . . And anything they wanna be . . . bisons . . . or anything. Bunny rabbits they could be, or anything. They could, but there's no bunny rabbit' " (Feldman 1989: 116). Here Emily unquestionably demonstrates that she knows the rules for making a certain narrative genre—that is, fantasy speech allows anything to be anything—and can state this rule explicitly. For this reason, Levy (1989: 155) claims that monologues are essentially metalinguistic exercises in a "developmental workspace," a place where a child can run though her knowledge of the code in an explicit way and solve the issues of representation without any of the pressures of public discourse in real life. This is practice in representationality.

Levy's (1989) point about the ultimate nature of speech for the self in young children evokes a broader construal of the language for thought and brings us back to the whole idea of computational run time, the control language, and mental orientation. As Nelson (1989a), Bruner and Lucariello (1989), and Feldman (1989) point out, Emily uses her monologues as problem-solving talk for the self; she is trying to make sense of her experience and order it through self-speech. More succinctly, she is trying to construct *a theory of her experiences*. Likewise, adults in the throes of cognitive breakdown deploy the language for thought to regain the balance of the self and reestablish their private theories about the facts at hand.

As is well known from the philosophy of science, a metalanguage is essential to the construction of such theories, and questions and answers are part of the metalanguage of theory building. Unsurprisingly, classic examples of the language for thought—the mental control metalanguage—are frequently structured around (self-directed) questions. A four-year-old bilingual Mandarin-English child, playing with a peg game, asks himself *Zhe da bu da?* 'Is this big?' (literally, 'This big not big?'; Saville-Troike 1988: 581). The A/not A form of the self-directed question is significant. In Mandarin, the A/not A form signals that the speaker is not predisposed to a particular answer and intends the question as a genuine request for information. This contrasts with other ways to ask questions, such as the sentence-final particle *ma*, which is compatible with a speaker's expectation about a possible answer (see Li and Thompson 1989: chap. 18). By using the A/not A form, the child is literally posing a real quandary to himself, one that requires an informative answer. Remarkably, no question in the monologues uses the *ma* form. So the child is arguably building a private theory here about the peg game by asking real questions with real answers via the mediational means Mandarin affords him.

Such private theory construction could not be carried out in the same way in an English control language, which sets quite different parameters for the asking of real information questions. What better illustration than this of the nature of speech for metaconsciousness and its dependence on the E-language/culture in which it is embedded and from which it is derived?

5.6   Computational Control and the Symptoms of the Machine Self

Up to this point I have discussed the nature, linguistic structure, cross-language manifestations, and development of the language for thought. Here I turn to the computational analogues. If our purpose is to develop a Vygotskyan cognitive science, we have to articulate the correspondence between computational representation and sociocultural, metacomputational representationality. There appears to be a natural connection in the way programming languages code and direct computational flow.

5.61 Who's a Vygotskyan?

Discussing the important but often unexamined role of control structures in mental computation, Pylyshyn (1985: 81) remarks, "Remembering often consists of arranging the environment to trigger appropriate processes at appropriate times. People used to tie knots in their handkerchiefs or set up unusual situations to act as general 'metareminders.' " This quote from a standard work on computational mind could have been taken verbatim from a standard work on sociocultural mind, Vygotsky's *Mind in Society* (1978: 51): "When a human being ties a knot in her handkerchief as a reminder, she is, in essence, constructing the process of memorizing by forcing an external object to remind her of something; she transforms remembering into an external activity." How could theorists so separated in space, time, and scientific ideology hit on the same argument in the same words? Is Pylyshyn a Vygotskyan?

The two converge on matters of mental control. For Vygotsky, the language for thought, in its minimal manifestation as private speech, provides external signals for recall, metareminders that regulate behavior by objectifying the task and tools. For Pylyshyn, one crucial aspect of mental computation is how the flow of data can be affected by external factors, so-called *interrupts,* and handled by mechanisms dedicated to control (see also Sloman 1993).

Two concepts of control organize the discussion that follows. The first is computational control proper, or the flow of execution in a program to sequence information, handle exceptions, and monitor subroutines, co-routines, and concurrence. The second is the by now familiar frame problem, not normally understood as a control issue (Hayes 1987) but which, as I will argue, can and should be.[7]

5.62 Control

Computational control concerns "the order of evaluation of expressions or of larger program units" (Fischer and Grodzinsky 1993: 249). Control specifies how information is managed or passed between instructions or chunks of instructions; it includes response to breakdown, since this is also a matter of data flow, whether from a failure internal to the program (e.g., a violation in the syntax of the code) or from an external disruption (e.g., a user-initiated interrupt).

Control is usually thought of as applying to computing via traditional programming languages (Pascal, C, etc.) and so is associated with the flow of the interior code or the language of thought, broadly construed. Connectionist systems are not typically given to control issues, but since they are generally network simulations written in symbolic code, they have information flow and can, like Turing machines, be said to instantiate instructions (Adams, Aizawa, and Fuller 1992). It is important not to dismiss control as a property of symbolic models only, especially when the line between symbolic and subsymbolic systems is ever more tenuous and productively compromised.

Kowalski (1979a, 1979b) argues that algorithms are composed of two distinct kinds of information: logic (data structures and procedures) and control (the manner in which the data structures and procedures are used). The former are the abstract terms and operations that define the information to be manipulated. The latter are the strategies of choice, direction, and execution of procedures. For example, in the programming language C, the term *int* represents a type of variable, integer, which can be given an arbitrary name, *int thisInt,* and assigned a value, *thisInt* = 5. These are matters of the logic of C. But this information can also be organized with respect to other aspects of the logic of C, by the terms *if, then,* and *else,* for example. These mark the flow of the data processing, not information per se, telling the machine how and when to evaluate statements. They are ways the language C allows users to organize instructions and direct the flow of computing.

Kowalski's separation of knowledge from its efficient use has two important consequences for control as an analogue of the language for thought. First, it is possible to modify the overall behavior of a system by changing *either* its logic or its control because they are essentially independent factors. Consequently, they can be dissociated, as in the unfortunate natural experiments of control disorders and aphasias described in Chapters 3 and 6. The language *of* thought is separable from the language *for* thought. Second, control can be implicit or explicit, depending on the programming language and the style of the programmer. As Kowalski (1979a: 429) writes, "The control component can either be expressed by the programmer in a separate control-specifying language, or it can be determined by the system itself." That is, control over the flow of code can be more or less a property of the code itself, depending on the trade-off between the *architecture of the code* and the programmer as a factor of the *programming context*.

In Chapter 5.5, I observed that the human control language is structured around the metarepresentational resources of language. Interestingly enough, *just as human representational control is metarepresentational, so computational control is metacomputational.* The *if/then/else* statements of C, for instance, instruct the program about how and where to search for other aspects of the program. In the same way that metasemantic and metapragmatic markers reflexively cue hearers to properties of the system and speech event, so control statements do not define data but refer to other statements and expressions in the program. They signal the manner of computation rather than the information computed. Human metarepresentational control positions an individual in a task; metacomputational procedures specify the machine's position or stance with respect to its own data structures. Control is the machine's processing style via its program.

5.621 A CATALOGUE OF CONTROL STRUCTURES

Control structures can be classified in a number of useful ways (see Fischer and Grodzinsky 1993: 248–310, Ghezzi and Jazayeri 1987: 173–223, and Teufel 1991: 69–87). There is a fundamental split between machine-level control, defined by the operation of the hardware, and high-level control, built out of and implemented in terms of machine-level control but nonetheless peculiar to the programming language itself (what Sloman 1993 calls *control of the virtual machine*). Booting a computer, for example, is a machine-level control process that instructs the machine to load the operating system and transfer control to it. Machine-level control is a hardware constraint on data flow determined by logic circuitry. The human machine—the brain—has this sort of control in the biological, wetware constraints on data flow. Thus, Pribram (1990) remarks that seriality, which characterizes all neurocognitive information flow, can be disrupted by a lesion anywhere in the brain (= machine). Wetware-level control, such as booting, executing, and seriating, appears to be part of basic consciousness.[8]

But frontal area lesions and trauma, of the sort discussed in Chapter 3, appear to affect computational flow at a different level. It is here that explicit, high-level computational control lies. High-level control structures come in two types, generally known as *statement-level* and *unit-level*.[9] The difference concerns the amount of code to which control applies and the range of its effects: statement-level control is local and affects individual statements and expressions in the program, while unit-level control is more global and affects chunks of a program or collections of statements and expressions. Significantly, just as the language for thought is *meta-representational,* so these high-level control operations are *metacomputational.* They signal the manner of computation rather than the information computed. The analogy, then, is that programming languages, like human representational systems, have a metafunctional vocabulary of control.

5.6211 Statement-Level Control Control at the statement level comes in three types: sequencing, selection, and repetition. Sequencing is the basic conjoining of code, and is not usually considered in detail in programming languages because its organization and effects are pretty much self-evident. Nonetheless, sequencing can be explicitly marked in a programming language, and groups of sequenced statements can also be bracketed so that serial data flow may be controlled by explicit metacomputational procedures. In Pascal, for example, the end of a statement is signaled by the semicolon, which also is a metainstruction to the machine to process the statements between the semicolon in sequence (see Ghezzi and Jazayeri 1987: 173–74).

Selection is the way choices among alternatives are managed in a program. There are two selectional control structures, *conditional* and *case,* and their use and form depend on the programming language in which they appear. The conditional comes in an *if/then/else* form and is composed of one or more conditions *(if)*, and, for each of these conditions, an expression or statement (see note 9) to evaluate if the condition is true *(then)* or false *(else)*. The exact control effects of the conditional depend on the nature of the code in a particular programming language. In functional languages, such as LISP, the information to be evaluated is always an expression (again, see note 9), and the conditional can be embedded in other code (technically, *nested*), producing a hierarchically structured, embedded conditional. But languages that lack conditional expressions— that is, have conditional statements—manage selectional control in a sequential way; in Pascal, for example, the conditional is a statement, not an expression, and so it communicates with the rest of the code *via the program environment,* not the memory stack. The larger point is that these code variations result in very different programming styles and on-line behavior as a function of how conditional control organizes the information flow (see Fischer and Grodzinsky 1993: 257–58). The analogy to natural language should also be clear: if the metarepresentational aspects of natural language are the mental control language, then differences in natural languages in this respect ought to have differential effects on mental information flow.

The second conditional control structure is *case*, "a structured control statement with multiple branches that implements this common control pattern in an efficient way" (Fischer and Grodzinsky 1993: 264). Suppose that a program has to do a number of actions that all depend on the value of a single expression (e.g., produce a number of outputs depending on the numerical value of a variable). Every time the program has to perform one of the actions, it has to reevaluate the expression, which is costly in computing time. To trace the multiple actions back to the single expression in an efficient way, *case* evaluates the condition only once and specifies in a single collection the multiple selections that depend on this evaluation. *Case* is thus a generalized and compact conditional control statement. Again, the natural language analogy should be clear: how do the metarepresentational resources of a language link multiple options to a single condition without forcing the individual to return to the condition each time?

In addition to selectional control, there is also repetition. Because computations must often be repeated, programming languages have ways to control this iteration, or *looping*. One way is via *counterdriven* loops, whereby repetition is controlled by a range of values that monitor reentry into the loop. For example, suppose that every time the program receives a value between 1 and 10, you want it to print out a certain result. This would require the program to loop through the integers from 1 to 10 and compare its current value to that set to determine the proper course of action. Counterdriven loops control such iteration by having it range over a finite set of values (e.g., *for* in languages such as Pascal or Basic).

Suppose, however, that the length of the data structure that controls the loop is not known. Suppose that whenever some kind of condition holds, you want the program to repeat one or more actions. This requires a *conditional* loop, which bounds the cycle of repetition by language-specific, iterative metamarkers and states the actions to be repeated. You might, for instance, want the program to repeatedly read the contents of a file and then print out what it encounters until it reaches a particular piece of information, say, the end of the file. Examples are the *repeat/until* loop in Pascal and the well-known *while,* both of which are metacomputational signals of reentry into the loop.

The natural language issue that arises here is the way metarepresentation and the language for thought allow individuals to manage iteration and simultaneity. One function of metamarkers might be to bound the cycles of repetition and indicate not only which information can be repeated under certain conditions, but also the very fact that the conditions and the cycle itself can occur at all.

5.6212 *Unit-Level Control*   In addition to having a vocabulary for controlling computation among individual statements, programming languages also have resources for controlling the flow of computation across entire sections of code, or what are otherwise known as *program units*. Unit-level control typically subsumes two situations, those where some program unit is called into operation and control is passed to that unit; and those where computing breaks down and control must be passed to some unit designed to recover and return control either to a program unit or to the user.

There are three kinds of program units that are involved in the first situation: subroutines, coroutines, and concurrent routines. A subroutine is a subordinate, coherent chunk of code that is explicitly invoked by a program, and to which control is transferred at the time of invocation. After the subroutine is run, control is transferred back to the main program which initially called the subroutine. Subroutines are the standard means of breaking a complex problem into manageable units for solution, and programming languages usually have a very straightforward vocabulary for invoking them: some kind of metacomputational instruction, such as Fortran's CALL, with the subroutine named and called as a unit.

One way to think about a subroutine is as a piece of code that is going to share data with the main program and operate on it in a specialized way to particular ends, which in turn requires some mechanism to ensure informational coherence between the data shared by the main program and the subprogram. This is done by *parameter passing:* the transfer of specific data between the main program and the subprogram. There are a number of ways to pass parameters, and these result in different styles of control. For example, the main program can pass the actual value of a parameter to a subprogram, a process known as *call by value,* whereby whatever changes the subprogram makes to the inherited data remain within the subprogram. There is also *call by reference,* which passes the memory address of the data, not the actual value, and thus achieves coherence more abstractly; the subprogram can change the value of the inherited data and send the change back to the main program because it operates on the level of the abstract address, not the actual data.

The importance of different types of parameter passing for the language for thought is that it gives us ways to think about the coherence of processing across mental domains and how the mental control language might facilitate its management. Human mental computation uncontroversially requires the invocation and management of subroutines, but how does the control flow and how is the information shared? Do subroutines communicate with the main program via actual data or abstract addresses? This is not an idle question because control aphasias suggest something like the latter. Patients who suffer from representational leakages (see Chapter 3) appear to be unable to control the values of the data from one task to the next. For instance, when asked to draw a circle and then a colon, they often produce a colon composed of two circles. Suppose that the main program is "draw," and the subroutines are "draw circle" and "draw colon." If the property of openness in the circle subroutine has been transferred to the main program of drawing and then passed on to the colon subroutine, the proper disordered behavior would result. In other words, the computational details of parameter passing and communication across subprograms might be a way of making sense of disruptions in the management of knowledge domains that characterize certain disorders.

There are ways of sharing data and having the computation flow across program units other than by subroutine. Suppose the main program and the subroutine partially activate each other. In this mutual invocation of code and symmetric transfer of control, known as a *coroutine,* computational control does not have to be totally passed over from one chunk of code to another but can be managed in a piecemeal trade-off, as long as there is an adequate metacomputational vocabulary for overseeing the mutual alternation (e.g., the programming language Simula 67 manages its coroutines by two such signals, *new* and *detach;* see Ghezzi and Jazayeri 1987: 203).

When part of a coroutine is activated and control is passed to the coroutine, the passing program is suspended. But suppose that when code is partially activated and two program units share data, the original code does *not have to suspend operation.* This asymmetric control across program units is known as *concurrence;* it is one way a serial processor can imitate parallel processing. As might be imagined, the management problems of concurrence are enormous. If two program units share data, and if each unit is partially activated and continues in activation while the other executes its procedures, how is the run time synchronized? The answers depend on where the programing language places the burden of control. For instance, the language might have an explicit signal in the respective program units to turn procedures on and off and synchronize processing, technically known as a *semaphore*. Or it might have a special program unit to oversee the shared data and access to it, a *monitor*. Or it might have the units involved signal each other as they operate so one can delay sharing data until the other is ready to allow it, a *rendezvous*.

The issue here for the language for thought is how human computation manages computational flow across domains that need to share data. Is there a separate monitor? Do knowledge domains signal one another? Answers to these questions may in turn depend on the architecture-context relations in the language for thought. Where metarepresentation is coded and so is part of the whole of the representations, control across domains may look more like a rendezvous or a semaphore; in places where metarepresentation is inferred and so is not a part of the representational system as such, control may look more like a monitor. As a separate control unit, a monitor should operate and break down differently from a semaphore or a rendezvous. In the end, these are empirical issues. Indeed, Sloman (1993: 85) argues that the analysis of human mental control must go well beyond "parameter adjustment" and address matters such as time sharing, the internal updating of knowledge domains, and more complicated issues of the interaction of knowledge structures. At present there are no observations or experiments in this regard.

We have seen three ways in which program units share data and manage control. What happens when computing breaks down and control must be reestablished? This is the problem of *exception handling*. Such breakdowns, or *interrupts*, have a number of causes. Some are hardware interrupts, as, for example, in an attempt to divide by zero; others are software interrupts, as, for instance, in reaching the end of a file or illegal code; still others are user interrupts, as in a request for a nonexistent file. In such cases, how does computing cope?

The nature of control under breakdown *depends on the programming language* (Teufel 1991: 84). What manifestly cannot be done is to ignore the interrupt, as some programming languages do for certain kinds of errors, because this can lead to disaster as the effects of the error accumulate, propagate, and ultimately surface. The usual solution is an *exception handler*, or a piece of code that is designed to respond to specific interrupts, transfer control appropriately, handle the exception, and resume computing. In some languages, when an interrupt terminates computing, control is passed to the exception handler, which resolves the problem, and returns computing to the point where the interruption occurred. In others, computing is terminated and the exception is handled, but computing does not return to the point of the interrupt. These two strategies naturally have different effects and place quite different demands on the system and user.

Again, issues of the language for thought come to bear immediately, especially here because private speech, inner speech, and metaconsciousness are intimately connected to cognitive breakdown. The language for thought surfaces when mental computing reaches impasses, and so one way to understand Vygotskyan theory is as an account of exception handling and the flow of control following interrupts. Does the language for thought terminate computation and force the speaker/thinker to resume computing outside the place of the interrupt? Can the language for thought terminate computing but return the speaker/thinker to the point of interruption? My feeling is that there are both kinds: boundary makers that signal severe breakdown and massive shift of attention; and continuation markers that indicate less severe breakdown and allow the individual to resume at the point of interruption. Different natural languages will also have different metarepresentational resources for implementing these kinds of error recovery.[10]

5.622 LANGUAGE FOR THOUGHT CORRELATES OF COMPUTATIONAL CONTROL

Kowalski (1979b: 129) observes that *natural language expressions*, such as computational algorithms, also separate logic from control. "The sentence 'If you want Mary to like you *then* give her presents and be kind to small animals' combines the declarative information 'Mary likes you *if* you give her presents and are kind to animals' with the advice that it be used top-down to solve problems of being liked by Mary to subproblems of giving her presents and being kind to animals." That is, the sentence signals both the information to be computed and the manner of computation, the latter by what we have elsewhere seen as metadiscourse signals of coherence and sequence (Chapter 5.55). What Kowalski argues in computational terms is otherwise a standard Vygotskyan socio-psycholinguistic claim: speech signals its truth and its perspective simultaneously, since language for thought forms appear side by side with forms for representational speech.

So how do the language for thought forms outlined in section 5.5 bring about the computational control effects we have seen in section 5.621?[11] A number of language for thought forms sequence information. One of the purposes of discourse markers, for instance, is to signal transitions across information states and to ensure both continuity and explicit marking of divergence. All languages have a default sequencer, the generic *and* of programming languages, but they also have a variety of more specific stance-related sequencers. Sissala (Blass 1990) has many discourse-level conjunctions that not only sequence information but also convey the manner of the sequencing: *ka* indicates sequencing of information that is *unexpectedly* conjoined. Hence, Sissala affords its speakers metarepresentational forms that effect both default and situation-specific sequential control.

Similar remarks hold for certain metalinguistic devices. Metatextual markers and reported speech forms sequence information by evoking it directly and citing it in the present context. Indeed, Bruner and Lucariello (1989) and Levy (1989) argue that these metalinguistic sequencers are the early signs of narrative and dialogical coherence in the speech of young children. Moreover, as we have seen, these forms surface early, and play a critical role, in children's self-directed monologue for cognitive control.

Selectional control seems to be particularly productive in the language for thought, with natural language exhibiting a variety of forms to signal choices and reasons for those choices. Perhaps the major linguistic device in this respect is the evidential, which, as we have seen, functions as a metasemantic instruction to the hearer to search the available choices in a referential space and make a selection on the basis of perspectival information. Evidentials signal the motivation for a choice of information at the expense of other information and thus work very much like computational control via *case*, where options are set out in an array under conditions to be met for their selection.

Consider, in this regard, the variety of meanings of the child's Mandarin private speech in section 5.53, *Wo yao dao Chicago le,* meaning:

1. I want to go to/will be in Chicago and I didn't want to/wasn't there before. (change)
2. What do you mean? I want to go to/will be in Chicago. (correction)
3. I have been wanting to go to/will have been in Chicago for some time now. (progress)
4. I want to go to/will be in Chicago, so now I . . . (determination)

5. So as I've said, I want to go to/will be in Chicago, and that's that. (closing)

These glosses constitute a multiple-branching choice space, keyed by the evidential marker *le*. Change, correction, progress, determination, and closing are the conditions that have to be met for each case to apply. *Le* is rather like a computational signal to begin searching the space 'I want to go to Chicago' with five cases and their conditions at hand. What is important here is that this kind of selectional control is carried by a meta-representational device that has been independently shown to be crucial to the structure of human mental control language.

Programming languages have a number of ways to monitor the passing of control from one computational domain to another and, in the process, to keep track of access to information shared by these domains. One way to think about focus, which we know has a seminal position in the language for thought, is as a device to manage the crossing of knowledge domains. Focus forms signal the existence of a piece of information in prior discourse, translate this information into a discourse variable, and then assert the information as a variable to be given a value in the present discourse. Seen this way, focus looks very much like call-by-reference parameter passing: presupposed information is passed into the present discourse as an address, not as an actual value; present discourse then operates on this information, even changes its value, and then passes this change back into the discourse. Thus, in terms of control, focus does not code the mere inheritance of past information by the present, but *mediates the active modification of data shared by the past and present.*

Consider again the German private speech from section 5.52:

> Zugaufenthalt . . . hm . . . ahm mit di ri . . . ah . . . ri na . . . wie heisst's hm denn noch ma . . . hm . . . ri . . . relay nee . . . layover layover oder . . . layover . . . quatsch . . . layover . . . doch beim Flugzeug heisst das so . . . hm . . . na nehm ich das ma eben.

> Layover . . . hmm . . . uh with di ri . . . uh . . . ri . . . no . . . what does it mean . . . hmm . . . ri . . . relay no . . . layover layover or . . . layover . . . shoot layover . . . with an airplane it does mean that . . . hmm well that'll do for now.

Here the speaker is trying to manage the presupposed association of the meaning of *Zugaufenthalt* with train travel and the meaning of its

English equivalent, *layover,* in the asserted context of airplane travel. The focus markers *noch* and *doch* pass the train travel sense into the present as a variable, and German allows its speakers to mark it in contrast to expectations—a potential change of value. Indeed, the speaker then changes the value of the equivalent and so asserts *layover* in its association with airplane travel. *Layover* can then be reinserted into the discourse with its proper change of value.

Even though focus can work like call-by-reference parameter passing that changes the value of a parameter and returns this changed parameter into the main program, it is not obliged to do so. There are plenty of instances of focus behaving like call by value, in which the present discourse shares past data in actual form. The examples from Spanish private speech in section 5.52 are illustrations. Here the children reassert presupposed information in its past form; this is focus with no counter to expectations.

Person markers might also be seen to work this way. At the local level, they bring about cohesion by indexing or tracking individuals across information states. When the individual remains the same from state to state—that is, when the value for the pronoun as a variable is passed directly from one state to another—languages use a typical range of devices to signal this continuity. It is possible, however, for the value to change across states, and again languages provide mechanisms to signal this, much as they have focus markers that indicate change of expectations. Perhaps the most well known such device is switch reference, which is a means to signal, across clauses, the discontinuity of individuals grammaticalized as the subject.

At the discourse level, too, the marking of person can signal continuity or divergence across information states. Givón (1983) has shown a correlation between referential form and continuity of topic across chunks of discourse. So, insofar as thematically unified sections of discourse constitute separate computational domains, languages provide mechanisms to monitor and track individuals as data structures shared by these domains.

A final and very important area where computational control and the language for thought converge is in breakdown and the handling of exceptions. One of the clearest and most uncontroversial functions of private speech is to signal that mental processing has reached an impasse and that the system is seeking recovery. In the Vygotskyan framework, breakdown requires that the system *pass control outside itself and into context.* This is another way of understanding what is meant by the Vygotskyan vocabulary of other-regulation and object-regulation in times of difficulty. A self-regulated individual uses an internal metacomputational control vocabulary to direct computing; an individual in processing distress must externalize control and elicit contextual help for recovery. In Vygotskyan theory, *an individual passes control in order to recover control.* In this matter there can be no clearer convergence of the social and computational minds.

Discourse markers signal the occurrence of an interrupt, the passing of control to context, and the resumption of processing. Let us reconsider the data from section 5.55, the private speech of an eight-year-old assembling a railroad track (Feigenbaum 1992: 192): "Now . . . Let's see . . . a different road . . . yeah . . . This stays here. Okay! This one . . . No. This one sticks. Where are the straight ones? Oh, yeah. There it is. Okay. Wait! Can't go this way. There. There it goes . . . Hey wait! What did I do wrong? . . . a few more curves . . . should get this one . . . Now this goes around . . . There!" Every point of breakdown is signaled by a discourse boundary marker: *Now, Let's see, Okay, No, Wait,* and so on. As I noted earlier, all these forms refer to properties of context and so signal that control has passed away from an internal solution to external circumstances: *Okay,* for instance, refers to actions in context.

These discourse markers essentially punctuate discrete episodes of otherwise smooth mental computing, much the way that an exception handler is engaged whenever (machine) computing reaches an impasse. Just as an exception handler mediates the computation and directs control and recovery—just as it is *not* a higher-order representation of the failed computation, although it may contain the exception as a name—so the discourse markers are symptoms of the flow of control and redirection of processing. They have the effect of returning control to the speaker, and every time the boundary marker appears, the processing proceeds.

Interestingly enough, frontal-lobe aphasics seem to have disorders of discourse that appear to vary the place to which their computing systems return control following an interrupt. Kaczmarek (1987) points out that some control aphasics perseverate on the initial propositions of their discourse and so always seem to be returned to the initial state of their tasks; other control aphasics produce discourse but always digress, suggesting that control is returned to the point of the error. That is, just like exception-handling mechanisms that resume computing at a brand-new state or at the state where the interrupt occurs, so the narratives of frontal-lobe aphasics seem to be characterized by a failure of development or a failure of internal control.

5.63 *The Frame Problem as a Control Issue*

This discussion of computational control returns us to the familiar frame problem. Even though the frame problem generally admits of logico-representational solutions—and logic is different from control—some recent proposals approach the frame problem through computational control. By analogy, cognitive control may be a way to solve the human (computational) frame problem.

5.631 REPRESENTATIONAL SOLUTIONS

In computational terms, the frame problem originates in the following predicament: most statements remain true of a state even after all actions have been performed, but only some of this information is relevant to a subsequent course of action. To put it another way, most information associated with a past state persists into a future state, but not all persists in the same way (see, e.g., Hanks and McDermott 1986). The frame problem is how to capture information about relevant persistence and change.

In fairness to both cognitive psychologists and computer scientists, the frame problem is a quandary mainly for the latter. As Hayes points out in a number of places (e.g., 1991: 72), humans clearly solve the frame problem all the time, since they do not find themselves spinning their inferential wheels and cycling through alternatives. But this is precisely why it is a problem for computation. Frame decisions are things humans make effortlessly and so have to be modeled, but modeling relevant persistence and change remains computationally intractable. This impasse, in turn, doubles back on cognitive psychology, since computational modeling is one way to make precise claims about the content and structure of the human mind. If frame information cannot be put in computationally tractable form, it is arguably irrelevant to accounts of human thinking.

Hayes argues in many places (e.g., 1987) that the frame problem is a matter of *expressing* the relevant information, a logic problem, how to *code* relevance. Indeed, one influential solution is to leave the code alone and assert that the frame problem is not a problem at all (the "sleeping dogs lie" solution; see McDermott 1982, 1987). Other proposals use frame axioms, or explicit statements as to which information holds from a past state and which is to be deleted. Somewhere between these seemingly ad hoc frame axioms and the laissez-faire "sleeping dogs lie" strategy are *explanation closure axioms,* which cast the frame problem as a matter of contrapositive inference on the basis of explicitly stated actions. If certain information is not present, changes do not occur, and persistence falls out as an inference from a negative state of affairs (see, e.g., Schubert 1990).

The technical problems of these logical solutions notwithstanding (e.g., is there a limit to the frame axioms?), scattered throughout these proposals are indications that control bears more on the frame problem than what purely representational solutions might allow. For example, Etherington, Kraus, and Perlis (1991) propose to limit the inheritance of information from state to state by logical scope, which restricts the range of effect of the content of one state on the content of another. This sounds very much like a control issue, a matter of data flow rather than data declaration. Similar comments are made by Dunn (1990) in his proposal for a relevance logic. For him, the frame problem turns on formalizing relevant persistence. Like scope, relevance logic asks, what past data are allowed to flow into the present information state? This, too, sounds very much like a control problem.

5.632 CONTROL-LIKE ASPECTS OF THE FRAME PROBLEM

Hayes (1987, 1991) argues an in-principle difference between frame and control. In his view, the former is representational, since it concerns the characterization of knowledge, and the latter is computational, since it concerns the organization of computing over given representations. Hayes argues that the philosophical community's general failure to separate the representational issues from the computing ones results in gross mischaracterizations of the frame problem; for instance, it is often cast as a matter of when computing stops, but this is technically a control issue.

In some ways Hayes is right, although he occupies very high and narrow ground, which tends to obscure two other points. First, there must necessarily be some representational—or, to be more in line with Hayes's apparent intentions, declarative—aspect to frame solutions. But control has its representational side, too: exception handlers and concurrence monitors are built around specific declarations. Moreover, the extent to which control is a matter of expression depends on the expressive possibilities of a particular programming language. So control cannot be excluded from the frame problem in principle simply because frame solutions require innovations in the expression of data.

Second, while the line between computing and representation is easily argued, it is not so easily maintained or implemented, as the successes of connectionist architectures demonstrate. Indeed, Kowalski (1979b), who, as we already know, has a vested interest in the logic/control dichotomy that Hayes respects, shows that control issues can have an essential bearing on the frame problem. Programs such as STRIPS (Fikes and Nilsson 1971) or PLANNER (Hewitt 1969) eliminate frame axioms and use special-purpose procedures to deal with the frame problem. But Kowalski (1979b) shows that different executions of frame axioms via alternative control structures can give frame solutions that are equivalent to—and sometimes better than—those of STRIPS or PLANNER. A Hayesian response to this control manipulation would surely argue that even in this case, most of the action still lies in the design of the frame axiom, a matter of expression. But Kowalski's (1979b) arguments do indicate that the frame problem can be made computationally tractable *by proper trade-offs between the expression of data and its management,* that is, that control can have an in-principle bearing on the frame problem.

The thinness of the line between expression and management has great importance in other proposals and, in turn, opens the frame problem to Vygotskyan claims about a language *for* thought. Nutter (1991) argues that frame solutions turn on mechanisms that inhibit the persistence of information across states. This is done by restricting algorithms and limiting the data they operate on, two basic functions of control structures. These "impoverishment mechanisms," as he calls them, are complemented by robust repair mechanisms that do not simply return a crashed system to square one, but alter the flow of processing according to what the system has already done and expects to do: another function of control structures. Moreover, when Nutter compares computing with natural language, he notes that the "impoverishment mechanisms" in the latter are focus, relevance, and salience, devices for contextual limitation and selection that give a humanly tractable version of a frame solution.

It takes little imagination to see the connections between the Vygotskyan language for thought and Nutter's computational solution to the frame problem. Informational inhibition through the contextual meta-forms of focus and salience are the functional and structural essence of the language for thought. When Tennenberg (1991) argues that one way to make the frame problem computationally tractable is to equip the system with evidentiality (statistically based modality, justification, and commitment), he further underscores the place of a Vygotskyan control language in solving the frame problem. Ford and Chang's (1989) attempt to give systems a logic of confidence based on personal construct theory from social psychology speaks directly to the Vygotskyan-Leont'ev concept of *smysl:* the personal significance of representations limits the inferences made on the representations.

Ultimately the frame problem is a human issue, not an engineering one.

The design questions have their force in terms of how they elucidate what a human mind is. Likewise, there are clear human frame effects. Children have to learn what information persists from state to state; they have to learn the impoverishment mechanisms and repair techniques that their societies and cultures allow. Moreover, there are disorders that disrupt this inhibition capability, as we shall see in Chapter 6. Given the lessons from control for the frame problem, what appear to be high-level logic dysfunctions might really be control problems.

The language for thought is the Vygotskyan solution to the human frame problem, but this version lacks the legitimacy of the standard Mc-Carthy and Hayes account (the cannibals and missionaries problem) because the former locates the solution in extramental factors, such as contextual meanings encoded in overt speech for self. In any case, if we want to consider the language for thought as a computational matter, then one way to do so is to read it as the development and mastery of a private code for choosing among informationally equivalent systems—precisely the definition that one computer scientist gives of the frame problem (Janlert 1987).

5.7 Run Time and Relativity

There is an important implication of all these observations: the language for thought is an instrument of individual variation. In the Vygotskyan framework, the development of a private mental control language out of public, social speech serves heterogeneity and the differentiation of the individual from the homogenizing forces of culture. The control language is thus an index of linguistic and cultural relativity. Since the language for thought has its computational analogue in control structures, is there any way to link computational control and human control under broader accounts of relativity? Or, to put it perhaps more unfathomably, can the Vygotskyan language for thought and the mechanists' computational control find a home in Benjamin Lee Whorf?

Programming languages can be classified by their run-time behavior (see Ghezzi and Jazayeri 1987: 59–81). To some extent this is traceable to the demands put on memory by each language's representational resources and obligations. For example, the memory demands of Fortran can be predicted in advance because, among other things, the amount of storage space needed for each variable is fixed. But this is not possible in Pascal because variables are dynamic, and the amount of storage space they need can change during execution of the program. Consequently, the run-time behavior of Fortran and Pascal differ markedly.

Other run-time variations follow from the control structures in programming languages. Functional languages allow control expressions and so have a hierarchical or nested style of execution. In contrast, procedural languages manage data flow through control statements and have a more sequential style. These differences affect the way programs in these languages are written, read, and compiled. For example, there is great benefit and power in the nesting of expressions because the forms that share transfer of control can be blocked together. But this readily leads to multiple nesting, and a programmer can easily forget to include all the delimiters in a block of expressions, causing the program to crash. Yet, the clear benefit in procedural languages of independent control statements that can redirect processing at any point has the detriment of easily produced spaghetti code, which, in turn, can prevent both readability and compiling.

Just as these cost-benefit trade-offs in control have an effect on how programs in different languages run, so the variations in control resources of natural languages can result in similar variations in the run-time behavior of metaconsciousness. As I argued in Chapters 3 and 4, where meta representation is coded, context and representation are stored together and the language for thought is automatic and rapid; where metarepresentation is calculated, context and representation interface, and the language for thought is slower and more deliberate. The varying computational properties attached to different representation-context relationships might be a way to chart the processing demands that different natural languages put on cognitive control.

This characterization of cognitive control in terms of the coding patterns of metaforms gives us a way of integrating both computational control and the Vygotskyan language for thought under Whorf's account of linguistic relativity, though Whorf's views must be understood a bit differently from their traditional, simplistic construal as the equation of language, culture, and thought. A close reading of Whorf shows that he believed that the form-meaning relationships of a language "condense experience, classifying together as 'the same' for the purposes of speech things which are in many ways quite different" (Lucy and Wertsch 1987: 73). These ready-made experience packages are used as guides in habitual thinking and trigger "associations which are not *necessarily* entailed by experience" (Lucy and Wertsch 1987: 73). In this way, the coding patterns of language direct the speaker out to the world and construct a worldview as habitual, on-line thinking through linguistic form. This is the real-time relativism that characterizes Whorf, not the pervasive straitjacketing of mind and culture by language that has reached the popular press (see Lucy 1992b).

For all intents and purposes, this account of Whorf sounds exactly like Vygotsky—on-line thinking is tied to the semantic and pragmatic associations of metaforms—with the exception that Vygotsky's views apply to abstract, higher thought (see Lucy and Wertsch 1987). So how do we get from habitual thought to abstract, higher thought? In Whorf's view (as elucidated by Lucy 1993), the connection lies in the paradox of reflexivity.

When a metalanguage is drawn from its object language, as is the case for metarepresentation in otherwise representational natural language, the metalanguage categories that serve as the basis for abstraction are typically borrowed directly from the categories in the object language. Thus, when speakers look out abstractly on the world, they find, to their astonishment, that the abstract world is a perfect match with the everyday world. The continuity between their representational means and their metarepresentational means fails to give contrasting cases, and so the distinctions in the former are rediscovered in the latter. Since the bases of higher thought are the metarepresentational resources of the ordinary language, higher thought suffers the same lack of contrasting cases. On-line *higher* thinking can be straightforwardly projected up from on-line habitual thinking.

The Whorfian hypothesis might thus be understood as a claim about how the metarepresentational resources of a language affect the run time of metaconsciousness as habitual thought grows into metathought. Just as control structures accord relativity to the running of programming languages, so the linguistic relativity and determinism that characterize habitual thinking are projected into the language for thought by virtue of the forms that construct the mental control language.

Another—but potentially very misleading—way of making sense of this convergence of Vygotsky, Whorf, and computational control is through *style,* which is a kind of nontechnical cover term for matters of individual variation and choice. Control affects the style of the programmer and the style of execution of the program. The language for thought is a symptom of cognitive style, the way an individual uniquely manipulates (mostly universal) mental representations. This might be an acceptable way of speaking if it were not also true that calling something *a matter of style* immediately demeans it. Is this a matter of style or substance? goes the proverbial query, with the expectation that if it turns out to be a matter of style, then it can be dismissed. Only substance is substantial enough to be important: style is, well . . . just style.

The irony here is that in programing languages, *style is a matter of substance*. There are no algorithms without control, and a language's style of management and tracking of representations is essential to the computation. So while there may be no human computation without representation, as Fodor has sloganized it, without human control you have *only* representation. Perhaps it would be more accurate to say *no computation with just representation*. But that does not ring quite so fashionably to the ear.

6

Control Disorders: Splitting the Computational from the Social

6.1 Logic/Control Dissociations

In the previous two chapters, I sketched out the basics of Vygotskyan cognitive science by looking at three kinds of subjectivity and the way reflexive language drives metaconsciousness. The principal lesson of these chapters is that the linguistic integration of computational and social mind hangs on the form and operation of the mental control language, the human analogue of computational control. In the present chapter we turn to the breakdown of that control language and try to read certain disorders of linguistic self-monitoring through the apparatus discussed in Chapters 4 and 5.

The clinical literature includes an increasing catalogue of syndromes that delink language from cognition generally. The study of some of these disorders has grown to fashionability since their congenital behavioral consequences speak directly to the line between learned and innate knowledge. But even with special focus on these conditions, no attention has been given to their effects on language for behavioral and mental control. On close examination, and with cognitive science informed by Vygotskyan principles, certain phenomenologies of these (otherwise quite diverse) disorders come together as problems in the attentional, metarepresentational, and individualizing functions of speech.

The linguistic deficits associated with these syndromes are best understood as *logic/control dissociations*. Here the results of Chapter 5, especially Kowalski's distinction between representation and control in computing systems, provide an explanation. The well-known sociocognitive deficits of these syndromes can be recast into the categories of metaconsciousness sketched in Chapter 4. Here, the linguistic and social deficits come together as problems in the language for thought.

234

6.2 A Catalogue of Control Disorders

Several syndromes with very different etiologies exhibit dissociations of linguistic knowledge from general cognitive abilities and, within language proper, a dissociation of syntax, morphology, and phonology on the one hand from pragmatics and certain areas of semantics on the other, roughly a form-function split. Most of these disorders also involve deficits in pragmatics proper, and so the syndromes do not appear to be simply access problems but look like disruptions in the informational structure of pragmatics itself. In what follows, these syndromes and what is known of their causes and typical manifestations are described briefly.

Williams syndrome, sometimes known as *hypercalcemia,* is a fairly rare genetic disorder, occurring once in every 25,000 or so live births. It involves abnormalities of the cardiovascular, renal, and musculoskeletal system, and results in a characteristic elfin appearance. Recent research suggests that the disorder is related to abnormalities in elastin production and the neuropeptide CGRP, which affects calcitonin, and so may be associated with hypercalcemia (Meyerson and Frank 1987; Udwin 1990; Udwin and Yule 1991; Bellugi, Wang, and Jernigan 1994; Karmiloff-Smith, Grant, and Berthoud 1993).

Individuals with Williams syndrome are hyperverbal and gregarious. Many studies report that they acquire language at a delayed rate (Thal, Bates, and Bellugi 1989; Bellugi, Sabo, and Vaid 1988), but ultimately with essentially normal outcome. The uncontroversial exception, however, is that Williams individuals perseverate in conversation, often shift rapidly from topic to topic, and in general fail to adhere to the normal appropriateness conditions on discourse.

In contrast to this hyperverbality, Williams individuals perform quite poorly on measures of general knowledge and problem-solving ability and on tests of nonverbal abilities, especially on tasks that require global spatial integration (Thal, Bates, and Bellugi 1989; Bellugi, Sabo, and Vaid 1988; Bellugi et al. 1990). The combination of high verbal abilities and essentially normal linguistic outcome with low nonverbal general problem-solving capacities invites the inference that the syndrome dissociates linguistic knowledge from general knowledge for performance. It most certainly shows that general problem-solving abilities and IQ are not prerequisites to speech. Moreover, with respect to language itself, Williams individuals seem to be unable to control the meaning and flow of discourse. Consequently, Williams syndrome is a classic illustration of the dissociation of language and cognition with attendant deficits in pragmatics.

Turner syndrome, which occurs once in about 2,500 live births, affects only females and results from abnormalities in the X chromosome. Turner girls typically have short stature, a webbed neck, broad chest, and gonadal dysgenesis; they also have a variety of skeletal, craniofacial, cardiovascular, and renal disorders, including scoliosis (spinal curvature), strabismus (crossed eyes), and aortic valve problems (White 1994, McCauley et al. 1987). Turner girls are very much like individuals with Williams syndrome. They are very verbal and gregarious, and while there are reports of developmental delay (Yamada and Curtiss 1981), their linguistic outcomes are essentially normal.

The exceptions for Williams syndrome repeat themselves for Turner girls, who are excessively verbal, show a marked dissociation of form and function (Yamada and Curtiss 1981), and seem to achieve their verbal skills at the expense of their nonverbal ones. Indeed, Temple and Carney (1993) report that the extent of verbal-nonverbal mismatch is a function of the severity of the syndrome (see also Garron 1977).[1] Turner girls have great difficulty with spatial integration and coding and transforming visual-spatial input (see Silbert, Wolff, and Lilienthal 1977; Downey et al. 1991; Rovet and Netley 1982; McGlone 1985, among the many studies). Consequently, Turner syndrome is viewed as another typical manifestation of language acquired without normal general cognitive skills.

Spina bifida with hydrocephalus is a congenital disorder of the spine resulting from a neural tube defect during the first month of intrauterine life. It occurs once in every 1,000 live births. In its most severe form (myelomeningocele), it involves a protruding (usually lumbar) cyst, accumulation of cerebrospinal fluid, and a variety of orthopedic and urological problems. Most cases also involve hydrocephalus—the accumulation of cerebrospinal fluid in the ventricles of the brain (Reigel 1993)—which requires surgical insertion of a shunt to relieve pressure.

Individuals with spina bifida with hydrocephalus have long been known to exhibit "cocktail party chatter," or rambling hyperverbosity (Tew 1979). They have normal linguistic form (Byrne, Abbeduto, and Brooks 1990), but are deficient in discourse and pragmatics (Culatta and Young 1992). Even with such apparently high verbal abilities, these individuals are markedly deficient in nonverbal skills (Hurley 1993), as shown by IQ tests, Piagetian performance measures (Cromer 1994), and tests of abstraction and world knowledge (Culatta 1993a). Hydrocephalus appears to be the cause of the separation of verbal and nonverbal performance (Fletcher et al. 1992). Still, because language is essentially normal in this syndrome—even supranormal in some cases—it supports the case for the separation of linguistic knowledge from all-purpose cognition; moreover, within language, linguistic form is preserved at the expense of pragmatic and discourse function.

Autism, which occurs, on the average, one to one and one-half times in every 1,000 live births, is a severe developmental pathology of essentially unknown etiology. Studies have implicated a variety of pathological correlates (e.g., hydrocephalus, tuberous sclerosis, Fragile-X phenomenon, rubella, and metabolic disorders) and neurobiological association (e.g., abnormalities in the temporal lobe, and, increasingly, the cerebellum; see Courchesne et al. 1994), but no single cause, or even cluster of causes, is the received explanation of the condition (Schopler 1994). Autistic individuals are characteristically self-contained, repetitive, and stereotyped in their activities. They have pervasive deficits in language and social knowledge and lack imaginative behaviors (Tager-Flusberg 1994: 175).

Despite their self-containedness, autistics often demonstrate quite high linguistic abilities, even though their language as a whole is delayed. They have good linguistic form (e.g., syntax), but are deficient in pragmatics and discourse functions (Sigman 1994, Tager-Flusberg 1991, 1994). Since autistics, almost by definition, have a deficit in social and world knowledge, the preserved linguistic abilities must be independent of general cognitive abilities. Thus, as Tager-Flusberg (1994) notes, autism is another case of form-function dissociation in the context of language-cognition independence.

Finally, a number of other syndromes manifest similar language-cognition dissociations. These conditions are frequently unnamed or very generally labeled. The condition reported by Yamada (1990), *Laura's syndrome,* as it were, and that described by Blank, Gessner, and Esposito (1979) as *language without communication* are typical of the unnamed conditions. Certain broadly labeled *nonverbal learning disabilities* (Rourke 1988) and *right hemisphere dysfunctions* (Kaplan et al. 1990) also manifest language-cognition delinkings. These syndromes are frequently of unknown etiology (except for right hemisphere trauma, of course) and have varying incidence. In all cases, however, linguistic performance is disconnected from world knowledge, and within language, form appears to be delinked from function. For example, Laura, in Yamada's (1990) study, manifests the classic, formally perfect but functionally deficient "cocktail party chatter" of Williams syndrome or spina bifida with hydrocephalus. At the same time, she is markedly deficient on measures of general cognition. Laura's linguistic knowledge must therefore not be dependent on all-purpose cognition, and within language, form must be dissociable from function.[2]

6.3   Logic versus Control

When we look in detail at how these disorders divide linguistic performance, we find that they all cut computation at its joints, as it were: they split representational logic from metarepresentational control. We can see this by examining the effects of these syndromes on the standard linguistic components: phonology, syntax, semantics, and pragmatics.

6.31   Phonology

None of the syndromes is marked by phonological disturbance. Quite the opposite: Williams, Turner, and spina bifida individuals and those with the unnamed disorders can be notoriously fluent (Cromer 1994, Yamada 1990: 59–61), even auditorily hypersensitive (Neville, Mills, and Bellugi 1994; Schopler 1994: 91). They are also excellent at verbal imitation. Spina bifida and Williams individuals are, in fact, better at verbal imitation that normals (Morrow and Wachs 1992; Karmiloff-Smith, Grant, and Berthoud 1993). Because individuals with spina bifida can repeat words as forms while failing to explain their meanings (Morrow and Wachs 1992), Dennis et al. (1987) propose that the disorder affects lexical semantics but preserves lexical phonology (how words as forms enter into the phonological system; this would also account for Karmiloff-Smith and associates' results).

The general absence of phonological disturbance in these syndromes is in line with a split of linguistic representation from linguistic metarepresentation for cognitive control. Phonology is a formal representational system and generally understood to constitute an autonomous computational component. Why, then, do we not see any control disruptions in phonology? Either phonological algorithms do not have a control component or phonological computation does not feed cognitive control. The first answer is very unlikely. The flow of phonological computation is clearly directed, since there are various levels of phonological representation that require management and tracking of representations. Within phonology itself there is phonological logic and phonological control, and the evidence suggests that this kind of intramodular control is not affected by these disorders. When Laura is given phonological parts of words—syllables, for example—she is able to complete the word normally on the basis of phonological information alone (Yamada 1990: 61). Thus, since she can manage phonological levels above the segment, such as the sequencing of syllables and the lexical item as a phonological unit, she appears to have preserved the ability to manage the flow of phonological data across representational levels—a classic instance of computational control.

It is more likely that phonological computation does not readily enter into *cognitive control*. The output of the phonological component interfaces with other formal linguistic modules (morphology, syntax, and some parts of semantics), but not directly with the conceptual system as such, and not with the metasemantic and metapragmatic functions of language that are associated with language for thought. The exception here is prosody, which is known to be associated with mental planning (see section 6.55). Indeed, Laura is reported to have problems with intonation and pausing and so may have a discernible split between phonological logic and phonological control. But on the whole, individuals with these disorders have preserved phonology because is it essentially not a metarepresentational system.

6.32 Morphology and Syntax

Similar facts hold for morphology and syntax: lexical and grammatical *form* are essentially unaffected by the disorders. Autistic children "are not impaired in their grammatical development. Thus far, research has not uncovered one area of deviance in the order of development or even in the process of development . . . in the domains of syntax and morphology" (Tager-Flusberg 1994: 190). Identical remarks have long been made about Williams syndrome (Thal, Bates, and Bellugi 1989), Turner syndrome (Yamada and Curtiss 1981), and spina bifida with hydrocephalus (Cromer 1994). The unnamed syndromes also manifest good morphology and syntax (Yamada 1990, Curtiss 1981).[3]

We might then ask, as with phonology, why there are no symptoms of control deficits. The same answer applies here: there are two kinds of control. Intramodular control is unaffected by the disorders. But where intramodular control stops and general cognitive control takes over, morphological and syntactic performance drops off.

Laura, for example, applies theta-roles absolutely correctly and appears to have all the mechanisms of logical form. She understands operators and the interrogative and can bind variables. She falters, however, in justifying her choice of values for the variables constrained by logical form, that is, where logical syntax interfaces with world knowledge:

[Experimenter]: What if the lion's face had been a monster's face?

[Laura]: A bear is scary. (Yamada 1990:52)

One way to explain this result is to say that, contrary to commonsense intuition, morphology and syntax are not cognitively and behaviorally strategic. Their control effects stay within the domains of formal knowledge. (Karmiloff-Smith et al. 1995 make a similar point in arguing that theory of mind preservation in certain of these disorders is traceable to the preserved interface between certain aspects of language and social knowledge. See also Frawley 1997.)

Perhaps the most compelling support for this interpretation lies in the fact that these disorders often preserve grammatical judgment and certain kinds of metalinguistic performance. Cromer's (1994: 150) subject performs perfectly well on tests of metalinguistic judgments of grammaticality and ungrammaticality.[4] Similarly, Laura exhibits metasyntactic and meta-morphological knowledge by spontaneously correcting her interlocutor's deliberate errors of production:

[Experimenter]: He wear his shirt.

[Laura]: He wears his shirt. (Yamada 1990: 36; cf. Cromer 1994: 150 for identical behavior in spina bifida)

Turner girls can do verbal completions and so must be aware of lexical and syntactic structure *as structure,* and Williams children are good at correcting grammatical anomalies (Bellugi, Wang, and Jernigan 1994: 28).

The natural conclusion is that these metalinguistic judgments, though reflexive by definition and thus a kind of control mechanism, must not involve the same sort of reflexivity and control that matters to overall cognitive functioning. These judgments lie *within* the formal components and reflect metaknowledge of code, not judgments at the interface of architecture and context. Another way to say this is that these syndromes preserve the kind of reflexive knowledge that Johnson-Laird (1988) and Jackendoff (1987) suggest is at the basis of consciousness: self-coding code upwardly projected from the modules. These judgments can be made without access to a context and so are not metaconscious per se.

6.33 Semantics

When we turn to disruptions in semantics, the facts differ in an interesting way. Not all semantics is architecture; some of the information is connected to cognition in context. It is at this point—where architecture meets context—that the syndromes affect performance.

These disorders all preserve the universal core of grammatical meaning: semantic logic, as it were. There are no clinical or experimental reports of problems in denoting (see Cromer 1994: 143 on spina bifida, Tager-Flusberg 1991 on autistics, and Bellugi et al. 1990 on Williams children). Because denoting is one of the elemental computations of semantic competence, and is essential to both formal models of meaning (the denoting function of model-theoretic semantics; see Bach 1989) and empirical studies of acquisition (the mapping of forms onto the world; see Golinkoff, Mervis, and Hirsh-Pasek 1994), these disorders do not affect the architectural basis of semantic learnability.

Moreover, all the syndromes appear to leave intact the form and relational organization of the mental lexical network. Laura understands synonymy and other lexical relations and can judge violations of selectional restrictions (Yamada 1990: 43). Williams, Turner, and spina bifida individuals are notorious for their lexical expressiveness or semantic fluency and show normal judgments of lexical categories and relational structure (Bellugi, Wang, and Jernigan 1994: 32; Temple and Carney 1993: 696).

Perhaps most crucial to the possibility of a universal representational semantics, the syndromes preserve what might be called *minimal content*—conceptual primitives that underlie the assignment of meaning to grammatical form—notions such as boundedness, specificity, animacy, and shape (Jackendoff 1990, Frawley 1992b, Spelke 1994). Sigman (1994: 142) reports that autistics are like normals on tests of categorization by color, form, and function. Tager-Flusberg (1994: 179 n. 4) reports: "Concepts and meanings that underlie the words they [autistics] use are identical to those of control groups." None of the data on Williams, Turner, spina bifida, or the unnamed syndromes suggests that this schematic grammatical content is disrupted (Yamada 1990: 43, McGlone 1985, Morrow and Wachs 1992).

But here the logic-control split reasserts itself. Williams and spina bifida children are semantically fluent to a fault, it turns out. On tests of semantic priming, Williams children exhibit hypersemantic excitation: the entire lexical network is activated by a prime (Bellugi, Wang, and Jernigan 1994:

49). The problem appears to be a deficit in the very sort of computational function that control structures perform: inhibition of computation and restriction of computation to a certain range of representations.

Analogous semantic control deficits are found in other syndromes. Tager-Flusberg (1991) reports that while autistics can mentally code meanings—execute the logic of semantic algorithms—they fail when asked to carry out strategic aspects of these semantic representations. They also have problems with semantic-pragmatic interactions, such as presupposition and deixis (Tager-Flusberg 1981, Cromer 1981), phenomena unquestionably at the code-context interface.

The semantic performance of Williams children also breaks down where semantic architecture has to link up to real-world context (Bellugi, Wang, and Jernigan 1994: 44). So while they have normal grammatical meaning and denotation, they have difficulty managing what these denotations further signify (Bellugi et al. 1990). Williams children thus appear to have a preserved semantic core but a deficit in the metasemantic ability to explain the applicability of such content.

Turner children also handle tasks that rely on minimal content but fail on those that require *strategic use* of minimal semantic content. Rovet and Netley (1982), for example, have found that while Turner children perform more poorly than normals on mental rotation of objects, the deficit appears to be one of *interference in strategies of rotation,* in managing the rotation of parts. Interestingly enough, the same kind of strategy interference does not surface in purely verbal verification tasks, which require algorithmic denotational decisions.

The split between local deterministic semantic processing and global semantic knowledge for cognitive control comes through especially clearly in these individuals' metasemantic judgments. As we know, these disorders preserve intramodular metajudgments such as decisions about lexical form. But on tasks demanding metajudgments that reflect the requirements of the mental control language, these individuals exhibit some notable deficits. For example, Tager-Flusberg (1991) observes that when autistics are asked to search mental semantic space for *appropriate* lexical items in recall tasks, their lexical performance, otherwise normal, markedly falls off. This kind of metajudgment involves both reflexivity and code-context trade-offs: the subject must assess the item's position in the semantic system because the task necessitates a (metasemantic) choice among items; the subject must also assess the fit of the item with the task as a context. If autism is in some respects a control disorder, then these two obligations ought to diminish performance.

A similar inability to manage semantic reflexivity is found in spina bifida children. Morrow and Wachs (1992: 488) report that spina bifida children, while semantically fluent, are unable to explain the meanings of the words they use. Dennis et al. (1987) find that spina bifida children do worse than normals on metasemantic judgments of anomaly. Cull and Wyke (1984: 181) note that spina bifida children have problems with word lists, though they otherwise exhibit high verbal IQ. Explaining meaning and judging anomaly are semantically reflexive by definition, and the processing of word lists requires the postulation of a metaproperty to unite the elements in the list *as a list*. (Bender, Linden, and Robinson 1989 report the same dysfunction *on lexical lists only* for Turner girls, who are otherwise quite normal in their lexical behavior.) For the same reason, then, that autistics fail on judgments of lexical appropriateness, spina bifida children fail on word lists and definitions: a control disorder manifests itself on tasks of metasemantic performance.[5]

6.34 Pragmatics

The dividing line between semantic and pragmatic information leads directly to dissociations of pragmatic logic and pragmatic control in these disorders. Pragmatic deficits and discourse problems have long been the unifying feature of these disorders (though Byrne, Abbeduto, and Brooks 1990 present some counters). This can be seen in the characteristic and well-documented "cocktail party chatter," elaborate, well-formed discourse that appears to have no topical integration to the context in which it occurs and no adherence to the rules of rational exchange:

> [Spina bifida individual asked about a button]: This is a button. It has two holes in it. It's like a lady's hat. You put them in a blouse or your apron, in case an apron has a button. That's big like this. You can roll it or throw it, but you never smash a window because if you have a button or a shape that goes on the wall or if you could take it and hang it on the dress that would be very nice. Would you do that for me? If you have a dress or coat you can hang it on it or you can keep it out to take it to the store. (Schwartz 1974: 466–67)

> [Turner syndrome individual asked if she has any brothers or sisters]: You guys were funny! Hey, I got it. After 12 I'm gonna say the number and I'll put out my fingers and each one of you has to say it together. (Yamada and Curtiss 1981: 107)

When we look more closely at the kinds of pragmatic and discourse phenomena that are affected, characterizing the syndromes in terms of a straightforward pragmatics-nonpragmatics cut does not appear to be totally accurate. The disorders often preserve a number of pragmatic abilities while other aspects of communicative competence are totally lost. In fact, they split pragmatics right at the *logic-control line*. Pragmatic representation is preserved, but metapragmatics, which ultimately feeds *smysl* and speech for cognitive control, is deficient. (Note that this would erroneously suggest a within-domain deficit in pragmatics; see note 3.)

Williams and Turner children are clearly able to execute the form of conversation (Bellugi, Wang, and Jernigan 1994, Yamada and Curtiss 1981). But they are unable to determine options within that form, manage turn taking and topic switching as routines, and signal, or detect signals of, the implications of these routines. Thus, Williams and Turner children tend to dominate conversations by always taking a turn and readily changing topics.

Similar facts hold for autism. Tager-Flusberg (1981) and Cromer (1981), citing substantial previous work, note that autistic children are able to execute the deterministic aspects of discourse: autistics have "developmentally primitive ways of maintaining a topic, such as routines, recodings, and simple responses to test questions" (Tager-Flusberg and Anderson 1991: 1131). But they have difficulty with the particulars of speaker-hearer shifts and the management of trade-offs between foreground and background knowledge (Tager-Flusberg 1981, Cromer 1981). They exhibit problems with speech act functions (i.e., metapragmatic judgments of informational significance and cuing) and with pronouns (i.e., information tracking devices; Tager-Flusberg 1994). Tager-Flusberg (1993) shows that autistics appear not to understand that discourse involves the exchange of *information*—a clear metapragmatic failure. Autistics are now understood to have a more general difficulty with interdigitating the flow of context, a problem traceable to cerebellar dysfunction (i.e., a design disorder). Significantly, the cerebellum is one of the brain's many "subselves"; it is a computational control system dedicated to ensuring smooth and timely data flow (Courchesne et al. 1994: 131–32).

These features also characterize the pragmatic abilities of Laura, who knows the discourse conventions of turn taking, responding, and extending topics, but is unable to work out the options within these parameters:

[Jeni]: You have a savings account?

[Laura]: Yesss!

[Jeni]: How do you earn your money?

[Laura]: Well, we were taking a walk, my mom, and there was this giant, like, my mother threw a stick. (Yamada 1990: 67)

Spina bifida children have problems with discourse focus and figure-ground structure (Culatta and Young 1992: 435); they also have problems with topic cohesion and expansion (Culatta 1993c: 178–79) and cannot link pictures to form a coherent story (Cromer 1994). Phrased more generally, these are difficulties in tracking information across domains, a classic issue in computational control.

What appears to be preserved in all these syndromes is the ability to *compute the formal representational aspects of pragmatics,* such as turn-taking routines and the fact of topic shift. But there is a *failure to control* the options within these routinized search spaces or to appreciate and convey the significance of these choices. It is therefore not "cocktail party chatter" per se that defines these disorders. After all, autistics—notoriously untalkative children—are grouped here with Williams children, and autism can even co-occur with Williams syndrome (Reiss et al. 1985). These are, rather, problems with the very features that anchor the mental control language.

In the end, the logic-control split provides a simple alternative to the existing explanations of the loquaciousness of these syndromes. Individuals with these disorders are verbose because their condition splits their algorithms and leaves them good at logic and deficient at control.[6]

6.4 Private Speech Disruptions

If these syndromes dissociate logic from control, then we ought to see deficits not only in metasemantic and metapragmatic functions, but also in the behavioral uses to which these functions are dedicated. Do individuals with these syndromes display problems with speech for thought? If humans learn to regulate mental computation by internalizing social discourse as personal control discourse, then a deficit in the building blocks of the language for thought should appear as a deficit in private speech.

The evidence for this prediction is mixed, if only because private speech is rarely tracked in the literature on these syndromes. Clinical and experimental reports indicate children with these disorders do use private speech in problem solving. Bellugi et al. (1990) observe: "Typically, the Williams syndrome subjects in these studies tended to talk their way through drawing tasks as if using their verbal skills to mediate the severely impaired act of drawing." Bellugi, Sabo, and Vaid (1988: 284) note the same ostensible verbal mediation: "Each one of the children verbalized before and while drawing." Yamada and Curtiss (1981: 100) also describe private speech by a Turner syndrome child building structures with sticks and shapes: "[She made] comment[s] as she manipulated the objects (e.g., 'Is this gonna work?', 'I made a house', 'OK, now I'm gonna make something with the sticks')." In my own clinical observations of a Turner syndrome child, I noted her using private speech while coloring during the clinical session. Parents of a Williams syndrome child I also observed told me that she talked to herself during tasks.

Tomasello, Kruger, and Ratner (1993: 504), however, find not a single mention of self-regulating speech in the literature on autism. Even when such speech is preserved, as in Williams syndrome, it lacks the properties of normal self-regulatory discourse and does not have the same circumstances of evocation. Normal private speech, we should recall from Chapter 5, must not only accompany action but gradually precede it as it comes to serve inhibition and planning; it must be self-directed and regulative. It also has certain structural characteristics, such as reduced syntactic and phonetic form, preservation of discourse focus, and metasemantic and metapragmatic markings. Many of these factors do not apply to the reported examples of private speech in these disorders. Two problems dominate: a tendency to denote and a failure of uptake and mediation.

The Williams children in Bellugi, Sabo, and Vaid's (1988: 284–85) study use private speech in an entirely denotative way. They simply *name their activities;* they do not use the private speech to plan and inhibit. The authors remark: "The examples of the children talking while drawing again demonstrate the dissociation between language and visuospatial skills. The children would often name the various parts of the model, and draw them as they named them, one next to the other" (285). Consequently, the children think of the drawing task as copying, not making a representation. Their private speech is also a kind of copying and so does not contribute to metacognitive integration.

In my own clinical observations, I noted a Turner girl using elaborate private speech as she occupied herself coloring while the doctor and her parents discussed her case in the same room. Two things were striking about her private speech. First, like the Williams syndrome children, she used private speech in a denotative way: "This is a blue one . . . This is a red crayon." (cf. Bellugi, Wang, and Jernigan 1994: 36: "The description

[of the drawing] is fluent and rich . . . 'It has long grey ears, fan ears.' ")
Second, the form of the private speech was abnormal: she regulated herself
in full sentences and in a very loud voice, making her speech for thought
indistinguishable from her usual loquacious social discourse. She seemed
to be simply performing privately, not regulating her thoughts and actions.
The speech had none of the earmarks of normal private speech in transition
from social discourse to monologue. Hence, it also was perfunctory and
ineffective.[7]

One way to understand this behavior is to say that in delinking logic
from control, the disorders leave the children with denotation, or logic,
not signification, or control (in Vygotskyan terms, *znachenie* is preserved
at the expense of *smysl*). This in turn has consequences for the uptake of
the private speech and its effectiveness as a mediational device.

Interestingly enough, Bellugi, Sabo, and Vaid (1988: 285) report that
in spite of using private speech ostensibly to mediate the drawing task, the
Williams children still fail to integrate the parts of the task into a functional
whole. This is because their self-regulatory discourse accompanies the task
and does not serve planning and inhibition. Indeed, in subsequent studies
of Williams children, Bellugi and her colleagues note this very failure of
uptake in the private speech: "WS subjects often talk their way through
drawings, as if using their verbal skills to mediate the severely impaired act
of drawing, *although the results often belie this effort*" (Bellugi, Wang, and
Jernigan 1994: 36; emphasis added). Similarly, the Turner girl I observed
used her private speech as a description of the events in which she was
engaged, not as a semiotic device to regulate her behavior in the task. She
simply spoke as she colored.

Lacking both significance and functional uptake, this private speech
serves no true cognitive mediation. It is private talking, not a tool and not
a vehicle for thinking. Although more work certainly needs to be done on
this line of inquiry—for example, do spina bifida children and autistics
manifest the same sorts of private speech?—it appears that these control
disorders do not leave individuals without private speech per se, but do
leave them without *effective* (internalized, monologic, metapragmatic)
self-regulatory discourse. Nowhere is this description clearer than in the
deleterious effects these syndromes have on metaconsciousness.

6.5   The Metaconscious Effects of Control Disorders

The foregoing account of these disorders as a delinking of logic from
control takes on very interesting characteristics if read through Vygotsky's

view of the function of language in thought, where reflexive language constructs, maintains, and regulates the self. If logic-control dissociations reflect a broader deficit in the language for thought, then we should find systematic disruptions in the properties of metaconsciousness outlined in Chapter 4. Indeed, when we look at individuals with these disorders, we see five kinds of control problems, traceable to a deficit in the language for thought.

6.51 Lack of Inhibition

Loquaciousness, hyperactivity, anxiety, impulsiveness, low adaptability, low persistence, low threshold to arousal, high distractability, and general attentional deficits are associated with all these disorders. They are some of the essential defining features of Williams syndrome (Tomc, Williamson, and Pauli 1991; Udwin 1990; Meyerson and Frank 1987). Some researchers have argued that the condition is only a general inhibitory-attentional problem: "Reduced visual memory may be related more to inefficient attention than to problems in retention or memory storage" (Crisco, Dobbs, and Mulhern 1988: 654). Turner syndrome has the same behavioral consequences (Downey et al. 1989, 1991; McCauley, Ito, and Kay 1986; Williams, Richman, and Yarbrough 1991), and for this reason looks very much like a nonverbal learning disorder (Williams, Richman, and Yarbrough 1991). Spina bifida (Horn et al. 1985, Schwartz 1974, Cull and Wyke 1984, Culatta 1993c) and the unnamed disorders (Yamada 1990) also manifest lack of inhibition and attentional control. Recent accounts of autism take this characteristic as basic and cast the disorder as an inability to control attentional shifts (Courchesne et al. 1994).

Here, the metaconscious consequences of dysfunction in the language for thought loom large. Such a deficit can surface as problems in attention, self-regulation, and ability to stay on task—the inhibitory and exclusionary functions of metaconsciousness. If, as we saw in section 6.4, there is no functional uptake of private speech—if private speech is merely denotative—then speech cannot mediate higher thinking. We should thus expect individuals with these syndromes to exhibit failures of inhibition and a lack of slow, deliberate thinking, since the mechanism that determines and ranks options in the problem space is ineffective.

Quite striking in this respect are the neuroanatomical studies of semantic priming in Williams syndrome children, which reveal uninhibited excitation of the neural network during lexical search (Bellugi, Wang, and Jernigan 1994). Williams individuals are hyperlexical because they lack the control mechanisms for inhibiting the lexical search space. Analogously, autistics can engage in joint attention, and so meet the prerequisite for situation definition and satisfactory social knowledge and performance. But their social referencing, as Courchesne et al. (1994) call it, appears to have no control effects or cognitive uptake. So the proper control behavior falls short of inhibitory function.

6.52   Inability to Choose among Alternatives

Very much related to lack of inhibition is another frequently reported control dysfunction: inability to choose among alternatives. Faced with an array of behavioral or cognitive options in a task, or several distinct and competing tasks, individuals with control disorders choose a limited number of options or break down altogether, as if they lacked a cognitive-behavioral dispatcher.[8]

Consider some standard results from experiments with spina bifida children. Horn et al. (1985) observe that such children have great difficulty in complex nonverbal tasks, such as sorting cards by type or feature. This kind of experiment requires the subject to manage multiple options under a single task. Horn et al. (1985) also report that, despite their high verbal abilities, spina bifida children fail on tasks of lexical identification in the presence of nonverbal distraction (e.g., in a decision about a known word presented against a "busy" nonverbal background). Cull and Wyke (1984) note that spina bifida children have problems with word lists *as lists,* though they otherwise exhibit high verbal IQ. The complex verbal background reduces their performance, unlike normals, for whom the list structures and assists performance. Even Byrne, Abbeduto, and Brooks (1990), who ultimately argue that spina bifida children and normals are not so different as usually reported in the literature, observe that as verbal tasks increase in processing demands, spina bifida performance declines.

It thus appears that spina bifida individuals cannot sort out relevant from irrelevant stimuli and have difficulty inhibiting irrelevant material in "busy" input. Horn et al. (1985: 719) suggest that these problems may lie in "receptive language use beyond the initial acquisition of the meaning of a word," that is, in lexical meaning beyond the elements of universal denotational space. This is another way of saying that the inability to choose among alternatives is connected to the Vygotskyan notion of *smysl:* word meaning beyond truth.

Similar behavioral patterns and explanations characterize the other control disorders. Autistics fail to use linguistic information effectively to retrieve information in word list tasks or to help in cognitive processing generally (Tager-Flusberg 1991). Sorting relevant from irrelevant stimuli has the same functional requirements as recalling word lists in that it needs a global heuristic strategy to exclude options. Indeed, one of the standard explanations of the self-contained repetitive behavior of autistics is that it is a compensatory strategy for a lack of perceptual constancy (Schopler 1994: 91), an attempt to impose structure on diverse input. (The autistic author Donna Williams 1992 poignantly describes her attempts to impose selectivity on the buzzing confusion of perceptual input in her memoir.)

Williams syndrome children are likewise reported to have a selectivity problem. Tomc, Williamson, and Pauli (1991) call this a standard characteristic of Williams temperament. Crisco, Dobbs, and Mulhern (1988: 654–55) suggest that Williams syndrome is marked by problems in perceptual selectivity and difficulty in sorting on varied input.

Interestingly enough, Williams syndrome and autism can co-occur, even though the two disorders seem polar opposites. The former produces extroverted, talkative individuals and the latter introverted, reticent individuals. But Reiss et al. (1985) report one case of their convergence (and Ghaziuddin, Bolyard, and Alessi 1994 report the convergence of autism and Noonan syndrome, the latter similar to Turner syndrome). If the problem with Williams and autism is not speech per se but computational control through the language for thought, then there is nothing problematic about this co-occurrence. Both produce dysfunction in metasemantic and metapragmatic speech for exclusion and individuation.

These clinical and experimental results come together nicely under the effects of computational control. Among the major management functions of control structures are filtering and ranking input, scheduling information for processing, and monitoring processing progress (especially in terms of demands on system resources) so as to anticipate errors and reset the system should breakdown occur. These are exactly the computational versions of the behavioral problems described earlier. If these syndromes involve a lack of uptake in speech for cognitive control, then problems in choosing among alternatives are to be expected. Moreover, they should be explained not simply as resource disorders, or problems compensated for by adding more memory or more attention. The language for thought orients the individual toward choices by providing metarepresentational *knowledge* for sorting out options, not just more mental space in which to make the choices. That is, control disorders are not reducible to performance problems (Frawley 1997).

6.53   Lack of Global Integration

Another widely observed characteristic of individuals with these disorders is an inability to integrate performance globally, with much more normal-like performance when the processing requires a local domain and a well-circumscribed solution. Instances of failure at global integration can be plucked from the literature almost at random. Williams syndrome produces well-known problems in spatial integration. Bellugi, Wang, and Jernigan (1994: 37) report that when Williams syndrome children are asked to copy pictures in a drawing task, they "reliably draw only the local features and do not configure them in the correct global arrangement." As a consequence, they produce exploded drawings of figures they are asked to copy (see also Bellugi, Sabo, and Vaid 1988).

Similar behavior typifies the discourse of Williams individuals, whose narratives adhere to the rules of local discourse organization and so have "good story structure" (Reilly, Klima, and Bellugi, 1991: 371) but lack overall topical coherence and purpose. Note how a Williams individual describes an elephant: "And what an elephant is, it is one of the animals. And what the elephant does, it lives in the jungle" (372). This narrative is a litany, a minimally structured list, not something that coheres to a larger narrative purpose.

But while the global-local cut characterizes visuospatial processing and some aspects of language in Williams syndrome, it does not at all apply to face recognition. Williams individuals are very good not only at standard tests of face recognition, but also at closure tests on faces and on identifying properties of completed faces, all assessment techniques that presumably require global integration. But on closure tests for non-face stimuli, such as ordinary objects, they perform quite poorly (Bellugi, Wang, and Jernigan 1994: 40–41). So the global-local cut applies only to some spatial domains; the face-object discrepancies follow the modular design properties of the brain/mind.

Similarly, Mervis and Bertrand (1993) have found that, contrary to expectation, Williams children process part-whole lexical relationships normally. One would anticipate poor performance in this respect since the task requires integration of the local semantic part into the global semantic whole. But part-whole lexical relations are arguably part of universal semantic space, which is preserved in Williams individuals. Moreover, denotation itself works by *whole-object* reference (Golinkoff, Mervis, and Hirsh-Pasek 1994). So, lexical-semantic wholes are not affected by the disorder in the same way that global face integration is unaffected in the fully preserved, biologically determined face-recognition module.

These findings support two broader points. First, the global-local cut certainly applies in Williams syndrome, but not as a resource deficit across the board, since these individuals can globally integrate within preserved domains. Second, and following from the first, they show that it is necessary to see exactly how and where control applies. Failures at global integration surface where code and context meet, as in narrative coherence. Consequently, the same deficit appears in the social cognition of Williams children, who, while strongly expressive, lack functional control over this ability (Thal, Bates, and Bellugi 1989; Udwin 1990).

Turner syndrome also produces failures in global integration alongside unexpected successes. IQ tests on Turner girls unwaveringly show failure on the block design and object assembly subtests, both of which require object manipulation with respect to a fully integrated spatial whole. More particularly, Yamada and Curtiss (1981: 98) report that their subject "seemed to have a great deal of difficulty drawing the parts of the picture in correct spatial relationship," but nonetheless could do closure tests with faces and figures. Downey et al. (1991: 37) note that Turner girls have difficulty visually picturing the completion of a spatial project, and so lack global visuospatial integration. Lewandowski, Costenbader, and Richman (1985: 145) find that Turner girls' depressed performance on design completion correlates significantly with their overall poor nonverbal performance.

Somewhat surprisingly, Silbert, Wolff, and Lilienthal (1977) find the usual difficulty with spatial wholes but no problem in certain ostensibly integrative aspects of the lexicon. When we look at the kinds of lexical tasks that they had the subjects perform, this result is not surprising. For lexical assessment, subjects had to do color naming and a Stroop interference test (the latter presents words printed in colored ink, and subjects are asked to identify the color); both test *lexical access*, not lexical integration (see Tanenhaus and Lucas 1987). Lexical access is an algorithmic process that taps the formal structure of the lexicon. Insofar as control disorders preserve the computational core of mind, lexical access should also be preserved. But lexical integration, in which words are coordinated with contexts, was not tested, and so the Turner girls in this case did not have to execute global integration at the architecture-context boundary.

Other control syndromes exhibit a marked inability to integrate information globally in certain domains but no such failure in others. Autistics and spina bifida children all manifest severe problems in sustaining topic coherence in discourse (Tager-Flusberg and Anderson 1991, Culatta 1993c: 178–79); even the unnamed syndromes are typified by such a lack of global integration in information (Blank, Gessner, and Esposito 1979; Yamada 1990). But, remarkably, spina bifida children can recall and integrate faces just like normals (Cull and Wyke 1984), and autistics have no problems with spatial integration (Bellugi, Wang, and Jernigan 1994: 47). Still, autistics do have marked difficulties integrating contextual and social information, the very place where control must manage the interaction of code and context.

All these findings speak to the effects of a breakdown in computational control. One of the major functions of control structures is to integrate processing by checking the smooth flow of computation across domains and the interaction of the computational system with the world outside the machine. Control crashes should thus manifest themselves as global and interactive dysfunctions.

These in turn evoke two properties of metaconsciousness: planning and stance. One way to think of planning is as the overall point of thinking, the ultimate scenario that unites local actions. Stance provides the cognitive frame or unifying point of view. If some parts of language drive the cognitive frame and anchor the overall metacognitive picture—the individual's theory of the world or situation definition—deficits in these aspects of language should result in stance and planning breakdowns.

6.54 Failure to Appreciate Significance beyond Meaning

Speech serves the development of significance, what Vygotsky called *smysl,* inferential meaning beyond both denotation and routinized implicature *(znachenie).* The metapragmatic and metasemantic aspects of speech free the individual from the social and so lead to context independence and individuation. But precisely the opposite behaviors are the common observations in these syndromes. Clinicians and experimenters unwaveringly report context dependence, situational restrictedness, literalness, and a general failure to appreciate significance beyond truth-conditional meaning.

Meyerson and Frank (1987: 261) note that Williams children, despite their loquaciousness, fail to grasp the significance of dialogue itself and the positions of the speakers in the exchange. For Williams children, discourse means only what it does in the circumstance of its expression. This dis-connection of discourse meaning from significance in fact clarifies one pe-culiar finding by Reilly, Klima, and Bellugi (1991). They note that Williams children tell elaborate and complicated stories, with too many affective and discourse markers. But if the syndrome dissociates logic from control, then Williams children should have the pragmatic logic of narrative but not metapragmatic control over the significance of the discourse. They *should fail* to control the very markers of meaning beyond the literal. Im-portant corollary support for this point lies in the fact that Williams chil-dren tend to *tell the same story to all audiences.* They do not adjust the structure of their discourse as a function of strategic linguistic value, sig-nificance, or contextual variation. All audiences for their narratives are es-sentially one audience.

A similar split between *znachenie* and *smysl*—and consequent literalness and contextual dependence—appears in Turner syndrome. McCauley et al. (1987) report that Turner girls are very good at recalling faces but fail to discriminate the affect on the face recalled. This result appears to be independent of the more general spatial problems of Turner girls because when spatial and attentional skills are experimentally controlled, the deficit in affective discrimination still surfaces. Lahood and Bacon (1985) report that on simple tasks of recall of spatial information, Turner girls are very much like normals. But on tasks that demand mental recoding, transfor-mation, and manipulation of spatial information, their performance mark-edly falls off (see also Rovet and Netley 1982). These findings make sense, however, in terms of a break between literalness and significance. Arguably, simple visual recall requires minimal recoding of the external world and so is, in a way, a context-dependent spatial task. But the deliberate mental transformation of spatial information demands context-independent ma-nipulations, and so we should expect the Turner girls to fail here.[9]

Contextual restriction and lack of uptake are very clear in the behavior of Laura, who shows remarkable literalness in situations that require her to calculate implicatures and act on the significance of information pre-sented to her. Yamada (1990: 138–39) reports an exchange among Laura, her mother, and her father in which she is invited to retell a story told earlier that day in school. Her mother says, "Let's hear it." In response, Laura interprets *hear* literally, as 'verbal sound', not as what is implicated: 'Please do tell the story'. So she tries to reproduce the events iconically and even asks about words to describe her imitation. She apparently grasps the locutionary foundation of the implicature, its representational base, but not its significance or appropriateness, its control function.

In the end, some of the strongest evidence for situational restrictedness and failure in significance comes from work on autism. For autistics, the more structured the social discourse situation, the better they perform (Tager-Flusberg and Anderson 1991); autistics have thus been called the "ultimate situation theorists" in that they seem totally tied to the external conditions of talk and performance (Leekam and Perner 1991).[10]

It is important to note that their situational restrictedness seems tied to specific discourse-related disorders that surface at the point of association between speech for thought and *smysl*. Tager-Flusberg (1993) shows that while autistics can engage in discourse, they appear not to understand that discourse involves the exchange of information. Like Williams syndrome, autism affects an appreciation of the very significance of discourse itself. Autistics also rarely use language to serve a social function and have problems with descriptions of mental and/or epistemic states and with attention generally, that is, they experience a deficit in propositional attitudes and mechanisms for focusing action through language (Tager-Flusberg 1992, 1993). Indeed, they tend to describe their internal states very much in external terms (Sigman 1994: 150).

While current psychological theory explains autism as a metarepresentational deficit, a failure in the development and use of secondary representation, and, consequently, a naive theory of mind (Perner 1991), a more general explanation for the theory of mind deficit itself can be traced to metaconsciousness and computational control. Stance, individuation, deliberateness, internalization, and representationality are tied to *smysl* and the liberation of the individual from the immediate social context.

The language for thought is a portable social structure that individuals carry into any task; it is the means by which the individual as a social self emerges from the social group and the contextual personae that the group affords. A disruption in the language for thought should therefore leave the individual in a kind of pure external state; it should also result in the need for *more external structure in problem solving* in order to have externally, not mentally, imposed limitations on the problem-solving space. Some intriguing data on spina bifida children support this expectation. Spina bifida children are no different from normals on almost all measures of social and verbal interaction in problem solving (Friedrich et al. 1991, van Hasselt et al. 1991), except that they use significantly more externalization strategies (van Hasselt et al. 1991: 76).

In a Vygotskyan cognitive science, we should expect the peculiar pragmatic deficits of these syndromes to appear as deficits in the ability to engage in true social discourse and to internalize social interaction as a self-regulatory mechanism. It is not surprising that individuals with disorders such as Williams syndrome display extremely sociable behavior but fail to harness this behavior in internalized form (i.e., fail to go from the intermental to the intramental). We might say that Williams individuals are expressively sociable and contextual *but not expressively social,* not able to manage the relationship between the individuated self and the external social group.

6.55 Lack of Goal-Directedness

An important purpose of control structures is to keep computing on track by monitoring the flow of information with respect to predetermined goals. Analogously, a major purpose of the language for thought is to support an individual's progress from mere behavior to behavior with a prercpresented outcome and smooth execution thereto. A control-language deficit should therefore leave an individual with severe problems in planning, imagining outcomes, and seeing tasks through to completion.

Again, the experimental and clinical literatures on the syndromes under consideration are rife with illustrations of just this sort of breakdown. Turner syndrome results in the inability to complete tasks and great difficulty in picturing the results of projects (Downey et al. 1989, 1991; McCauley, Ito, and Kay 1986; Williams, Richman, and Yarbrough 1991). Downey et al. (1991: 37) in fact report this problem as the only difference between Turner girls and normals on a self-evaluation of performance in everyday spatial tasks.

Similar results characterize the findings on spina bifida. Landry et al. (1990: 306) observe that spina bifida children have problems with "planning the actions necessary to carry on [an] activity . . . [and] persisting in these actions in order to achieve an identified goal." Their experiments show that "children with spina bifida show less task-oriented behavior" (309) and difficulties "sustaining this behavior" (310). While some of this is surely traceable to the limitations on mobility incurred by children with spina bifida, it is important to note that lack of goal-directedness is not characteristic just of physical motion in these individuals. As Culatta (1993c: 181–82) reports, an inability to appreciate goals and plans runs throughout all behavior, not just motoric performance.

Problems with goal-directed behavior and difficulty in sustaining behavior toward a desired end also surface in autism. This is perhaps surprising since autism appears, at least on the surface, as *extremely controlled behavior*—unidirectional and overly self-directed. But this self-directedness is evidently compensation for a loss in control. Sigman (1994: 144) reports a number of results which show that autistics have difficulty on tasks that "require individuals [to] use internally formulated plans and set aside more habitual actions evoked by the external context. Autistic individuals have been shown to have difficulty in guiding their behavior in terms of foreseeable consequences." Moreover, this planing deficit seems to be a consequence of autism per se since it is characteristic of nonretarded autistics and so is not associated with any other mental deficit (Sigman 1994: 145).

A nice final illustration of this deficit and its connection to the language for thought appears in the behavior of Laura. Yamada (1990) reports throughout her study that Laura fails to stay on task or keep to a desired end, and this is one of the reasons why her discourse seems so rambling. Interestingly enough, although her language is generally quite good, Laura does appear to have prosodic problems (Yamada 1990: 61). The same sort of prosodic difficulties have also been observed in Turner girls, for whom Silbert, Wolff, and Lilienthal (1977: 18) report significantly lower scores than for normals on tests of rhythm and tonal memory and auditory figure-ground structure. It is well known that pausing and prosody are reliable indications of planning (Garman 1990: 121–33). As the individual engages in slow, deliberate thought, prosody (itself a coherence device) marks the organizational chunks, and pausing "allows the speaker to plan ahead" (Garman 1990: 130). Thus, bizarre prosody and pausing and difficulty with rhythm are natural correlates of planning problems.[11]

All these characteristics are associated with speech for higher thought, metaconsciousness, and computational control. The ability to complete tasks, for example, is connected to the ability to plan solutions in a symbolic way and to execute action toward this represented outcome. The metasemantic and metapragmatic bases of the language for thought are the symbolic means an individual uses to plan and sustain action toward a symbolically represented end (see, e.g., Wertsch 1991). A deficit in this control language should surface as a deficit in goal-directedness.

We might, in fact, recast this whole matter of goal-directedness into Leont'ev's activity theory. As we know from Chapter 3, Leont'ev distinguishes action from activity. The former is bare or mere behavior, not directed to any apparent end outside itself. Action is the sort of thing that Landry et al. (1990: 309) describe as typical of spina bifida children in situations that would otherwise evoke goal-directedness in normals: "[They] spent more time in simple manipulation of the play materials."

Activity, by contrast, is action with a predetermined symbolic end: self-speech constructs metaconsciousness and the mentally projected outcomes of situations that allow the individual to think deliberately without being at the mercy of others or of circumstance. Activity is the very thing that Landry et al. (1990: 310) report as absent in spina bifida children: "It may be that staying on task, which encompasses understanding what steps need to be taken to move toward a goal and the sequence in which they occur, is especially difficult for spina bifida children."

Curiously, this description of what spina bifida children lack is virtually identical to what Ghezzi and Jazayeri (1987: 173) say is essential to efficient computation: "control structures—the mechanisms by which programmers can specify the flow of execution . . . language units that are used to order the sequence in which individual statements are executed." Control might thus be understood as the way computing itself progresses from simple computational action to computational activity.

6.6 Two Final Clarifications

We now have a picture of the effects on behavior and thinking that result from disruptions in the mental control language. But this wide-ranging discussion of ostensibly very different disorders requires two final clarifications that return us to the particulars of computationalism, metaconsciousness, and the way sociocultural mind might be given a computational interpretation.

First, we might wonder what is gained by all this control language talk? Why not think of these syndromes just as disorders of social knowledge, without casting them as computational disruptions? After all, these individuals appear to lack some crucial knowledge of the world. For example, Tomasello, Kruger, and Ratner (1993: 504) characterize autistic children as "basically acultural, reflecting a general deficit in the ability to acquire culturally conventional human behaviors."

The literature is full of rather curious reports that these individuals do possess (sometimes extensive) sociocultural knowledge. Williams syndrome children are very sociable and are quite eager to display all sorts of social and cultural knowledge. Laura clearly has considerable social knowledge, as the exchanges about Thanksgiving and death in Yamada's book (1990: 137–42.) reveal. There are reports of Turner girls having superior social judgment (Lahood and Bacon 1984)—a strange result if they otherwise lack social knowledge! Autistics are reported to be able to engage in fundamental social behavior: "[They] are not as socially unresponsive as originally thought" (Sigman 1994: 146).

Individuals with these syndromes have the logic of social-knowledge algorithms but not the control. That is, they lack *effective social knowledge,* not social knowledge per se. Turner girls have difficulty seeing the appropriateness of social rules even though they can expertly judge social information. So the issue appears to be more subtle than just the absence of social knowledge. If these are control disorders, then the problems lie in the uptake and use of sociocultural information, not in the paucity of the information itself.

These disorders may, in fact, be better understood as a generalized problem with interface management, a typical control function in computational systems. Tager-Flusberg's (1994: 6) view of DH, the well-known case of spina bifida (Cromer's famous subject), approaches this characterization. She argues that DH has both social and linguistic modules intact but still behaves as if she lacked social knowledge. The problem lies in the integration and monitoring of these knowledge domains, one of the very purposes of the language for thought (see Frawley 1997).

These observations lead to the second clarification. As control disorders, these syndromes are not just resource or performance problems. Again, it would be convenient to think of them as such since social tasks put these individuals at a great disadvantage, and one might then argue that their mental computing systems in such circumstances crash from overload. But this would be the wrong view of both the syndromes and control. Put simply, control is not a resource. It is part of the algorithm. As Kirsh (1992) points out, resource deficits can be compensated for by increasing the mental resources available to an individual (e.g., adding to memory resources by giving external memory aids). But these control disorders cannot be so rectified. One cannot bypass the disorders of Williams syndrome, for example, by somehow modifying the processing capacity of the individual. Control disorders remain disorders of knowledge, not resource. They are deficits in the metarepresentational, control aspect of algorithms.

Epilogue: Is Everything Cognitive Science?

Against Grand Schemes

Vygotskyan cognitive science requires that certain units of internal formal mind be external sociocultural units *and* that these external sociocultural units be implemented as internal computational units. Phrased as such, Wittgenstein's problem might bring a great sinking feeling with it. When the contrasts of human thinking find a single home—when ethnography tells us as much about computational mind as automata theory tells us about socioculturalism—cognitive science becomes the ultimate discipline. Is there anything that is *not* cognitive science?

We run the risk of creating a *grand scheme monster,* a metatheoretical "just so story" in which every fact falls in place. Grand schemes solve every problem, usually by not solving very many in particular. The devil may be in the details, but so are the angels. Have we made a kind of gentle monster here, one that lets in every fact and hypothesis and so advances none?

Even though sociocultural and formal mind are compatible, not everything is cognitive science because not every pursuit of mind requires a *design limitation* account of *computable representations.* The study of biological information processing privileges accounts that describe wetware engineering constraints on structures and inner code: cognitive science is thus the study of representation engineering (see Sloman 1993 for some nice points in this respect).

In this way, proposals that make no essential reference to the mind's design limitations on computable representations, in spite of their appeals to cognitive structure, are just not cognitive science. Consider Turner's (1991) book on literary theory in which he argues that literature is built out of ordinary language, and so both its production and its reception are traceable to the structures that motivate language itself. These are mental

261

image schemas, derived from the physical and spatial organization of the human body in the world and mentally generalized by means of meta-phorical transfer (e.g., fundamental concepts of the body may be analo-gized to other "higher" conceptual domains; Lakoff 1987). Because lit-erary language follows the image-schematic organization of ordinary language, its study is a part of cognitive linguistics and so is a branch of cognitive science.

There are a number of problems with this line of thinking, ones that return us to our fear of the grand scheme monster. For one thing, it is decidedly anticomputational. Turner (1991: 17) writes, "Human lan-guage is an expression of uniquely human forms of thought, forms not available, for example, to a contemporary digital computer." This is just wrong, as the survey of Chapter 2 shows. Anyhow, if the brain/mind is not a computing device, then what is it?

For another thing, there does not seem to be *any* experimental support of the image-schematic view of mental organization. Everything cited as evidence is really just linguistic analysis claiming to be cognitive science. And the computational models that Turner ironically cites (1991: 21 n. 15)—basic connectionist systems—do not use these kinds of mental image schemas as the content of their representations. To say that an analogical model, like a neural net, can accommodate image schemas and their ana-logical transfer is not to say that they do.

The real problem here is that Turner (and, I would add, those he cites) confuses conceptual analysis with cognitive analysis and then calls it all *cognitive science*.[1] But *how* is literature a function of the design limitations of the computable representations of the mind/brain? What exactly is *mind/brain computed?* The angel is in the details, and as Courbet famously said, show me an angel and I'll paint it.

The (ultimately trivial) fact that a human activity, such as literature, is the product of a human mind does not necessitate cognitive science as the proper method of its analysis. Should there then be a *cognitive science* of politics? Of the stock market? Of subatomic theory? Of guilt? Of baseball? Perhaps there could be a *conceptual* analysis of these, but now I think I hear the grand scheme monster knocking at the door.

Is Vygotskyan cognitive science design discourse? The usual social re-ductionist reading of Vygotsky says no. But the foregoing arguments of the book have tried to show that it is an explanation of the *design of higher thought*, compatible with both sociocultural knowledge external to mind and internally computed representations. When we say, for example, that

Williams syndrome is a congenital delinking of the language for thought from the language of thought, we are making a claim about design breakdown. When we say that the language for thought is a control structure, we are making a claim about the design of part of the code of the mind's software.

Vygotskyan cognitive science is entirely in accord with the computational-engineering explanations that characterize mainstream cognitive science. This yields a double lesson: Vygotskyans have to be responsible computationalists, but only as much as computationalists are responsible socioculturalists.

Sociocomputationalism

What this book has *not* argued is that the mind is in the world. This is obviously true and, in the end, misleading because embedding the mind in the world neither produces a sociocultural cognitive science nor guarantees that the world will have any effect on the mind's operation (i.e., not be causally efficacious, to use Pylyshyn's phraseology). There are many theories of how the world is organized, many about how the mind computes, and many about how the mind computes *in* the world. There are far fewer theories of how the world actually *is* computationally effective. Vygotskyan cognitive science is a claim about *how the world is in the computational mind*. More particularly, it is about how the world is in the mind by means of certain parts of language that have computational landing sites. Vygotskyan cognitive science is an account of *computationally effective sociocultural information*. This is what I call, at the risk of jargonizing, *sociocomputationalism*. Vygotsky called it *internalization*.

Let us consider an example of the need to respect the details of how the world can be in the computational mind. McClamrock's (1995) book on the contextual situatedness of otherwise computational mind is very much in the spirit of the present one, but not all that much in the letter.[2] In his view, cognitive science has lost track of the importance of regularities external to the mind, or what he forcefully calls *existential cognition*. In his view, some causal mechanisms for mind lie outside the organism; context makes local parts of the environment salient to mind as it satisfices—takes its best behavioral shot by assessing the environment and the task at hand, without deploying an optimal model. Mind and its analysis have no overriding theory of tasks and plans: the experience of organized instances provides the best cognitive fit.

So far so good. But *how* does all this happen? In many cases, existential cognition drifts out of cognitive science and becomes an account of mind in the world, not the world in the mind. It perpetuates the *boundary* of the mind and world rather than the integration of the two.

Consider McClamrock's (1995: 113) point that the mind can exploit the environment without representing and computing over this representation of it. As he says, the world is its own model (113). He argues, for instance, that the perceived stability and fullness of the visual field is not traceable to the internal mechanisms that construct visual consciousness because they are unstable (185). The eye moves constantly, and visual information changes with every movement, so the seamlessness and fullness of the visual field must be "in a very strong sense the stability of the environment" (183). The regularity of vision lies in the regularity of the external visual database. The visual world is its best model.

Intriguing as this proposal is, it overlooks the otherwise accepted neurocomputational account of the unity of visual experience. If an experimental subject is shown two successive points of light at an interval of less than 0.1–0.2 seconds, she will experience the points as simultaneous even though they are "actually" successive; a slight increase in the interval will result in the experience of successive points. Remarkably, this cognitive interval in which visual experience is continuous and unified has a neural correlate in the dominant rhythm of the visual cortex at about 0.15 seconds (Varela, Thompson, and Rosch 1991: 73; see also Iwasaki 1993).

The computation of the representations given as a consequence of the mind's design limitations, in concert with the input, determines the "unified visual now." This visual binding affords the organism default stretches of experience: *models*. The visual world is not its best model. Only the *effectively computed* visual world is the best model. The world may take care of things for the mind which we sometimes think the mind does, but unless those proxies are computed, the world has not taken care of much.

A more apposite lesson emerges from an issue on which existential cognition and Vygotskyan cognitive science more obviously dovetail: how the environment controls thinking. McClamrock (1995: 107) observes that thinking can involve two kinds of control: internal (what he calls *access* across modules) or external (what he calls *penetrability* of modules by external or top-down information). (There is a similar discussion in Chapter 3 on kinds of control breakdown.) Moreover, external control can be either *reactive* (responsive to the enforced structure of the environment) or *opportunistic* (responsive to aspects of the structured environment it is prepared for; 85–90). It is the last of these that is made viable by socio-computationalism. *How* does opportunism work?

Consider the printer attached to your computer. When you instruct it to print a file, the printer and the CPU, modules of the system, exchange information. Control of this exchange is what McClamrock calls *access*. Now, suppose that in the middle of printing, you want the printer to stop. How do you do it? How do you bring about a user-initiated interrupt?

One way is to pull the plug. In this case, the printer module experiences external control *(penetrability)* and simply *reacts* to the experience by stopping. The printer does not "expect" to have the plug pulled, and certainly has no memory of previous plug pulls to remind it what to do. Still, when the plug is pulled, the printer stops. In this way, it successfully "thinks" without a representation.

A more computationally sophisticated way of stopping the printer is to send it a command to do so. You could start hitting the keys while the printer is running to try to stop the printing. But, as those of you who have done so will attest, not every keystroke causes the printer to stop. Only some keystrokes are meaningful to the system.[3] Only user interrupts that the internal code is ready to receive are effectively computed (i.e., manifest *opportunism*). Only some keystrokes *remind* the printer of its printing options.

Which signals work? Sociocomputationalism is an account of the details of the opportunistic environmental control of thinking by certain aspects of language. Why don't all the keystrokes of human sociocultural interaction initiate a user-initiated interrupt? Only some of them are sociocomputationally effective. Only some have a landing site in minds. Only some have a role in the language *for* processing and can remind a human about her own thinking. Sociocomputationalism reminds us that grand schemes of the *mind in the world* need to be responsible to specific claims about *how the world could be in the mind*.

Two Prospects for Sociocomputationalism

Where can we use sociocomputationalism? Apart from the illustrations in the previous chapters, this integration of the social and computational might find a place in two current research programs: "theory of mind," which is an account of how higher thinking might be a kind of metacomputation; and computational architectures with mechanisms that would support something like higher thought.

Theory of Mind

In Chapter 6 I briefly discussed the influential proposal that a significant part of mental development involves the construction of a "theory of mind" (hereafter TOM), a personal account of one's own and others' mental states (see, e.g., Wellman 1990, Perner 1991). Since TOM is a comprehensive picture of *thought about thought*, it looks like a natural place for Vygotskyan cognitive science. But the two overlap only in part, and where they converge and diverge is an interesting lesson in the benefits of sociocomputationalism.

While there is much debate about the details of TOM (Leslie and Roth 1993, Perner 1993, Hobson 1993), advocates essentially agree that it is a high-level metarepresentational construct built on some ontogenetically prior construct, such as a nonrepresentational desire psychology (Wellman 1993) or mechanisms of attention and goal detection (Baron-Cohen 1993). The rudiments of TOM emerge around the end of the first year, when children exhibit an understanding of the difference between self-caused and externally caused action. TOM changes over the second year as children begin to understand person-object relations and learn that objects can be the focus of attention (a kind of proto-intentionality). At about the age of three, TOM settles fully into place as children productively differentiate people's insides from outsides, judge the privacy of their own thoughts, and become confident that internal beliefs influence external behavior (Wellman 1993).[4]

The properties of TOM bear a remarkable resemblance to those proposed for metaconsciousness. TOM involves metarepresentations, internal-external relations, and awareness of mental stance. It is connected to the development of knowledge of persons and has a variety of executive functions. Despite these similarities, metaconsciousness and TOM diverge on several crucial counts, which underscore the need for sociocomputationalism.

In Leslie's view (1987, Leslie and Roth 1993), TOM is a *metarepresentational data structure* built on an agent's attitude toward a represented aspect of reality (a primary representation) that is decoupled from reality into an imaginary situation (metarepresentation). Put this way, TOM gets a computational flavor as a kind of mental formula: AGENT *[has]* ATTITUDE *[to]* PRIMARY REPRESENTATION *[such that]* '*it is a* METAREPRESENTATION' (e.g., I pretend that this pencil 'is a spaceship'). Much rides on the decoupling of the primary representation from reality, which is notationally signaled by the bracketing of the metarepresentation as a proposition about the primary representation: *'it is a METAREPRESENTATION'*. In Leslie's terms, the bracketing *quarantines* the imaginary situation and raises it to a second-order representation, an expression about reality.

Autism, Leslie argues, is a deficit of this second-order data structure. His evidence is that autistic individuals have great difficulty with false belief—an incorrect model of a state of affairs—because it requires discontinuity between primary and secondary representation. If they had an intact TOM, they would be able to coordinate representational and metarepresentational data structures.

Here the clarifications of sociocomputationalism come to bear. There are two aspects to metarepresentation—content and bracketing (cf. Wellman 1993: 30)—and thus two possible higher-thought disruptions. Classic TOM disorders are data structure deficits, problems with higher-order content. As such, they are entirely endogenous and purely computational, built on the proliferation of representational data structures.

But there could also be bracketing disorders, such as the control syndromes described in Chapter 6. Metaconsciousness is higher-thought but *not* a data structure, not a representation *of* another representation. It is awareness of a representation *as* a representation, originating in the sociocultural resources for reflexivity, chiefly speech. Control disorders are located in TOM's mechanisms of reflexive focusing, not in its higher-order content. Thus, TOM may be essentially a data structure, and disorders of TOM may be data structure deficits, but metaconsciousness and its disorders are not: they involve the self-referential bracketing that signals representationality itself.[5]

This clarification of TOM brings order to several surprising findings about TOM breakdown, which in turn suggests some new things about the language for thought. Autism appears *not* to be a problem of reflexive focusing (Perner 1993: 119). In fact, reflexive focusing appears to bring the performance of autistic individuals up to a normal level in the crucial experiments on false belief (Baron-Cohen 1993: 60n.). Thus, it might be argued that autistic individuals have difficulty with *representation of* but have no problem with, and indeed benefit from the signals of, *representation as*. This seems to be what Perner (1993) argues when he says that autistic individuals have a database deficit, not a decoupling problem, and it would stand to reason if autism were a disorder of *only one aspect of metaknowledge*.[6]

Experimental findings also suggest that TOM, unlike metaconsciousness, is not related to planning or inhibition. Autistic individuals can plan and inhibit (Leslie and Roth 1993, Harris 1993), but they have difficulty with perspective and stance (Leslie and Roth 1993). Apparently, not all executive functions are equal, a result that would again stand to reason, given two kinds of higher thought disruption. If TOM is representational and exhibits patterns of perspectival breakdown, then perspective and stance may be matters of content. But planning and inhibition, immune as they appear to be to TOM disruptions, may be issues of representation-*ality* not representation; that is, they may be more properly issues of activity than of data.

If these speculations are in any way correct, then one way to think about autism might be as bracketing without content, control without logic, or, more strongly, *a language for thought with a disrupted language of thought.* We might further argue that autism involves an *overdeveloped* language for thought, or at least one unconstrained by content. This may be why autistic individuals are so self-contained and overly self-regulated. They overfocus and overbracket. With no second-order content to bracket, they evince representational problems, but they nevertheless benefit from bracketing help. They can inhibit and plan, but they cannot take a stance. If autism preserves bracketing and focusing but not internal second-order representations, then its characterization as a deficit in cultural learning (Tomasello, Kruger, and Ratner 1993) may not be accurate. Quite the opposite: the external origins of metaconsciousness and the hyper–self-regulation of autistic individuals might suggest that they have been *overenculturated*, or that they have too rapidly internalized the external world. Their sociocomputational control mechanisms run independently of the representations that normally harness them.

Sociocomputational Architectures

The second prospect for sociocomputationalism concerns the computational architectures that might support the ideas of Vygotskyan cognitive science. Much is made of the computational tractability of TOM (Leslie 1987) and metaprocesses generally (Karmiloff-Smith 1986, 1992: 190). Does sociocomputationalism have any true computational analogue? Can metaconsciousness be computed?

The past decade or so has seen substantial work on architectures that might accommodate explicit, self-reflexive focusing. For instance, hybrid connectionist-control architectures combine networks with explicit rules.

Blackboard architectures have an independent workspace and explicit control algorithms. Both give a central role to explicit computational control. We will look briefly at the latter as an illustration.

Blackboard architectures (Hayes-Roth 1985) have three components: a database that provides the knowledge that the system manipulates; an independent, multiply accessible, dynamic workspace for problem solving, the *blackboard;* and a control unit that monitors both the database and the blackboard (Nii 1989). While much of the influence of blackboard systems derives from the idea of the blackboard itself, equally if not more important are the mechanisms of control. Indeed, the first blackboard system, Hearsay, is significant for both its problem-solving results and its agenda-based control (Hayes-Roth 1989).

It would seem straightforward to link sociocomputationalism with the blackboard, the central workspace for problem solving. But we should recall that higher thinking is not problem solving per se but its management. The *control mechanisms* in blackboard systems are the most likely correlates of sociocomputational mechanisms.

Interestingly enough, the overall advantages of blackboard systems often hang on how control works in a particular implementation. For example, blackboard systems allow multiple lines of reasoning to converge on an emergent solution to a problem in a large solution space. Critical to this performance is the monitoring of both the blackboard and the database and the exclusion and inhibition of options as the problem solving proceeds. Thus, a blackboard implementation involves a kind of trade-off between the openness and dynamism of on-line reasoning and the restrictiveness of control. This trade-off, in turn, produces a clear lesson about the computational analogues of metaconsciousness.

In Chapter 3 we saw that social and computational mind might be brought together under a larger framework of trade-offs between architectures and contexts. The relative contextualization of social metaknowledge can vary from culture to culture—that is, from implementation to implementation—and should have measurable effects on speed and performance. This very problem, in purely computational terms, has been the focus of empirical studies of alternative control systems for blackboard architectures.

Garvey and Hayes-Roth (1989) report on a comparison of two kinds of blackboard control: one in which the control is explicit and directly coded in a module distinct from the database and the blackboard (this is the standard blackboard model); and one in which control is implicit and embedded in the task-specific procedures themselves. In the former implementation, control and problem solving interface, and so the metaprocesses are in a set-membership relation to the rest of the system; they are clearly demarcated as a control context for the rest of the architecture. In the latter implementation, control and problem solving are similarly coded and so form a part-whole relation: the contextual metaprocesses are not clearly demarcated from the rest of the architecture.

Significantly, these architecture-context manipulations of control in blackboard systems produce results that mirror those reported in Chapter 3 for the same manipulations with respect to human processing of the lexicon. When control and the rest of the system interface, performance is slow; when control is part of the whole of the system, performance is fast (Garvey and Hayes-Roth 1989: 50). It thus appears that the very framework proposed for unifying social and computational mind to begin with applies to computational architectures that seek to characterize metaknowledge.[7]

Does Internalism Win Out?

Considerations of computational architecture return us to the original question of this book. As architectures, they are *inside stories*. Not everything is cognitive science—that's for certain. But must all those things that are cognitive science—sociocomputationalism included—be internal? In avoiding the grand scheme monster by shooting narrowly and clearly, have we let internalism back in?

In a necessary and ultimately harmless sense, we have. Individualism could not but be right on one score: the *direct mechanisms* of mind are internal, and the most regular of external worlds must be neurologically mediated. This amounts to saying that we do not think unless we think, and that is fine by me. In fact, the discomfort of representationless cognitive science is that it makes it sound as if we do not have to think in order to think.

The proper way to reconvene the internalist-externalist debate in the context of sociocomputationalism is in the terms of Chapter 1. How and where do we draw the mind-world boundary? What and where are the trade-offs? Where is the bulk of the influence? What is the best story for particular mind-world facts?

Consider, again, Universal Grammar (UG). Even the most ardent UG adherent acknowledges that input plays some role in language development. But its influence is so minimal that *input* is a misnomer. Exposure to linguistic data triggers the unfolding of an internal process, much as the immune system is triggered into effectiveness from the experience of pathogens. How else could we make sense of the fact that in deaf children the internal push toward language is so strong that speech seeps right out of their fingers? For UG, it does not make sense to say that much has been internalized because environmental "conditions are not the source of [UG's] internal organization" (Cosmides and Tooby 1994: 69 n. 11). UG is best told as an inside story.

This is not the case for control structures. They most certainly have some genetic substrate: the machine-level control on which unit-level and statement-level control is built. But we simply cannot tell the tale of the management of thinking, metarepresentation, inhibition, recovery from breakdown, self-talk, stance in problem solving, theory of mind development and breakdown, and the frame problem as an inside story. The internal structure of these things *is* traceable to environmental conditions: the metarepresentational and metacomputational properties of the programming language to be learned. A purely inside story of control is just not rich enough.

Only a story of some parts of thinking as an externally regulated speech activity—only an outside story—could possibly explain a memorable incident in my son's development. When he was about three, we had the following curious exchange:

"Where's Mommy?" he asked.

"I don't know," I said truthfully. I really did not know where she was at that moment. But this did not help him at all.

"Noooo," he insisted. "Where *is* she?"

"I don't *know*," I repeated, with equal insistence. How could he not believe me?

"Nooooooooo!!!! Where *is* she???!!"

This was escalating rapidly. And it was not an inside problem, not a matter of his representations alone. Otherwise the truth should have been enough. He believed that I knew the contents of his mind—or, better, that his mind was indistinct from mine, that he was me. And since I knew the answers, he had to know too. This was a sociocomputational control problem, an external-internal regulatory affair, not an issue of content. So not just any old answer would do. It had to be one that could close debate, right his capsized computational boat, and return his mind to its proper footing.

"Noooooo!!!! WHERE IS SHE???!!?"

"On the moon," I said.

"On the moon? Oh, good," he said. "The moon," he whispered to himself—very, very happy.

.

Notes

Bibliography

Index

Notes

1. Internalism and the Ideology of Cognitive Science

1. Recall from the Introduction that this stark distinction between internalism and externalism deliberately simplifies the situation in order to organize the field of competing research programs. Discussions based on more subtle versions of each side of the distinction can be found in Chapters 2 and 4, for example.

2. Dennett and Searle do, however, acknowledge the potential importance of externals. Dennett (1984a: 145) writes, "Frame-making . . . machinery might be guided by its previous experience," and he notes the role of cultural relevance in beliefs (1987: 29). Searle (1992: 127–28) writes: "I am convinced that the category of 'other people' plays a special role in the *structure* of our conscious experiences . . . But I do not yet know how to . . . analyze the structure of the social element in individual consciousness."

3. The individualism-nonindividualism split has the expected variety of intermediate positions. A principally individualistic theory but with a conservative acknowledgment of the world is the idea of *narrow content* (which Fodor adopts; see the papers in Loewer and Rey 1991). Technically, narrow content is a function that maps from possible contexts onto wide content. Informally, it is minimal formal information about the world that is intrinsic to an internal representation. For example, in the Twin Earth problem my double and I differ on wide content but share narrow content in that we both have the same function that maps from the possible contexts of our thoughts about our cats to the actual wide contexts where our thoughts differ. Although this seems to be a formalist trick, and looks very much like just another formal syntactic manipulation that returns mind to individualistic syntax (see Block 1991, Stich 1991), the important lesson is that intermediate positions on content can be developed (see also the papers in Grimm and Merrill 1985).

4. All Dennett's proposed "stances," or explanatory viewpoints, are thoroughgoing internalist positions. Not only is the intentional stance, as shown earlier, but so is the *design stance* (that we can explain an organism by its internal configuration) and the *physical stance* (that we can explain a system by its material constitution). Even what Dennett calls the "enabling assumptions"

(1987: 153) of his approach, autophenomenology and heterophenomenology, are essentially tied to internalism. The former is a first-person perspective on phenomena, the view from the inside, discovering the internal through self-report; the latter is a third-person perspective, the view from the outside, discovering the internal through report on or by others (and the reporter's own self can count as an other). Although these enabling conditions acknowledge the place of externalism, they nonetheless refer to the position of the explainer, not to the content of the explanation, which remains decidedly internal. To borrow Chomsky's (1986: 19–24) phraseology, they are still I-Stances.

2. From Plato's Problem to Wittgenstein's Problem

1. There is some controversy over whether this knowledge is computational (i.e., formal manipulation). Searle (1992: 197–226) argues that the brain/mind is not computational because nothing is intrinsically a computer, and so the brain/mind does not "process information" as such. The later Wittgenstein would have agreed with this view, given that his only response to reading Turing's famous paper on computation was that machines do not calculate. For the purposes of the present argument, it is not important whether the brain/mind is computational. Plato's answer does not require computationalism, only obligatory, purely internal, prewired "stuff." Even though I use the terms *computational* and *formal* interchangeably in what follows, this is a matter of convenience. If the brain/mind turns out not to be a computing device, Plato's answer is not much the worse for wear.

2. This is not to deny that we learn things about our language for our entire lives; that is, some things about language *are* revised. We certainly hear new words and learn new meanings; we hear new pronunciations and adjust our own. But these revisions are very minor compared to what we never modify or hear. We never hear a new part of speech or a new sentence type. We never revise the syllable structure or stress pattern of our language. We never form plurals in a new way, by, say, prefixing rather than suffixing. We never change the way we denote things in the world, even though we do modify what we denote. Crucially, at one time in our lives, between birth and about age five or six, we *did* make such changes, but they were systematic and very conservative, and then we stopped making them. What allows the child to stop computing the structure of language?

3. Certainly there are many other schools of linguistics that have also laid claim to acquisition. My choice of government binding as an illustration is not meant to undercut those schools, which, in any case, get their identity as alternatives to it.

4. Object scope is an empirical version of the fundamental semantic principle of extension, that the meaning of an expression can be determined from an enumeration of the individuals to which the expression applies. Crucially, object

scope precedes designation by features, or *intension*—truth by a description of properties of individuals.

5. Such radical Platonism is not as bizarre as it might appear. After all, the virtual-machine paradigm views language as a mathematical object and the mind as a formal-result device. What properties of language allow it to be manipulated and the right formal results to fall out? Do numbers have to be instantiated in a mind—that is, conceptualized—in order to be real? Does the truth of $(A + B) + (C) = (A) + (B + C)$ depend on the equation being grasped by a mind? Real-time, contingent conceptualization of mathematics in fact obscures the ideality of numbers and interferes with mathematical knowledge. Such Platonism is essentially identical to the views of one of the historical predecessors of mainstream cognitive science, Gottlob Frege, who held that the universal truths of logic and arithmetic do not depend on our cognizing them; logic, unlike ordinary human thought, is free from contradictions (Leiber 1991: 37–39).

This position gets additional support from an unlikely externalist sympathizer, Putnam (1988), who points out that in mathematics there is no need to decide between two extensionally equivalent systems. Thus, when linguistics adduces psychological data to make such decisions about equivalent grammars, it vitiates the mathematical nature of the object. Putnam (1980) argues that if the grammar is anything, it is an external object, in the language itself, just as the grammar of predicate calculus lies in the system of logic. He uses this argument to bolster his externalist views. For him there are no essences, only historical identities. So while the grammar may be in the language, it is not a timeless ideality. Nonetheless, Putnam's overall point fits tightly into Katz's (1981) objections. If language were a true formal object, it would not need psychobiological explanatory adequacy to arbitrate its grammars.

6. Here, Wittgenstein sounds like Chomsky's twin: actual language would fall out from logically possible language, and the latter would show its truth and correctness by its form. In formal linguistics, the best model of language—the one that is explanatorily adequate—shows its superiority to others by its formal simplicity. Its truth is displayed and does not need to be stipulated.

7. His logical program is very much like Frege's, though Frege confessed not to understand it. For Wittgenstein, unlike Frege, a proposition could have sense (descriptive meaning) without reference (extensional object); in fact, a proposition can only assert its sense, not reference. (How can a proposition assert an object?) This necessary world connection may be one reason for their misunderstanding. At the same time, it is also quite different from Russell's beliefs and those of the logical empiricists, who embraced the *Tractatus* as their apologia. Wittgenstein later remarked that Russell's introduction to the book missed the mark completely. While he and Russell were concerned with examining the limits of reason from within—and both had transcendental leanings—Wittgenstein sought what cannot be said while the empiricists sought only what can. As Janik and Toulmin (1973) so aptly remark, the *philosophy* of

the *Tractatus* is to show the limits of modeling facts, but the *worldview* of the book is to show the impossibility of modeling value.

8. There are both more and less fashionable, but equally jargonized, ways of linking Vygotsky and Wittgenstein through postmodern theories of social action. See any of the hundreds of exposés (e.g., Jameson 1991, Lyotard 1984). I use Derrida and deconstruction here because they add to the philosophical continuity: Derrida's work goes back to Husserl, who wrote during the same period as Wittgenstein and Vygotsky. But another way to link Vygotsky and Wittgenstein through modern social action theory is through Bourdieu (1977), whose notion of *practice* is very much like Derrida's deconstructive attitude and Wittgenstein's forms of life (Margolis 1987: 148 makes a similar observation). Practice is structure in real time, and social analysis (including the analysis of language) involves the examination of the actual performance of individuals in their practical, open-ended, and contradictory relations with one another; these are ordered and limited by the forces of social reproduction—a "habitus," in Bourdieu's words. In some ways Bourdieu's account is a better modern analogue of Wittgenstein 2 than is deconstruction because it evokes the real machine through notions such as timing and execution (though Bourdieu would object to the latter term) and stresses linguistic *style* as the key to self and position. In the end, the choice of theoretical link between Vygotsky and Wittgenstein on the one hand and modern social and cognitive theory on the other is less important than the fact of the link itself. This embarrassment of riches turns out to be a real embarrassment. If there are so many possible links, why have they not been made before?

9. If all this sounds very much like mainstream cognitive science, it should. The *noema* is something like the representational content of mental states, and much of Husserl's program is dedicated to spelling out the details of this content. Such representationalism and idealism lead Dreyfus (1982) to argue that Husserl is the true progenitor of cognitive science and artificial intelligence; he likens Husserl to Fodor and contrasts him with Searle, Fodor's opponent. This is all the more evidence for seeing Derrida as a complement to Husserl, just as Vygotsky and Wittgenstein 2 emerge as complements to representational cognitive science.

10. Interestingly enough, one can almost hear Putnam (1988: 11): "Meanings have an identity through time but no essence." We get identity not by tabulating similarities but by "discounting differences" (1988: 104).

11. Chomsky (1986) argues that Wittgenstein's sense of *rule*—with Kripke's (1982) modifications—is unacceptable to linguistics. He characterizes the Wittgenstein-Kripke view of rules and rule-following as having four features: (1) rules are conscious, (2) rules can be followed blindly, (3) rules need public criteria for ratification and utility, and (4) rules must be ascribable to the follower even to apply. To Chomsky (1986), features 1, 3, and 4 are false; 2 can be true without any effect on the present conception of linguistic rules. So the popularized Wittgensteinian idea that rules have to be socially applied and

conscious to be rules is just wrong when one is measuring linguistic rules. If the deconstructive reading of Wittgenstein is correct, however, these criticisms simply do not apply. Wittgenstein is not talking about rules—predetermining forms instantiated on occasions—at all. He is talking about *rulings,* which indeed are conscious, blindly followed, publicly ratified, and determinately ascribable. But these apply, as I will later argue, to metalinguistic knowledge in the service of metaconsciousness, not to universal grammar and the computational mind. In other words, the Derridean reading of Wittgenstein lets Wittgenstein and Chomsky live peaceably together. The same will go for Fodor's justification of a private language of thought against Wittgenstein's private language counters. There can be a *public language for thought* that complements a *private language of thought* (see Chapter 5).

12. Russell (1987), reading Wittgenstein 2 in much the same way as Staten, suggests a connection with Piaget and calls for a "Wittgensteinianized Piagetianism" in developmental psychology. He sees a productive association of the two in accounts of intuition, "mental orientation," and metathought, with sociolinguistic expression organizing one's "inner voice" (45, 46). Insofar as Vygotsky and Wittgenstein 2 are close partners, one might also call for a Vygotskyan Piagetianism—an ironic term, as those who are familiar with the Vygotsky-Piaget debate will affirm.

3. Architectures and Contexts

1. One of Globus's (1992) points in this regard strikes me as a bit extreme. In bringing Derrida fully into cognitive science, he proposes deconstructing the brain, too. Technically we must stop privileging the (computational) brain as positive being and hold it up against its noncomputational complement (whatever that is! For Globus it is connectionism, if I understand him). My epistemological insecurities tell me not to go this far—I still want the brain as positive being—but I may be saying more about myself than anything else. In fact, Brown (1990) argues that the concept of the brain as a structure is an illusion imposed by researchers on physical activity in tissue. For Brown, the brain is a kind of emergent property of neurochemistry: it disappears on examination!

2. Connectionist accounts, unlike representationalist ones, are also *designed to be simulations by computer.* So when we say that connectionism *models the mind,* we mean it literally in that there is a working implementation. The necessary association of connectionism with simulation means that connectionist accounts of notions such as 'model', 'learning', and 'understanding' are quite different from those of their rivals. Representationalism has no such modeling obligation. Even though some of its critics argue that this absence is a fatal one, implementation is certainly not a necessary criterion for an account of mind.

3. One putative exception is the school of situated action, founded on many of the principles outlined by Winograd and Flores (1986) in their proposals for

social-based computer understanding. Situated action has been discussed in Chapter 1, but it, too, is partial to the inner code (and has to be!), though its advocates deny it.

4. Apologies to the Churchlands and other mind-brain identity theorists. To be more accurate, I should say that functionalism is the dominant metatheory for those versions of cognitive science where mind is still accorded existence and thought of as a device.

5. Whether computation is syntactic or semantic is a matter of great dispute. Some argue for the priority of syntax—contentless unit manipulation (Pylyshyn 1985, Stich 1983). Others argue that syntax presupposes semantics (Mellor 1989). Still others mingle the two, as in Harnad's (1990) idea of grounded computation. No one questions the relevance of semantics, just its proper place.

6. As a result IQ, which to some people (not myself) measures computational intelligence, is thought of as a capacity and measured as such by its speed. (Some allow this capacity to be genetically given and go around measuring speed differences by birth history and inherited characteristics, such as height, which has a correlation with IQ!) In my view, this presumes that intelligence is what you do when you know how to do something—the faster, the better. I follow Vygotsky and Bakhtin here (thanks to Caryl Emerson for pointing this out in a lecture): intelligence is what you do when you *don't know what to do*. Cognitive framing is slow and deliberate but the most important part of the task.

7. I say *usually* here because there is no necessary reason why representationalism and modularity belong together. Anderson's (1983) ACT system, for example, uses a representational logic, but the algorithms are general purpose, and so the format does not look anything like the format of modular systems in Fodor's sense.

8. Churchland goes on (1986: 358): "Functionalism as it lives and breathes, however, is another matter," often aligned with antireductionism. But this overstates the facts. Chomsky, a dyed-in-the-wool mental-sentence-cruncher, in Churchland's terms, has said often that linguistics is a branch of neurobiology. But fear of reduction does underscore the tendency for computationalists to speak as if there were no brain, just as the brain sciences sometimes operate as if there were no mental states to be explained.

9. *Vygotskyan* thus means 'the Vygotsky-Luria-Leont'ev amalgamation' (see the Introduction). It is also tempting to include Bakhtin in this alliance, since his work comes closest to the postmodern line that brings Vygotsky and Wittgenstein together. But, as James Wertsch has pointed out to me, Bakhtin was an orthodox Christian, an anti-Marxist, and a disbeliever in Enlightenment rationality—not exactly three compatibilities with Vygotsky! Just as the term *Chomskyan* can misleadingly unite all versions of formal grammar, so *Vygotskyan* does not easily embrace every Russian social-mind theorist.

10. This emphasis on development and change makes Vygotsky a ready-made can-

didate for adoption into the fashionable process-over-product rhetoric in the West. But though he is a kind of social functionalist, his sympathies are quite different from those of adherents to the more familiar dynamic-interactionist view of thought. Newman and Holzman's (1993) study of Vygotsky's work is especially good on this count.

11. Toulmin (1985: 4) holds a similar view: "It would have been strange if, in the long run, human psychology had *not* proved to be one of the 'humanities,' *as well as* one of the 'sciences.' "

12. Another way to think about this is to say that social dialogue condenses to monologue, since speech for oneself collapses the speaker and hearer into a single person and so gives the appearance of noninteractive speech. The use of *monologue,* however, unnecessarily suggests removal from dialogical context, which misrepresents the Vygotskyan view of the social embeddedness of all speech.

13. The historical context of the idea that speech controls thinking is itself a lesson in the merger of computation and culture. The regulatory function of meta-thought is traceable in Vygotsky's work to his reading of Spinoza, in whose ethics mind seeks improvement by uniting reason and intellect to control the passions via understanding (see van der Veer 1991: 239–41). The modern, though still dated, version of this is cybernetics, Norbert Wiener's theory that self-compensating systems operating by feedback, control, and purpose could model human behavior (Haugeland 1985: 168–76).

14. For this reason, self-reflexive approaches to social action, such as deconstruction or Bourdieu's sociology, are needed to link Vygotsky with Wittgenstein and ultimately to computationalism. Only in these kinds of theories are an individual's contradictions benign, even useful.

15. Lave (1993) notes the pervasiveness of this last factor in elementary school mathematics instruction. She remarks on a third grade class in which the students, in group workbook sessions and other settings without the teacher, solve problems and come to important mathematical discoveries by talking over their difficulties with one another. But when asked whom they consult when they have problems, the students inevitably report that it is the teacher they turn to, even though this is clearly not so. American culture scripts school as arbitrated by the teacher and so assigns the teacher the highest position in the context's hierarchy of participants.

16. Consider some linguistic evidence. Strictly within the inner code, phonological representations are embedded in the context of lexical representations, which in turn occur in the context of syntactic ones. But these are not equal relationships. In the phonological-lexical congruity, sounds *are part of the whole* of the word, whereas in the lexical-syntactic one, words *are members of the set* of grammatical categories (note, e.g., that a sound is not a member of the set *word*). Because sounds belong to their representational contexts differently from the way words belong to theirs, the processing relationships differ, yielding contrasting architectural effects. Words give feedback to sounds, but sen-

tences do not give feedback to words, and so phonological-lexical relationships look interactive while lexical-syntactic ones look modular. Crucially, this difference lies in the architecture-context *relations via feedback,* not in the inherent design of the architecture (see Tanenhaus and Lucas 1987; Tanenhaus, Dell, and Carlson 1987).

17. Lexical processing provides a nice example of these distinctions. Words with the same overt form but different meanings can be either polysemous (a single entry in the mental lexicon with the different meanings subsumed thereunder) or homonymous (separate entries for each sense). For example, the word *gas* in the meanings 'leaded' and 'unleaded' is polysemous: the meanings are distinct senses under a single word. But *gas* in the senses 'petroleum product' and 'substance in neither liquid nor solid form' is homonymous: there are two words, *gas*$_1$ and *gas*$_2$. Processing experiments show that context feeds back onto the senses of polysemous words, presorting them for contextual appropriateness, precisely because a polysemous word is a single entry in the mental lexicon with its multiple senses stored together as part of the whole of the word as a meaning unit. In contrast, homonyms exhibit modular effects with a computed relation to context. Their senses are selected, not presorted, for contextual appropriateness because the cost of finding the right context for separate words with distinct senses is quite high, compared to finding the context for a single word with related senses (see Jones 1989).

18. Bakhtin (1981: 293) puts the idea as follows: "Language, for the individual consciousness, lies on the borderline between oneself and the other."

4. Subjectivity

1. I use the term *nonconscious* instead of *unconscious* to avoid the associations of the latter with psychotherapeutic discourse.

2. Johnson-Laird's Craikian automaton is not exactly an experiencer with awareness, however. A Craikian automaton is characterized by symbol manipulation, and so Johnson-Laird appears to equate, or at least to make cohabitate, symbolic computation and consciousness. But this construal seems incorrect. Input systems are, in representationalist views, computationally symbolic but still zombies. Low-level vision is symbolic but does not have awareness per se: visual awareness is supported by, or emerges out of, this elemental symbol manipulation. Therefore, operation via an internal model does not ensure or induce awareness. There must be properties other than symbol manipulation, then, that determine consciousness (see section 4.3).

3. Technically, I have made the *absent qualia* argument here: that is, zombies are humans without qualia. In doing so, I have left aside many important issues and counters (e.g., the *inverted qualia* argument) and have no doubt offended many. Whatever the ultimate status of the absent qualia argument, I think it is a good illustration of the nature of awareness. If recourse to qualia turns out

to be simply a way of speaking vaguely about some sort of neurological process, then that is fine with me. Flanagan (1992: chap. 4) nicely defends qualia, at least as a working idea.

4. Note that I do not simply match the three forms of subjectivity in Vygotsky's work—*znanie, soznanie,* and *osoznanie*—with nonconscious processing, consciousness, and metaconsciousness. *Znanie* and nonconscious processing may be compatible since both are tied to elementary processes, though Vygotskyan theory and computationalism take different stances even about what is elemental. But *soznanie* and consciousness are not analogous: *soznanie* (co-knowing) requires other minds, whereas computational consciousness can be individualistic. Metaconsciousness and *osoznanie* do look compatible, which is why this connection is explored here.

5. Nonconscious processing, consciousness, and metaconsciousness fall along what linguists call an *implicational hierarchy,* a series of concepts in asymmetric dependency such that the earlier members of the series are simpler, more common, and necessary to the later members; the autonomy of each member of the series extends incrementally and continuously upward (i.e., only the earlier ones can stand alone):

Nonconscious Processing → Consciousness → Metaconsciousness

6. These representational continuities between conscious and nonconscious processes lead Searle (1992: chap. 7; see also 1991) to argue against the sharp demarcation of the two. His usual foil is Chomskyan linguistics, where the goal of analysis is to uncover the structure of unconscious grammatical representations. For Searle (1992: 132), "every unconscious intentional state is at least potentially conscious" because unconscious *unintentional* states—those that do not represent, like the pumping of the heart—make no contribution to mental states. So it is the representationalism of cognitive science that forces it into the analysis of consciousness.

7. With respect to the locality of disruptions of metaconsciousness, Bisiach (1988: 472) remarks, "Even severe mental deterioration does not necessarily imply anosognosia [lack of metaknowledge] for a disorder ensuing from local brain damage." The specificity of metaknowledge therefore protects it from global thought disorders; metaconsciousness, like consciousness, is not a general property of the mind/brain.

8. For this reason, trauma to consciousness can have varied effects on metaconsciousness. Many patients with cortical blindness are also *aware of their own syndrome* (Young and de Haan 1990), so their metaknowledge appears to be preserved. Other patients, however, lack such metaknowledge (Young and de Haan 1990), which may be the result of the severity of the trauma and disruption of the shared features of the three modes of subjectivity. Bisiach (1988b) reports variations in metaknowledge with respect to hemineglect, the

failure to describe or recognize the side of the body contralateral to a lesion. Some patients deny the syndrome; others are aware of it; some with more than one disorder deny one and acknowledge the other(s) (471). For Bisiach, the verbal reports of hemineglect patients (which fail to describe the spatial information on the side contralateral to the lesion) suggest that language can operate "without thought" because it can be misfed (471) by the nonlinguistic modules of space. It might also suggest that in cases where metaknowledge is not present, speech then fails to feed metaconsciousness.

9. For this reason, Johnson-Laird's (1983, 1988) proposal to derive self-consciousness from a self-modeling operating system cannot be entirely correct. This would be second-order representation without knowledge of the representational system per se.

10. See also White (1991: chap. 5–6) on the unity of the self and the association of self, person, and externals, especially the idea of *metapsychological relativity,* a concept that evokes both Vygotsky and Harré, though White does not cite either. For White (1991: 186), personhood and self-consciousness are connected by their tie to facts outside the individual. In his view, self-consciousness is not a property of individuals at all but a feature of group mediation of thinking (1991: 172), another quite transparently Vygotskyan point. Also lurking in the background is Wittgenstein 2, for whom the idea of the public being, the self with public criteria for identity and true beliefs—the person—is the essential complement to the privately constituted logic machine.

11. Here Vygotsky and Searle part ways. For Vygotsky, the background must be representational because social-semiotic mediation is basic to higher thought. It is not clear whether this puts the two essentially at odds, since Vygotsky locates this representational support *outside mind* while Searle's account remains internal.

12. Contrary to Fodor's (1983) dismissal of higher-thought processes as isotropic and unamenable to scientific analysis, there can be a science of central processes. See also Shallice (1988b).

13. Actually, in Zhang and Norman's (1994) study the problem is reversed, with the disks initially arranged from smaller to larger. This is done for design consistency and does not affect the overall structure of the problem.

14. Interestingly enough, working memory is a kind of short-term memory, which, as we know, is associated with consciousness. So to say that internal representations tap working memory is to say that internalism taps consciousness, a point I have made in a number of ways with respect to the interiority of conscious processing. Planning and externalism are known to be associated with metathought.

15. Coincidentally, Premack (1988: 53, 63) points out that the only apparent cognitive benefit of teaching apes language is that some of the words they learn focus attention on and stabilize distinctions necessary to problem solving. For apes (as for humans?), language does not confer new content so much as *new orientation* or bracketing of existing content.

5. Control and the Language for Thought

1. As if NSS were really muttering during the task, *Oh, yes, how easy that is, he thought.* This would raise the famous mind's eye regress: where is the mind that is saying "he thought"?

2. Another way to think about this is in terms of Sperber and Wilson's (1986) ergonomic theory of communication. In their account, communication seeks the greatest contextual effect with the least processing effort. This cost-benefit ratio is carried by a trade-off between direct coding and indirect inference. These, in turn, have their effects against two kinds of context: given context, where coding and inference add incrementally to a prior contextual base, and chosen context, where coding and inference select a context appropriate to their informational output. These distinctions sound remarkably like my own and suggest that architecture-context relationships are part of a general processing account of human language whereby different contextual effects feed into and are fed by differences between coding and inference.

3. According to formal semantics, identifying the properties themselves and determining what aspects of the world or culture fill out the property set are not linguistic or logical problems (see Bach 1989) but questions for disciplines such as anthropology and physics, which seek to uncover the structure of the external world. While I disagree with this extremism (Frawley 1992b), its acceptance does not vitiate the universal structure of predication per se as reference to property sets.

4. If this analysis of the role of focus in the language for thought is correct, it casts a different light on the observation that private speech "degrades" into inaudible muttering in its course of abbreviation. The principal means for any language to indicate focus is stress, and so muttering and otherwise inaudible self-directed discourse may be less a reduction of overt form than a surfacing of the universal focus marker of prosodic prominence. That is, with focus as the controlling variable, the progressive reduction of surface form to muttering is less remarkable than the fact that speech surfaces at all! And when it does so as muttering, this might be seen as the *retention of form through focal stress.*

5. A native German speaker tells me, in fact, that if *eigentlich*, which means 'change of perspective', were used instead of *denn*, the private speech would be contradictory.

6. Some of these languages also accord highest evidential status to the other (= you) and so seem to recruit the metasystem as a whole to privilege the other (see Frawley 1992b: 412 n. 6; also Schlichter 1986 and Harré and Mühlhäusler 1990: 106–7). The cognitive and metacognitive consequences of these facts are as yet unexplored.

7. There is a third notion of control, the management of real-time computing, where a system monitors input and output continuously in order to produce an appropriate response under actual-time restrictions. Real-time computing is certainly relevant to a Vygotskyan cognitive science, since the language for

thought is an index of on-line thinking, but this is beyond the scope of the present discussion.

8. Alzheimer's disease might be considered a deterioration of machine-level control structures. Harré and Gillett (1994: 31–32), in fact, say as much, though not in computational terms, when they suggest that the discourse of Alzheimer's patients may be disordered in the real-time linking and sequencing of statements.

9. These terms can be misleading because some programming languages lack statements as such but nonetheless have control structures. A statement is technically a form that does not return a value, in contrast to an expression, which does. Some programming languages, known as *functional languages* (e.g., LISP), lack statements; other languages, known as *procedural or sequential languages* (e.g., C), have both statements and expressions. Both kinds of languages have control but, because of the nature of their constituent expressions, execute data flow differently. Because functional languages are composed of forms that deliver outputs, order is communicated and passed via the memory stack, where the outputs are recorded. But procedural languages do not have to manage control via the memory stack since they have forms that do not deliver outputs; such languages are said to communicate via the program environment. The point, however, is that the nature of coding in these languages affects the way data flow is managed.

10. We have not considered GOTO, one of the earliest and eventually most controversial means of effecting control. This is an unrestricted statement that directs the computing to virtually anywhere in the program. Since it has such wide-ranging effects, it lies conceptually between local, statement-level control and global, unit-level control.

On the one hand, GOTO has unquestionable benefits, since it is a kind of control escape clause, allowing control to pass freely and immediately throughout the program. If processing needs to be directed to an expression or collection of expressions outside the immediate programming environment, then such an all-purpose jump mechanism to do this is, if unbeautiful, at least useful. But as Dijkstra (1968) has argued, and convinced the rest of the programming community, GOTO can have terrible consequences because it can pass control at any point to any other point, thus producing what is known as *spaghetti code*, which can have a number of harmful effects. Because GOTO lets the flow of computation cross and recross parts of code, a program may develop unexpected bugs and be difficult to compile. The problems of spaghetti code have led to the banishment of GOTO altogether—or at least to its isolation—and a greater emphasis on structured programming, or the grouping of sections of code that *belong together* computationally or that are involved in the transfer of control.

All of this raises some interesting questions about the language for thought and the human management of mental computation. Do humans have an all-purpose, metarepresentational GOTO for transferring cognitive control to any part of the mental code? My own feeling is that there is no such thing because control disorders, such as frontal lobe aphasias and various disruptions of the language for thought, leave their sufferers with behavior that looks remarkably like the behavior of a program with spaghetti code: that it, GOTO is a *consequence* of the damage. In such disorders, unrelated representations are inadvertently linked, processing is slow or it crashes, modification of existing code (learning) is problematic and unpredictably curtailed. Moreover, young children have to learn how to control their thinking, and prior to acquiring their culture's language for thought, they struggle with computational control and evince behavior that suggests that their mental computation has to overcome spaghetti code. Perhaps only after they have mastered the resources of the language for thought can they debug their mental code and think as if their language of thought were written as a structured program. This would make much sense in terms of theory of mind literature and arguments about theory of mind deficits and disorders.

11. One caution: we cannot simply pair up a language for thought form with, say, a single statement-level or unit-level control phenomenon. Human computation is more complex than machine computation, and so its control language will be larger and more varied than that found in programming languages. Unlike markers of computational control, which straightforwardly serve only the purposes for which they are designed, natural-language control markers always come with a stance. Moreover, a single language for thought form might bring about several different kinds of control. The language for thought is a more complicated control language because its history and purposes are more complicated, as are the representations and data flow it manages.

6. Control Disorders

1. This observation ultimately provides support for a modular mental architecture, where domains interface but do not intermix. Individuals with the most severe form of Turner syndrome, in which the second sex chromosome is deleted (45 X0), differ from normals only on nonverbal measures; individuals with less severe versions, such as the mosaic or partial deletion pattern, have both verbal and nonverbal performance depressed (Garron 1977: 111). Why should the most severe form of the disorder result in the lesser cognitive impairment? If the syndrome operates over a modular mental architecture, then the more severe the disruption, the more the verbal is freed from the nonverbal; the less severe the disruption, the more the verbal and nonverbal continue to borrow from each other in an impaired fashion. The more severe condition unconstrains the verbal, and so the verbal measures look normal; the less severe depresses performance overall. In this way, the syndrome may best be understood as an interface disorder rather than a specific knowledge impairment. I pursue this line of thought further in Frawley (1997).

2. Another syndrome that may be cognitively and linguistically related to the five

discussed here is *Noonan syndrome,* a Turner-like genetic disorder but without chromosomal abnormality. It occurs once in about every 1,000 live births and so is rather frequent: "second in frequency of occurrence among disorders with multiple congenital abnormalities" (Hopkins-Acos and Bunker 1979: 494). Individuals with Noonan syndrome are characterized by a distinct oral-facial pattern, short stature, cardiac problems, strabismus, gonadal malformations, and skeletal abnormalities (Nora et al. 1974).

Assessments of the cognitive functioning of Noonan individuals vary widely, ranging from reports of "some with doctoral degrees to others who are only educable" (Nora et al. 1974: 53). This finding is all the more remarkable since intellectual impairment appears in about 68 percent of the cases (Wilson and Dyson 1982). The very few studies of the language of individuals with Noonan syndrome show delayed language and behavioral milestones but relatively well developed communicative structure, though lacking linguistic metafunctions such as self-commentary and metalinguistic practice (Wilson and Dyson 1982). Hopkins-Acos and Bunker (1979) report similar observations in a subject lacking most speech but who could carry out the usual functions of language nonverbally. Ghaziuddin, Bolyard, and Alessi (1994) report some dissociation of language and world knowledge in Noonan syndrome and one case of verbal skills exceeding nonverbal ones. Noonan syndrome thus appears to split language from general cognition and leave pragmatic deficits in the former, but the lack of definitive research on the disorder calls for a more conservative assessment at present.

3. The one exception is Karmiloff-Smith, Grant, and Berthoud's (1993) study of gender knowledge in French-speaking Williams children, whose performance is well below normal. The authors take this to indicate that Williams syndrome can have within-domain deficits (within morphology), and they call into question the whole idea of a modular architecture, which should not have within-domain effects. But there is another explanation. In many morphological theories, morphology does not exist as an autonomous component because it involves the interaction of so many distinct kinds of information. Indeed, Karmiloff-Smith and associates observe that French gender depends on the interaction of a number of features not tied to morphology proper. So their results may be the exception that proves the rule: there may be no autonomous morphology module for the disorder to affect, and the ostensible within-domain deficits are the result of cross-domain interactions. One way to sort all this out would be to test the relative weights of the factors affected. Those that are clearly domain-specific should be less affected than those that cross domains (see Frawley 1997).

4. Cromer (1994: 150) remarks that the only case in which this individual fails to perform normally is on double-object constructions (nonprepositional datives). But this in fact proves the larger point about control. The acceptability of double objects hangs on the management of information not wholly contained within the formal linguistic system. So it might be argued that double

objects are difficult precisely because they require control structures other than those preserved by the syndrome. See also note 3.

5. The dissociation of semantic logic and semantic control might shed light on the debate in spina bifida studies over whether these individuals have a deficit in abstract semantic information. A variety of studies report that spina bifida individuals are better at concrete language than abstract language (Hurley et al. 1990, Culatta and Young 1992, Culatta 1993a and b). But the deficits seem to hang on only one sense of *abstract*. Culatta and Young (1992: 436) find, contrary to most of the reported literature, no difference between children with spina bifida and controls on tests of verbalization about *distal* phenomena (*abstract* as 'removed'). But spina bifida children do have difficulty with quantifiers and relational terms (*abstract* as 'abstracted' or 'intangible').

   Culatta (1993a and b) reports that spina bifida children say things like "This is the same" and "Everything is behind" to refer to physically present objects (respectively, cookies and physical objects). The abstraction problem here is thus not one of removal. In point of fact, these expressions of relational terms are odd because they fail to code the spatial landmarks against which the asserted items are to be judged: The same as *what?* Behind *what?* This is arguably not a semantic issue at all but one of focus in discourse. What is deleted—defocalized—in each expression is given information: *This [cookie] is the same [as that cookie]* and *Everything is behind something ('covering or blocking the view of something else')*. Focus is a metapragmatic problem, a matter of control, not logic. So, in fact, these apparent deficits in abstraction may really be symptoms of control disruptions. It is no wonder, then, that spina bifida children have problem-solving difficulties associated with these relational terms, since focus feeds perspective on problem solving (Culatta 1993b; see also Chapter 5).

6. If computationalism is correct, all the results described herein for language should hold for other domains of knowledge, since the representations define domain-independent automata, not specific kinds of content. (I am grateful to Dan Chester for this observation.) This would mean that, assuming these control disorders are not exclusively language disorders (which they are not), we should see logic-control dissociations in other domains. Perhaps individuals with these syndromes are able to compute music and faces as a form but unable to execute control aspects of music and face recognition, such as managing musical and facial choices or interpreting musical and facial expressions. There does seem to be some evidence for this prediction.

   Williams individuals are notoriously good at face recognition, even better than normals at recognizing unfamiliar faces and faces in noncanonical position (Bellugi et al., 1990; Bellugi, Wang, and Jernigan 1994: 38). This ability is traceable to a domain-specific module defined by its representations. Turner syndrome children can also recall faces quite well, but fail to discriminate the affect on the face (McCauley et al. 1987). The same findings hold for autistics, who have difficulty reading emotions on faces (Sigman 1994: 147). This suggests that where they need to deploy social significance, their ability breaks down. Again, what might look like a within-domain deficit is really a logic-control problem. While face *recognition* involves finite computation in a genetically determined module, face *interpretation* requires control.

Moreover, Williams syndrome children taught to read do better if taught through phonetics—bottom-up, representational processes—rather than through a nondeterministic global-language approach (Udwin, Yule, and Martin 1987; MacDonald and Roy 1988). Again, this can be explained by an appeal to logic versus control. Phonetics is representational whereas the whole-language approach is sensitive to metarepresentational control.

7. Money (1994: 148) comments, however: "A Turner girl's degree of handicap [on spatial rotation] may be lessened by the device of transliteration from shapes and directions into silently spoken language." It is not clear whether this is a report of clinical success or a speculation. If the former, it would be a counter to the foregoing argument.

8. One reason why this problem manifests itself widely in these conditions is that the experimental tasks which have elicited the behavior vary widely. If the language for thought is sensitive to differential task requirements and surfaces as a tracking and management device under the processing strains that such task variation causes, then clearly a problem in this mechanism ought to arise under such diverse circumstances of assessment.

9. The inability to transform spatial phenomena has an unexpected advantage. Turner girls do not rotate reversible letters (b→ d) when learning to read, as most children do (Money 1994: 148–49).

10. Indeed, virtually the same characterization has been given of all the other control disorders. Turner individuals need much structure to socialize and complete tasks and move away from the circumstances of the moment (McCauley, Ito, and Kay 1986: 405). Landry et al. (1990) suggest that spina bifida children could benefit from more differentiating social structure provided by others. Thal, Bates, and Bellugi (1989: 499–500) argue that Williams syndrome is a pathology of extreme expressive style and context dependence.

11. I have seen no other data on the prosody of individuals with the other control disorders described herein, but I suspect that a fine analysis of their speech would reveal similar disruptions in prosody and in the simultaneous construction of mental goals. This finding would be very significant not only because of the planning implications, but also because individuals with these syndromes are known for their *hyperphonology*. Prosodic problems would thus give further evidence for the modularity of mind, since it would mean that mind mirrors phonological theory by separating prosody from segmental phonology.

Epilogue

1. I should also add that I have no problem with this kind of conceptual analysis per se. I think it has done much for linguistics and deserves to be part of more

mainstream formal analysis (see Frawley 1992b). But this is different from calling it *cognitive science* in itself.

2. For the record, I read McClamrock's book *after* I had completely finished writing Chapters 1–6, so his points had no bearing on how I thought about those issues. Any coincidence between his ideas and mine is just that.

3. So McClamrock (1995: 126) cannot be entirely correct when he says that meaning is not a mental state but systematically related behavior. You could systematically hit keys, but unless they matched the "mental" state of the machine, they would be meaningless. A lot hangs on the word *related:* does this mean 'internalized'?

4. At about age three, my son began to realize that other people have mental states and that the effectiveness of his own behavior sometimes depended on its mental registration by others. For example, he was very interested in the fact that he could hide from other people and could speak but not be heard by others. He often said to me with great joy, "They can't see us!" and "They can't hear us!" He sometimes told me to stop singing a song and "just think it." At the age Wellman's theory predicts, he had insights into the importance of people's private knowledge of overt actions.

5. One way to draw the distinction might be to say that while TOM is a *theory* of mind, metaconsciousness is a *metatheory* of mind. Following the terminology of philosophy of science, TOM proper would concern the ontology of the theory of mind, and metaconscious control would concern the method and epistemology of the theory of mind. Whether this is a useful way of talking remains to be seen. But, as independent evidence for the distinction, Jackendoff (1987: 265–72) observes that central processes come in two types: those that subserve thought and those that fine-tune it. These appear to be Jackendoff's analogues of the content and bracketing aspects of TOM.

6. By contrast, Bruner and Feldman (1993: 280) report that autistic individuals' narratives lack focus markers and other kinds of reflexive language. This absence of linguistic signals of bracketing in autistics' speech needs further investigation.

7. Work in computation theory on the role of self-knowledge in machine learning also has suggestive correspondences to the claims for sociocomputationalism. Case (1994: 6) argues that a robot can get complete low-level self-knowledge without infinite regress by projecting a copy of itself externally, that is, by moving outside the architecture proper. Moreover, this external projection for self-referentiality is related to computational control: the usual control structures of programs (e.g., if-then-else) are complements to the control structures of self-knowledge, built as they are on Kleene recursion (see Case 1994: 8). Thus, the idea that human self-knowledge and metaconsciousness are derived from control information external to the self is entirely compatible with the requirements of the theory of computation.

Bibliography

Adams, Fred, Kenneth Aizawa, and Gary Fuller. 1992. Rules in programming languages and networks. *The symbolic and connectionist paradigms: Closing the gap,* J. Dinsmore, ed., 49–67. Hillsdale, N.J.: Erlbaum.

Agre, Philip. 1993. The symbolic worldview: Reply to Vera and Simon. *Cognitive Science* 17:61–69.

Aissen, J. 1992. Topic and focus in Mayan. *Language* 68:43–80.

Aizawa, Kenneth. 1992. Biology and sufficiency in connectionist theory. *The symbolic and connectionist paradigms: Closing the gap,* J. Dinsmore, ed., 69–88. Hillsdale, N.J.: Erlbaum.

Aksu-Koç, Ayhan and Dan Slobin. 1986. A psychological account of the development and use of evidentials in Turkish. *Evidentiality: The linguistic coding of epistemology,* W. Chafe and J. Nichols, eds., 159–67. Norwood, N.J.: Ablex.

Allport, Alan. 1988. What concept of consciousness? *Consciousness in contemporary science,* A. Marcel and E. Bisiach, eds., 159–82. Oxford: Oxford University Press.

Anderson, John. 1983. *The architecture of cognition.* Cambridge, Mass.: Harvard University Press.

——— 1987. Methodologies for studying human knowledge. *Behavioral and Brain Sciences* 10:467–77.

Apple, Michael. 1982. *Education and power.* London: Routledge.

Arbib, Michael. 1989. Modularity, schemas, and neurons: A critique of Fodor. *Computers, brains, and minds,* P. Slezak and W. Albury, eds., 193–219. Dordrecht: Kluwer.

Arcavi, Abraham and Alan Schoenfeld. 1992. Mathematics tutoring through a constructivist lens: The challenges of sense-making. *Journal of Mathematical Behavior* 11:321–35.

Azmitia, Margarita. 1992. Expertise, private speech, and the development of self-regulation. *Private speech,* R. Diaz and L. Berk, eds., 101–22. Hillsdale, N.J.: Erlbaum.

Baars, Bernard. 1988. *A cognitive theory of consciousness.* Cambridge: Cambridge University Press.

Bach, Emmon. 1989. *Informal lectures on formal semantics.* Albany: SUNY Press.

Baker, C. L. and John McCarthy, eds. 1981. *The logical problem of language acquisition*. Cambridge, Mass.: MIT Press.

Bakhtin, Mikhail. 1981. *The dialogic imagination*. Austin: University of Texas Press.

Banfield, Ann. 1982. *Unspeakable sentences: Narration and representation in the language of fiction*. Boston: Routledge & Kegan Paul.

—— 1993. Where epistemology, style, and grammar meet literary history: The development of represented speech and thought. *Reflexive language*, J. Lucy, ed., 339–64. Cambridge: Cambridge University Press.

Barnden, John. 1992. Connectionism, generalization, and propositional attitudes: A catalogue of challenging issues. *The symbolic and connectionist paradigms: Closing the gap*, J. Dinsmore, ed., 149–78. Hillsdale, N.J.: Erlbaum.

Baron, Robert. 1987. *The cerebral computer*. Hillsdale, N.J.: Erlbaum.

Baron-Cohen, Simon. 1993. From attention-goal psychology to belief-desire psychology: The development of a theory of mind, and its dysfunction. *Understanding other minds: Perspectives from autism*, S. Baron-Cohen, H. Tager-Flusberg, and D. Cohen, eds., 59–82. Oxford: Oxford University Press.

—— 1995. *Mindblindness: An essay on autism and theory of mind*. Cambridge, Mass.: MIT Press.

Barwise, Jon and Robin Cooper. 1981. Generalized quantifiers and natural language. *Linguistics and Philosophy* 4:159–219.

Bechtel, William and Adele Abrahamsen. 1990. *Connectionism and the mind*. Cambridge, Mass.: Blackwell.

Bellugi, U., A. Bihrle, D. Trauner, T. Jernigan, and S. Doherty. 1990. Neuropsychological, neurological, and neuroanatomical profile of Williams syndrome. *American Journal of Medical Genetics* 6 (Suppl.):115–25.

Bellugi, U., H. Sabo, and J. Vaid. 1988. Spatial deficits in children with Williams syndrome. *Spatial cognition: Brain bases and development*, J. Stiles-Davis, M. Kritchevsky, and U. Bellugi, eds., 273–98. Hillsdale, N.J.: Erlbaum.

Bellugi, U., P. Wang, and T. Jernigan. 1994. Williams syndrome: An unusual neuropsychological profile. *Atypical cognitive deficits in developmental disorders*, S. Broman and J. Grafman, eds., 23–56. Hillsdale, N.J.: Erlbaum.

Bender, Bruce, Mary Linden, and Arthur Robinson. 1989. Verbal and spatial processing efficiency in 32 children with sex chromosome abnormalities. *Pediatric Research* 25:577–79.

Berk, Laura. 1986. Relationship of elementary school children's private speech to behavioral accompaniment to task, attention, and task performance. *Developmental Psychology* 22:671–80.

—— 1992. Children's private speech: An overview of theory and the status of research. *Private speech*, R. Diaz and L. Berk, eds., 17–53. Hillsdale, N.J.: Erlbaum.

Bernstein, Richard. 1983. *Beyond objectivism and relativism*. Philadelphia: University of Pennsylvania Press.

Bever, Thomas. 1992. The logical and extrinsic sources of modularity. *Modularity and constraints in language acquisition,* M. Gunnar and M. Maratsos, eds., 179–212. Hillsdale, N.J.: Erlbaum.

Biederman, Irving. 1990. Higher-level vision. *Visual cognition and action: An invitation to cognitive science,* vol. 2, D. Osherson, S. Kosslyn, and J. Hollerbach, eds., 41–72. Cambridge, Mass.: MIT Press.

Bisiach, E. 1988a. The (haunted) brain and consciousness. *Consciousness in contemporary science,* A. Marcel and E. Bisiach, eds., 101–20. Oxford: Oxford University Press.

——— 1988b. Language without thought. *Thought without language,* L. Weiskrantz, ed., 464–84. Oxford: Oxford University Press.

Blakemore, Diane. 1987. *Semantic constraints on relevance.* Oxford: Blackwell.

Blank, M., M. Gessner, and A. Esposito. 1979. Language without communication: A case study. *Journal of Child Language* 6:329–52.

Blass, Regina. 1990. *Relevance relations in discourse.* Cambridge: Cambridge University Press.

Block, Ned. 1991. What narrow content is not. *Meaning in mind: Fodor and his critics,* B. Loewer and G. Rey, eds., 33–64. Oxford: Blackwell.

——— 1992. Begging the question against phenomenal consciousness. *Behavioral and Brain Sciences* 15:205–6.

Bloom, Paul. 1990. Subjectless sentences in child language. *Linguistic Inquiry* 21:491–504.

Borer, Hagit and Kenneth Wexler. 1987. The maturation of syntax. *Parameter setting,* T. Roeper and E. Williams, eds., 123–72. Dordrecht: Reidel.

Bourdieu, Pierre. 1977. *Outline of a theory of practice.* Cambridge: Cambridge University Press.

Bowerman, Melissa and Soonja Choi. 1994. Linguistic and nonlinguistic determinants of spatial semantic development. Paper presented at the Boston University Conference on Language Development, November.

Bozhovich, L. I. 1979. Stages in the formation of the personality in ontogeny. *Soviet Psychology* 17:3–24.

Bronckart, Jean-Paul and Madeleine Ventouras-Spycher. 1979. The Piagetian concept of representation and the Soviet-inspired view of self-regulation. *The development of self-regulation through private speech,* G. Zivin, ed., 99–131. New York: Wiley.

Brooks, Rodney. 1991. Intelligence without representation. *Artificial Intelligence* 47:139–59.

Brown, Jason. 1977. *Mind, brain, and consciousness.* New York: Academic Press.

——— 1987. The microstructure of action. *The frontal lobes revisited,* E. Perecman, ed., 251–72. Hillsdale, N.J.: Erlbaum.

——— 1990. Preliminaries for a theory of mind. *Contemporary neuropsychology and the legacy of Luria,* E. Goldberg, ed., 195–210. Hillsdale, N.J.: Erlbaum.

——— 1991. *Self and process: Brain states and the conscious present.* Berlin: Springer.

Bruner, Jerome and Carol Feldman. 1993. Theories of mind and the problem of autism. *Understanding other minds: Perspectives from autism,* S. Baron-Cohen, H. Tager-Flusberg, and D. Cohen, eds., 267–91. Oxford: Oxford University Press.

Bruner, Jerome and Joan Lucariello. 1989. Monologue as narrative recreation of the world. *Narratives from the crib,* K. Nelson, ed., 73–97. Cambridge, Mass.: Harvard University Press.

Bruyer, Raymond. 1991. Covert face recognition in prosopagnosia: A review. *Brain and Cognition* 15:223–35.

Burge, Tyler. 1979. Individualism and the mental. *Midwest Studies in Philosophy* 4:73–121.

——— 1986. Individualism and psychology. *Philosophical Review* 95:3–46.

Butterworth, George. 1993. Context and cognition in models of cognitive growth. *Context and cognition: Ways of learning and knowing,* P. Light and G. Butterworth, eds., 1–13. Hillsdale, N.J.: Erlbaum.

Byrne, K., L. Abbeduto, and P. Brooks. 1990. The language of children with spina bifida and hydrocephalus: Meeting task demands and mastering syntax. *Journal of Speech and Hearing Disorders* 55:118–23.

Cam, Philip. 1989. Notes toward a faculty theory of cognitive consciousness. *Computers, brains, and minds,* P. Slezak and W. Albury, eds., 167–91. Dordrecht: Kluwer.

Campione, Joseph, Ann Brown, Roberta Ferrara, and Nancy Bryant. 1984. The zone of proximal development: Implications for individual differences and learning. *Children's learning in the "zone of proximal development,"* B. Rogoff and J. Wertsch, eds., 77–91. San Francisco: Jossey-Bass.

Carey, Susan. 1985. *Conceptual change in childhood.* Cambridge, Mass.: MIT Press.

Case, John. 1994. Infinitary self-reference in learning theory. *Journal of Experimental and Theoretical Artificial Intelligence* 6:3–16.

Caton, Steve. 1993. The importance of reflexive language in G. H. Mead's theory of self and communication. *Reflexive language,* J. Lucy, ed., 315–37. Cambridge: Cambridge University Press.

Chafe, Wallace. 1974. Language and consciousness. *Language* 50:11–33.

Chafe, Wallace and Johanna Nichols, eds. 1986. *Evidentiality: The linguistic coding of epistemology.* Norwood, N.J.: Ablex.

Chierchia, Gennaro. 1985. Formal semantics and the grammar of predication. *Linguistic Inquiry* 16:417–43.

Choi, Soonja and Melissa Bowerman. 1992. Learning to express motion events in English and Korean. *Lexical and conceptual semantics,* B. Levin and S. Pinker, eds., 83–121. Cambridge, Mass.: Blackwell.

Chomsky, Noam. 1959. Review of B. F. Skinner's *Verbal behavior. Language* 35:26–58.

——— 1986. *Knowledge of language.* New York: Praeger.

——— 1992. A minimalist program for linguistic theory. MIT Occasional Papers in Linguistics 1.

Churchland, Patricia. 1986. *Neurophilosophy: Toward a unified science of the mind-brain.* Cambridge, Mass.: MIT Press.

Churchland, Patricia Smith. 1988. Reduction and the neurobiological basis of consciousness. *Consciousness in contemporary science,* A. Marcel and E. Bisiach, eds., 273–304. Oxford: Oxford University Press.

Churchland, Paul. 1985. *Matter and consciousness.* Cambridge, Mass.: MIT Press.

Clancey, William. 1993. Situated action: A neuropsychological interpretation response to Vera and Simon. *Cognitive Science* 17:87–116.

Clark, Andy. 1993. *Associative engines.* Cambridge, Mass.: MIT Press.

Clifton, Charles and Fernanda Ferreira. 1987. Modularity in sentence comprehension. *Modularity in knowledge representation and natural-language understanding,* J. Garfield, ed., 277–90. Cambridge, Mass.: MIT Press.

Cocking, Rodney and K. Ann Renninger. 1993. Psychological distance as a unifying theory of development. *The development and meaning of psychological distance,* R. Cocking and K. Renninger, eds., 3–18. Hillsdale, N.J.: Erlbaum.

Cole, Michael. 1990. Alexandr Romanovich Luria: Cultural psychologist. *Contemporary neuropsychology and the legacy of Luria,* E. Goldberg, ed., 11–28. Hillsdale, N.J.: Erlbaum.

Cosmides, Leda and John Tooby. 1994. Beyond intuition and blindness: Toward an evolutionarily rigorous cognitive science. *Cognition* 50:41–77.

Courchesne, Eric et al. 1994. A new finding: Impairment in shifting attention in autistic and cerebellar patients. *Atypical cognitive deficits in developmental disorders,* S. Broman and J. Grafman, eds., 101–37. Hillsdale, N.J.: Erlbaum.

Crick, F. H. C. and C. Asanuma. 1986. Certain aspects of the anatomy and physiology of the cerebral cortex. *Parallel distributed processing: Explorations in the microstructure of cognition,* vol. 2, *Psychological and biological models,* J. McClelland, David Rumelhart, and the PDP research group, eds., 333–71. Cambridge, Mass.: MIT Press.

Crick, Francis and Christof Koch. 1990. Towards a neurobiological theory of consciousness. *Seminars in the Neurosciences* 2:263–75.

Crisco, J., J. Dobbs, and R. Mulhern. 1988. Cognitive processing of children with Williams syndrome. *Developmental Medicine and Child Nuerology* 30:650–56.

Cromer, R. 1981. Developmental language disorders: Cognitive processes, semantics, pragmatics, phonology, and syntax. *Journal of Autism and Developmental Disorders* 11:57–74.

——— 1994. A case study of dissociations between language and cognition. *Constraints on language acquisition: Studies of atypical children,* H. Tager-Flusberg, ed., 141–53. Hillsdale, N.J.: Erlbaum.

Culatta, Barbara. 1993a. Developing abstract concepts. *Teaching the student with spina bifida,* F. Rowley-Kelly and D. Reigel, eds., 125–43. Baltimore: Paul H. Brookes.

——— 1993b. Building mathematic skills. *Teaching the student with spina bifida,* F. Rowley-Kelly and D. Reigel, eds., 145–70. Baltimore: Paul H. Brookes.

——— 1993c. Intervening for language-learning disabilities. *Teaching the student with spina bifida,* F. Rowley-Kelly and D. Reigel, eds., 171–91. Baltimore: Paul H. Brookes.

Culatta, Barbara and Carol Young. 1992. Linguistic performance as a function of abstract task demands in children with spina bifida. *Developmental Medicine and Child Neurology* 34:434–40.

Cull, C. and M. Wyke. 1984. Memory function of children with spina bifida and shunted hydrocephalus. *Developmental Medicine and Child Neurology* 26:177–83.

Curtiss, S. 1981. Dissociations between language and cognition: Cases and implications. *Journal of Autism and Developmental Disorders* 11:15–30.

D'Andrade, Roy G. 1981. The cultural part of cognition. *Cognitive Science* 5:179–95.

Davidson, Donald. 1975. Thought and talk. *Mind and language*, S. Guttenplan, ed., 7–23. Oxford: Oxford University Press.

Davydov, V. V. and L. A. Radzhikovskii. 1985. Vygotsky's theory and the activity-oriented approach in psychology. *Culture, communication, and cognition*, J. Wertsch, ed., 35–65. Cambridge: Cambridge University Press.

de Haan, Edward, Andy Young, and Freda Newcombe. 1987. Face recognition without awareness. *Cognitive Neuropsychology* 4:385–415.

Dennett, Daniel. 1984a. Cognitive wheels: The frame problem of AI. *Minds, machines, and evolution*, C. Hookway, ed., 129–51. Cambridge: Cambridge University Press.

——— 1984b. *Elbow room: The varieties of free will worth wanting*. Cambridge, Mass.: MIT Press.

——— 1987. *The intentional stance*. Cambridge, Mass.: MIT Press.

——— 1988. Quining qualia. *Consciousness in contemporary science*, A. Marcel and E. Bisiach, eds., 42–77. Oxford: Oxford University Press.

——— 1991. *Consciousness explained*. Boston: Little Brown.

Dennett, Daniel and Marcel Kinsbourne. 1992. Time and the observer: The where and when of consciousness in the brain. *Behavioral and Brain Sciences* 15:183–247.

Dennis, M. et al. 1987. Language of hydrocephalic children and adolescents. *Journal of Clinical and Experimental Neuropsychology* 9:593–621.

Denny, J. Peter. 1988. Contextualisation and differentiation in cross-cultural cognition. *Indigenous cognition: Functioning in cultural context*, J. Berry, S. Irvine, and E. Hunt, eds., 213–29. Dordrecht: Nijhoff.

Diaz, Rafael. 1992. Methodological concerns in the study of private speech. *Private speech*, R. Diaz and L. Berk, eds., 55–81. Hillsdale, N.J.: Erlbaum.

Diaz, Rafael and Laura Berk, eds. 1992. *Private speech*. Hillsdale, N.J.: Erlbaum.

Dijkstra, E. W. 1968. Goto statement considered harmful. *CACM* 11:147–49.

Dinsmore, John. 1992. Thunder in the gap. *The symbolic and connectionist paradigms: Closing the gap*, J. Dinsmore, ed., 1–23. Hillsdale, N.J.: Erlbaum.

Dixon, Roger. 1987. Wittgenstein, contextualism, and developmental psychology. *Meaning and the growth of understanding: Wittgenstein's significance for developmental psychology*, M. Chapman and R. Dixon, eds., 49–67. Berlin: Springer.

Downey, J., A. Ehrhardt, R. Gruen, J. Bell, and A. Morishima. 1989. Psychopathology and social functioning in women with Turner syndrome. *Journal of Nervous and Mental Disease* 177:191–201.

Downey, J., E. Elkin, A. Ehrhardt, H. Meyer-Bahlburg, J. Bell, and A. Morishima. 1991. Cognitive ability and everyday functioning in women with Turner syndrome. *Journal of Learning Disabilities* 24:32–39.

Dreyfus, Hubert. 1972. *What computers can't do.* New York: Harper & Row.

───── 1982. Introduction. *Husserl, intentionality, and cognitive science,* H. Dreyfus, ed., 1–27. Cambridge, Mass.: MIT Press.

Dreyfus, Hubert and Stuart Dreyfus. 1986. *Mind over machine.* New York: Free Press.

───── 1987. How to stop worrying about the frame problem even though it's computationally insoluble. *The robot's dilemma,* Z. Pylyshyn, ed., 95–11. Norwood, N.J.: Ablex.

Drozd, K. 1994. A discourse analysis of child English "no." Boston University Conference on Language Development, November.

Dunn, J. Michael. 1990. The frame problem and relevant predication. *Knowledge representation and defeasible reasoning,* H. Kybourg, R. Loui, and G. Carlson, eds., 89–95. Dordrecht: Kluwer.

Elman, Jeffrey. 1992. Grammatical structure and distributed representations. *Connectionism: Theory and practice,* S. Davis, ed., 138–78. Oxford: Oxford University Press.

Etherington, David, Sarit Kraus, and Donald Perlis. 1991. Limited scope and circumscriptive reasoning. *Reasoning agents in a dynamic world: The frame problem,* K. Ford and P. Hayes, eds., 43–54. Greenwich, Conn.: JAI Press.

Feigenbaum, Peter. 1992. Development of the syntactic and discourse structures of private speech. *Private speech,* R. Diaz and L. Berk, eds., 181–98. Hillsdale, N.J.: Erlbaum.

Feldman, Carol. 1989. Monologue as problem-solving narrative. *Narratives from the crib,* K. Nelson, ed., 98–119. Cambridge, Mass.: Harvard University Press.

Fikes, R. and N. Nilsson. 1971. STRIPS: A new approach to the application of theorem proving to problem solving. *Artificial Intelligence* 2:189–208.

Fischer, A. and F. Grodzinsky. 1993. *The anatomy of programming languages.* Englewood Cliffs, N.J.: Prentice-Hall.

Flanagan, Owen. 1991. *The science of the mind.* Cambridge, Mass.: MIT Press.

───── 1992. *Consciousness reconsidered.* Cambridge, Mass.: MIT Press.

───── In press. Prospects for a unified theory of consciousness or what dreams are made of. *Scientific approaches to the question of consciousness. Twenty-fifth Carnegie symposium on cognition,* J. Cohen and J. Schooler, eds. Hillsdale, N.J.: Erlbaum.

Fletcher, J. et al. 1992. Cerebral white matter and cognition in hydrocephalic children. *Archives of Neurology* 49:818–25.

Fodor, Jerry. 1972. Some reflections on L. S. Vygotsky's *Thought and language. Cognition* 1:83–95.

───── 1975. *The language of thought.* New York: Crowell.

―――― 1981. *Representations*. Cambridge, Mass.: MIT Press.

―――― 1983. *The modularity of mind*. Cambridge, Mass.: MIT Press.

―――― 1986. Frames, fridgeons, sleeping dogs, and the music of the spheres. *Modularity in knowledge representation and natural language*, J. Garfield, ed., 25–36. Cambridge, Mass.: MIT Press.

―――― 1989. Why there *still* has to be a language of thought. *Computers, brains, and minds*, P. Slezak and W. Albury, eds., 23–46. Dordrecht: Kluwer.

Fodor, Jerry and Zenon Pylyshyn. 1988. Connectionism and cognitive architecture: A critical analysis. *Connections and symbols*, S. Pinker and J. Mehler, eds., 3–71. Cambridge, Mass.: MIT Press.

Ford, Kenneth and Paul Chang. 1989. An approach to automated knowledge acquisition founded on personal construct theory. *Advances in artificial intelligence research*, M. Fishman, ed., 83–131. Greenwich, Conn.: JAI Press.

Frauenglass, M. and R. Diaz. 1985. Self-regulatory functions of children's private speech: A critical analysis of recent challenges to Vygotsky's theory. *Developmental Psychology* 21:357–64.

Frawley, William. 1992a. Lexicography and mathematics learning: A case study of *variable. Applied Linguistics* 13:385–402.

―――― 1992b. *Linguistic semantics*. Hillsdale, N.J.: Erlbaum.

―――― 1997. A reconsideration of language in global knowledge disorders. Paper presented at the Linguistic Society of America, Chicago, January.

Frawley, William and James Lantolf. 1985. Private speech and self-regulation: A commentary on Frauenglass and Diaz. *Developmental Psychology* 22:706–8.

Frazier, Lyn. 1987. Theories of sentence processing. *Modularity in knowledge representation and natural-language understanding*, J. Garfield, ed., 291–307. Cambridge, Mass.: MIT Press.

Friedrich, W., M. Lovejoy, J. Shaffer, D. Shurtleff, and R. Beilke. 1991. Cognitive abilities and achievement status of children with myelomeningocele: A contemporary sample. *Journal of Pediatric Psychology* 16:423–28.

Furrow, David. 1984. Social and private speech at two years. *Child Development* 55:355–62.

―――― 1992. Developmental trends in the differentiation of social and private speech. *Private speech*, R. Diaz and L. Berk, eds., 143–58. Hillsdale, N.J.: Erlbaum.

Fuson, Karen. 1979. The development of self-regulating aspects of speech. *The development of self-regulation through private speech*, G. Zivin, ed., 135–217. New York: Wiley.

Gallistel, C. R., A. Brown, S. Carey, R. Gelman, and F. Keil. 1991. Lessons from animal learning for the study of cognitive development. *The epigenesis of mind: Essays on biology and cognition*, S. Carey and R. Gelman, eds., 3–37. Hillsdale, N.J.: Erlbaum.

Gal'perin, P. 1969. Stages in the development of mental acts. *A handbook of contemporary Soviet psychology*, M. Cole and I. Maltzman, eds., 249–73. New York: Basic Books.

————— 1979. The role of orientation in thought. *Soviet Psychology* 18:84–99.

Gardner, Howard. 1983. *Frames of mind: The theory of multiple intelligences.* New York: Basic Books.

Garman, M. 1990. *Psycholinguistics.* Cambridge: Cambridge University Press.

Garnham, Alan. 1993. Is logicist cognitive science possible? *Mind and Language* 8:49–71.

Garron, David C. 1977. Intelligence among persons with Turner's syndrome. *Behavior Genetics* 7:105–27.

Garvey, Alan and Barbara Hayes-Roth. 1989. An empirical analysis of explicit vs. implicit control architectures. *Blackboard architectures and applications,* V. Jagannathan, R. Dodhiawala, and L. Baum, eds., 43–56. San Diego: Academic Press.

Gazzaniga, Michael. 1988. Brain modularity: Towards a philosophy of conscious experience. *Consciousness in contemporary science,* A. Marcel and E. Bisiach, eds., 218–38. Oxford: Oxford University Press.

Gee, James Paul. 1989. Two styles of narrative construction and their linguistic and educational implications. *Discourse Processes* 12:287–307.

Gerhardt, Julie. 1989. Monologue as a speech genre. *Narratives from the crib,* K. Nelson, ed., 171–230. Cambridge, Mass.: Harvard University Press.

Gerken, LouAnn. 1991. The metrical basis for children's subjectless sentences. *Journal of Memory and Language* 30:431–51.

Ghaziuddin, M., B. Bolyard, and N. Alessi. 1994. Autistic disorder in Noonan syndrome. *Journal of Intellectual Disability Research* 38:67–72.

Ghezzi, Carol and Mehdi Jazayeri. 1987. *Programming language concepts.* New York: Wiley.

Gibson, James. 1979. *The ecological approach to visual perception.* Hillsdale, N.J.: Erlbaum.

Girotto, Vittorio and Paul Light. 1993. The pragmatic basis of children's reasoning. *Context and cognition: Ways of learning and knowing,* P. Light and G. Butterworth, eds., 134–56. Hillsdale, N.J.: Erlbaum.

Givón, Talmy. 1983. Topic continuity in discourse: An introduction. *Topic continuity in discourse,* T. Givón, ed., 5–41. Amsterdam: John Benjamins.

Globus, Gordon. 1990. Heidegger and cognitive science. *Philosophy Today* 34:20–29.

————— 1992. Derrida and connectionism: Différance in neural nets. *Philosophical Psychology* 5:183–97.

Glucksberg, S., R. J. Kreuz, and S. Rho. 1986. Context can constrain lexical access: Implications for models of language comprehension. *Journal of Experimental Psychology: Learning, Memory, and Cognition* 12:323–35.

Glymour, Clark. 1987. Android epistemology and the frame problem: Comments on Dennett's "Cognitive wheels." *The robot's dilemma,* Z. Pylyshyn, ed., 65–75. Norwood, N.J.: Ablex.

Goffman, Erving. 1981. *Forms of talk.* Philadelphia: University of Pennsylvania Press.

Gold, E. M. 1967. Language identification in the limit. *Information and Control* 10:447–74.

Goldberg, Elkhonon and Robert Bilder. 1987. The frontal lobes and hierarchical organization of cognitive control. *The frontal lobes revisited*, E. Perecman, ed., 159–87. Hillsdale, N.J.: Erlbaum.

Goldberg, Gary. 1987. From intent to action: Evolution and function of the premotor systems of the frontal lobe. *The frontal lobes revisited*, E. Perecman, ed., 273–306. Hillsdale, N.J.: Erlbaum.

Goldman, Alvin. 1990. Action and free will. *Visual cognition and action: An invitation to cognitive science*, vol. 2, D. Osherson, S. Kosslyn, and J. Hollerbach, eds., 317–40. Cambridge, Mass.: MIT Press.

Golinkoff, R., C. Mervis, and K. Hirsh-Pasek. 1994. Early object labels: The case for lexical principles. *Journal of Child Language* 21:125–55.

Golinkoff, Roberta et al. 1992. Young children and adults use lexical principles to learn new nouns. *Developmental Psychology* 28:99–108.

Gomberg, Jean Emile. 1992. *Metalinguistic development*. Chicago: University of Chicago Press.

Goodluck, Helen. 1991. *Language acquisition*. Cambridge, Mass.: Blackwell.

Goodnow, Jacqueline and Pamela Warton. 1993. Contexts and cognitions: Taking a particular view. *Context and cognition: Ways of learning and knowing*, P. Light and G. Butterworth, eds., 157–77. Hillsdale, N.J.: Erlbaum.

Goudena, Paul. 1987. The social nature of private speech of preschoolers during problem solving. *International Journal of Behavioral Development* 10:187–206.

——— 1992. The problem of abbreviation in private speech. *Private speech*, R. Diaz and L. Berk, eds., 215–24. Hillsdale, N.J.: Erlbaum.

Greenfield, Patricia. 1993. Representational competence in shared symbol systems: Electronic media from radio to video games. *The development and meaning of psychological distance*, R. Cocking and K. Renninger, eds., 161–83. Hillsdale, N.J.: Erlbaum.

Greeno, James and Joyce Moore. 1993. Situativity and symbols: Response to Vera and Simon. *Cognitive Science* 17:49–59.

Griffin, Donald. 1981. *The question of animal awareness*. New York: Rockefeller University Press.

——— 1984. *Animal thinking*. Cambridge, Mass.: Harvard University Press.

Grimm, Robert and Daniel Merrill, eds. 1985. *Contents of thought*. Tucson: University of Arizona Press.

Gruber, Jeffrey. 1967. Subject and topicalization in child language. *Foundations of Language* 3:37–65.

Grumet, Gerald. 1985. On speaking to oneself. *Psychiatry* 48:180–95.

Hacker, P. M. S. 1990. *Wittgenstein: Meaning and mind*. Cambridge, Mass.: Blackwell.

Haegeman, Liliane. 1991. *An introduction to government and binding theory*. Cambridge, Mass.: Blackwell.

Hanks, S. and D. McDermott. 1986. Default reasoning, nonmonotonic logics, and the frame problem. *Proceedings of fifth national conference on artificial intelligence,* T. Kehler et al., eds., 328–33. Los Altos, Calif.: Morgan Kaufman.

Harnad, Stephen. 1982. Consciousness: An afterthought. *Cognition and Brain Theory* 5:29–47.

—— 1990. The symbol grounding problem. *Physica D* 42:335–46.

Harré, Rom. 1987. Persons and selves. *Persons and personality: A contemporary inquiry,* A. Peacocke and G. Gillett, eds., 99–115. Oxford: Blackwell.

Harré, Rom and Grant Gillett. 1994. *The discursive mind.* Thousand Oaks, Calif.: Sage.

Harré, Rom and Peter Mühlhäusler. 1990. *Pronouns and people.* Oxford: Blackwell.

Harris, Paul. 1993. Pretending and planning. *Understanding other minds: Perspectives from autism,* S. Baron-Cohen, H. Tager-Flusberg, and D. Cohen, eds., 228–46. Oxford: Oxford University Press.

Haugeland, John. 1985. *Artificial intelligence: The very idea.* Cambridge, Mass.: MIT Press.

—— 1987. An overview of the frame problem. *The robot's dilemma,* Z. Pylyshyn, ed., 77–93. Norwood, N.J.: Ablex.

Hayes, P. 1987. What the frame problem is and isn't. *The robot's dilemma,* Z. Pylyshyn, ed., 123–37. Norwood, N.J.: Ablex.

—— 1991. Commentary on "The frame problem: Artificial intelligence meets David Hume." *Reasoning agents in a dynamic world: The frame problem,* K. Ford and P. Hayes, eds., 71–76. Greenwich, Conn.: JAI Press.

Hayes-Roth, Barbara. 1985. A blackboard architecture for control. *Artificial Intelligence* 26:251–321.

—— 1989. Control in blackboard systems. *Blackboard architectures and applications,* V. Jagannathan, R. Dodhiawala, and L. Baum, eds., 3–7. San Diego: Academic Press.

Heil, John. 1981. Does cognitive psychology rest on a mistake? *Mind* 90:321–42.

—— 1992. *The nature of true minds.* Cambridge: Cambridge University Press.

Hemphill, Lowry. 1989. Topic development, syntax, and social class. *Discourse Processes* 12:267–86.

Hewitt, C. 1969. PLANNER: A language for proving theorems in robots. *Proceedings of the International Joint Conference on Artificial Intelligence,* D. Walker and L. Norton, eds., 295–301. Los Altos, Calif.: Walter Kaufmann.

Hickmann, Maya. 1993. The boundaries of reported speech in narrative discourse. *Reflexive language,* J. Lucy, ed., 63–90. Cambridge: Cambridge University Press.

Hirschfeld, Lawrence and Susan Gelman, eds. 1994. *Mapping the mind: Domain specificity in cognition and culture.* Cambridge: Cambridge University Press.

Hirsh-Pasek, K. et al. 1986. "Daddy throw": On the existence of implicit negative evidence for subcategorization errors. Paper presented at the Boston University Conference on Language Development, November.

Hobson, Peter. 1993. Understanding persons: The role of affect. *Understanding other minds: Perspectives from autism,* S. Baron-Cohen, H. Tager-Flusberg, and D. Cohen, eds., 204–27. Oxford: Oxford University Press.

Holyoak, Keith. 1990. Problem solving. *Thinking: An invitation to cognitive science*, vol. 3, D. Osherson and E. Smith, eds., 117–46. Cambridge, Mass.: MIT Press.

Hopkins-Acos, P. and K. Bunker. 1979. A child with Noonan syndrome. *Journal of Speech and Hearing Disorders* 44:494–503.

Horgan, Terence and John Tienson. 1992. Structured representations in a connectionist system? *Connectionism: Theory and practice*, S. Davis, ed., 195–228. Oxford: Oxford University Press.

Horn, D., E. Lorch, R. Lorch, and B. Culatta. 1985. Distractability and vocabulary deficits in children with spina bifida and hydrocephalus. *Developmental Medicine and Child Neurology* 27:713–20.

Hunt, Earl and Mahzarin Banaji. 1988. The Whorfian hypothesis revisited: A cognitive science view of linguistic and cultural effects on thought. *Indigenous cognition: Functioning in cultural context*, J. Berry, S. Irvine, and E. Hunt, eds., 57–84. Dordrecht: Nijhoff.

Hurley, Anne. 1993. Conducting psychological assessments. *Teaching the student with spina bifida*, F. Rowley-Kelly and D. Reigel, eds., 107–23. Baltimore: Paul H. Brookes.

Hurley, Anne et al. 1990. Cognitive functioning in patients with spina bifida, hydrocephalus, and the "cocktail party" syndrome. *Developmental Neuropsychology* 6:151–72.

Hyams, Nina. 1992. A reanalysis of null subjects in child language. *Theoretical issues in language acquisition*, J. Weissenborn, H. Goodluck, and T. Roeper, eds., 249–67. Hillsdale, N.J.: Erlbaum.

Hyams, Nina and Kenneth Wexler. 1993. On the grammatical basis of null subjects in child language. *Linguistic Inquiry* 24:421–59.

Ingram, David. 1989. *First language acquisition*. Cambridge: Cambridge University Press.

Iwasaki, Syoichi. 1993. Spatial attention and two modes of visual consciousness. *Cognition* 49:211–33.

Jackendoff, Ray. 1987. *Consciousness and the computational mind*. Cambridge, Mass.: MIT Press.

——— 1992. *The languages of the mind*. Cambridge, Mass.: MIT Press.

Jacobsen, William. 1986. The heterogeneity of evidentials in Makah. *Evidentials: The linguistic coding of epistemology*, W. Chafe and J. Nichols, eds., 3–28. Norwood, N.J.: Ablex.

Jacoby, L. and C. Kelley. 1992. Unconscious influences of memory: Dissociations and automaticity. *The neuropsychology of consciousness*, A. Milner and M. Rugg, eds., 201–34. San Diego: Academic Press.

Jaeggli, Oswaldo and Kenneth Safir, eds. 1989. *The null subject parameter*. Dordrecht: Kluwer.

Jameson, Fredric. 1991. *Postmodernism, or the cultural logic of late capitalism*. Durham: Duke University Press.

Janik, Allan and Stephen Toulmin. 1973. *Wittgenstein's Vienna*. New York: Touchstone Books.

Janlert, Lars-Erik. 1987. Modeling change—the frame problem. *The robot's dilemma*, Z. Pylyshyn, ed., 1–40. Norwood, N.J.: Ablex.

Johnson-Laird, Philip. 1983. *Mental models*. Cambridge, Mass.: Harvard University Press.

———— 1988. *The computer and the mind*. Cambridge, Mass.: Harvard University Press.

Jones, Janet Lee. 1989. Multiple access of homonym meanings: An artifact of backward priming? *Journal of Psycholinguistic Research* 18:417–32.

Just, Marcel and Patricia Carpenter. 1992. A capacity theory of comprehension: Individual differences in working memory. *Psychological Review* 99:122–49.

Kaczmarek, B. L. J. 1987. Regulatory function of the frontal lobes: A neurolinguistic perspective. *The frontal lobes revisited*, E. Perecman, ed., 225–40. Hillsdale, N.J.: Erlbaum.

Kahneman, D. and A. Tversky. 1973. On the psychology of prediction. *Psychological Review* 80:237–51.

Kaplan, J., H. Brownell, J. Jacobs, and H. Gardner. 1990. The effects of right hemisphere damage on the pragmatic interpretation of conversational remarks. *Brain and Language* 38:315–33.

Karmiloff-Smith, Annette. 1986. From meta-processes to conscious access: Evidence from children's metalinguistic and repair data. *Cognition* 23:95–147.

———— 1992. *Beyond modularity*. Cambridge, Mass.: MIT Press.

Karmiloff-Smith, A., J. Grant, and I. Berthoud. 1993. Within-domain dissociations in Williams syndrome. Paper presented at the Society for Research in Child Development, New Orleans, March.

Karmiloff-Smith, Annette, Edward Klima, Ursula Bellugi, Julia Grant, and Simon Baron-Cohen. 1995. Is there a social module? Face processing and theory of mind in individuals with Williams syndrome. *Journal of Cognitive Neuroscience* 7:196–208.

Katz, Jerrold. 1981. *Language and other abstract objects*. Totowa, N.J.: Rowman and Littlefield.

———— 1990. *The metaphysics of meaning*. Cambridge, Mass.: MIT Press.

Kean, Mary-Louise. 1992. On the development of biologically real models of human linguistic capacity. *Formal grammar: Theory and implementation*, R. Levine, ed., 402–15. Oxford: Oxford University Press.

Keil, Frank. 1992. The origins of an autonomous biology. *Modularity and constraints in language acquisition*, M. Gunnar and M. Maratsos, eds., 103–37. Hillsdale, N.J.: Erlbaum.

Kinsbourne, Marcel. 1988. Integrated field theory of consciousness. *Consciousness in contemporary science*, A. Marcel and E. Bisiach, eds., 239–56. Oxford: Oxford University Press.

Kirsh, David. 1992. PDP learnability and innate knowledge of language. *Connectionism: Theory and practice*, S. Davis, ed., 297–322. Oxford: Oxford University Press.

Klein, Harriet. 1986. Styles of Toba discourse. *Native South American discourse*, J. Sherzer and G. Urban, eds., 213–35. Berlin: Mouton de Gruyter.

Kohlberg, L., J. Yaeger, and E. Hjertholm. 1968. Private speech: Four studies and a review of theories. *Child Development* 39:691–736.

König, Ekkehard. 1991. *The meaning of focus particles.* London: Croom Helm.

Kowalski, R. 1979a. Algorithm = logic + control. *CACM* 22:425–36.

——— 1979b. *Logic for problem solving.* Amsterdam: North Holland.

Kozulin, Alex. 1986. Vygotsky in context. L. S. Vygotsky, *Thought and language,* xi–lvi. Cambridge, Mass.: MIT Press.

Kripke, Saul. 1982. *Wittgenstein on rules and private language.* Cambridge, Mass.: Harvard University Press.

Kuhn, Thomas. 1962. *The structure of scientific revolutions.* Chicago: University of Chicago Press.

Lachter, Joel and Thomas Bever. 1988. The relation between linguistic structure and associative theories of language learning: A constructive critique of some connectionist learning models. *Connections and symbols,* S. Pinker and J. Mehler, eds., 195–247. Cambridge, Mass.: MIT Press.

Lahood, Barbara and George Bacon. 1985. Cognitive abilities of adolescent Turner's syndrome patients. *Journal of Adolescent Health Care* 6:358–64.

Lakoff, George. 1987. *Women, fire, and dangerous things.* Chicago: University of Chicago Press.

Landry, S., D. Copeland, A. Lee, and S. Robinson. 1990. Goal-directed behavior in children with spina bifida. *Developmental and Behavioral Pediatrics* 11:306–11.

Lave, Jean. 1991. Situating learning in communities of practice. *Perspectives on socially shared cognition,* L. Resnick, J. Levine, and S. Teasley, eds. 63–82. Washington, D.C.: American Psychological Association.

——— 1993. Word problems: A microcosm of theories of learning. *Context and cognition: Ways of learning and knowing,* P. Light and G. Butterworth, eds., 74–92. Hillsdale, N.J.: Erlbaum.

Lebeaux, David. 1988. Language acquisition and the form of the grammar. Ph.D. diss., University of Massachusetts.

Lee, Benjamin. 1985. Intellectual origins of Vygotsky's semiotic analysis. *Culture, communication, and cognition,* J. Wertsch, ed., 66–93. Cambridge: Cambridge University Press.

Lee, Benjamin and Maya Hickmann. 1983. Language, thought, and self in Vygotsky's developmental theory. *Developmental approaches to the self,* B. Lee and G. Noam, eds., 343–78. New York: Plenum.

Leekam, S. and J. Perner. 1991. Does the autistic child have a metarepresentational deficit? *Cognition* 40:203–18.

Legrenzi, P., V. Girotto, and P. N. Johnson-Laird. 1993. Focussing in reasoning and decision making. *Cognition* 49:37–66.

Leiber, Justin. 1991. *An invitation to cognitive science.* Cambridge, Mass.: Blackwell.

Leitch, Vincent. 1983. *Deconstructive criticism.* New York: Columbia University Press.

Leont'ev, A. A. 1978. Some new trends in Soviet psycholinguistics. *Recent trends in Soviet psycholinguistics,* J. Wertsch, ed., 10–20. Armonk, N.Y.: M. E. Sharpe.

Leont'ev, A. N. 1978. *Activity, consciousness, and personality.* Englewood Cliffs, N.J.: Prentice-Hall.

—— 1981. The problem of activity in psychology. *The concept of activity in Soviet psychology,* J. Wertsch, ed., 37–71. Armonk, N.Y.: M. E. Sharpe.

Leont'ev, D. A. 1990. Personal meaning and the transformation of a mental image. *Soviet Psychology* 28(2):5–24.

Leslie, Alan. 1987. Pretense and representation: The origins of "theory of mind." *Psychological Review* 94:412–26.

Leslie, Alan and Daniel Roth. 1993. What autism teaches us about metarepresentation. *Understanding other minds: Perspectives from autism,* S. Baron-Cohen, H. Tager-Flusberg, and D. Cohen, eds., 83–111. Oxford: Oxford University Press.

Levinson, Stephen. 1983. *Pragmatics.* Cambridge: Cambridge University Press.

Levy, Elena. 1989. Monologue as development of the text-forming function of language. *Narratives from the crib,* K. Nelson, ed., 123–70. Cambridge, Mass.: Harvard University Press.

Lewandowski, L., V. Costenbader, and R. Richman. 1985. Neuropsychological aspects of Turner syndrome. *International Journal of Clinical Neuropsychology* 7:144–47.

Li, Charles and Sandra Thompson. 1989. *Mandarin reference grammar.* Berkeley: University of California Press.

Lieberman, Philip. 1991. *Uniquely human.* Cambridge, Mass.: Harvard University Press.

Lillo Martin, Diane. 1992. Comments on Hyams and Weissenborn: On licensing and identification. *Theoretical issues in language acquisition,* J. Weissenborn, H. Goodluck, and T. Roeper, eds., 301–8. Hillsdale, N.J.: Erlbaum.

Llinás, Rodolfo, and Patricia Churchland, eds. 1996. *The mind brain continuum: Sensory processes.* Cambridge, Mass.: MIT Press.

Lloyd, Dan. 1992. Toward an identity theory of consciousness. *Behavioral and Brain Sciences* 15:215–16.

Loewer, Barry and Georges Rey, eds. 1991. *Meaning in mind: Fodor and his critics.* Oxford: Blackwell.

Lucy, John. 1992a. *Grammatical categories and cognition.* Cambridge: Cambridge University Press.

—— 1992b. *Language diversity and thought: A reformulation of the linguistic relativity hypothesis.* Cambridge: Cambridge University Press.

—— 1993. Reflexive language and the human disciplines. *Reflexive language,* J. Lucy, ed., 9–32. Cambridge: Cambridge University Press.

Lucy, John and James Wertsch. 1987. Vygotsky and Whorf: A comparative analysis. *Social and functional approaches to language and thought,* M. Hickman, ed., 67–86. Cambridge: Cambridge University Press.

Luria, A. R. 1973. *The working brain.* New York: Basic Books.

—— 1980. *Higher cortical functions in man*. New York: Basic Books.

—— 1982. *Language and cognition*. New York: Wiley.

Luria, Alexander. 1976a. *Cognitive development*. Cambridge, Mass.: Harvard University Press.

—— 1976b. *The nature of human conflicts*. New York: Liveright (originally 1932).

Lust, Barbara, ed. 1986. *Studies in the acquisition of anaphora*, vol. 1. Dordrecht: Reidel.

Lutz, Catherine. 1992. Culture and consciousness: A problem in the anthropology of knowledge. *Self and consciousness: Multiple perspectives*, F. Kessel, P. Cole, and D. Johnson, eds., 64–87. Hillsdale, N.J.: Erlbaum.

Lyotard, Jean-François. 1984. *The postmodern condition*. Minneapolis: University of Minnesota Press.

MacDonald, G. and D. Roy. 1988. Williams syndrome: A neuropsychological profile. *Journal of Clinical and Experimental Neuropsychology* 10:125–31.

Maratsos, Michael. 1992. Constraints, modules, and domain specificity: An introduction. *Modularity and constraints in language acquisition*, M. Gunnar and M. Maratsos, eds., 1–24. Hillsdale, N.J.: Erlbaum.

Margolis, Joseph. 1987. Wittgenstein's "forms of life": A cultural template for psychology. *Meaning and the growth of understanding: Wittgenstein's significance for developmental psychology*, M. Chapman and R. Dixon, eds., 129–49. Berlin: Springer.

Marr, David. 1982. *Vision*. San Francisco: Freeman.

Marslen-Wilson, William and Lorraine K. Tyler. 1987. Against modularity. *Modularity in knowledge representation and natural language understanding*, J. Garfield, ed., 37–62. Cambridge, Mass.: MIT Press.

McCarthy, John. 1980. Circumscription—a form of nonmonotonic reasoning. *Artificial Intelligence* 13:27–39.

McCarthy, John and Patrick Hayes. 1969. Some philosophical problems from the standpoint of artificial intelligence. *Machine intelligence*, vol. 4, B. Meltzer and D. Michie, eds., 463–502. Edinburgh: Edinburgh University Press.

McCauley, E., J. Ito, and T. Kay. 1986. Psychosocial functioning in girls with Turner's syndrome and short stature: Social skills, behavior problems, and self-concept. *Annual Progress in Child Psychiatry and Development*, S. Chess and T. Alexander, eds., 394–409. New York: Brunner/Mazel.

McCauley, E., T. Kay, J. Ito, and R. Treder. 1987. The Turner syndrome: Cognitive deficits, affective discrimination, and behavior problems. *Child Development* 58:464–73.

McClamrock, Ron. 1995. *Existential cognition*. Chicago: University of Chicago Press.

McClelland, J., D. Rumelhart, and G. Hinton. 1986. The appeal of parallel distributed processing. *Parallel distributed processing: Explorations in the microstructure of cognition*, vol. 1, *Foundations*, D. Rumelhart, J. McClelland, and the PDP research group, eds., 3–44. Cambridge, Mass.: MIT Press.

McDermott, Drew. 1982. A temporal logic for reasoning about processes and plans. *Cognitive Science* 6:101–55.

———— 1987. We've been framed: Or, why AI is innocent of the frame problem. *The robot's dilemma*, Z. Pylyshyn, ed., 113–22. Norwood, N.J.: Ablex.

McElree, Brian and Thomas Bever. 1989. The psychological reality of linguistically defined gaps. *Journal of Psycholinguistic Research* 18:21–36.

McGinn, Colin. 1991. *The problem of consciousness.* Oxford: Blackwell.

McGlone, J. 1985. Can spatial deficits in Turner's syndrome be explained by focal CNS dysfunction or atypical speech lateralization? *Journal of Clinical and Experimental Neurology* 7:375–94.

McRoberts, Gerald. 1994. Prosodic bootstrapping: A critique of the argument and evidence. Paper presented at the Boston University Conference on Language Development, November.

Mead, George Herbert. 1934. *Mind, self, and society from the standpoint of a social behaviorist.* Chicago: University of Chicago Press.

Mellor, D. H. 1989. How much of the mind is a computer? *Computers, brains, and minds,* P. Slezak and W. Albury, eds., 47–69. Dordrecht: Kluwer.

Mercer, Neil. 1993. Culture, context, and the construction of knowledge in the classroom. *Context and cognition: Ways of learning and knowing,* P. Light and G. Butterworth, eds., 28–46. Hillsdale, N.J.: Erlbaum.

Mervis, Carolyn and Jacquelyn Bertrand. 1993. Early lexical development: Universals and alternate paths. Ms., Emory University.

Meyerson, M. and R. Frank. 1987. Language, speech, and hearing in Williams syndrome: Intervention approaches and research needs. *Developmental Medicine and Child Neurology* 29:258–70.

Money, John. 1994. Specific neurocognitional impairments associated with Turner (45,X) and Klinefelter (47,XXY) syndromes: A review. *Social Biology* 40:147–51.

Morgan, James. 1986. *From simple input to complex grammar.* Cambridge, Mass.: MIT Press.

Morrow, Judy and Theodore Wachs. 1992. Infants with myelomeningocele: Visual recognition memory and sensorimotor abilities. *Developmental Medicine and Child Neurology* 34:488–98.

Murdoch, John. 1988. Cree cognition in natural and educational contexts. *Indigenous cognition: Functioning in cultural context,* J. Berry, S. Irvine, and E. Hunt, eds., 231–56. Dordrecht: Nijhoff.

Nagel, Thomas. 1986. *The view from nowhere.* Oxford: Oxford University Press.

Napoli, Donna Jo. 1989. *Predication theory.* Cambridge: Cambridge University Press.

Neisser, Ulrich. 1992. The development of consciousness and the acquisition of self. *Self and consciousness: Multiple perspectives,* F. Kessel, P. Cole, and D. Johnson, eds., 1–18. Hillsdale, N.J.: Erlbaum.

Nelson, Katherine. 1989a. Monologue as the linguistic construction of self in time. *Narratives from the crib,* K. Nelson, ed., 284–308. Cambridge, Mass.: Harvard University Press.

——— ed. 1989b. *Narratives from the crib*. Cambridge, Mass.: Harvard University Press.

Neville, H., D. Mills, and U. Bellugi. 1994. Effects of altered auditory sensitivity and age of language acquisition on the development of language-relevant neural systems: Preliminary studies of Williams syndrome. *Atypical cognitive deficits in developmental disorders*, S. Broman and J. Grafman, eds., 67–83. Hillsdale, N.J.: Erlbaum.

Newman, Fred and Lois Holzman. 1993. *Lev Vygotsky: Revolutionary scientist*. London: Routledge.

Nii, H. Penny. 1989. Introduction. *Blackboard architectures and applications*, V. Jagannathan, R. Dodhiawala, and L. Baum, eds., xix–xxix. San Diego: Academic Press.

Nora, J. et al. 1974. The Ullrich-Noonan syndrome (Turner phenotype). *American Journal of Diseases of Childhood* 127:48–55.

Norman, Donald. 1988. *The psychology of everyday things*. New York: Basic Books.

——— 1993. *Things that make us smart*. Reading, Mass.: Addison-Wesley.

Nutter, Terry. 1991. Focus of attention, context, and the frame problem. *Reasoning agents in a dynamic world: The frame problem*, K. Ford and P. Hayes, eds., 171–88. Greenwich, Conn.: JAI Press.

Oatley, Keith. 1988. On changing one's mind: A possible function of consciousness. *Consciousness in contemporary science*, A. Marcel and E. Bisiach, eds., 369–89. Oxford: Oxford University Press.

O'Grady, William. 1986. *Principles of language and learning*. Chicago: University of Chicago Press.

Penfield, W. and L. Roberts. 1959. *Speech and brain mechanisms*. Princeton: Princeton University Press.

Perner, J. 1991. *Understanding the representational mind*. Cambridge, Mass.: MIT Press.

Perner, Josef. 1993. The theory of mind deficit in autism: Evidence from deception. *Understanding other minds: Perspectives from autism*, S. Baron-Cohen, H. Tager-Flusberg, and D. Cohen, eds., 112–37. Oxford: Oxford University Press.

Pettito, Laura. 1992. Modularity and constraints in early lexical acquisition: Evidence from children's early language and gesture. *Modularity and constraints in language acquisition*, M. Gunnar and M. Maratsos, eds., 25–58. Hillsdale, N.J.: Erlbaum.

Pickering, Martin and Guy Barry. 1991. Sentence processing without empty categories. *Language and Cognitive Processes* 6:229–59.

Pinker, Steven and Paul Bloom. 1990. Natural language and natural selection. *Behavioral and Brain Sciences* 13:707–84.

Pinker, Steven and Alan Prince. 1988. On language and connectionism: Analysis of a parallel distributed processing model of language acquisition. *Connections and symbols*, S. Pinker and J. Mehler, eds., 73–193. Cambridge, Mass.: MIT Press.

Premack, David. 1988. Minds with and without language. *Thought without language*, L. Weiskrantz, ed., 46–65. Oxford: Oxford University Press.

Pribram, Karl. 1990. The frontal cortex—a Luria/Pribram rapprochement. *Contemporary neuropsychology and the legacy of Luria*, E. Goldberg, ed., 77–97. Hillsdale, N.J.: Erlbaum.

Putnam, Hilary. 1975. *Mind, language, and reality*. Cambridge: Cambridge University Press.

——— 1980. What is innate and why: Comments on the debate. *Language and learning*, M. Piattelli-Palmarini, ed., 287–309. Cambridge, Mass.: Harvard University Press.

——— 1988. *Representation and reality*. Cambridge, Mass.: MIT Press.

Pylyshyn, Zenon. 1985. *Computation and cognition*. Cambridge, Mass.: MIT Press.

——— ed. 1987. *The robot's dilemma*. Norwood, N.J.: Ablex.

Radzikhovskii, L. A. 1991. Dialogue as a unit of analysis of consciousness. *Soviet Psychology* 29(3):8–21.

Ramirez, Juan. 1992. The functional differentiation of social and private speech: A dialogic approach. *Private speech*, R. Diaz and L. Berk, eds., 199–214. Hillsdale, N.J.: Erlbaum.

Reigel, Donald. 1993. Spina bifida from infancy through the school years. *Teaching the student with spina bifida*, F. Rowley-Kelly and D. Reigel, eds., 3–30. Baltimore: Paul H. Brookes.

Reilly, J., E. Klima, and U. Bellugi. 1991. Once more with feeling: Affect and language in atypical populations. *Development and psychopathology* 2:367–91.

Reiss, A., C. Feinstein, K. Rosenbaum, M. Borengasser-Caruso, and B. Goldsmith. 1985. Autism associated with Williams syndrome. *Journal of Pediatrics* 106:247–49.

Ribiero, Branca. 1993. Framing in psychotic discourse. *Framing in discourse*, D. Tannen, ed., 77–113. Oxford: Oxford University Press.

Rieber, Robert and Aaron Carton, eds. 1987. *The collected works of L. S. Vygotsky*, vol. 1. New York: Plenum.

Roazzi, Antonio and Peter Bryant. 1993. Social class, context, and cognitive development. *Context and cognition: Ways of learning and knowing*, P. Light and G. Butterworth, eds., 14–27. Hillsdale, N.J.: Erlbaum.

Rogoff, Barbara and James Wertsch, eds. 1984. *Children's learning in the "zone of proximal development."* San Francisco: Jossey-Bass.

Romani, Cristina. 1992. Are there distinct input and output buffers? Evidence from an aphasic patient with an impaired output buffer. *Language and Cognitive Processes* 7:131–62.

Roskies, Adina and C. C. Wood. 1992. Cinema 1-2-many of the mind. *Behavioral and Brain Sciences* 15:221–23.

Rourke, Byron. 1988. The syndrome of nonverbal learning disabilities: Developmental manifestations in neurological disease, disorder, and dysfunction. *Clinical Neuropsychologist* 2:293–330.

Rovet, J. and C. Netley. 1982. Processing deficits in Turner's syndrome. *Developmental Psychology* 18:77–94.

Rubin, Kenneth. 1979. Impact of the natural setting on private speech. *The development of self-regulation through private speech,* G. Zivin, ed., 265–94. New York: Wiley.

Rugg, M. D. 1992. Conscious and unconscious processes in language and memory—a commentary. *The neuropsychology of consciousness,* A. Milner and M. Rugg, eds., 263–78. San Diego: Academic Press.

Rumelhart, D. and J. McClelland. 1986. PDP models and general issues in cognitive science. *Parallel distributed processing: Explorations in the microstructure of cognition,* vol. 1, *Foundations,* D. Rumelhart, J. McClelland, and the PDP research group, eds., 110–46. Cambridge, Mass.: MIT Press.

Russell, James. 1987. Rule-following, mental models, and the developmental view. *Meaning and the growth of understanding: Wittgenstein's significance for developmental psychology,* M. Chapman and R. Dixon, eds., 22–48. Berlin: Springer.

Ryle, Gilbert. 1949. *The concept of mind.* London: Hutchinson.

Sacks, H., Emmanuel Schegloff, and Gail Jefferson. 1974. A simplest systematics for the organization of turn-taking in conversation. *Language* 50:696–735.

Saville-Troike, Muriel. 1988. Private speech: Evidence for second language learning strategies during the "silent" period. *Journal of Child Language* 15:567–90.

Saxe, Geoffrey, Maryl Gearhart, and Steven Guberman. 1984. The social organization of early number development. *Children's learning in the "zone of proximal development,"* B. Rogoff and J. Wertsch, eds., 19–30. San Francisco: Jossey-Bass.

Schank, Roger and Robert Abelson. 1977. *Scripts, plans, goals, and understanding.* Hillsdale, N.J.: Erlbaum.

Schiffrin, Deborah. 1987. *Discourse markers.* Cambridge: Cambridge University Press.

Schlichter, Alice. 1986. The origins and deictic nature of Wintu evidentials. *Evidentials: The linguistic coding of epistemology,* W. Chafe and J. Nichols, eds., 46–59. Norwood, N.J.: Ablex.

Schoenfeld, Alan. 1983. Beyond the purely cognitive: Belief systems, social cognitions, and metacognitions as driving forces in intellectual performance. *Cognitive Science* 7:329–63.

——— 1987a. Cognitive science and mathematics education: An overview. *Cognitive science and mathematics education,* A. Schoenfeld, ed., 1–31. Hillsdale, N.J.: Erlbaum.

——— 1987b. What's all the fuss about metacognition? *Cognitive science and mathematics education,* A. Schoenfeld, ed., 189–215. Hillsdale, N.J.: Erlbaum.

——— 1988. When good teaching leads to bad results: The disasters of "well-taught" mathematics courses. *Educational Psychologist* 23:145–66.

Schoenfeld, Alan et al. 1992. Toward a comprehensive model of human tutoring in complex subject matter domains. *Journal of Mathematical Behavior* 11:293–19.

Schopler, Eric. 1994. Neurobiologic correlates in the classification and study of autism. *Atypical cognitive deficits in developmental disorders,* S. Broman and J. Grafman, eds., 87–100. Hillsdale, N.J.: Erlbaum.

Schubert, Lenhart. 1990. Monotonic solution of the frame problem in the situation calculus: An efficient method for worlds with fully specified axioms. *Knowledge representation and defeasible reasoning*, H. Kybourg, R. Loui, and G. Carlson, eds., 23–67. Dordrecht: Kluwer.

Schwartz, E. 1974. Characteristics of speech and language development in the child with myelomeningocele and hydrocephalus. *Journal of Speech and Hearing Disorders* 39:465–68.

Scott, Thomas. 1992. Taste, feeding, and pleasure. *Progress in Psychobiology and Physiological Psychology* 15:231–91.

Scribner, Sylvia. 1985. Vygotsky's uses of history. *Culture, communication, and cognition*, J. Wertsch, ed., 119–45. Cambridge: Cambridge University Press.

Searle, John. 1969. *Speech acts*. Cambridge: Cambridge University Press.

———— 1979. *Intentionality*. Cambridge: Cambridge University Press.

———— 1991. Consciousness, explanatory inversion, and cognitive science. *Behavioral and Brain Sciences* 13:585–641.

———— 1992. *The rediscovery of the mind*. Cambridge, Mass.: MIT Press.

———— 1995. *The construction of social reality*. New York: Free Press.

Seidenberg, Mark and Michael Tanenhaus. 1986. Modularity and lexical access. *From models to modules*, I. Gopnik and M. Gopnik, eds., 135–57. Norwood, N.J.: Ablex.

Sejnowski, Terrence. 1986. Open questions about computation in cerebral cortex. *Parallel distributed processing: Explorations in the microstructure of cognition*, vol. 2, *Psychological and biological models*, J. McClelland, D. Rumelhart, and the PDP research group, eds., 372–89. Cambridge, Mass.: MIT Press.

Shafir, Eldar. 1994. Uncertainty and the difficulty of thinking through disjunction. *Cognition* 50:403–30.

Shallice, Tim. 1988a. Information-processing models of consciousness: Possibilities and problems. *Consciousness in contemporary science*, A. Marcel and E. Bisiach, eds., 305–33. Oxford: Oxford University Press.

———— 1988b. *From neuropsychology to mental structure*. Cambridge: Cambridge University Press.

Siegel, Irving. 1993. The centrality of a distancing model for the development of representational competence. *The development and meaning of psychological distance*, R. Cocking and K. Renninger, eds., 141–58. Hillsdale, N.J.: Erlbaum.

Sigman, Marian. 1994. What are the core deficits of autism? *Atypical cognitive deficits in developmental disorders*, S. Broman and J. Grafman, eds., 139–57. Hillsdale, N.J.: Erlbaum.

Silbert, Annette, Peter Wolff, and Janet Lilienthal. 1977. Spatial and temporal processing in patients with Turner's syndrome. *Behavior Genetics* 7:11–21.

Silverstein, Michael. 1985. The functional stratification of language in ontogenesis. *Culture, communication, and cognition*, J. Wertsch, ed., 205–35. Cambridge: Cambridge University Press.

———— 1993. Metapragmatic discourse and metapragmatic function. *Reflexive language*, J. Lucy, ed., 33–58. Cambridge: Cambridge University Press.

Sloman, Aaron. 1993. The mind as a control system. *Philosophy and cognitive science,* C. Hookway and D. Peterson, eds., 69–110. Cambridge: Cambridge University Press.

Smith, David W. 1986. The structure of (self-)consciousness. *Topoi* 5:149–56.

Smolensky, Paul. 1986. Neural and conceptual interpretation of PDP models. *Parallel distributed processing: Explorations in the microstructure of cognition,* vol. 2, *Psychological and biological models,* J. McClelland, D. Rumelhart, and the PDP research group, eds., 390–431. Cambridge, Mass.: MIT Press.

———— 1988. On the proper treatment of connectionism. *Behavioral and Brain Sciences* 11:1–74.

Smolucha, Francine. 1992. Social origins of private speech in pretend play. *Private speech,* R. Diaz and L. Berk, eds., 123–41. Hillsdale, N.J.: Erlbaum.

Sokolov, A. 1972. *Inner speech and thought.* New York: Plenum.

Spelke, Elizabeth. 1990. Origins of visual knowledge. *Visual cognition and action: An invitation to cognitive science,* vol. 2, D. Osherson, S. Kosslyn, and J. Hollerbach, eds., 99–127. Cambridge, Mass.: MIT Press.

Spelke, Elizabeth. 1994. Initial knowledge: Six suggestions. *Cognition* 50:431–45.

Sperber, Dan and Deirdre Wilson. 1986. *Relevance.* Oxford: Blackwell.

Stalnaker, Robert. 1993. How to do semantics for the language of thought. *Meaning in mind: Fodor and his critics.* B. Loewer and G. Rey, eds., 229–37. Oxford: Blackwell.

Staten, Henry. 1984. *Wittgenstein and Derrida.* Lincoln: University of Nebraska Press.

Sterelny, Kim. 1989. Computational functional psychology: Problems and prospects. *Computers, brains, and minds,* P. Slezak and W. Albury, eds., 71–93. Dordrecht: Kluwer.

Stich, Stephen. 1983. *From folk psychology to cognitive science.* Cambridge, Mass.: MIT Press.

———— 1991. Narrow content meets fat syntax. *Meaning in mind: Fodor and his critics,* B. Loewer and G. Rey, eds., 239–54. Oxford: Blackwell.

Stillings, Neil et al. 1987. *Cognitive science: An introduction.* Cambridge, Mass.: MIT Press.

Straus, Terry. 1989. The self in Northern Cheyenne language and culture. *Semiotics, self, and society,* B. Lee and G. Urban, eds., 53–68. Berlin: Mouton de Gruyter.

Stuss, D. and D. Benson. 1987. The frontal lobes and control of cognition and memory. *The frontal lobes revisited,* E. Perecman, ed., 141–58. Hillsdale, N.J.: Erlbaum.

———— 1990. The frontal lobes and language. *Contemporary neuropsychology and the legacy of Luria,* E. Goldberg, ed., 29–49. Hillsdale, N.J.: Erlbaum.

Suchman, Lucy. 1987. *Plans and situated actions.* Cambridge: Cambridge University Press.

———— 1993. Response to Vera and Simon's "Situated action: A symbolic interpretation." *Cognitive Science* 17:71–75.

Tager-Flusberg, H. 1981. On the nature of linguistic functioning in early infantile autism. *Journal of Autism and Developmental Disorders* 11:45–66.

—— 1991. Semantic processing in the free recall of autistic children: Further evidence for a cognitive deficit. *British Journal of Developmental Psychology* 9:417–31.

—— 1992. Autistic children's talk about psychological states: Deficits in the early acquisition of a theory of mind. *Child Development* 63:161–72.

—— 1993. What language reveals about the understanding of minds in children with autism. *Understanding other minds: Perspectives from autism*, S. Baron-Cohen, H. Tager-Flusberg, and D. Cohen, eds., 138–57. Oxford: Oxford University Press.

—— 1994. Dissociations in form and function in the acquisition of language by autistic children. *Constraints on language acquisition: Studies of atypical children*, H. Tager-Flusberg, ed., 175–94. Hillsdale, N.J.: Erlbaum.

Tager-Flusberg, H. and M. Anderson. 1991. The development of contingent discourse ability in autistic children. *Journal of Child Psychology and Psychiatry* 32:1123–34.

Tanenhaus, Michael, Gary Dell, and Gregory Carlson. 1987. Context effects in lexical processing: A connectionist perspective on modularity. *Modularity in knowledge representation and natural-language understanding*, J. Garfield, ed., 87–108. Cambridge, Mass.: MIT Press.

Tanenhaus, Michael and Margery Lucas. 1987. Context effects in lexical processing. *Cognition* 25:213–34.

Tannen, Deborah. 1993. What's in a frame. *Framing in discourse*, D. Tannen, ed., 14–56. Oxford: Oxford University Press.

Teghtsoonian, Robert. 1992. In defense of the pineal gland. *Behavioral and Brain Sciences* 15:224–25.

Temple, C. M. and R. A. Carney. 1993. Intellectual functioning of children with Turner syndrome: A comparison of behavioral phenotypes. *Developmental Medicine and Child Neurology* 35:691–98.

Tennenberg, Josh. 1991. Abandoning the completeness assumptions: A statistical approach to the frame problem. *Reasoning agents in a dynamic world: The frame problem*, K. Ford and P. Hayes, eds., 231–57. Greenwich, Conn.: JAI Press.

ter Hark, Michel. 1990. *Beyond the inner and the outer: Wittgenstein's philosophy of psychology*. Dordrecht: Kluwer.

Tuefel, Bernd. 1991. *Organization of programming languages*. New York: Springer.

Tew, B. 1979. The "cocktail party syndrome" in children with hydrocephalus and spina bifida. *British Journal of Disorders of Communication* 14:89–101.

Thal, D., E. Bates, and U. Bellugi. 1989. Language and cognition in two children with Williams syndrome. *Journal of Speech and Hearing Research* 32:489–500.

Tomasello, Michael, Ann Cale Kruger, and Hilary Horn Ratner. 1993. Cultural learning. *Behavioral and Brain Sciences* 16:495–552.

Tomc, S., N. Williamson, and R. Pauli. 1991. Temperament in Williams syndrome. *Williams Syndrome Association Newsletter* Fall:32–39.

Toulmin, Stephen. 1979. The inwardness of mental life. *Critical Inquiry* 6:1–16.

——— 1985. *The inner life: The outer mind.* Worcester, Mass.: Clark University Press.

Tul'viste, P. 1982. Is there a form of verbal thought specific to childhood? *Soviet Psychology* 21:317–27.

Turner, Mark. 1991. *Reading minds: The study of English in the age of cognitive science.* Princeton: Princeton University Press.

Tversky, A. and D. Kahneman. 1974. Judgment under uncertainty: Heuristics and biases. *Science* 185:1124–31.

Udwin, O. 1990. A survey of adults with Williams syndrome and idiopathic infantile hypercalcemia. *Developmental Medicine and Child Neurology* 32:129–41.

Udwin, O. and W. Yule. 1991. A cognitive and behavioural phenotype in Williams syndrome. *Journal of Clinical and Experimental Neurology* 13:232–44.

Udwin, O., W. Yule, and N. Martin. 1987. Cognitive abilities and behavioural characteristics of children with idiopathic infantile hypercalcemia. *Journal of Child Psychology and Psychiatry* 28:297–309.

Ulmità, Carlo. 1988. The control operations of consciousness. *Consciousness in contemporary science,* A. Marcel and E. Bisiach, eds., 334–56. Oxford: Oxford University Press.

Urban, Greg. 1989. The "I" of discourse. *Semiotics, self, and society,* B. Lee and G. Urban, eds., 27–51. Berlin: Mouton de Gruyter.

Valsiner, Jaan. 1988. *Developmental psychology in the Soviet Union.* Bloomington: Indiana University Press.

van der Veer, Rene and Jaan Valsiner. 1991. *Understanding Vygotsky.* Oxford: Blackwell.

van Gelder, Tim. 1992. Comment: Making conceptual space. *Connectionism: Theory and practice,* S. Davis, ed., 179–94. Oxford: Oxford University Press.

van Gelder, Timothy. 1990. Compositionality: A connectionist variation on a classical theme. *Cognitive Science* 14:355–84.

van Hasselt, V. et al. 1991. Assessment of social skills and problem behaviors in young children with spina bifida. *Journal of Developmental and Physical Disabilities* 3:69–80.

Varela, Francisco, Evan Thompson, and Eleanor Rosch. 1991. *The embodied mind.* Cambridge, Mass.: MIT Press.

Velmans, Max. 1991. Is human information processing conscious? *Behavioral and Brain Sciences* 14:651–726.

Vera, Alonso and Herbert Simon. 1993. Situated action: A symbolic interpretation. *Cognitive Science* 17:7–48.

Verster, John. 1988. Cognitive competence in Africa and models of information processing: A research prospectus. *Indigenous cognition: Functioning in cultural context,* J. Berry, S. Irvine, and E. Hunt, eds., 127–56. Dordrecht: Nijhoff.

Vološinov, V. 1986. *Marxism and the philosophy of language.* Cambridge, Mass.: Harvard University Press.

Vygotsky, L. S. 1962. *Thought and language.* Cambridge, Mass.: MIT Press.
———— 1978. *Mind in society.* Cambridge, Mass.: Harvard University Press.
———— 1979. Consciousness as a problem in the psychology of behavior. *Soviet Psychology* 17(4):3–35 (originally 1925).
———— 1986. *Thought and language,* rev. Cambridge, Mass.: MIT Press.
———— 1987. *The collected works of L. S. Vygotsky,* vol. 1, *Problems of general psychology.* New York: Plenum.
Wassmann, Jürg and Pierre Dasen. 1994. Yupno number system and counting. *Journal of Cross-Cultural Psychology* 25:78–94.
Weinberg, Amy. 1987. Modularity in the syntactic parser. *Modularity in knowledge representation and natural-language understanding,* J. Garfield, ed., 259–76. Cambridge, Mass.: MIT Press.
Weiskrantz, L. 1986 *Blindsight: A case study and implications.* Oxford: Oxford University Press.
Weissenborn, Jürgen. 1992. Null subjects in early grammars: Implications for parameter-setting theories. *Theoretical issues in language acquisition,* J. Weissenborn, H. Goodluck, and T. Roeper, eds., 269–99. Hillsdale, N.J.: Erlbaum.
Wellman, Henry. 1990. *The child's theory of mind.* Cambridge, Mass.: MIT Press.
———— 1993. Early understanding of mind: The normal case. *Understanding other minds: Perspectives from autism,* S. Baron-Cohen, H. Tager-Flusberg, and D. Cohen, eds., 10–39. Oxford: Oxford University Press.
Wertsch, James. 1979. The regulation of human action and the given-new organization of private speech. *The development of self-regulation through private speech,* G. Zivin, ed., 79–98. New York: Wiley.
———— 1981. The concept of activity in Soviet psychology: An introduction. *The concept of activity in Soviet psychology,* J. Wertsch, ed., 3–36. Armonk, N.Y.: M. E. Sharpe.
———— 1985. *Vygotsky and the social formation of mind.* Cambridge, Mass.: Harvard University Press.
———— 1991. *Voices of the mind.* Cambridge, Mass.: Harvard University Press.
Wertsch, James and Jenifer Bivens. 1993. The social origins of individual mental functioning. *The development and meaning of psychological distance,* R. Cocking and K. Renninger, eds., 203–18. Hillsdale, N.J.: Erlbaum.
Wertsch, James and Maya Hickmann. 1987. Problem-solving in social interaction: A microgenetic analysis. *Social and functional approaches to language and thought,* M. Hickmann, ed., 251–66. Cambridge: Cambridge University Press.
Wertsch, James and C. Addison Stone. 1985. The concept of internalization in Vygotsky's account of the genesis of higher mental functioning. *Culture, communication, and cognition,* J. Wertsch, ed., 162–79. Cambridge: Cambridge University Press.
Wexler, Kenneth. 1982. A principle theory for language acquisition. *Language acquisition: The state of the art,* E. Wanner and L. Gleitman, eds., 288–315. Cambridge: Cambridge University Press.
Wexler, Kenneth and Peter Culicover. 1981. *Formal principles of language acquisition.* Cambridge, Mass.: MIT Press.

White, Beverly. 1994. The Turner syndrome: Origin, cytogenetic variants, and factors influencing the phenotype. *Atypical cognitive deficits in developmental disorders,* S. Broman and J. Grafman, eds., 183–95. Hillsdale, N.J.: Erlbaum.

White, Stephen. 1991. *The unity of the self.* Cambridge, Mass.: MIT Press.

Wierzbicka, Anna. 1992. *Semantics, culture, and cognition.* Oxford: Oxford University Press.

Williams, Donna. 1992. *Nobody nowhere.* New York: Times Books.

Williams, J., L. Richman, and D. Yarbrough. 1991. A comparison of memory and attention in Turner syndrome and learning disability. *Journal of Pediatric Psychology* 16:585–93.

Wilson, M. and A. Dyson. 1982. Noonan syndrome: Speech and language characteristics. *Journal of Communication Disorders* 15:347–52.

Winograd, Terry and Fernando Flores. 1986. *Understanding computers and cognition.* Norwood, N.J.: Ablex.

Wittgenstein, Ludwig. 1956. *Remarks on the foundations of mathematics.* Oxford: Blackwell.

—— 1968. *Philosophical investigations.* New York: Macmillan (originally 1953).

—— 1969. *On certainty.* New York: Harper.

—— 1974a. *Tractatus logico-philosophicus.* Atlantic Highlands, N.J.: Humanities Press (originally 1921).

—— 1974b. *Philosophical grammar.* Berkeley: University of California Press.

Worthington, B. A. 1988. *Selfconsciousness and selfreference: An interpretation of Wittgenstein's Tractatus.* Aldershot: Avebury.

Wright, Crispin. 1989. Wittgenstein's rule-following considerations and the central project of theoretical linguistics. *Reflections on Chomsky,* A. George, ed., 233–64. Oxford: Blackwell.

Yamada, J. 1990. *Laura: A case for the modularity of language.* Cambridge, Mass.: MIT Press.

Yamada, J. and S. Curtiss. 1981. The relationship between language and cognition in a case of Turner's syndrome. *UCLA Working Papers in Cognitive Linguistics* 3:93–115.

Young, Andrew and Edward de Haan. 1990. Impairments of visual awareness. *Mind and Language* 5:29–48.

Yuille, A. L. and Shimon Ullman. 1990. Computational theories of low-level vision. *Visual cognition and action: An invitation to cognitive science,* vol. 2, D. Osherson, S. Kosslyn, and J. Hollerbach, eds., 5–39. Cambridge, Mass.: MIT Press.

Zhang, Jiajie and Donald Norman. 1994. Representations in distributed cognitive tasks. *Cognitive Science* 18:87–122.

Zimmermann, R. and K. Schneider. 1987. Dialogical aspects of individual lexical search. *Multilingua* 6:113–30.

Zinchenko, V. P. 1985. Vygotsky's ideas about units for the analysis of mind. *Culture, communication, and cognition,* J. Wertsch, ed., 94–118. Cambridge: Cambridge University Press.

—— 1990. The problem of the "formative" elements of consciousness in the activity theory of the mind. *Soviet Psychology* 28(2):25–40.

Zivin, Gail. 1979. Removing common confusions about egocentric speech, private speech, and self-regulation. *The development of self-regulation through private speech*, G. Zivin, ed., 13–49. New York: Wiley.

Index

Abbeduto, L., 236, 243, 249
Abelson, R., 17, 32
Abrahamsen, A., 68, 69
Achromatopia, 46, 146
Action. *See* Activity theory
Activation. *See* Connectionism
Activity. *See* Activity theory
Activity theory, 100–101, 154–155, 257–258. *See also* Leont'ev, A. N.
Adams, F., 215
Addresses. *See* Memory
Affordances. *See* Gibson, J.
Agency, feelings of, 105–106
Agre, P., 25
Aissen, J., 192
Aizawa, K., 69, 215
Aksu-Koç, A., 201
Alessi, N., 250, 288
Algonkian, 204
Algorithm. *See* Control
Alien hand syndrome, 104
Allport, A., 121, 138
Alzheimer's disease, 286
Anderson, J., 14, 56, 78, 116, 280
Anderson, M., 253, 255
Animacy hierarchy, 153–154
Apple, M., 23
Arbib, M., 81
Arcavi, A., 167
Architecture, 69, 78–82, 268–270; connectionist-control, 3, 268; central processes in, 79; modular, 79–80; interactive, 80–82; neural, 84–86

Architecture-Context relations, 5–7, 106–117, 131–132, 164–165, 185–187, 281–282, 285
Artificial intelligence. *See* Frame problem
Asanuma, C., 83–84, 85
Associationism. *See* Behaviorism; Connectionism
Attentional deficits. *See* Control
Autism, 7, 235–259, 289, 291
Autophenomenology, 161, 276. *See also* Dennett, D.
Awareness, 6, 126. *See also* Con sciousness
Azmitia, M., 183

Baars, B., 121, 122, 126–127, 139, 147
Bach, E., 189, 241, 285
Background, of consciousness, 17, 144
Bacon, G., 254, 258
Baker, C. L., 38
Bakhtin, M., 3, 179, 280, 282
Banaji, M., 204
Banfield, A., 179
Barnden, J., 69
Baron, R., 82–86
Baron-Cohen, S., 9, 266, 267
Barry, G., 71
Barwise, J., 189
Bates, E., 235, 239, 252, 290
Bechtel, W., 68, 69